STARTING SOCIOLOGY

STARTING SOCIOLOGY

THIRD EDITION

JACK LEVIN
Northeastern University

JAMES L. SPATES
Hobart and William Smith Colleges

HARPER & ROW, PUBLISHERS, New York
Cambridge, Philadelphia, San Francisco,
London, Mexico City, São Paulo, Singapore, Sydney

1817

PHOTO CREDITS

Chapter 1 opener: © Spratt, Picture Group / p. 8 left: DeWys; right: The Granger Collection / p. 13: The Bettman Archive, Inc. / p. 18: UPI, Bettmann / p. 21: Culver Pictures / p. 32 left: AP, Wide World Photos; right: Michel Casson / Chapter 2 opener: Ritscher, Stock, Boston / p. 41 left: Henle, Photo Researchers; right: Malave, Stock, Boston / p. 49: Harrington, Photo Trends / p. 62: Driskis, Jeroboam / p. 67 left: Novositi, Sovfoto, Eastfoto; right: Lazarus, Photo Researchers / p. 75 top: Charles Gatewood; bottom: Tannenbaum, SYGMA / p. 85 top: Marjorie Pickens; center: Herwig, Stock, Boston; bottom: AP, Wide World Photos / Chapter 3 opener: Hammid, Photo Researchers / p. 90 top: © Popper, Picture Group; bottom: Skytta, Jeroboam / p. 92: © The Boston Globe / p. 94: Culver Pictures / p. 99: The Granger Collection / p. 103 top: Moon, Stock, Boston; center: Marion Bernstein; bottom: Seitz, Woodfin Camp / p. 109: Dean Williams, American Broadcasting Companies, Inc. / p. 113: Culver Pictures / p. 124: Herwig, Stock, Boston / Chapter 4 opener: Forsyth, Monkmeyer / p. 134: Beckwith Studios / cartoon p. 135: Reprinted by permission, Tribune Media Services, Inc. / p. 151 top: Dietz, Stock, Boston; bottom left: Monroe, DPI; bottom right: Monroe, Photo Researchers / p. 159 top: © Meyers, 1980 Picture Group; bottom: Vannucci, DeWys / p. 163 top: AP, Wide World Photos; bottom: AP, Wide World Photos / p. 166 top: Vanderbes, DeWys / Chapter 5 opener top: Eckert, EKM, Nepenthe; bottom: Bailey, Jeroboam / p. 171: Culver Pictures / p. 175: Albertson, Stock, Boston / p. 176: The Granger Collection / p. 180: AP, Wide World Photos / p. 183 top: Corry, DPI; bottom left: AP, Wide World Photos / p. 187 top: Colin Davey, Photo Trends; center: Menzel, Stock, Boston; bottom: © 1981, Hazel Hankin / Chapter 6 opener: © Kelley, Picture Group / p. 210 top: New York Public Library Picture Collection; bottom: Southwick, Stock, Boston / p. 215 top: Marion Bernstein; bottom: Eagan, Woodfin Camp / p. 220: Bob Combs, Free Vision / p. 221: Photo Trends / p. 226 top: Franken, Stock, Boston; bottom: Wong, Contact, DeWys / Chapter 7 opener: © Reno, Jeroboam / p. 253: AP, Wide World Photos / p. 258: The Bettman Archive, Inc. / p. 259: AP, Wide World Photos / p. 262: AP, Wide World Photos / p. 276: UPI, Bettmann / p. 283 top: Culver Pictures; bottom: AP, Wide World Photos / Chapter 8 opener: Pavlovsky, SYGMA / p. 300 top: © Hazel Hankin 1984; bottom: © Hazel Hankin 1983 / p. 316 left: Balzer, Stock, Boston; right: Marjorie Pickens / p. 318 top: DeWys; bottom left: Lukas, Photo Researchers; bottom right: Hammid, Photo Researchers / p. 319: Chip Morel / p. 324: Culver Pictures / p. 325: DeWys / Chapter 9 opener: Siteman, Stock, Boston / p. 334: Herwig, Stock, Boston / p. 335: Lon Wilson, Photo Trends / p. 340: Cove, Photo Researchers / p. 350 top left: Bodin, Stock, Boston; top right: Corry, DeWys; bottom: Corry, DeWys

Sponsoring Editor: Alan McClare
Project Editor: Brigitte Pelner
Text and Cover Design: Betty L. Sokol
Cover Photo: Leo De Wys
Text Art: Fineline Illustrations, Inc.
Photo Research: Mira Schachne
Production Manager: Jeanie Berke
Compositor: ComCom Division of Haddon Craftsmen, Inc.
Printer and Binder: R. R. Donnelley & Sons Company

Starting Sociology, Third Edition

Library of Congress Cataloging in Publication Data
Levin, Jack, 1941-
  Starting sociology.

  Bibliography: p.
  Includes index.
  1. Sociology. 2. United States—Social conditions.
I. Spates, James L.   II. Title.
HM51.L359 1985   301   84-25140
ISBN 0-06-044004-1
85 86 87 88 89 9 8 7 6 5 4 3 2 1

CONTENTS

COLLECTIVE BEHAVIOR 251

SOCIAL CHANGE 293

CONTROVERSIES IN SOCIOLOGY 333

PREFACE

Our purpose in writing the first edition of *Starting Sociology* was to provide a flexible organizing tool for the introductory course in sociology. We designed our book to accommodate a wide range of approaches and supplementary materials while emphasizing the concepts that are central to sociological analysis. At the same time, we sought to explain and illustrate the sociological perspective as it bears on the lives of students taking their first course in sociology. We had precisely the same concerns in writing the second edition of the text.

In this, the book's third edition, we have been careful to maintain our original purpose. We have not eliminated any of the effective learning aids contained in the earlier editions such as boxed inserts, materials from newspapers and magazines, end-of-chapter questions and projects, and running and concluding glossaries. We have, however, updated our examples, clarified or expanded our discussions of various concepts and once again added new material. Specifically, at the urging of instructors, we have completely revised Chapter 5, "Social Stratification," including recent research in this area and updated Chapter 7, "Social Change," to include discussions of major trends now affecting American society—continuing suburbanization and the women's movement. Other modifications, too numerous to mention, have been made throughout the text. We will now briefly indicate our reasons for organizing the book as we have.

In the first chapter, "What is Sociology?," we begin with an overview of what the discipline takes as its main objective of study

—social life—and suggest how it must be approached if reliable information is to be obtained. This accomplished, we next turn to the foundational concepts of the discipline. If there is one key finding that social science has made in its brief existence, it is the discovery of "culture" and its great influence on human life. Consequently, a discussion of this concept and its related concepts form the basis of Chapter 2. If, as we argue in Chapter 2, culture is *the* social phenomenon that creates the human experience as we know it, it then becomes central to our endeavor to explain how it is transmitted to human beings. Hence, "socialization" becomes the focus of Chapter 3. Because this chapter indicates how culture becomes an internal, subjective reality in human existence, it also implicitly suggests, *à la* Durkheim, that culture must be an external, objective reality. That is, culture is not only *in* us, but *outside* of us as well. To explain this aspect of social reality then, we have focused on three major conceptual areas of sociological thought— "The Structure of Social Interaction" in Chapter 4, "Social Stratification" in Chapter 5, and the relationship between subjective and objective social reality in Chapter 6, "Social Institutions." As a balance to these three chapters, all of which emphasize enduring social structures, we return to an examination of the dynamic elements found in most modern societies—"Collective Behavior" in Chapter 7 and "Social Change" in Chapter 8. In conclusion, we return to our starting place once again, to focus on the discipline itself, with a deeper understanding of it and its subject matter, and consider its continuing dynamic development in Chapter 9, "Controversies in Sociology."

Many people have helped to make this book a reality. We are grateful to the staff at Harper & Row for their help in all three editions of our book. We also wish to acknowledge the assistance of Professors Dorothy Martin, Lorain County Community College; Geoffrey Kapenzi, Babson College; Eugene Rigney, College of Charleston; Charles Richardson, Oakland Community College; Janet Hermans, Southeastern University; and Randy Thomson, North Carolina State University, many of whose suggestions were helpful in producing the final version. Perhaps most importantly, we express our heartfelt thanks to our wives, Flea Levin and Tracy V. Spates, for their helpful suggestions and constant encouragement throughout the project.

This edition, like the last, is dedicated with love to our children, Michael Steven, Bonnie Lynn, Andrea Ilene Levin, and Jamie Mark Spates, who are part of the foundation of an increasingly humane society.

Jack Levin
James L. Spates

STARTING SOCIOLOGY

WHAT IS SOCIOLOGY?

1

THE SUBJECT MATTER OF SOCIOLOGY

It is winter 1984. The wife of the suburban family, in her early thirties, is becoming increasingly disconsolate. She has been married for 8 years, has two lovely children, all she ever wanted materially, and a husband who makes an excellent living. Yet something is missing. The endless routine of housework, clubs, entertaining, even vacationing, has begun to wear *very* thin. Her husband is deeply involved in his work and doesn't seem to understand her complaints and the "old solaces," the church and friends, don't seem to help. She doesn't know what to do. Finally, while shopping one afternoon, she sees a poster advertising a discussion session held by a group of women in the city. Taking a chance, she attends the next session. There, she learns that her discontent is not unique, that women throughout the country are finding their "expected pattern" of life restrictive. After attending a few more group meetings, she becomes convinced that not only women, but also men and children in America are all locked into an unexamined regimen of life that, in the long run, is quite frustrating to what she now calls "personal growth." Her husband, friends, and relatives are unimpressed with this new philosophy. Her frustration deepens and, some months later, with no change in attitude at home (and none on the horizon), she leaves, gets a job in the city, works out a "sharing the children" arrangement with her husband, and becomes an active member of the city's women's movement.

The scene shifts back in time. It is a decade and a half earlier, spring 1971. American involvement in the war in Vietnam has escalated and a rash of student protests has shut down college classrooms across the country. At the small, liberal arts college he attends, the disheveled-looking young man with long hair, a beard, and bright hippie-style clothes has been instrumental in organizing students against the war for the past 3 years. He is nationally known and is by far the most radical member of his class. Two months later, in May, his class graduates. At the commencement ceremony, one of the young man's professors looks for him among the robed students, half expecting to find him along the sidelines, carrying a placard, protesting to the end, or not being there at all. To his amazement, he finds the young man smack in the middle of the class, looking almost unrecognizable. His hair is shorn, his beard gone, and his eyes are fixed attentively on the speaker, a member of the administration in Washington whom the student had so recently and vehemently opposed. Incredulous, the professor asks him after the ceremony what happened. The student responds that, first of all, his parents were there and would not appreciate their son, the first in their family to graduate college, organizing a disruptive protest. And second, he has a job beginning Monday in the sports department of a large metropolitan newspaper and his hippie attire and appearance would certainly not be apropos there. Third he says, "Well . . . the sixties *are* over. We all have to grow up sometime!"

Here are two true to life cases, each strikingly different from the other: In one, the last described, an obviously nonmainstream individual suddenly decides to become mainstream; in the other, a person in one of the most traditional roles—"the American housewife"—gradually becomes radical and forsakes that role for another. Each case illustrates the subject matter of sociology, relating something about the breadth of the sociologist's interest in human affairs.

Before beginning the first course in sociology, most students have some idea (however vague) about sociologists and the work they do. More specifically, they might associate sociology with the "helping services" such as social work, community planning, or urban development. Or they might relate the discipline to the analysis of specific human problems such as the place of minority groups in America, the development of delinquent gangs, or the changing sexual patterns of college students.

And the students would be right. Sociologists do all these things and more. For example, sociologists are involved in studying the following topics as well as those just mentioned:

- The effect of religious beliefs on the life-style of different groups.
- The universal characteristics of human nature.
- The manner in which people use their hands while conversing with one another.
- The reason that many males in American society feel they must be a "success" in their life work.
- The reasons that many females in American society feel they must marry successful men.
- The current computer mania sweeping the country.
- The fact that three out of every four Americans live in urban areas.

The key fact is this: Sociologists are interested in how social influences and social processes of *any* type shape human behavior. Why, for example, does a dedicated political radical "change his stripes" on graduation from college? Why does a "woman with everything" throw it all over for a nontraditional life-style? Finding the answers to such questions is not always easy.

Human behavior is extremely complex and can be examined in many different ways. Consequently, a number of different *approaches* to its study have developed over the years, each claiming to make a unique contribution to our knowledge.

Economics and political science, for example, seek to understand the nature of human behavior in specialized contexts. Thus the field of economics focuses on forms of human behavior such as the operation of supply and demand, fluctuations in the business cycle, or the law of diminishing returns. Behavior beyond the scope of these economic exchanges is left to other fields to explore. In a similar way, political science investigates specifically political phenomena, such as the sources of power and control, international relations, voting behavior, and international conflict, leaving nonpolitical behavior to other analysts.

Sociology is much broader than economics and political science in its scope of inquiry. As Pitirim Sorokin (1947) once suggested, *the social elements of human behavior are present any time that two or more people encounter one another.*

> Sociology sees . . . generic social phenomena appearing in practically all social processes: economic, political, artistic, religious, philosophical . . . The same is true of such social processes as competition and exploitation, domination and subordination, stratification and differentiation, solidarity and antagonism, and so forth. Each of these processes appears not only in single compartments of the [social order as a whole] but in practically all compartments of sociocultural life, and as such requires a [separate] study of its generic form[s]. . . . Such a study transcends the

boundary lines of any compartmentalized discipline. (1947, p. 7)

The Perspective of Sociology

sociology The scientific study of the behavior of people when they interact with one another, and of the characteristics that people develop as a result of such interaction.

Despite its broad scope, **sociology** still has a definite perspective: It is *the scientific study of the behavior of people when they interact with one another, and of the characteristics people develop as a result of such interaction.* Let us take a moment to say a few words about the key aspects of this definition: *social interaction and social characteristics.*

Social Interaction. Sociology examines the behavior that results from encounters between as few as two people all the way to the behavior that results from encounters between nations. Some key questions that sociologists ask about the nature of social interaction are: How does interaction emerge and develop? What keeps it going? How does continued interaction affect the individuals involved? What must individuals do in order to maintain interaction? Under what conditions does interaction become unstable or change?

It should be noted that sociologists use the word **social** in a special sense. As Peter Berger (1963, pp. 26–27) has put it, the use of the word must be "sharpened" for sociological purposes.

social The primary quality of human interaction. A social situation is one in which individuals orient their behavior toward one another.

> In common speech it may denote . . . a number of different things—the informal quality of a certain gathering ("this is a social meeting—let's not discuss business"), an altruistic attitude on somebody's part ("he had a strong social concern in his job"), or, more generally, anything derived from contact with other people ("a social disease"). The sociologist will use the term more narrowly and more precisely to refer to the quality of interaction, interrelationship, mutuality. Thus two men chatting on a street do not constitute a "society," but what transpires between them is certainly "social." . . . As to the exact definition of the "social," it is difficult to improve on Max Weber's definition of a "social" situation as one in which people orient their actions towards one another. *The web of meanings, expectations and conduct resulting from such mutual orientation is the stuff of sociological analysis.* [Our emphasis.]

Social Characteristics. The sociologist's concern with this "web of meanings, expectations, and conduct" is just what we mean when we say that the second main focus of sociology is on the characteristics that people develop as a result of social interaction. One thing is clear: When people take notice of one another (interact), their behavior is changed from what it was before they took notice. For example, two people walking casually down the street may suddenly recognize one another and immediately begin acting very differently: Their faces change, they stop, shake hands, and speak in a prescribed and predictable manner. In another social encounter, a British citizen walking down the street may suddenly meet the Queen of England out shopping with her retinue. Although this person's behavior is also likely to change very suddenly, in this encounter the casual "greetings between friends" routine is not employed but another routine entirely is used: The individual bows, calls the Queen "Your Majesty," and quickly passes out of her way. The Queen, for her part, is likely to smile rather formally, but otherwise take little interest in the person.

The only way we can begin to explain these very different reactions in very similar social situations—two people meeting on the street—is to recognize that, for different situations, different social characteristics have been developed and learned. Because of the widespread existence of such varied social characteristics, sociologists spend a great deal of effort trying to understand the different webs of meanings, expectations, and conduct that people have invented for different types of social interaction—for example, between members of families, between men and women courting one another, or between upper-class people and their servants.

Indeed, the different social characteristics that individuals develop in interaction have led to whole subdivisions of sociology. For example, there are the study of human population characteristics and settlement patterns (human ecology) and the study of the relatively permanent features of social life such as social class and people's beliefs (often called the study of social structure).

Moreover, it is this interest in *all* types of social interaction and social characteristics that distinguishes sociology from other behavioral sciences. The economist is interested only in economic interaction and characteristics, the political scientist only in political interaction and characteristics. Although some historians are interested in explaining many different social interactions and characteristics, they typically are interested in these only as they cast light on specific historical events—the War of 1812—or specific historical trends—the rise of democracy in American society. In comparison to these disciplines, then, sociology is a generalizing discipline, ultimately trying to make statements about how *all* people will behave when they interact with one another, or about the essential social characteristics of *all* societies, *all* wars, or *all* families.

Sociology and Psychology

Since both psychology and sociology study general aspects of human behavior in everyday life, the essential difference between these fields of study may be particularly hard to see. Psychology and sociology study the same phenomena, but their focus on these phenomena is quite different.

According to Radcliffe-Brown (1957), although the sociologist is primarily concerned with the relations *between* two or more people when they interact, the psychologist is primarily concerned with the relations *within* any one individual from one moment to the next. In other words, whereas the sociologist is interested in the general principles that apply to *group process,* the psychologist is interested in the general principles that apply to the *mental process of an individual,* those personal characteristics of behavior located within the individual, whether on a conscious or an unconscious level.

Thus the sociologist takes the psychology of an individual for granted and is interested in the nature of one person's psychological makeup as such *only* when it changes the pattern of social interaction. Indeed, the sociologist would say that you can have a perfectly adequate explanation of most human interactions without focusing on individual psychological traits at all. For example, teachers and students everywhere tend to interact within the purely social conventions of "how to transmit and acquire knowledge in a relatively formal setting," despite the fact that each teacher and each student may have very different psychological characteristics.

The psychologist, on the other hand, takes the fact that all individuals live in society for granted and is interested in the nature of a particular social convention *only* when it changes how the person being examined thinks; for example, how a specific teacher was very influential in Mary Jones's life. This distinction between the sociological and psychological perspectives is depicted in Figure 1–1.

To put it another way, sociology does not explain everything of relevance about human behavior, but it does study something not adequately investigated by any other discipline. As one of the principal founders of the discipline, Emile Durkheim (1964, p. 3), has argued, "What is social about human behavior is . . . a category of facts with very distinctive characteristics; [they] consist of ways of acting, thinking, and feeling, external to the individual, and [are] endowed with a power of coercion, by reason of which they control him."

In fact, the influence of what Durkheim calls "social facts" is so great, and most sociologists would agree, that they even *condition*

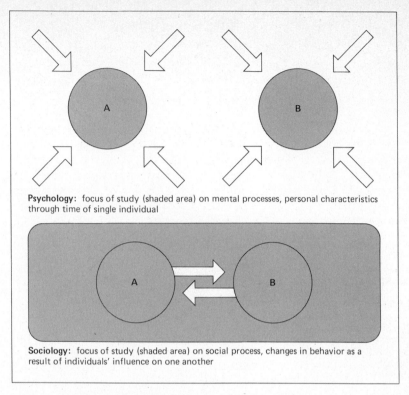

Figure 1–1 **The Perspectives of Psychology and Sociology**

much of our individual psychology. In Box 1–1, there is an example of a person going to school and learning geometry. Clearly, how this individual's thoughts develop as a result of this process is a psychological problem, but the very fact that the person desired to learn geometry at all, knew that school was the place to learn it, and learned it in a certain way are all internal thoughts that have been strongly conditioned by the society in which the individual lives. Similarly, our thoughts about how to organize our day —from waking to sleeping—are all shaped by our knowledge of social life (we wear certain types of clothing, are at certain places at certain times, think about how to present an argument to another person, and so on).

Obviously, if these social facts are so influential in our lives, they are worthy of careful study. It is with this in mind that we now turn to a consideration of how sociologists practice their trade.

HOW SOCIOLOGISTS DO THEIR WORK

The central objective of sociological inquiry is to understand the social aspects of human behavior. How do sociologists attempt to

The difference between what sociologists and psychologists study is nicely summarized by these two examples of French art. Above is the well-known "Moulin de la Galette" by painter Auguste Renoir. Its subject matter is classically sociological: people interacting with one another in different ways in a social setting, in this case a street café. The dancers in the background, the people chatting in the lower right-hand portion of the painting, are all acting *socially;* their behavior is changed because they recognize the presence of others. On the right is sculptor Auguste Rodin's most famous piece, "The Thinker." It depicts a single person lost in thought. Psychologists take as their central focus of study just such a subject—the thoughts of a person and how they come to be ordered as they are.

Box 1-1 SOCIAL AND PSYCHOLOGICAL RELATIONSHIPS

The relations of a man coming into a store to buy a hat or of a woman to buy a beefsteak with the clerk, with the cashier, with the storeowner—these are social relationships. The relationships *in* a man between coming to realize he needs a new hat and making up his mind to buy one, or *in* a woman realizing she is hungry and deciding to buy a beefsteak—these are psychological relationships. No relationship *between two persons* can . . . be a psychological relation. The only psychological relations are those which exist within one mind. . . .

If I go to school and learn geometry and later become an engineer and apply this learning, the relationship between what I learned and how I use it is specifically a psychic relationship. An exchange of ideas, on the other hand, is clearly a social relationship. The moment an exchange of symbols is involved, there is a social relation. That you are angry at a man is a psychological relation between your own mental states; but if you show your anger, swear at him, you establish a social relation. The very fact that one enters into communication with another shows that certain modifications of the interests of two people are taking place. The interest of two people may be in fighting one another; you cannot play a game of chess unless you have an opponent. An enmity of that sort is a conjunction of interests; there is a social relationship. If you are concerned with the psychological system, obviously there are relations under the skin of one individual; [however the] moment you get outside the skin of that individual, you have no longer psychological, but social relations.

Source: A. R. Radcliffe-Brown, *A Natural Science of Society* (New York: Free Press, 1957), p. 47.

accomplish their goal? By what method of inquiry do they operate as sociologists?

Components of the Scientific Method

Most sociologists seek to gather information and answer questions about the social aspects of human behavior by using the techniques of systematic and objective observation and analysis prescribed by the **scientific method.** The emphasis on this method is what separates the approach of the sociologist from that of the average person. Rather than relying on common sense, personal judgment, or the opinion of an authority, sociologists seek to establish the validity of their ideas by systematically testing them in actual social settings. In this way sociologists attempt to minimize the possibility that any personal bias or preconception will interfere with the conclusions they reach. The attempt doesn't always work, of course. As we shall see, sociological methods of research are far from perfect; they do not always eliminate the influence of an investigator's biases on her or his conclusions. Still, a scientific attitude and the pursuit of scientific goals provide the best possible

scientific method A method of inquiry based on systematic and objective observation.

opportunity for investigators to test their ideas effectively and to gain insights into the nature of human behavior.

According to Babbie (1973), there are three major components of scientific activity: description, the discovery of order, and the development of theory.

Description.   A scientist attempts to observe and describe accurately the objects or events being studied. For the physical scientist, such as a physicist or an astronomer, this might involve the measurement of the velocity of falling objects or the wavelength of emissions from a star. For the sociologist, description might include gathering statistics on the rate of suicide among the members of a particular group or observing what happens to people when they change jobs in an industrial setting.

concept A basic idea of a discipline. Sociological concepts include role, status, norm, primary group, and culture.

Scientific description is made possible by the use of a specialized language in which the basic ideas or **concepts** of a discipline can be expressed. Specialized language enables the sociologist to label social phenomena in order to communicate information about them. As this book will amply demonstrate, sociology is rich in concepts such as value, role, norm, status, institution, primary group, subculture, anomie, and culture, to mention just a few.

Discovery of Order.   Many phenomena *vary* in different situations, at different times, and under the influence of different factors. Once phenomena have been identified and defined (described), the scientist becomes involved in the second task of scientific activity—to discover the regular patterns that underlie the seeming chaos of experience. For example, in studying the temperature of objects, the physical scientist will not only make precise measurements of any variations, but will also attempt to identify the factors that cause or influence the variations.

hypothesis A statement of relationship between two or more phenomena that can be submitted to test.

This task is generally accomplished by forming a **hypothesis,** that is, a statement of relationship between two or more phenomena that can be submitted to test. Based on many observations, the physical scientist might tentatively propose that there is a relationship between the temperature of an object and its solidity and then design experiments to determine if such a relationship does in fact exist and, if so, the nature of the relationship. The sociologist might hypothesize a relationship between family structure and delinquency, such as "children from one-parent families tend to engage in more delinquent behavior than do children from two-parent families," or between sex and suicide, such as "males are more likely than females to commit suicide."

variable A concept capable of having two or more aspects.

In the formation of hypotheses the phenomena to be studied are known as **variables.** These are concepts capable of having two or more aspects. Some examples of sociological variables are social class (lower, middle, or upper), family structure (one-parent or two-parent), and institution (family, political, economic, religious, or educational). The variable to be explained or accounted for is known as a **dependent variable** and its presumed cause or an influential factor is known as an **independent variable.** The investigator thus hypothesizes that variations in the independent variable cause an alteration in the dependent variable. In the hypothesis "children from one-parent families tend to engage in more delinquent behavior than do children from two-parent families," the type of family structure (one-parent vs. two-parent) is regarded as the causal or independent variable and the amount of delinquency is the dependent variable.

dependent variable A variable to be explained or accounted for.

independent variable A variable presumed to be a cause or an influential factor.

Development of Theory.   The third task of scientific activity is the formulation of more generalized statements concerning the relationships the investigator has discovered. A **theory** is a statement of relationships among variables that explains a number of seemingly unrelated observations or hypotheses.

As an illustration, consider the possibility that medical science might soon develop a theory that explains a good deal about the nature of cancer in human beings. At the present time, only a number of separate hypotheses regarding the incidence of cancer have been generated and tested. For example,

theory A general statement of relationships among variables that explains a number of observations or hypotheses.

1. Prolonged exposure to the sun increases the likelihood of skin cancer.
2. Cigarette smoking increases the likelihood of lung cancer.
3. Pipe smoking increases the likelihood of lip cancer.
4. Excessive use of saccharin increases the likelihood of stomach cancer.

A theory of the nature of cancer would be able to interrelate and explain these independent hypotheses. For example, a theory of cancer might state that the disease is caused by the influence on the processes of cell division of a particular virus that emerges when some part of the body is subjected to constant irritation (Figure 1–2). This general theory of "irritant cancer" links together the previously unrelated hypotheses and explains why the observed relationships exist. Heavy smoking irritates the lungs, prolonged exposure to the sun irritates the skin, and so forth.

In a similar way, sociologists seek to develop theories that explain the nature of social phenomena. A classic example of sociological theory is found in the work of the well-known French sociologist, Emile Durkheim (1855–1917). Durkheim studied statistics of suicide to see if he could detect any relationship between

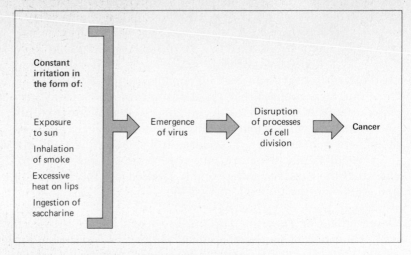

Figure 1–2 A Hypothetical Theory of Cancer

a person's propensity for suicide and his or her social characteristics. For example, he observed the following:

1. Soldiers are more likely than civilians to commit suicide.
2. Officers are more likely than enlisted men to commit suicide.
3. Volunteer soldiers are more likely than draftees to commit suicide.
4. Men are more likely than women to commit suicide.
5. Protestants are more likely than Catholics to commit suicide.
6. Single persons are more likely than married persons to commit suicide.
7. Divorced or widowed persons are more likely than married or single persons to commit suicide.
8. Persons are more likely to commit suicide during periods of rapid economic change, either boom or bust, than during periods of economic stability.
9. Persons are more likely to commit suicide during periods of rapid social change than during periods of social stability.

From his study of the suicide rates of different groups of people in different time periods, Durkheim developed a single theoretical concept that linked together all these hypotheses regarding suicide. He proposed that suicidal behavior is related to the amount of *social integration* experienced by an individual; that is, the nature and depth of a person's involvement with a social group affects that individual's propensity to commit suicide. Durkheim's theory is outlined in Figure 1–3.

Emile Durkheim (1855–1917) is usually regarded as one of the three or four greatest sociologists. His classic work *Suicide* (1897) was the first sociological study to carefully employ the methods of science in the understanding of a social phenomenon.

According to Durkheim, the amount of social integration is causally related to suicide in three different ways in three different types of suicide: altruistic, egoistic, and anomic. In **altruistic suicide**, the individual's amount of social integration is extremely high. The individual's commitment to a group supersedes the satisfaction of personal desires. The commitment may be so strong that the individual is willing to give up his or her life for the group's continuance. Durkheim identifies this type of self-destruction as altruistic suicide.

The concept of altruistic suicide provides an explanation for Durkheim's first three observations previously listed. First, military life demands a strong sense of group loyalty at the expense of individual liberty. The propensity for suicide is thus great-

altruistic suicide The variety of suicide that occurs when the individual's social integration is excessively high.

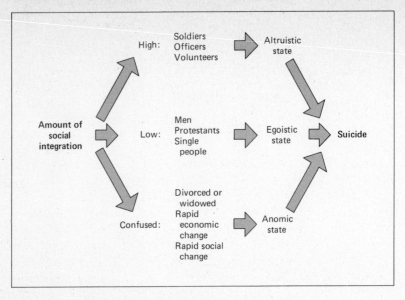

Figure 1–3   Durkheim's Theory of Suicide

er than in civilian life where the individual's commitment is diffused among many groups. There are numerous cases of soldiers who throw themselves on enemy grenades in order to save their fellow soldiers. A similar, highly publicized example of this type of suicide was the Japanese kamikaze pilot of World War II.

Second, since the amount of social integration (commitment to military goals) tends to increase as military rank increases, officers are more likely to give up their lives for "the cause" than are enlisted men. The well-known phrase "The captain goes down with his ship" illustrates this point. The same reasoning can be applied to the difference between the suicide rates of volunteers and draftees, the third observation. In contrast to soldiers who are drafted, volunteers tend to be people who are ready and willing to accept a great degree of loyalty to military life. Their high suicide rate is a result of that loyalty.

egoistic suicide The variety of suicide that occurs when the individual's social integration is excessively low, so that life loses meaning.

What Durkheim labeled **egoistic suicide,** on the other hand, is motivated by an excessively low level of social integration. In modern societies there are individuals who belong to fewer social groups than others. Moreover, even in the groups to which these people belong, their commitment may be weak because either it is their choice or the group requires few duties of its members. Such an individual, Durkheim calls egoistic—one who depends "only on himself and recognizes no other rules of conduct than what are founded on his private interests" (Durkheim, 1951, p. 209). Such independence may be in some respects a positive attribute. However, it also means that such an individual is more likely to feel isolated, alone, unwanted, or that his or her life has no meaning, than individuals who are strongly attached to many social groups. Consequently, for an egoistic person, life's regular trials and tribulations are likely to assume a much greater significance in day-to-day life, perhaps to the point of seeming insurmountable or not worth the effort needed to correct them. In such a situation, one ultimate response may be to commit egoistic suicide.

The state of egoism provides the basis for explaining Durkheim's findings (observations 4, 5, 6) that suicide is more likely among men than women, among Protestants than Catholics, and among single persons than married persons. When compared to other members of society, it is found in all these cases that the amount of social integration is low. In our society, for example, the role of the male frequently demands individualism and self-reliance which are not expected of the female. As a result, American males are more likely than their female counterparts to commit egoistic suicide. Similarly, Protestantism emphasizes self-reliance and independence for the individual more than Catholicism does. The Protestant is supposed to communicate directly and personally with God, however difficult that may be. The Catholic's relation to the Deity is spelled out in much more literal terms and mediated by the group structure. For example, Catholics have a formal mechanism for regularly "confessing their sins," a mechanism that can relieve them of considerable guilt. Protestants have no such mechanism and thus have to "bear their sins" privately. Consequently, Protestants are more likely than Catholics to commit egoistic suicide. Similarly, since single persons tend to be less integrated into the social order than their married counterparts, they are more likely to commit egoistic suicide.

Observations 1 to 6 explained, Durkheim then turned to a consideration of another possible variation in social integration to explain observations 7, 8, and 9. He argued that all members of society, whatever their social position, live day to day by working out an intricate pattern of behaviors that attempt to match their means to their needs. Thus rich and poor, black and white, famous and unknown people, all develop deeply habitualized routines by which they organize their lives. Occasionally, however, sudden changes may occur in social circumstances—for example, physical catastrophes, war, loss of family, friends, or fortune—that upset this established routine. In such situations, which Durkheim called a state of **anomie,** people affected by the crisis suddenly find their patterns of social integration disrupted and are confused about how to act. Old routines may be perceived as either useless or uninviting; new routines have not yet been accepted and, in com-

anomie A state of society where, because of sudden or continuing social change, knowledge of the correct ways to behave is disrupted.

parison to the old routines, seem foreign or frightening. Such confusion, in the extreme, my lead some people to commit **anomic suicide.**

The condition of anomie provides an explanation for Durkheim's observations 7, 8, and 9; self-inflicted death is more likely among divorced or widowed persons and in times of rapid economic or social change. The widower, for example, suddenly loses that individual around whom his whole life-style has been organized. Other social relations may remain the same, but suddenly "nothing makes sense anymore." Similarly, persons may experience anomie after losing their life's earnings in a stock market crash. Witness the large number of suicides following the Wall Street crash of 1929. However, in this context, Durkheim (1951, p. 253) is quick to point out that sudden economic crises of a *positive* kind—"booms"—can create an increase in anomic suicide as well.

> With increased prosperity desires increase. At [this] very moment . . . traditional rules [lose] their authority [and] the richer prize offered these appetites stimulates them and makes them [harder to] control. The state of de-regulation or anomie is thus further heightened by passions being less disciplined, precisely when they need more disciplining.

Imagine a very poor person suddenly winning a million dollars in the state lottery. What would happen to that person's daily routines? Let us say a man worked for $3 an hour at a gas station. What would happen to his relationships with other poor friends? Now rich, but never "bred" to be rich, how could he now interact with other rich people in society? (See Box 1–2.) Finally, consider the dislocations brought about by rapid social change. For example, a school vice-president who has held that position for 30 years may unexpectedly find the position has been eliminated in favor of a review board for school operations. Finding that her services are no longer needed and unable to find another equivalent job, she may experience severe anomie and become a prime candidate for suicide.

In summary, then, Durkheim's theory of suicide is an excellent example of the application of the scientific method to explain social aspects of human behavior. We see, reviewing Babbie's components of scientific activity that, first, Durkheim *described* the phenomenon under consideration (suicide—all self-inflicted deaths); second, he *discovered* that the phenomenon was clearly *ordered* (e.g., suicide tends to be committed more often by males than females); and, third, he *developed a theory* that explained

Box 1–2　LOTTERY WINNERS

Individuals who experience anomie are confused about how to behave. Their old routines have been disrupted, and they are left without rules for living.

Sociologist H. Roy Kaplan (1978) interviewed more than 100 big-money lottery winners including many instant millionaires in five states. He found that the "lucky winners" had experienced anomie because of dramatic changes in their ways of living.

For one thing, many had gone from poverty to affluence. Before winning, they had little money or education. Now, they were millionaires or at least wealthier than they ever dared imagine. Before winning, they had worked at low-level jobs requiring little training or skill. Now, they were able to quit their jobs and buy expensive homes in exclusive neighborhoods.

Despite the wealth, not all of the big winners confessed to being entirely happy with their new status in life. According to Kaplan, some had trouble coping with their new joblessness. They tried in vain to fill the hours of the day by watching television, working around the house, and entertaining at home; but they attended few concerts or lectures and rarely visited museums or the theatre. Few of them enrolled in colleges or performed community service. Most were unable to find challenging work because they lacked marketable skills. As a result, many suffered from boredom and monotony.

To make matters worse, many big winners were the targets of con men and shysters. They were bombarded with mail asking for charity or loans. Their former co-workers became jealous and hostile. Long-lost relatives appeared to collect their share of the winnings; and children of the winners felt less than satisfied with the amounts they received.

In many cases, the lottery winners felt compelled to change their residence in order to maintain privacy and insulate themselves from hostility. After moving, they often avoided revealing to their new neighbors and friends exactly how they had acquired their new-found wealth.

Despite all the anomie, none of the instant millionaires interviewed by Kaplan expressed regrets about winning so much money. Instead, they emphasized how their winnings had relieved the financial burdens of life. Indeed, many of them continued to buy lottery tickets on a regular basis—and in larger amounts than ever!

H. Roy Kaplan, *Lottery Winners: How They Won and How Winning Changed Their Lives* (New York: Barnes & Noble, 1978).

that order (suicide varies with the type of social integration experienced in a society).

We now turn to a consideration of how the scientific method has developed in sociology itself.

The Scientific Method in Sociology

The scientific method can be and has been applied to the study of almost everything in the universe, including baseball, extrasen-

San Francisco's Golden Gate Bridge is beautiful, massive, and in one of the world's most spectacular settings. This bridge has become a world renowned place for suicide attempts as well. Why? For a partial explanation see the box, "The Social Elements of Suicide."

sory perception, astrology, the social organization of apes, and transcendental meditation. It has long been used in such established disciplines as physiology, physics, and chemistry. Among the fields of study employing this method, however, sociology is relatively new, being less than a century and a half old as a separate field.

Auguste Comte (1798–1857), a French mathematician and philosopher, coined the name "sociology" and was the first to argue that students of society should utilize the methods of science in gathering information about human behavior. Comte realized that a science of social life would be difficult to achieve because the social aspects of human behavior are extremely complex and varied. Nevertheless, he argued that such a study must be undertaken if humankind were ever truly to understand itself. With the objective knowledge generated by a science of society, human life

Box 1-3 THE SOCIAL ELEMENTS OF SUICIDE

Once *San Francisco Magazine* ran an article reporting the results of an interview done with four of the eight known survivors of suicide attempts from San Francisco's Golden Gate Bridge. At the time of the article 536 suicides had been reported at the site and the bridge was unquestionably the "favorite location for death by suicide in the entire Western world." It is interesting, in considering Durkheim's theory, to examine the social characteristics of these four survivors.

All were male, unmarried, under 30 years of age, and unsettled in their lifestyles. One was a 16-year-old runaway with no money and no job, who had just had a serious argument with the only friend he had in a strange city. The second was 18, lived alone with his mother, had few friends, and had lost his two closest friends in the previous weeks very suddenly—one by murder, another by suicide. The third was a 29-year-old hippie, who, while high on LSD and disillusioned by the failure of his culture to transform the world, thought as he went over the bridge: "If there isn't going to be a Utopia, why pursue this motley, mortal existence?" The fourth was a 21-year-old homosexual with a temporary job at the post office. Unable to find a meaningful relationship with others for years, he felt suicide would be "an escape into something else."

Two interesting sociological observations may be made from the above information. First, without exception, these young men shared significantly in the characteristics which Durkheim relates to either egoistic or anomic suicides: all were either directly or indirectly cut off from what they perceived to be meaningful social relationships or had had such relationships suddenly broken immediately before their suicide attempts. In the article, no mention is made of suicide attempts by people not sharing these characteristics.

Second, the four men attempted to carry out their decisions to commit suicide according to a well-known, socially defined pattern, that is, they went to a place commonly associated with spectacular, self-inflicted deaths and committed their act in a way that hundreds of others had before them: they walked to the middle of the bridge and leaped off. As the editors of the magazine say,

> Over the years, as we [San Franciscans] have watched millions of tourists drawn to our photogenic Bridge, we have also watched a suicide mystique grow up around it. Instead of just swallowing too many pills in their bathroom, or putting a bullet through their frontal lobe in the backyard, death-wishers have been known to travel miles, at great inconvenience, to leap toward death in the Bay. Such a jump is spectacular, guaranteeing newspaper headlines, and although it may not be as easy as some people think, over five hundred suicides have proved that it certainly can be done.

Psychiatrist David Rosa, who interviewed the four survivors, comments in the article on some of his findings regarding the social attraction of the Bridge.

> The Golden Gate Bridge survivors' suicide plans involved *only* the Golden Gate Bridge. For *all* of them, the Bridge had a special and unique meaning; often this was related in a symbolic way to the association of the Bridge with death, grace and beauty. The fact that the Golden Gate Bridge leads the world in suicides should be knowledge enough for us to begin to deromanticize suicide, specifically as it relates to the Bridge. I underscore and concur wholeheartedly with the . . . recommendation that a suicide barrier should be constructed on the Golden Gate Bridge.

Source: *San Francisco,* April 1975, vol. 17, no. 4.

could move to a level of unparalleled development. Without it, however, human life would likely remain subject to the "slings and arrows of outrageous fortune" (as Shakespeare so succinctly put it), as it had been since time immemorial.

Despite the cogency of Comte's appeal, early sociologists, including Comte himself, took what has been called an "armchair approach" to the study of social phenomena; that is, they tended to draw their conclusions about the social world from their philosophical musings about how society supposedly worked rather than from direct observations. Comte, for example, never studied Paris, or France, or any other society systematically.

Another armchair approach was to build social theories on information supplied by nonscientists. Herbert Spencer, a noted nineteenth-century British sociologist, used the reports of missionaries to build a theory of how societies "evolved." Not surprisingly, using such reports (whatever their good intentions, it must be remembered that missionaries went out to convert the "heathen"), and his own personal biases, Spencer concocted a theory that suggested rather strongly that *his own society* was the most evolved on earth. With few exceptions, this armchair approach to the study of social life prevailed for the first 50 to 75 years of sociology's existence.

During the early part of the twentieth century, however, a number of sociologists (including Emile Durkheim) began to recognize that personal perceptions of the social world are frequently inaccurate and that reliance on secondhand information alone may lead to erroneous conclusions. Sociologists started to advocate that a certain amount of fieldwork should be done by anyone attempting to describe a particular group or society. More specifically, they advised that investigators go to the physical location of the groups they were interested in studying, so that they could examine firsthand the manner in which these groups began, perpetuated themselves, or changed. Only by the direct application of the methods of scientific inquiry could sociologists ever hope to view social situations objectively and to develop adequate explanations of human behavior. As a result of these endeavors, sociologists have developed a useful repertoire of research methods with which they can test their ideas about the social aspects of human behavior. Such methods include the experiment, survey, participant observation, and content analysis.

Research Methods in Sociology

experiment A method of research in which the investigator manipulates an independent variable.

The Experiment. In an **experiment** the sociologist actually manipulates the independent variable being studied. For instance, an experimenter attempting to test the hypothesis that

Auguste Comte (1798–1857) is considered by many to be the founder of sociology. His major work, *The Positive Philosophy*, contended that it was the prime occupation of a social science to discover the laws by which regular social events occurred. If this were done properly, he felt that for the first time in history, a true science of humanity would result, with which humankind could both understand and better itself.

frustration (the independent variable) increases prejudice against minorities (the dependent variable) might first employ some testing device to determine the level of prejudice among the subjects. Then the investigator might manipulate the independent variable by assigning a difficult (i.e., frustrating) examination to the **experimental group** while allowing the **control group** to relax or to take an easy examination. If a subsequent retesting indicates more prejudice in the experimental group than in the control group, this difference could be attributed to the influence of frustration.

But how can the experimenter be sure that the experimental and control groups are identical to begin with? How is it possible to obtain comparable groups from the beginning of the study? The answer lies in a procedure known as **randomization,** whereby subjects are assigned on a random basis to the experimental and control conditions, so that the groups differ by chance alone. Randomization might be achieved, for example, by assigning subjects to either the experimental or the control group by a flip of a coin. Random assignment provides relative assurance on a probability basis that the groups are in fact comparable. An example of a simple experiment that produced some fascinating results is contained in Box 1–4.

experimental group The subjects in an experiment who are exposed to the changing conditions devised by the experimenter.

control group The subjects in an experiment not exposed to changing conditions devised by the experimenter.

randomization An experimental procedure whereby subjects are assigned on a chance basis to the experimental or control groups to ensure that the groups differ by chance alone.

Box 1–4   HELPING YOURSELF TO A CHEESEBURGER: AN EXPERIMENT

We know that the presence of others in an emergency situation inhibits people from coming to the aid of persons in need of help (i.e., you're more likely to get help from someone on a relatively untraveled road than on a busy highway, holding everything else constant). Does the presence of others also reduce the opportunity to help oneself rather than other people? Specifically, are individuals less likely to help themselves to a free lunch when other people are around than when they are alone?

To find out, Petty, Williams, Harkins, and Latane (1977) conducted an experiment in which they gave elevator riders at Ohio State University the opportunity to help themselves to a coupon good for a complimentary Quarter Pounder with cheese. Upon entering the elevator, riders confronted a poster reading "Free McDonald's Burger" and a pocket underneath it in which coupons for one Quarter Pounder were located.

Fifty-six people entered the elevator alone. Of this number, 26 were randomly permitted to ride without other passengers, while 16 rode with one other passenger and 14 rode with two other passengers (all of the "other passengers" were actually confederates of the experimenters who decided on a random basis whether subjects rode with two, one, or no other riders).

Results obtained by Petty et al. showed that individuals riding alone were much more likely to help themselves to a cheeseburger than were riders in the presence of other passengers. Of those individuals riding by themselves, 81 percent took a free coupon. With one other passenger present, however, only 38 percent took a coupon; and with two other passengers present, only 14 percent helped themselves to a coupon.

These results seem to indicate that people will inhibit doing something—even something to their advantage—in order to avoid the embarrassment that results from calling attention to themselves in a public setting. In addition, individuals often employ one another as models for appropriate behavior. Until someone else acts, everyone in an elevator may be led to assume that taking a free coupon is improper.

survey A method of research in which a record of behavior is obtained by the investigator, after it has occurred.

The Survey. The central advantage of the experiment is that researchers can exercise a great deal of control over the situation; they have a direct hand in producing the effect that is predicted to occur. By contrast, **survey** research is *retrospective*, the investigator records behavior after it has occurred rather than observing it directly or manipulating it. In a study of the impact of frustration, for example, a researcher might compare a number of persons on the basis of the existence of severe deprivation or frustrating experiences in their history, such as physical disabilities, social isolation, poverty, or poor grade-point average. The survey obtains the reports of a set of respondents by means of either a self-administered *questionnaire* or an *interview* in which the presence of a trained interviewer is required.

Sometimes surveys can attempt to find out information about every member of a population. One example is the U.S. census, taken every decade. Despite the fact that it is always somewhat imperfect (e.g., the poor, rural people, immigrant groups, and illegals are often incompletely surveyed), the census produces much useful information about our society. Thus the 1980 census showed conclusively that women and blacks were entering the work force in greater numbers and at better paying positions. Although in both cases the percentage of women and blacks in the work force did not equal their percentage in the population generally (52 percent for women, 14 percent for blacks), advances were made over the previous decade. For instance, the percentage of women employed as editors in journalism rose from 40 to 49 percent between 1970 and 1980 and blacks, who were virtually nonrepresented in construction in 1970, held 7 percent of the construction jobs in 1980 (*New York Times,* April 24, 1983, pp. 1, 18).

However, most researchers do not have the financial and labor resources of the U.S. government at their disposal. As a result, the typical survey researcher investigates only a **sample,** a smaller number of individuals who are presumed to be representative of a population. For example, a sociologist who is interested in the population of a large urban center might be able to make accurate statements about that whole urban complex based on a study of only several hundred city residents. In a similar manner, a communications researcher might generalize to the population of millions of television viewers or a political analyst might predict the voting behavior of millions of Americans based on carefully sampled surveys of only a few thousand persons. The Nielson television ratings, for example, are based on the viewing habits of a thousand carefully sampled American homes; similarly, the Harris and Gallup polls have on occasion been accurate within a tenth of a percent in their predictions of the voting behavior of all Americans based on only a few thousand interviews.

A well-designed and well-executed sampling plan is essential to ensure that the sample will represent the population. The most effective way to obtain a representative sample is *random sampling,* whereby every member of a population has the same chance to be chosen for the sample. For instance, a researcher attempting to obtain information about a given population of

sample A small number of individuals who are somehow representative of a larger population, used in research as the basis for generalizations about the larger population.

prison inmates might decide to interview every tenth inmate on a complete list of all inmates. The researcher can be reasonably sure that the hundred randomly selected respondents will provide an adequate representation of total inmate feelings or behavior. Thus the survey can be an extremely effective way to arrive at **generalizations** about a population without expending the time, money, and effort required to poll the entire population. Just as importantly, survey research well done allows sociologists to make predictions with greater certainty about how a given population is likely to act in the future or how similar populations, as yet unsurveyed, may act. An interesting example of survey research that examined the so-called "generation gap" is reported in Box 1–5.

Participant Observation.   Another widely used method in the study of social aspects of human behavior is **participant observation,** in which the sociologist "participates in the daily life of the people under study, either openly in the role of researcher or covertly in some disguised role, observing things that happen, listening to what is said, and questioning people, over some length of time" (Becker and Geer, 1970, p. 133).

participant observation
A method of research in which the sociologist participates in the activities of the group under study.

Participation observation gives the researcher the chance to learn the meaning of social behavior from *within* the group. For example, the observer is able to study the use of words in their context and to explore their meanings under a variety of conditions or to learn the complex rituals of the group and the manner in which they are defined by group members. An interesting illustration of the technique is provided by Festinger, Riecken, and Schachter's *When Prophecy Fails* (1956), a study of a small group of people who predicted the destruction of the world. The 25 to 30 participants in this group gathered around a woman who claimed to be receiving written messages from outer space. One message brought news of an impending flood that would engulf the continent. Subsequent messages revealed that only group members would be saved: They would be carried away by flying saucers at a designated time.

Before predicting the impending disaster, the group was characterized by extreme secrecy and suspicion of nonbelievers. Therefore, to investigate the group's behavior, Festinger, Riecken, and Schachter sent trained participant observers to join the group, posing as ordinary members who believed as the others did in the validity of the messages from outer space. Their observations were carried out over a 3-month period (2 months before

Box 1–5   HAS THE GENERATION GAP WIDENED?

Is the "generation gap" between teenagers and their parents any wider now than it was 50 years earlier? In their widely acclaimed study of a midwestern community in the 1920s (called Middletown), Robert and Helen Lynd (1929) administered questionnaires on "the life of the high school population" to students in all high school sophomore, junior, and senior English classes.

The original study of Middletown was conducted in 1924. Some 53 years later, during the winter of 1977, sociologist Howard M. Bahr and his associates (1980) went back to Middletown high schools, where they administered a survey questionnaire containing the original Lynd questions and some additional items about school and family life. For example, students marked a list of 13 topics about which they agreed or disagreed with their parents. The authors' results were based on a random sample of questionnaires obtained from an estimated population of 4,000 Middletown students.

Bahr's results were surprising when compared with those obtained decades earlier by the Lynds. For example, in both time periods 1924 and 1977, more than 40 percent of the students reported having disagreements with their parents concerning "the hours you get in at night." Similarly, the frequencies of disagreement about grades, spending money, and student organizations were also the same in 1977 as in 1924.

Certain topics did in fact generate greater conflict between parents and high schoolers in the more recent time period. For example, there was more family disagreement in 1977 about helping with household chores or doing yardwork. On the other hand, there was also less reported conflict in 1977 than in 1924 about the use of the family car, the number of times a student wanted to go out on school nights, and peers chosen as friends.

In sum, results obtained by Bahr did not support the belief that disagreements between high school students and their parents—the so-called generation gap—was any wider in the seventies than it had been during the twenties. Although some of the topics of disagreement may have changed, the overall level of disagreement between teenagers and parents was comparable in 1924 and 1977.

the predicted disaster and 1 month after it did not occur) without the knowledge or consent of group members.

When the prophecy failed to occur as predicted, Festinger, Riecken, and Schachter's observers reported an extremely interesting set of events. First, after struggling for some time with the possible explanation that they had been wrong, the members found an alternative explanation that would protect them from thinking that the tremendous time and effort they have lavished on this group and its beliefs had been wasted. The new explanation was in the form of a "message from God" (actually from the woman who had been communicating with outer space all along).

It said, in effect, "that He had saved the world and stayed the flood because of this group and the light and strength they had spread throughout the world" (Festinger, 1957). Second, after receiving this message, the group members did something they had never done before: They avidly sought publicity and tried to make converts. By convincing more and more people of the "correctness" of their interpretation of the nonflood, they would not have to face the fact that appeared to others to be indisputable—that they had been wrong in predicting the end of the world.

The suspicions of Festinger, Riecken, and Schachter's subjects about outsiders dictated that the researchers assume a disguised role to participate as fully as possible in the behavior under observation. By contrast, John Dollard, in his classic study of race relations in a small southern community, *Caste and Class in a Southern Town* (1937), engaged in only the "casual participation possible [for] a 'Yankee down here studying Negroes.' " For most of the 5 months he spent as a participant observer, Dollard operated openly in the role of researcher, observing what people said, did, and seemed to feel, but avoided direct interrogation by the town's people. Dollard observed a complex pattern of race relations that generated important economic, sexual, and prestige gains for the white, middle-class residents of the town. He was also able to identify several forms of aggression—among blacks, against whites, and against blacks—that resulted from race prejudice.

On another level, the difference between the Festinger-Riecken-Schachter approach to participant observation and that of Dollard throws into high relief the question of sociological ethics, a controversy that has not been resolved in a half-century. Should sociologists always identify themselves as such when doing participant observation? Some sociologists argue that the answer is always "yes," because not to do so would deceive the people under study and violate their basic rights as human beings. On the other hand, if they were always to identify themselves as sociologists, people might refuse to cooperate and no information could be gained. Or, perhaps, those under study may consciously or unconsciously change their behavior in the presence of the sociologist, thereby creating "new" behavior which is not what the researcher is trying to understand. (Do *you* act completely naturally when you know your voice is being recorded?) Consequently, some sociologists argue that if the information is not to be used in a destructive way or if they "disguise" the group under study—calling the town "Smithville" rather than referring to its actual name—"unacknowledged" participant observation is both ethical *and* necessary in order to accumulate accurate social knowledge. What do you think?

Content Analysis.   Content analysis is the study of messages of communication in various forms, such as books, magazines, newspapers, films, radio and television broadcasts, photographs, cartoons, letters and diaries, verbal interaction between two individuals, political propaganda, and music. Such messages give clues to many phenomena of interest to the sociologist. For example, sociologists have employed content analysis to investigate changing sex roles as reflected in advice to the lovelorn columns, conceptions of romantic love as depicted in popular song lyrics, changes in concern with wealth as found in the platforms of the two major parties for presidential elections, and the values of the recent youth counterculture.

In an early study of majority and minority Americans in magazine fiction, for example, Berelson and Salter (1946) analyzed the content of a sample of 198 short stories published in eight of the most widely read magazines of 1937 and 1943. They compared "Americans," that is, white Protestants of no distinguishable foreign origin, with characters having foreign or minority status, such as blacks, Jews, Italians, Poles, and Orientals. Dramatic group differences emerged. There were many more "Americans" and fewer minority characters in these stories than in the population of the United States at the time the study was conducted. Moreover, minority characters who did appear were given obscure or undesirable dramatic roles and were stereotypically portrayed. For example, Berelson and Salter report finding images of the "amusingly ignorant Negro," the "Italian gangster," the "sly and shrewd" Jew, the "emotional" Irishman, and the "primitive and backward" Pole. Such findings of stereotyped characters suggest that content analysis can be a very effective method for uncovering the subtle (and not so subtle) messages that people in a society communicate to one another.

Other Sociological Methods.   Although the preceding methods —the experiment, the survey, participant observation, and content analysis—are among the most commonly used in the discipline, there are others, too numerous to discuss in detail, that sociologists use. One particularly interesting one is **comparative analysis**. In this approach sociologists take known characteristics about one group or country—for example, population statistics or religious beliefs or attitudes about cleanliness—and compare them with other groups or countries to arrive at better understandings of social processes.

Consider beliefs about cleanliness: An American visitor to

content analysis A method that studies forms of communication, such as books, films, radio or TV broadcasts, diaries, and the like.

comparative analysis A method that examines the characteristics of groups or countries and compares them with other groups or countries.

Cairo is likely to observe, if he or she stays there long enough, an Arab putting a finger by one of his nostrils and blowing his nose directly into the street. How horrible we think! How unsanitary! Yet a more curious observer might ask the Arab why this is done? He would reply that, in his society, mucous in the nose is regarded as unsanitary and that the best way to discard it is to get it away from the body altogether, into the hot street where it will evaporate quickly. In contrast, the Arab may be incredulous at *our* habits of supposed cleanliness, when he learns that Americans generally blow their noses into linen handkerchiefs, look at the results, carefully fold the handkerchief, and put it in their pockets! Worse, the handkerchief is used again and again! How horrible! How unsanitary! The lesson, of course, is clear: Different groups have decidedly different social beliefs about cleanliness, beliefs that make sense in their *own* social context.

unobtrusive measures A method of observation that does not require the cooperation of the respondent.

Another technique is the examination of social facts by the use of what are called **unobtrusive measures** —measures that "do not require the cooperation of a respondent" (Webb et al., 1966). For example, the sociologist might observe, not necessarily as a participant, such things as the clothes people wear or the ways they decorate their rooms for social effect. Similarly, a researcher might be able to determine the amount of studying done by various members of a class by leafing through their textbooks. If the pages of the books of one group of students are a bit soiled, bent, profusely underlined and the like, he or she might predict that that group would do better on the final exam than another group whose textbooks remained in pristine condition to the last day of the course.

simulation A method that creates artificial social conditions.

Lastly, of increasing interest to sociologists is the use of the method known as **simulation,** or the creation, under artificial conditions, of social situations to see what happens when variables are manipulated. Haney, Banks, and Zimbardo (1973), for example, created a simulation to see what would happen if noncriminals (in this case, normal college students) were put in an artificial prison-type setting and asked to "play the roles" of prisoners or guards. They found that, in a very short period of time, the students who were *randomly designated* as guards began acting tyrannical and had an obsessive concern with order, whereas the students who were *randomly assigned* as prisoners began acting docile and developed an attitude of "self-survival" at the expense of fellow prisoners. They concluded that simulated prisons appear to have a great ability to call forth true prison-type social behavior even among people who had never experienced such social settings before. Furthermore, their research demonstrated once again the power social situations can exert on our lives if we are uncritical participants.

THE USES OF SOCIOLOGY

We have been examining what sociologists try to do and how they go about doing it. But why should we study sociology? What is the relevance of the field to living in our world?

The Question of Relevance

The word "relevance" can be used to refer to several different things. Most students taking their first course in sociology are concerned about sociology's relevance to everyday life, society's problems, or career goals.

Relevance to Everyday Life.   The goal of sociology is to increase our understanding of ourselves as social beings. In fact, the desire for self-understanding is often a motivating factor in people's interest in the field of sociology. There is little doubt, furthermore, that sociology can provide such relevant information. To take a current and crucial example, many people are learning through the application of sociological findings that the traditional sex roles in American society—the independent, aggressive, unemotional male and the dependent, mild-mannered, emotional female—are arbitrary inventions of our social order. Research has shown that these characteristics have no innate or biological basis (see "Socialization and Human Nature," Chapter 3). The fact that many men and women conform to these role characteristics is only an indication that the members of certain groups expect them to act in the traditional ways. Obviously, this type of information has great relevance to our everyday lives. It can make us aware of the social forces that have been and still are shaping us in certain directions, allow us to decide if changes in these forces would be beneficial, and give us the knowledge necessary for making such changes. As the American sociologist Lester Frank Ward expressed it over 75 years ago, "I would have never taken any interest in sociology if I had not conceived that it . . . gives [people] the means of self-orientation. With this information to start with [they] are in a position to consider [the] future" (1906, p. 20).

Relevance to Society's Problems.   Sociology may also help us to deal with the issues of our time and place. In the example of sex role behavior we can see not only the relevance of the discipline to an individual's everyday life, but also implications for society as a whole. Sociological findings are applicable to many current problems, such as the impact of pornography on society, busing as a mechanism for achieving integrated schools, the causes of crime and delinquency, the effects of television on children, the use of power in politics, the changing role of the aged, race relations and poverty, public housing, and many others. In short, anything identifiable as a social problem is highly appropriate material for sociological analysis.

Relevance to Career Goals.   The ability of an individual to deal with the social aspects of human behavior is an important factor for the fulfillment of many careers, including business management, law and law enforcement, public relations, medicine, social service, urban planning, advertising, and teaching. Although the largest number of career sociologists teach at the college level, a significant number hold positions in marketing and consumer research, social policy and planning, high school teaching, industrial relations, government, and social research. In addition, many business and professional organizations encourage their prospective employees to take courses in sociology as a means of becoming more aware of their social environment. Box 1–6 lists just a few of the careers in which sociological learning is especially relevant.

Sociology and Common Sense

Students taking their first course in sociology sometimes feel that their commonsense observations of social behavior tell them as much as any sociological analysis can. Typical remarks include "I knew that before taking this course" or "I would have guessed that anyway."

This problem can be expected to arise to some extent whenever an introductory course attempts to teach the language of its discipline. For example, what do students of anatomy learn when they are taught to refer to their collarbone as the "clavicle" or to their kneecap as the "patella"? They have not acquired new factual knowledge, but they are learning to use the tools of communication of a field. As previously mentioned, accurate communication among scientists is possible only because they agree to employ the same specialized and highly precise language.

But sociology is often attacked as being merely a restatement of commonsensical information using a specialized vocabulary. Unlike the phenomena studied by the physical sciences, the social world is directly experienced by all human beings on an everyday basis. All of us have developed opinions about our social

---

Box 1-6 APPLIED SOCIOLOGY

The topics covered in *Applied Sociology* (1983), a recent book sponsored by the American Sociological Association, illustrate the broad range of interests found among professional sociologists outside the academic world. Some of these topics in the areas of business, government, education, and health and human services are the following:

Business
   Social research in industry
   Corporate marketing
   Consumer and advertising research

Source: Howard E. Freeman, Russell R. Dynes, Peter H. Rossi, and William Foote Whyte (eds.), *Applied Sociology* (San Francisco: Jossey-Bass, Inc., 1983).

Government
   Demographic analysis
   Government policy research
   Legislative consultation
   Law and criminal justice
   Military studies
   Housing and environmental planning

Education
   Research on educational programs

Health and Human Services
   Program evaluation
   Human services planning
   Health service administration and research
   Research on aging

---

world, many of which are deeply ingrained and difficult to modify. We all like to think that we really understand "the truth" about living in society; most of us feel we know quite a lot about the nature of racism, poverty, and political power, simply because we have been exposed to these problems so often throughout life. Such "overexposure" to subject matter does not usually happen in fields such as physics and chemistry (see Box 1–7).

Another factor contributing to the feeling of "already knowing" the subject matter is that much of the information students do have before they enter a course in sociology has in fact been developed within the discipline. The findings of the behavioral sciences have a way of becoming part of the background assumptions on how we live. Yet relatively few people are aware of the origin of such ideas. Even fewer have read the works of those sociologists, psychologists, and anthropologists who have had such a profound influence on their behavior and attitudes.

Consider how deeply ingrained in our culture are many of Freud's discoveries relating to unconscious sexual and aggressive motivation. These ideas have influenced the way that we think about one another and our view of human nature. In a similar

From the time of Comte and Durkheim, sociology has been concerned with the different problems societies develop and how these problems affect individuals. Two such contemporary problems are the efficiency of bureaucratic functioning (above) and the relationship between the sexes (right). For more on the former problem see Chapter 4; for more on the latter, see Chapters 3 and 7.

way, awareness of the presence in American society of inequality based on social class has been greatly heightened by popularized accounts of sociological work such as Vance Packard's best-selling books of the 1950s. Popular anthropological writings (e.g., by Margaret Mead and Ashley Montagu) have apprised the members of our society of the rich variety of customs (from cannibalism to polygamous marriage) found in other societies of the world.

Still another source of the feeling that sociology and common sense overlap to a large extent is that almost any conclusion (or its opposite), whether true or false, can be justified *after the fact* on the basis of logic or arbitrary judgment. Consider the following sets of contradictory "facts" that can easily be rationalized by the use of common sense:

- *Fact:* Did you know that during World War II soldiers were more eager to return to the states while the fighting continued than they were after the enemy surrendered?
- *Rationale:* Of course! Everybody knows there is an inborn drive toward self-preservation. Who wants to die, anyway?

Box 1–7   A CHALLENGE TO CONVENTIONAL WISDOM

If people really knew what was going on between them, sociology would have far less reason for existence than it does. But much of what people "know" is in fact a series of folk statements, a set of comfortable prejudices, a closet full of oversimplifications. Sociology and sociologists function as a challenge to stereotyped ways of understanding social reality. But there is a catch. We can't live without some simplifications, or at least most people can't. Sociology thus can be uncomfortable to people.

Let me give you an example. Whenever I teach political sociology we spend quite a bit of time on the problem of just how much power and influence America's giant corporations have. I make sure the students understand that the *structure* of the social situation—including the role of these companies—should not be confused with the personalities of the individuals who head them up. With a series of real-world consumer issues I try to illustrate the real conflicts of interest that arise. What is sad is this—sometimes the bright son or daughter of a high-level corporate executive starts the course parroting the line of the corporation. By the end of the course the student's viewpoint has changed somewhat—not convinced, but at least willing to see more than one side of these issues. Then she goes home, and gets into a real and basic argument that

summer with her father. "For *this* I'm spending so much tuition money!" he exclaims. Just in this way—not to supplant one set of stereotypes with another, but to open up as questions what were previously the closed doors of conventional wisdom, is one of the main gifts of sociology.

But again, note that the gift has another kind of price. A high one, at that. You will never see the world the same again. Regardless of how insane sociology can seem at times, how burdened with the wordy jargon of pedants, how full of textbooks, there is a core to it, a challenge, a training in the reinspection of the things that have made your life comfortable as well as the things that have made it uncomfortable. Why eat of the apple from the tree of knowledge? Look what happened to Adam and Eve! Yet we do have curiosity. We are born with it as a very strong motivating force, in fact, according to all the new studies that directly observe small children. We have a natural curiosity about society—the same curiosity that must have driven the great founders of the field to do *their* work, to ask the first great questions about how and why a society is set up the way it is. And if curiosity and the challenging of old assumptions have a price, well, I encourage you to pay it. The irritation you may cause others by your questions and the pain you may experience as you reexamine your own assumptions will more than be repaid by a deeper, more genuine understanding of the world out there.

Source: Elliott Krause, *Why Study Sociology?* (New York: Random House, 1980), pp. 165–166.

But what if the "fact" had been the opposite?

- *Fact:* Did you know that during World War II soldiers were more eager to return to the states after the enemy surrendered than they were while the fighting continued?
- *Rationale:* Of course! Everybody knows that combat morale was very high. Who would have wanted to stay after the job had been done, anyway?

Or, consider these "facts":

- *Fact:* Did you know that individuals tend to look for a mate whose personality characteristics they find lacking in themselves?
- *Rationale:* Of course! Just think of the old saying, "Opposites attract."
- *Fact:* Did you know that individuals tend to look for a mate whose personality characteristics they find in themselves?
- *Rationale:* Of course! Just think of the old saying, "Birds of a feather flock together."

As it turns out, a sociological survey of soldiers during World War II determined that soldiers actually were more eager to return home after the Germans surrendered than during the fighting. Combat morale did tend to be high during that war. (It is interesting to conjecture whether the same finding would have been obtained during the Vietnam War.) Concerning factors in mate selection, sociologists have found that "opposites attract" in personality needs but that "birds of a feather flock together" in terms of ethnicity, religion, and socioeconomic status. Unfortunately, neither adage concerning mate selection is precise enough to permit the kind of predictions that sociologists seek to make.

In short, what appears to be common sense frequently is not something that individuals *objectively* know to be true. Instead they believe it to be true on the basis of personal opinion, assumptions taken for granted by members of their group, or after the fact rationalization. The sociologist cannot be satisfied with such judgments. All ideas regarding the social world, whether or not obvious, must be subjected to the rigorous requirements of scientific inquiry. Common sense is not enough; frequently it is very wrong.

SUMMARY

Human behavior can be studied in different ways by employing a number of different approaches. Disciplines such as economics and political science compartmentalize behavior by isolating one aspect of behavior from the whole. Sociology has a broader scope of inquiry in seeking to understand social phenomena that appear in all social processes, whether economic, political, religious, educational, or any other.

Sociology can be regarded as the scientific study of the social aspects of human behavior, that is, as the study of the behavior that people exhibit when they *interact* together. It is also the study of the *characteristics* that people acquire as a result of such interaction. History also studies social aspects of behavior, but usually as unique historical occurrences rather than as general social patterns. Psychology studies general aspects of behavior but focuses on its personal influences and consequences within the mind of an individual, whereas sociology focuses on the exchanges between individuals.

Most sociologists attempt to gather and analyze information about the social aspects of behavior using the scientific method. Three major components of scientific activity can be identified: (1) description, the accurate observation and measurement of objects or events; (2) discovery of order, the statement of relationships between phenomena in the form of hypotheses; and (3) development of theory, the statement of broader relationships that explains a number of hypotheses.

Among disciplines using the scientific method, sociology is relatively young. Early sociologists tended to take an armchair approach, deriving their conclusions from personal judgment and the unsystematic observations of others. Contemporary sociology has developed a set of more sophisticated research methods with which to test its ideas about social life. Such methods include the experiment, the survey, participant observation, and content analysis.

Many students are concerned about the relevance of the field of sociology, but its relevance is unquestionable in that it increases our self-understanding in many aspects of everyday life, provides information and insights necessary to deal with society's problems, and contributes to knowledge and skills that can be applied in the fulfillment of many career goals.

Often students approaching sociology for the first time feel that their commonsense observations of social behavior could provide the same knowledge. Sociology is particularly vulnerable to this attack for several reasons. First, introductory courses must first teach the vocabulary of the field which may appear to be merely giving new names to familiar events. Second, sociology is frequently concerned with matters directly experienced by students and about which they already hold deeply ingrained opinions. Third, students are often unaware that much of the knowledge they take for granted before they enter a course in sociology was in fact developed within the field. And, fourth, many conclusions about social life, whether objectively true or false, can be justified after the fact on the basis of logic or judgment. We must therefore be skeptical of the obvious and willing to submit our most accepted ideas to systematic, scientific test.

QUESTIONS, EXERCISES, PROJECTS

1. What distinguishes the perspective of sociology from that of other behavioral sciences such as economics, political science, history, and psychology?
2. What is meant by the goal of scientific objectivity?
3. Define and illustrate the three components of scientific activity.
4. How would you go about testing the hypothesis, "Competition between groups tends to increase intergroup conflict and hostility"? Describe how at least two research methods could be employed to study this hypothesis.
5. Emile Durkheim said that all social crises tended to increase the rate of anomic suicide but one. Which one? Why?
6. Why is random sampling so important in scientific inquiry? If you were conducting a study of attitudes in your dormitory, how would you employ the principle of randomness to ensure an accurate picture?
7. Should sociologists engaging in participant observation always identify themselves and their interests to their subjects? If you were writing a term paper on "dorm life" or "family behavior" and had to use participant observation to get your data, would you identify yourself as a "sociologist"? What would happen if you did?
8. Discuss the ways in which sociology might be relevant to the life of a student taking his or her first course in it.
9. Why can't sociologists rely on common sense to explain human

social behavior? Give two examples in which commonsense explanations are problematical.
10. What are the questions likely to be asked by a psychologist, an economist, and a sociologist who are studying the behavior of a married couple contemplating a divorce?

CULTURE

how, they were different. True, our bodies function similarly to those of other species—dogs and cats, for example—our intelligence is matched in some ways by some species—dolphins and whales, for instance—and we even *look* like another species—the great apes. Nevertheless, we are not convinced. In some way, people stand apart.

Such musings are more than wishful thinking, more than human beings trying to invent something about themselves that will give special meaning to their lives. Human beings *are* different, and in a most important and fundamental way. Social scientists are convinced they understand what that difference is. Consider the following.

INSTINCT VERSUS INTERPRETATION

The Character of an Instinct

Much of animal behavior consists of a predictable set of responses to stimuli in the environment. Reactions are on the basis of **instinct:** that is, they are inborn, automatic, and unvarying from one situation to another. Take the behavior of a cornered rat. When a rat senses a threat to its well-being and is backed into a spot from which it cannot escape, its reaction is immediate and automatic. It will raise up on its haunches, bare its teeth, and fight ferociously

instinct An inborn, automatic, and unvarying response to stimuli.

no matter what size or kind of enemy the attacker may be, no matter what its ultimate chances for success are. Fighting is the only possibility open to it. In other words, the instinct of self-preservation takes over the organism completely and the rat acts aggressively. Moreover, this instinctual response is invariable, appearing every time this particular circumstance (cornering) arises.

Another example of the operation of instinct can be seen in the birth process of animals. For example, a female dog about to give birth knows exactly how to proceed, even if it is her first litter and she has never observed the process of birth before. First, she will find a safe, quiet place to have the litter. When the first pup arrives, she immediately licks off the amniotic sac in which it was born. Then she finds and bites off the umbilical cord that still fastens the pup to her. Finally, she eats the afterbirth. All this is done completely automatically, instinctually. There is no *choice* in the matter.

No less remarkable is the behavior of the newborn pup itself. As soon as the amniotic sac has been broken and all the mucous has been cleaned from its nostrils by the mother's licking, it begins to breathe. Within seconds, even though it may still be attached to the umbilical cord, the pup begins crawling toward the mother in order to locate her milk sacs. Upon reaching its destination and having rooted about until it latches onto a nipple, the pup begins to suck hungrily. The whole process—the tremendous effort involved in crawling, locating, and sucking—is totally instinctual.

The Human Response

Although nature takes care of other animals' problems by providing them with instinctual responses for many occasions, it does not do so for human beings. Whereas rats and dogs can (without thought) take care of themselves, human beings must be cared for (thoughtfully) during the first few years of life and later must decide for themselves which actions are appropriate for each situation that arises. To make these decisions, they must rely on their intelligence and their memory. The crux of the matter is this: As far as we know, *human beings do not have instincts*, at least not in the sense other animals do.*

Humans do exhibit a few minor "instinctoids" that disappear

*A few sociologists would disagree with this statement. To a greater or lesser degree, they believe that some instincts, however weak they may be and however modifiable they are by social influences, still exist in human beings. These sociologists are often called "sociobiologists" or "biosociologists." The evidence for their position is considered in Chapter 9.

The newborn of other animals (above) know how to respond to their situation instinctively—that is, they respond by means of a built-in mechanism. Human babies (right), in comparison, have no such apparatus. They must be shown how to nurse. It is similar with virtually all other human responses: People must learn, via the process of interpretation, how to respond to the world.

shortly after birth. For example, babies curl their toes when they are tickled and make vague sucking motions if their mouth is pinched. In addition, the human body exhibits several reflex actions such as the classic knee jerk that occurs when a doctor taps a person's leg in the appropriate place below the knee cap. But, other than these reflexes and a few others, people exhibit no demonstrable, completely automatic responses to incoming stimuli. Nature may "take care of its own" as far as other animals are concerned, but it lets humans fend for themselves.

Compare, for instance, the behavior of human babies with that of other mammals. As we found in the case of the newborn pup, other infant mammals make a great effort to crawl to their mothers and begin nursing. The newborn human baby, in contrast, does almost nothing. In the first place, it is not physically capable of crawling and will not be for some time. This alone indicates the degree of its helplessness. The best it can do is to flail its arms and legs a bit and cry. In the second place, even when the infant child is placed on its mother's breast, it does not automatically begin to nurse. In most cases the child has to be directed to the nipple and have its cheeks pinched a little before it will begin sucking. Even then, it continues this process only when it learns that sucking reduces its hunger.

In short, the human infant is devoid of the self-help instincts of the puppy. It can survive only if it is *helped* by other human beings and *learns* the appropriate behavior. This constitutes one essential difference between human beings and other animals. Whereas other animals act automatically, humans must learn how to act. This complex mental process, the process of **interpretation**, that humans must go through to produce action, has three steps. (1) Human beings must *think*, that is, produce conscious reflections concerning the stimuli that reach the brain. (2) They must *organize* their thoughts about the incoming stimuli. (3) They must *evaluate* their thoughts and *choose* a course of action. In short, people must find their own answers to questions about how to act in the world.

interpretation The process whereby human beings think, organize, and evaluate their thoughts and choose a course of action appropriate to the stimuli.

Variety in Human Behavior

The absence of instincts in human beings leads to a variety in human behavior not observed in other animals. Whereas a cornered rat always exhibits the same automatic and predictable aggressive reaction, a "cornered" human being may not necessarily act the same way. Imagine, for example, that a young man walking in the woods one day happens upon a bear cub. He does not know that it is dangerous to be near the young of wild animals. When the young man sees how playful the cub is, he begins to run and play with it. Shortly, the mother bear returns and finds this fellow cavorting with her cub. The adult bear, *instinctively* perceiving a threat to her young, *automatically* reacts. She growls and makes other noises indicating her intent to attack and then chases the man through the woods into a small box canyon. The young man finds himself "cornered" and must finally turn to face his adversary. What will he do?

Since he is human, it is not easy to say. He has no built-in response as the rat does. He must, however hurriedly, think about his situation, organize his thoughts, evaluate them, and choose a course of action. For example, he may think about fighting the bear head on. He may think about running wildly about the canyon screaming for help in the hope that someone will hear him. He may fall to the ground and weep. He may consider trying to "talk" the bear out of its attack. He may think of fending the bear off by using a stick or by throwing stones at it. But then he may see a large tree nearby, evaluate the possibility that he may be able to reach it before the bear overtakes him, and decide that it is his best chance of escape. He sets out for it and reaches it just before the bear arrives behind him (thank goodness!).

Patterns of Human Behavior

If people are capable of behaving differently at each new encounter, can we hope to find any *patterns* of behavior by studying them? Would not any consistency observed in their actions merely be due to chance? Despite the possibility for variation in human conduct, human beings actually do not exercise this capacity for variation all the time. On the contrary, *human life is marked by a remarkable degree of consistency and order.* Consider the following patterns of behavior involving millions of Americans on a routine basis: (1) driving in the 5 o'clock rush hour traffic, (2) eating with a knife and fork, (3) drinking a cup of coffee with breakfast, (4) observing Sunday as a day of rest, (5) eating three meals a day, (5) watching several hours of television a week, and (6) marrying only one person at a time.

Now, since human beings do not have instincts, there is no *biological* reason for millions of Americans to comply with the foregoing patterns of behavior. At any time individual Americans could decide to stagger their work hours, eat with their hands or with chopsticks, drink beer with breakfast, work on Sunday, eat five meals daily, give up television, or marry (or live with) several persons at a time. The choice exists, but the patterns persist.

What is more, even the changes that human beings manifest tend to be patterned. Witness the rapid growth of the suburbs over the past few decades as millions of people "simultaneously" decided to move from the cities. Or consider the tremendous popularity of fads and fashions in American society that have determined changes in the length and texture of hair, appropriateness of mustaches and neckties, size of shoe heels, color of nail polish, length of dresses, and width of cuffs, to mention just a few.

THE CONCEPT OF CULTURE

The reason that there is so much patterning in social life is that groups of people share the same **culture**. That is, they have created a way of life that can be learned, shared, and passed from one generation to the next. Before we go into a detailed discussion of this concept, however, it is important to make two points.

First, it is important to keep in mind that there is a significant distinction between the popular, everyday use of the word "culture" and the sociological definition just mentioned. For many people in our society, the word "culture" is frequently used to refer to activities associated with art forms, such as literature, painting, ballet, and classical music, or to refer to the life-style of a particular group or community, such as "They are a highly cul-

culture A way of life that is learned and shared by human beings and that endures from one generation to the next.

tured family" or "Boston is a great cultural city." For the sociologist, however, this usage is much too narrow: The concept "culture" indicates *all* activities and behavior patterns that are learned and shared by a group of people. Thus, in sociological understanding, a baseball game is as much a part of culture as is Brahms' Piano Concerto no. 2; similarly, *all* families and cities are cultural, although perhaps their cultural content is quite different from one another.

Second, most sociologists would agree that it is the human capacity to form culture that is the second major "difference" between human beings and other species that we alluded to at the beginning of this chapter. As far as we know, no other animal has been able to improve on its biological capacity or transmit information in forms other than direct communication (individual-to-individual). But by inventing culture, human beings have been able to do all these things. They can fly by using the aircraft they created and can communicate with each other over extremely vast distances. For example, because of the media of television and radio, it is estimated that 95 percent of the American population knew of President Kennedy's assassination in 1963 within *one hour* of the shooting in Dallas; similarly, because of the invention of writing and later of printing books, people today can be influenced by the thinking of the ancient Egyptians or the plays of William Shakespeare. The *smartest* dogs, dolphins, or chimpanzees have never been able to accomplish such feats.

Material Culture

material culture Products of human activity.

Culture can be conceived as having two major aspects, material and ideational. **Material culture** consists of the products of human activity (artifacts) that do not occur naturally in the physical universe. It is directly observable, tangible, and concrete. For instance, books, chairs, tree houses, sculpture, lipstick, light bulbs, cities, stereos, bubble gum, and so on are all parts of material culture. They can be viewed or handled; all are created by human beings.

Material culture has been invented, first and foremost, as an attempt to provide solutions to the problems of living that humans' biological inheritance has not provided them. For example, people lack the protective equipment that is frequently built into the anatomy of other animals: warm fur, powerful claws, or great speed. However, having the ability to interpret the world, human beings have solved this kind of problem. In the place of warm fur, they have invented clothing and shelters of various kinds. In the place of powerful claws, they have invented weapons and machines of different sorts. In the place of great speed, they have invented extremely complex means of transportation, such as the automobile, the train, and the airplane.

On another level, material culture has been invented not only for mere survival, but for convenience as well. Torches are one way of providing light in the dark, but lamps filled with whale oil are more convenient, and electricity is still more convenient.

The crucial element in material culture, then, is not the artifact itself, but what we know and what we think about it. The proper use of any cultural artifact depends on our understanding of its operation and function. Given an artifact that we have never before seen, we would probably have no idea what to do with it. As an example, consider an artifact that was commonly used in American society less than a hundred years ago (see Figure 2–1).

Since this item is now rarely used, a contemporary urban American encountering it for the first time might be hard pressed to figure out what it does and how it works. It is an empty barrel with a stick through the top, but what goes in it, what does one do with the stick, how long does one do whatever it is one does? Quite clearly, its utility depends on our ideas regarding its function and operation. This leads us to a consideration of the second and more important aspect of culture: The *ideas* that people learn and share.

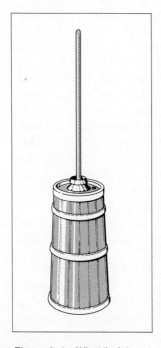

Figure 2–1   What Is It?

Ideational Culture

ideational culture A
learned and shared set of
ideas that provide general
knowledge about the world
and guidelines for social
behavior.

Ideational culture consists of a set of ideas, learned and shared by members of a group, that provides them with either general knowledge about the world or guidelines for behavior in social situations. In order to understand ideational culture, we must examine its elements in detail.

Ideational Culture Is a Set of Ideas.   Ideational culture is not directly observable or a tangible object such as an item of material culture. It is *symbolic,* existing in the minds of group members, and therefore must be studied indirectly. We come to know it only by being told what it is by others or by observing what people do in everyday life. For example, we may enter a series of classrooms in American colleges. By observing the interaction that takes place there, we may notice that in most of these classrooms one person, the teacher, does most of the talking. We may also observe that when other members of the class wish to speak, they first raise their hands and usually wait for the teacher to recognize them before speaking. From these observations, we would infer that the members of this group, teacher and students, share at least two cultural ideas: (1) It is expected the teacher will speak more than the students and (2) when students wish to speak they will raise their hands so the teacher can give them "permission" to speak. If we ask the teacher and students *why* this pattern exists, we may get the response that it is appropriate that classroom interaction proceed in this manner because (1) the teacher knows more than the students about the subject being discussed and has a job to impart that knowledge and (2) in order that questions be answered while the topic is at hand and the classroom kept orderly, students raise their hands before speaking. However, as anyone who has been in a classroom in an American college knows, the "intangible" quality of these cultural agreements—that is, the fact that they are hidden from view and usually unspoken—in no way detracts from their ability to influence our lives. We may avoid doing something that we have an idea is unacceptable to our society just as surely as we may avoid a rock wall looming in our path.

Ideational Culture Is Shared.   In order for information to become general and guide the behavior of more than one person, it must be recognized and understood by more than one person. An idea held by only one individual is a psychological phenomenon, not a cultural one. The sharing of an ideational culture is essential for the maintenance of order and consistency in a group. It provides its members with a common world view for the interpretation of incoming stimuli. For instance, in the classroom example just mentioned, the entire interaction pattern is made possible by the fact that all group members, teachers and students alike, agree, at least most of the time, on the ideas described. This sharing of ideas is what makes social life predictable most of the time to its participants and, from another perspective, to the sociologist.

Ideational Culture Is Learned.   Because of our instinctless biological state, we are born without knowledge of the world or of how to behave properly in any given situation. We acquire this information through our experiences with others. All of us, particularly when we are young, spend much of our time acquiring the information necessary for life in society. Once again, our classroom example may serve as a good illustration. Certainly none of the people in this group was born with an instinctive knowledge of how to act in complex, large group learning situations. Rather, from kindergarten on, each person has most likely picked up, day-by-day, year-by-year, the central cultural ideas for appropriate classroom behavior.

The importance of learning shared cultural ideas cannot be exaggerated; for it is in the acquisition of culture that human beings become whatever variation of humanity their group has developed. Furthermore, this "process of becoming" has extremely important consequences for each individual.

We have already established that almost everything human beings do involves thought and that almost all the content of our thoughts comes from our encounters with the social world. As a result, human beings can be said to be, in an important sense, cultural "products." Ideational culture is a major determining factor in human existence. It gives order to our lives and allows us to attain some ends and pursue others. It allows us, in other words, freedom from ignorance and the blind, irrational struggle for sustenance. Therefore ideational culture is an indispensable element of human existence.

However, ideational culture is, by necessity, only a *selection* from the range of ideas that could shape human activity. Given this perspective, we must realize that although ideational culture is, on the one hand, a liberating influence on human life, allowing us to attain our ends more easily and develop our human potential, it is also, by necessity, a *restrictive* influence on our lives as well. It presents us with only one (or at most a few) alternative courses of action from the very many in which human beings have the potential to engage.

Usually, the restricted set of alternatives presented by a culture is so deeply learned by those of us who are members of that culture that we have a very strong tendency to perceive it as the *only correct* way to behave. Consequently, we have difficulty understanding, let alone engaging in, other behaviors that may be equally, or more, efficient. A good example of this is provided by simple eating habits. Members of most Western countries are taught to eat their food utilizing three items of material culture—knives, forks, and spoons. This cultural idea concerning proper eating behavior has held sway for a long time and millions of people have adopted it. However, the adoption by an individual of this behavioral pattern has certain consequences that are inevitable over a long period of time. For example, the person engaged in this behavior develops deeply ingrained patterns of eye-to-hand-to-mouth movement, finger placement, utensil manipulation, and so forth. In contrast, members of many Far Eastern societies have learned to eat their food with chopsticks, utensils that are, in these societies, culturally defined as being appropriate. The adoption of chopsticks also has consequences for eye-to-hand-to-mouth movements, finger agility, and the like. Thus Westerners attempting to use chopsticks have great difficulty holding and manipulating the utensils and the same problem arises for the Easterner using Western utensils for the first time. In order to become proficient in the use of another culture's eating utensils, individuals must learn a good deal.

Another consequence of being restricted by ideational culture is the development of an ethnocentric attitude toward other people's cultures. **Ethnocentrism** refers to the tendency for a person to regard his or her own culture as superior and to evaluate other cultures in terms of his or her own. (see photo) An ethnocentric American might think that people who eat with chopsticks are inefficient and those who eat with their hands are barbaric (ignoring, of course, the American tendency to eat hors d'oeuvres with toothpicks and the most recent meal at Kentucky Fried Chicken. As another example, consider bathing practices in Japan and the United States. Americans visiting Japan have difficulty with the Japanese practice of going into a bathroom, sitting on a stool, washing oneself with soap and water from a bowl, and then, rinsed, settling into an astonishingly hot tub. They are embarrassed further when they learn that *each member* of the household goes through the same routine and settles into the *same* hot water tub after washing. The Japanese visitor to America, in contrast, has problems understanding an American's bathing habits. On the one hand, when an American takes a bath, he or she washes and then soaks in his or her own dirty water! On the other hand, if a person takes a shower (a much cleaner alternative from the Japanese viewpoint), he or she wastes an incredible amount of hot water and doesn't get the salubrious effects of soaking in a hot tub. Box 2–1 takes cultural variation one step further: It suggests that what groups make of human smells is by no means universal.

ethnocentrism The tendency for a person to regard his or her own culture as a standard for judging any other culture.

Look carefully at this photograph. What is your deep subjective reaction to it? If the photograph seems to make you feel as if the people depicted are somehow "strange," "different," "unusual," "not me," then you are experiencing what sociologists would call an ethnocentric reaction. Human beings, because they have different cultures, vary greatly in how they look, dress, and so on. Over a period of time, experiencing life in one culture, a person rather inevitably comes to feel that his or her culture is "right," or "normal." This feeling has both positive and negative aspects to it (see text).

One of the easiest ways to perceive the amount and type of ethnocentric bias of a group is to listen to its members characterize both their own and other people's groups. Usually their own group is referred to in glowing terms while the other is referred to in derogatory terms by the use of slurs (see Box 2–2).

Ethnocentrism is closely related to the common practice of **stereotyping**, the willingness to characterize members of a group according to some traits that all members of that group are presumed to have. The key fact about stereotyping is that it is based on (often wildly inaccurate) generalizations. People are not judged on their own terms, as individuals, but are put, willy-nilly, into the stereotypic category. For example, many Americans regard all communists as "dangerous" and Africans as "backward." It does not take much imagination to see that such beliefs may lead to

stereotyping. Characterizing members of a group according to traits that all members are presumed to possess.

Box 2–1 ODOR AS A CULTURAL VARIABLE

According to Largey and Watson (1970), many people have used odors to indicate the moral character of others. In fact, odors have been used widely to distinguish the "good" from the "evil." The bad guys are regarded as skunks, because they are the individuals or the groups we want to avoid. For example, we might describe someone who cannot be trusted as a "real stinker" or a "stinkpot." Another example is the heavily perfumed woman who is thought to be promiscuous and immoral. During the Middle Ages, it was widely believed that sorcerers and heretics could be detected by their evil odor.

In addition to serving as a mark of moral impurity, odor has also been used to indicate virtue or moral value. Just as we try to avoid skunks, so we are attracted to anyone who smells like a rose. At the extreme,

for example, a particularly holy person might be described as emitting the odor of sanctity; and Eskimos often show intimacy by their nose-kissing and sniffing. Even in our society, we have made a practice of sending flowers or scented letters as a symbol of love and respect. There have been very important, sometimes elaborate, procedures for determining odor as an indicator of virtue or excellence. For instance, the intermediaries responsible for arranging a Middle Eastern marriage would often make sure to smell the prospective bride. They would reject her if she didn't smell right.

Are we so different? Millions of Americans try to improve their public image by consuming products to get rid of bad breath, "ugly" perspiration, and "feminine odor."

major consequences, often of a disastrous nature, on the level of foreign policy.

The social benefit of ethnocentric and stereotypic beliefs is that they produce **in-group solidarity,** a positive feeling among members of a group that their way of doing things is right. By so doing, the group rejects criticism of its beliefs and activities and protects its members against the realization that these beliefs and activities are perhaps no better than those of other groups. This is important because if group members were continually questioning the beliefs and activities of the group and trying alternatives to them, the group would find it very difficult to attain its goals. The problem with ethnocentric beliefs is that simultaneously, as we have already seen, they have a tendency to produce **out-group hostility,** a negative feeling among members of a group toward the ways other groups have of doing things. We need not go too deeply into the history of black–white relations in our own culture to see both in-group solidarity and out-group hostility prominently and tragically on display.

Sociologists who hope to increase their understanding of other cultures cannot afford to be ethnocentric. Fortunately, most sociologists are keenly aware of this possibility and attempt to study

in-group solidarity The positive feeling among members of a group that their way of doing things is right.

out-group hostility The negative feeling members of a group have about other groups.

Box 2–2 ETHNOCENTRISM

One of the great early American sociologists, William Graham Sumner (1840–1910), catalogued a series of ethnocentric praises and slurs in his book *Folkways* (1906). Although these examples are nearly three-quarters of a century old, they can easily be supplemented from contemporary life. Try, after reading them, to think of how ethnocentrism occurs in contemporary America, in your home town, on your college campus, even in the dorm where you live.

> When Caribs were asked whence they came, they answered, "We alone are people." The meaning of the name Kiowa is "real or principal people." The Lapps call themselves "men," or "human beings." The Greenland Eskimos think that Europeans have been sent to Greenland to learn virtue and good manners from the Greenlanders. Their highest form of praise for a European is that he is, or soon will be, as good as a Greenlander . . .

Source: William Graham Sumner, *Folkways* (Boston: Ginn and Co., 1906), p. 14.

The Jews divided all mankind into themselves and Gentiles. They were the "chosen people." The Greeks and Romans called all outsiders "barbarians." In Euripides' tragedy of *Iphigenia in Aulis* Iphigenia says that it is fitting that Greeks should rule over barbarians, but not contrariwise, because Greeks are free, and barbarians are slaves. . . . In 1896, the Chinese minister of education and his counselors edited a manual in which this statement occurs: "How grand and glorious is the Empire of China, the Middle Kingdom! She is the largest and richest in the world. The grandest men in the world have all come from the Middle Empire." In the literature of all the states equivalent statements occur, although they are not so naively expressed. In Russian books and newspapers the civilizing mission of Russia is talked about, just as, in the books and journals of France, Germany, and the United States, the civilizing mission of those countries is assumed and referred to as well understood. Each state . . . regards itself as the leader of civilization, the best, the freest, and the wisest, and all others as inferior.

any culture in terms of the standards of its members. This doctrine of **cultural relativism** does not ask that sociologists abandon their personal ideas about what is proper and improper, right and wrong, but it does require that they try to make sense of any other culture they study *on its own terms* and base their understanding on that culture's historical and environmental circumstances.

cultural relativism The doctrine that other cultures can only be understood on their own terms.

As we have seen, then, at the same time that cultural ideas liberate us, they harness us to certain modes of thinking and acting. To the extent that we cannot easily accept other possibilities as we encounter them, we may speak of the *binding aspect of culture.* Taken as a whole, the group members' lifelong exposure to the content of their culture is the most important element in structuring their social lives.

COMPONENTS OF IDEATIONAL CULTURE

Given the foregoing introduction to the shared and learned aspects of ideational culture, we now turn to a discussion of its important components: general knowledge and guidelines for behavior.

General Knowledge

general knowledge That component of ideational culture that provides the basic data about reality that enables individuals to conduct their everyday affairs.

Many cultural ideas contain information about various aspects of reality that are generally known and accepted among the members of a group. **General knowledge** does not inform a person what socially proper behavior is; instead, it provides the basic data on the basis of which individuals conduct their everyday affairs. The most commonplace elements of general knowledge are *facts* ("President John F. Kennedy was elected in 1960") and *usages* (the pronunciation of words, the function of a chair). General knowledge also serves to explain the elements of material culture to the members of a group (how to operate a churn or a washing machine). Overall, it provides information about the setting within which social situations take place.

Guidelines for Behavior: Values

guidelines for behavior That part of ideational culture that suggests how the members of a group should or should not act in social situations.

values Concepts of the desirable that indicate what activities are good to do and what kind of person it is good to become.

Cultural ideas also outline how the members of a group should or should not act in social situations. They serve as **guidelines for** much of our **behavior.** There are two chief varieties of such guidelines: values and norms.

Clyde Kluckhohn (1951) has said that **values** are "concepts of the desirable" that indicate what activities are good to do and what kind of person it is good to become. Values are general ideas existing within a group that indicate the proper orientation and goal of social situations. In the truest sense, values represent ideals that people believe in or work toward. There are at least two varieties of values: value orientations and general system values.

value orientations Concepts that give members of a group the basic answers to the core problems of human existence.

Value Orientations. **Value orientations** refer to those general ideas that give members of a group the basic answers to the existential questions of human life, without which concerted action would be impossible. According to Florence Kluckhohn and Fred Strodtbeck (1961), there are five major questions that must be meaningfully answered before an individual can feel "at home" in a social group (see Figure 2–2).

1. What is the nature of *time?* Kluckhohn and Strodtbeck say there are really only three possible answers to this question. A social group may be oriented toward the *past* (as the Daughters

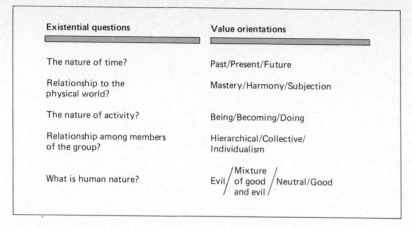

Figure 2–2   Kluckhohn and Strodtbeck's (1961) View of the Existential Questions of Human Life and Their Value Orientations

of the American Revolution are), the *present* (as participants are in making love), or the *future* (as farmers are when planting seeds).

2. What is the nature of the group's *relationship to the physical world?* Again, only three possibilities present themselves. The group may attempt to gain *mastery over* the physical world (as the medical profession does in attempting to conquer cancer), to live in *harmony with* that world (as ecological conservation groups do), or to exist in *subjection to* that world (as religious groups do in submitting to God's will).

3. What is the nature of *activity?* There are three alternatives: *being,* where individuals are exhorted to express their impulses or desires (spontaneously) in culturally specified ways (e.g., the Spanish fiesta); *becoming,* where individuals are encouraged to focus on personality or spiritual development (as in many Eastern religions); and *doing,* where the members of the group are evaluated with respect to their achievements (most Americans believe in "working hard" to get benefits in life).

4. What is the nature of the *relationship among members of the group?* Three possibilities present themselves. A society's members can relate to each other in a *hierarchical* fashion, where some members are accorded higher status than others and must be obeyed (as in any military organization); a *collective* fashion, where all members are essentially equal in status and work together (as in a New England town meeting); or in an *individualistic* fashion, where each individual is seen as responsible only for his or her own interests (as in much of American business).

5. What is *human nature?* Here Kluckhohn and Strodtbeck see

four basic possibilities. Human nature may be regarded as *evil* (the view held by early Protestant denominations such as Calvinism; see the discussion of the "Protestant Ethic" in Chapter 8); as a mixture of *good and evil* (Kluckhohn and Strodtbeck feel this orientation characterizes most modern Americans); as *neutral*—that is, a product of the forces that shape it (many contemporary sociologists hold this view); or as *good*— that is, loving, kind, generous (the hippies of the 1960s had this perspective).

Kluckhohn and Strodtbeck indicate that answers to these questions must be provided before any group can orient or guide its members in a meaningful way. Moreover, they suggest that certain consistent patterns emerge among the value orientations in any group. For example, it would make little sense for a group's members to believe in "mastery over" nature and have a "being" perspective on activity. They are mutually contradictory viewpoints. Rather, one would expect the "doing" activity orientation to complement most effectively, and therefore to be found with the "mastery over" nature orientation.

To illustrate this idea of value orientations, let us look at one example in depth. Elaborating on Kluckhohn and Strodtbeck's evidence, we have good reason to assume that much of American business subscribes to the following value orientations (see Box 2–3):

- Time: future ("Plan ahead.")
- Nature: mastery over ("Progress is our most important product.")
- Activity: doing ("Work hard.")
- Relational: individualistic ("Every man for himself," "Dog eat dog.")
- Human nature: evil ("You can't trust anyone," "Watch out for the other guy.")

Taken together, these orientations provide a strong foundation for the unceasing emphasis on achievement, progress, and profit making of much of American, capitalistic activity. Where would the momentum for highly competitive activities be if American business subscribed to the *following* pattern of value orientations?

- Time: present ("Enjoy yourself.")
- Nature: harmony ("Everyone is just a part of the All.")
- Activity: being ("It's not what you do, but who you are that counts.")
- Relational: collective ("All people are brothers and sisters.")

Box 2–3   STUDY: BOSSES FAIL TO NURTURE WORK ETHIC

By Steve Curwood
Globe Staff

Contrary to popular myth, the American work ethic is alive and strong in the 1980s, but it's being sabotaged by conventional American management.

That's the conclusion of a three-year study of American workers and managers by Daniel Yankelovich and John Immerwahr of the Public Agenda Foundation in New York. The study was released today in conjunction with the nation's 101st celebration of Labor Day.

More than three-quarters of the 845 people surveyed said they do not work as hard as they can at their jobs—but it's not because they're lazy, said Yankelovich.

The problem arises because management has largely failed to recognize that the nature of work and work incentives has changed, say the two authors of "Putting the Work Ethic to Work: A Public Agenda Report on Restoring America's Competitive Vitality."

Yankelovich is a veteran pollster, chairman of the public opinion research firm Yankelovich, Skelly and White Inc., and co-founder of Public Agenda Foundation with former Secretary of State Cyrus Vance. Immerwahr is a philosophy professor at Villanova University in Philadelphia.

Their study found that more than 70 percent of workers endorse the work ethic, and 52 percent said they have an inner need to do the best job possible, regardless of pay. Only 17 percent said they hate work and wouldn't work if they didn't need the cash.

"The conventional wisdom of a deteriorating work ethic is badly off target [as] the American work ethic is strong . . ." said Yankelovich. "But rather than rewarding the work ethic, many American managers ignore it or intentionally undercut it."

For example, "73 percent say job effort has declined because people frequently receive the same pay increases regardless of how hard they work."

The study also found that almost four workers in five (78 percent) feel there is no direct relationship between how hard they work and how much they are paid, and even more (83 percent) don't think they would be the primary beneficiary if they worked harder.

In contrast, other studies have shown only 7 percent of Japanese workers feel they would not benefit from working harder.

This puts the United States at a competitive disadvantage in the world economy, as US productivity growth has faltered badly since 1968, Yankelovich noted.

Source: Boston Globe, September 5, 1983, pp. 1, 8.

- Human nature: good ("People are beautiful; be kind to and love everyone equally.")

Obviously, American business would not last long in the world marketplace if these were its orientational attitudes. These attitudes did characterize one recent American group, however—the hippies of the late 1960s and early 1970s. It would be hard to find a group more different from American business in its basic orientation and consequent life-style.

Kluckhohn and Strodtbeck indicate that value orientations may be differentially preferred within a social group, especially a complex group. For example, members of an American business firm may subscribe to the first pattern, previously described, all year, but on the day of the annual Christmas party they may adopt a pattern of value orientations not unlike that of the hippies. Also, within any group, individual differences in value orientations are likely to occur. In the case of a business firm perhaps 85 percent of its members may be oriented to the future (those who work toward long-range goals), whereas 10 percent may be oriented to the present (quick profit takers), and 5 percent may be oriented to the past (those who dwell on how things used to be done in the "good old days"). Kluckhohn and Strodtbeck suggest that there is usually a dominant value orientation that characterizes a group as a whole. Preferences in addition to the dominant pattern in a group may be called *secondary value orientations.* Box 2–3 illustrates this concept.

general system values
Concepts that identify the desirable goals of the group and specify the appropriate behavior of group members as they work toward those goals.

General System Values.   **General system values** are concepts that identify the desirable goals of the group and specify the appropriate behavior of group members as they work toward those goals. For example, the business firm already mentioned would more than likely have a general system value directed toward making a profit. Much of the activity within the firm would be oriented toward the attainment of that value, whether the particular objective involved sales policy, turning off lights when not in use, sending people home when they were not needed for business, or whatever. Similarly, any member of that firm who subscribed to its general system value would participate in such activities and those who worked hardest toward the profit-oriented goal, that is, those who best exemplified the value, would be likely to be the most highly revered members of the firm.

General system values provide the major guidelines for action for large as well as small groups, even though they may be more broadly defined in a larger group. For example, Talcott Parsons and Winston White (1964) have claimed that a general American value involves the building of the "good society." There are two value patterns to which most Americans are committed in their quest for a good society. Parsons calls the first the **instrumental complex.** This value pattern, related to the set of ideas known as the Protestant ethic (see Chapter 8), emphasizes concepts such as hard work, progress, and the like. Instrumental values orient the behavior of most Americans to the most efficient use of means in attaining the good society. In other words, everything is evaluated

instrumental complex A value pattern emphasizing the most efficient use of means in attaining the ends of society.

with respect to its potential usefulness in progressing toward the goal. Specifically, there appear to be three major instrumental values held in American society.

1. *Achievement.* Each individual is expected to be a success at whatever he or she does, and everyone is exhorted to "do his best" in all of life's endeavors.
2. *Rationality.* In order to achieve most effectively in American society, each individual is expected to examine alternative courses of action and to select the ones most advantageous to the goal. In the pursuit of the goal it is expected that people will "control their emotions" and "use their heads."
3. *Economic-occupational endeavor.* In order that the goal of society be attained there is extremely strong pressure for the individual American to achieve within a specific context of socially approved activities, namely, the capitalistic (business and industry) or professional (medicine, law, etc.) spheres.

The other major pattern of American general system values can be regarded as the **democratic-humanitarian complex.** These values, a direct product of the original, widespread migration to America in search of freedom and opportunity, are historically legitimized by the American Constitution and the Bill of Rights. Specifically, there seem to be four values in the democratic-humanitarian complex.

democratic-humani-tarian complex A value pattern that stresses democracy, equality, justice, freedom, and humanitarianism.

1. *Democracy.* The right of the people to govern themselves by majority rule. The American political system as well as great numbers of smaller social systems (e.g., high school and college student governments) are oriented by this value.
2. *Freedom.* The right of each individual to live his or her life as he or she sees fit (freedom of life-style), to say what he or she wishes (freedom of speech), to worship, admire, or believe as he or she chooses (freedom of belief), and so on. This value is constantly being invoked when individuals or groups of Americans feel their "rights" are being taken away, and it is embodied in such activist groups as the American Civil Liberties Union (ACLU).
3. *Equality and Justice.* The right of each individual to be "inherently" as good as any other individual and to have access by his or her efforts to all areas of American society; the right to be fairly treated under the law regardless of race, religion, creed, and the like. This value, along with that for "freedom," was the focus of the Civil Rights movement of the 1960s and is the clarion call of the more recent women's movement.
4. *Humanitarianism.* This value stresses a concern for the welfare

of others and the desire that those with "less" in whatever fashion be given "every chance" so that they may be able to live their lives as they choose. From this emphasis, many Americans get their willingness to fight for groups they see as "oppressed" (e.g., in the Korean War of the 1950s), and their willingness to allow immigration of the "oppressed peoples" into the country most of the time (e.g., the Hungarian refugees of the 1950s, the Cuban refugees of the 1960s, and Polish refugees in the 1980s). Also linked to this value is the American willingness to allow political asylum to virtually anyone who wishes it (e.g., to Soviet author and dissident Alexander Solzhenitsyn).

Not all general system values hold equal weight among all the members of a group. Like value orientations, they become differentially preferred by group members, making it possible to speak of *dominant* and *secondary* patterns. For instance, given the orientation of the business firm toward profit making, the instrumental pattern is likely to be dominant in the participants' minds and responsible for guiding much of their behavior. Democratic-humanitarian values would be secondary. Among members of Congress, charged as they are with upholding the Constitution and its provisions, one would expect the democratic-humanitarian pattern to be dominant and the instrumental pattern secondary.

It is this question of general system value dominance that explains the furor surrounding ex-President Nixon's role in the infamous Watergate affair in the early 1970s. In sociological terms Nixon was charged with being more oriented toward instrumental than democratic-humanitarian priorities. He was accused of being more concerned with his own reelection at any cost (an instrumental priority) than with making sure that the law was upheld and a standard of ethical behavior maintained (a democratic-humanitarian concern). After the break-in at Democratic National Committee headquarters at the Watergate Hotel had been discovered and made public, Nixon was charged with concealing the involvement of his closest aides, thus protecting his administration and himself (an instrumental concern), rather than informing the country of his involvement as he was charged to do by oath of office and the Constitution (a democratic-humanitarian concern).

Was Mr. Nixon behaving "abnormally" by putting instrumental concerns over democratic-humanitarian concerns? Probably not: He was merely doing what a great many Americans do, but in an *inappropriate* social context. Consequently, in the years since President Nixon's resignation, Presidents Ford and Carter, the House of Representatives, the Senate, and the judicial system have all attempted to institute what is popularly known as "the post-Watergate morality"—in our terms, a return to democratic-humanitarian values as priorities for public servants. People who have not lived up to this redefinition, such as Congressman Wilbur Mills, and the government officials involved in the Abscam payoffs scandal, have all been dealt with severely by other members of the government (see the discussion of "Negative Sanctions" later in this chapter).

Are American Value Priorities Basically Instrumental or Democratic-Humanitarian? A Value Analysis.   Between 1971 and 1977 Spates, one of the coauthors of this book, asked his introductory sociology classes to rank a list of American general system values according to the value preferences of their own parents. The list included both instrumental and democratic-humanitarian components as well as a series of other values suggested by sociologist Robin Williams (1971), for example, individualism, material comfort, and group superiority/racism. In the seven classes studied the results were essentially the same. Students perceived their parents as being concerned primarily with instrumental values and secondarily with democratic-humanitarian values; the other values were not found to form any consistent pattern. Although these results were provocative, they could not be used to describe American society as a whole because of sample limitations. Only 700 students were sampled over the 7-year period, and most of these students came from middle- to upper-class backgrounds.

The consistency of the results, however, suggested that a more extensive study be undertaken. To this end, Spates conducted a content analysis (see the discussion of "the content analysis technique" in Chapter 1). He designed a category system of values that included the instrumental, democratic-humanitarian, and other values as previously described. He then sampled the most highly circulated magazines as they appealed to different social classes. For the upper-middle class, *Saturday Review* was chosen; for the middle class, *Reader's Digest;* and for the working class, *National Enquirer.* Each magazine was sampled during the following time periods, 1957 to 1959, 1967 to 1969, and 1977 to 1979. Four issues of each magazine were randomly drawn from each year. Then two articles were randomly selected from the table of contents and six sentences from each article. A total of 1296 sentences were coded according to the value expressed in them.

As shown in Table 2–1, the general interest magazines in all time periods showed a marked preference for instrumental themes over both democratic-humanitarian and other concerns. For example, these magazines presented their readers with advice regarding financial investments and taxes, lessons from the careers of persons who had achieved occupational success, and similar subjects. Far fewer addressed themselves to such democratic-humanitarian concerns as starvation and poverty or the goals of the Civil Rights movement in America. Moreover, these findings held for each magazine. That is, whether considering *Saturday Review, Reader's Digest,* or *National Enquirer,* instrumental concerns appeared more frequently than did democratic-humanitarian ones. This suggests that the "instrumental priority" holds across social class lines as well. Readers from all classes are getting more instrumental "messages" in their favorite magazines. Finally, Table 2–1 indicates that there has been a slight increase in instrumental content in these magazines over the decades sampled (from 45 percent in 1957 to 1959 to 48 percent in 1977 to 1979). But this increase has been matched by a corresponding increase in democratic-humanitarian content (from 20 percent in 1957 to 1959 to 23 percent in 1977 to 1979). Thus the instrumental priority remains about the same: There is approximately twice as much instrumental content as democratic-humanitarian content in American mass-circulated magazines.

These results clearly indicate that in the magazines studied, instrumental values are of dominant concern, whereas democratic-humanitarian values are of secondary importance. If this is the preference generally shared by the American population, it may help to explain why we are so slow at implementing such clearly humanitarian concerns as cleaner air, the removal of cancer-causing agents from food and hair dyes, or automobile safety: They would cost too much, decrease profits, and thereby threaten individual and corporate definitions of "success." Similarly, such a value priority system may explain partially the great resistance minority groups such as blacks, homosexuals, and women have met in trying to attain equal treatment in American society. Such democratic concerns may be clearly secondary to instrumental questions, such as hiring practices, group and business images, and neighborhood composition.

Table 2–1 AMERICAN GENERAL SYSTEM VALUES IN GENERAL INTEREST MAGAZINES BY TIME PERIOD

| | *Time Period* | | |
Value	1957–1959	1967–1969	1977–1979
Instrumental	45%	47%	48%
Democratic-humanitarian	20	22	23
Other	34	30	27
Unidentified[a]	1	1	2
Total	100%	100%	100%
(N = 1296)	(432)	(432)	(432)

[a]A category of unidentified was added to account for the few sentences that could not be categorized as having value content, such as "It rained today."

These findings suggest one reason that value priorities may be so hard to change. The readers of these magazines are being exposed approximately twice as frequently to instrumental messages as they are to democratic-humanitarian ones. This implies that the *reinforcement* is twice as strong for one set of values as it is for the other. Overall, this effect is probably not unlike the well-known effect of repeated advertising: It creates a rather indelible impression in the recipient's mind. If such "dunning" is occurring not only with regard to values, but also with regard to attitudes toward other groups—such as blacks, homosexuals, and women—it can help explain the depth of ethnocentric feelings about these groups by majority groups—whites, heterosexuals, and men. Finally, it can help explain why even members of discriminated against groups often have such negative feelings about their own group.

Guidelines for Behavior: Norms

Norms are behavioral guidelines that inform group members in specific terms what is right and proper to do in a particular social situation. In other words, norms are cultural "rules" whose function is to help ensure that behavior in social situations proceeds as specified by the values of the group. Thus, as already seen, there are norms for how to greet strangers and for how to act in a classroom. There are also norms for how to buy clothes, for how to ride on a subway, for how to fight a war, and so on. In fact, there are complex sets of norms for virtually every social interactive situation; they are, in fact, what make human life in society possible.

Sometimes norms are consciously formulated—as for example, when baseball was invented: "Let's see, we'll need nine players, and one will play here, another over there . . ." and so on. Just as frequently, however, they emerge tacitly, almost surreptitiously, as people experiment in social situations with various ways of behaving. Similarly, the linkage of norms with values is almost palpable —as in the *Fortune* magazine ad that says "Drive yourself today and tomorrow you may not have to." Could a more exact linkage to the American achievement value be imagined? At other times the norm-value connection may be more subtle—such as when small children in grade school get little stars on their foreheads for good behavior. (Again, what's being taught is the value of achievement.)

To illustrate the widespread influence of norms in everyday life, consider the system of norms that frequently governs the behavior of individuals during their "family dinner." For the evening meal, family members agree that it is proper that all members sit at the

norms Those guidelines for behavior that inform the participants in social situations specifically what is right and proper to do.

table at the same time and begin eating from plates, with knives, forks, spoons, and so on. It is also agreed that, if a family member wishes something that is out of reach, it is proper to ask others to "Please pass the butter." Consider also the arbitrary nature of these norms. There is no biological reason for the people in a family unit to eat together at the same time. They are not responding instinctually to the need to satisfy hunger; in fact, such an eating arrangement probably means that not all family members will eat when they are hungriest. There is no biological reason to eat from dishes, using knives and forks; it might be more efficient if they all just ate their food with their hands from a single large bowl. Lastly, it may often be a "waste of time" and an imposition on others to ask someone to pass an object that could easily be grabbed from across the table.

Family members could make the choice to dump their food off their plates, begin eating with their hands, and start grabbing for things out of reach. Is this not how babies behave when they first get solid food? Yet older family diners do not behave in this way.

Why do the members of one society eat with chopsticks, whereas the members of another eat with knives and forks? Why don't we all eat with our hands from one large bowl and just grab things that are out of reach?

To these individuals, such things are just "not done." It even sounds a trifle (and what could be worse?) "uncivilized."

The key thing to realize here is that agreed-upon norms make social behavior relatively well ordered, secure, and predictable. Without these norms, as we just tried to indicate in the example of the family dinner where the norms are dispensed with, chaos would likely reign. No one would know what another person was going to do from moment to moment.

Ideal Versus Actual Norms. The family dinner is only one example of a system of norms within a social group. We could have used literally thousands of other examples to illustrate the same concept (see Box 2–4). At this point, however, it is important to distinguish between two different types of norms, both of which may apply in any given social situation. First, there are **ideal norms** that specify the behavior that individuals ought to exhibit if they are to live up to all the expectations of their group. When you ask an individual to tell you the rules of behavior for his or her group, you will usually receive a recitation of the ideal norms as an answer. They are the rules to which violators may be referred when they are being chastised for behavior "unbecoming" a member of the group.

ideal norms Concepts that specify the precise behavior that individuals are expected to exhibit, if they are to fulfill group ideals.

To give a particular example, the ideal norms of police work specify that police officers should always arrest someone who breaks the law regardless of mitigating circumstances. A lawbreaker is a lawbreaker and according to the general system value of equality of justice, no special considerations should be given to particular lawbreakers, whether they are relatives, friends, or persons of great wealth.

In reality, however, the police do not always arrest everyone who breaks the law. That is, in any given situation they may follow not the ideal norms of that situation, but a second set of less rigid **actual norms.** These actual norms specify (sometimes only vaguely) the amount of latitude a participant in a social situation may take with the ideal norms without becoming subject to the hostility of other group members. Thus the police officer faced with a speeder on a highway may decide to use a warning, rather than to give a ticket, in the hope that a warning will be enough to keep the offender from repeating the offense. Or, the police officer may decide to "forgive" an offender who is rushing home to a family emergency or who is a powerful leader in the community. These circumstances, as well as others (see accompanying cartoon), may sway the police officer from strict compliance with the ideal norms to employment of the actual norms.

actual norms Concepts that specify the amount of latitude a participant may take with the ideal norms without becoming subject to the hostility of other group members.

Box 2–4 NORMS FOR ATTENDING FOOTBALL GAMES

As everyone who has attended high school or college football games knows, there are usually appropriate sides of the field for the observers from each school—the home team fans sit on one side of the field and the visiting team fans sit on the other.

Quite clearly, this seating arrangement is a purely social invention. After all, there is nothing inherent in a football field that makes it amenable to one type of person on one side and to another type of person on the other. Any norms for seating have to be invented by the people using the field. Yet, despite the fact that the seating arrangement is contrived, it has great power over the behavior of large numbers of people. In fact, its power is so great that the seating arrangement is frequently held to quite rigidly, in spite of other reasons for adjusting it.

For example, let us assume that two friends attend the game. One is from the school of the home team and the other is from the school of the visiting team. Thinking only in terms of their strong liking for each other as individuals, a casual observer might expect the two friends to sit together during the game. However, upon arriving at the field, the two friends part company and each progresses to his or her "proper" side of the field. Because of the social demands that fans from opposing schools sit on opposite sides of the field, the personal desires of the friends are overruled, and each sits where he or she is "supposed to." Everyone knows this. And it is precisely because everyone *does* know this—because it is a norm concerning proper behavior at football games—that the personal choices of the friends succumb to the social choices.

Now let us assume that the two friends decide to rebel against these arbitrary rules and proceed with one another to seats on the home side of the field. How can we expect each of them to feel, having defied a strong social convention? We might expect the fan from "the wrong side of the field" to feel very much out of place. Being a loyal supporter of the visiting team, he or she will have a strong tendency to cheer or "boo" various plays on the field when the fans on the home side are doing the opposite. The fans on "the right side of the field" may think this behavior "out of place" and respond with negative glances, words, or gestures. The home team fan's "traitorous" decision to bring one of the opponent's supporters into "the home camp" may be a source of some embarrassment. Even those persons who defy norms are influenced by them.

Unlike their ideal counterparts, actual norms are generally informal, unwritten, and learned only by experience. In many cases they are discretionary; that is, it is up to the individual whether or not to employ them. Therefore actual norms allow the flexibility in social situations that is needed in order to adapt to new or special circumstances.

Mores Versus Folkways.   The American sociologist William Graham Sumner (1906) provides us with another important way to distinguish between types of norms. Sumner distinguished between mores and folkways. **Mores** are *rules* of behavior to which

mores Norms that specify essential behavior and to which the members of a group demand conformity.

The potential conflict between ideal and actual norms is well illustrated by this cartoon. The police are ideally supposed to arrest speeders. Occasionally, however, the speeder is not an "average citizen," but rather a high-ranking, government official who, if offended or embarrassed by a speeding ticket, might call the police officer's captain and complain, thereby putting the officer in a difficult situation with his superiors just for doing his job. In such situations, it is not infrquently found that actual norms are applied. A situation such as that depicted in the cartoon should also suggest some thoughts about social stratification, or people's ranking in society. We will deal with this topic in some depth in Chapter 5.

the members of a group *demand* conformity. Compliance is regarded as essential; violation is seen as a threat to the group and therefore is strongly disapproved by its members. In American society mores include prohibitions against murder, theft, cannibalism, and political subversion.

Folkways are the rules for conducting ordinary, everyday affairs in the traditionally accepted way. There are folkways to cover a broad range of routine activities, including how to eat dinner, dress for the beach, invite guests to a party, order from the menu in a restaurant, behave in an elevator, write a letter, and introduce a stranger (see Box 2–5).

Since conformity to folkways is regarded as appropriate rather

folkways Norms that state the traditionally accepted way of conducting the routine affairs of everyday life.

Box 2-5   FOLKWAYS AS GUIDELINES FOR BEHAVIOR

Mores assure a measure of social control. All cultures punish those individuals who defy their most important conventions. A social function of folkways is to provide cultural guidelines for behavior, so that our lives are predictable and orderly. In the absence of folkways for a particular situation, participants may feel confused regarding appropriate behavior and may turn to external authorities for guidance. Take the case of a 14-year-old girl who wrote to Amy Vanderbilt for advice concerning the correct way to eat an eclair. She asked.

When you are served an eclair on a dessert plate with the eclair in one of

those paper frills, should you remove the frill before you eat the eclair or cut into the eclair with your fork while it is still in the frill? If you remove the frill, what do you do with it?

Amy Vanderbilt's response to this 14-year-old girl was a precisely worded rule of behavior specifying both how to eat an eclair and how to dispose of the frill.

Eat the eclair in the frill. Tiny eclairs are sometimes offered as a finger-food dessert. When they are served like this, you should take one, frill and all, using the frill to protect your fingers. You then crumple the frill and dispose of it in some convenient way —in a nearby wastebasket or in a large ashtray.

Source: Amy Vanderbilt, *Ladies Home Journal,* August 17, 1970, p. 23.

---

than essential behavior, their violation produces only mild forms of hostility and punishment. At worst, violators may be viewed as eccentric or idiosyncratic. At best, they may be overlooked or regarded as individualists who refuse to "follow the crowd."

Guidelines for Behavior: Sanctions

As suggested in the foregoing discussion, conformity to cultural rules is often seen as obligatory. As we know, however, since human behavior is not governed by instinct, individuals may, for whatever reason, interpret a situation differently from other members of a group and decide to act differently from that group. The result may be **deviant behavior,** any behavior that violates the norms or values of a group. All societies have developed an agreed-upon set of ideas and actions, which sociologists call sanctions, that are employed to keep such "misinterpretation" and therefore deviant behavior at a minimum.

deviant behavior Any behavior that violates the norms or values of a group.

Sanctions. Sanctions are of two types: positive and negative. *Positive sanctions* are rewards; they are ideas and actions that when learned by members of a group, appear so satisfying to their personal needs that members are inspired to work hard for the goals of the group without questioning the framework within which the

sanctions Rewards and punishments that are employed to keep deviant behavior at a minimum.

work is accomplished. Perhaps the most commonly used positive sanctions are tangible rewards, praise, and affection.

Tangible rewards are any material possessions that members of a group regard as valuable. In our society, tangible rewards include job promotions, bonus money or raises, or vacations ("Because you got all A's this term, I will take you to Florida for vacation.").

Praise is the generally verbal acknowledgment by one or more members of a group that another member has fulfilled group expectations. It can range from the praise given by parents at their child's first steps, to the "Latin praise" given with some college degrees *(summa cum laude, magna cum laude, cum laude),* to the kudos that are given prominent members of organizations when they lecture to the public.

Affection is also used as a positive sanction in the form of an

All societies have evolved ways to sanction their members both positively and negatively. In Russian society, where agricultural skills are highly acclaimed, people such as Alexei Steptsov (shown above) may be accorded high public praise for their ability to drive tractors. On the other hand, in most complex societies, a form of publicly recognized ostracism —prison (right)—has developed to keep people who are deemed to be serious deviants out of the everyday interaction of the society.

overt demonstration of love from one or more individuals to another when that individual does what is expected particularly well. This can range over a broad spectrum from parents hugging and kissing their children for some feat to one person agreeing to marry another because the other "finally" got the "right kind" of job.

Negative sanctions are employed primarily when there is some indication that a member of the group either has not or will not conform to the group's expectations. Such sanctions are ideas and actions that appear to offer such punishment to an individual that the individual is discouraged from engaging in nonconformist or deviant behavior.

Negative sanctions vary in type and severity of punishment according to the group's estimation of the degree of actual or potential transgression of the norms or values. A relatively mild form of negative sanction, for example, is *criticism*, the personal communication from one individual to another that the second individual's behavior is not viewed with pleasure. Such communication can be transmitted in many ways, from the relatively subtle raising of one's eyebrows when someone else says something we consider wrong, to the attempt to publicly discredit the offender in both his or her own eyes as well as the eyes of the group.

Box 2–6   WHAT'S IN A NAME?

Plenty! What people call you can influence everything from your grades to your popularity. Research indicates that children with unusual or unpopular names may actually be treated worse by teachers and friends than are children with "desirable" names.

Groups are very conscious of the impact of names. The most dramatic example of a group rejecting its label is the case of so-called freaks—giants, dwarfs, Siamese twins, circus-style fat ladies—who regard the term "freak" as a badge of shame and a reminder that they have long been excluded from the rest of humanity.

The history of black America shows us just how important it is in terms of group consciousness-raising for a group to be comfortable with its identity and with those names symbolizing group spirit. Black may be beautiful; but the term "colored" now suggests inequality and submission. How different it was prior to the Civil Rights movement of the fifties and sixties when the word "black" was hardly ever used to identify race, except in a negative sense.

A great many persons who have some physical disability—for example, people in wheelchairs or those who are deaf or blind—simply do not like the name "handicap." The reason is that handicap at one time literally meant cap-in-hand; lots of disabled people had no alternative but to beg in the streets, actually holding out their caps for the purpose of collecting money. It should come as no surprise that disabled people today who try hard to maximize their independence may resent being labeled in a derogatory way.

Another relatively mild form of negative sanction employed when it appears that the transgressor is going to persist in rule breaking is the *convincing argument.* An attempt is made to appeal to logic, thereby demonstrating to the offender the folly of his or her ways: "Everyone would lose out if he or she did what he or she wanted. So you can see that the best way is to. . . ." Another form of the convincing argument is the appeal to evidence: *"Everybody* does it! Can't you see that? There's nothing *wrong* with it!"

If criticism or convincing argument fails to bring the offender back into line, a more severe type of negative sanction may be called into play, the *threat.* The threat attempts to dissuade the offender by either promising to withdraw or withhold something strongly desired ("If you don't eat your supper, you can't go out and play.") or by suggesting the imposition of punishment ("If you keep hitting your brother like that, I'll have to spank you.").

If all the preceding negative sanctions fail, actual *physical violence,* one of the two most severe sanctions, may be employed. Physical punishment may range in degree from pinching someone to severe beating, torture, lynching, murder, or war (see Box 2–7).

If the individual persists in adhering to deviant ways (and physical death is ruled out as a possibility), the extreme sanction of *ostracism* may be used. Ostracism is an attempt to maintain group order by casting out the disruptive deviant member. This both punishes the member and prevents the "contamination" of other

---

Box 2–7 ANN LANDERS

How He Trained His Wife

Dear **Ann Landers:**

I'll admit that the man who wanted to wire his wife's bedspring so he could press a button and give her a slight electric shock to get her up in the morning to fix his breakfast was a little far-out, but in principle he was perfectly right. I was surprised you weren't on his side.

A husband who works hard all day is entitled to a hearty breakfast to get him off to a good start.

Some women are like dumb animals.

You have to show them who's boss or they aren't worth a damn. I trained mine right from the beginning and, believe me, there are no arguments in our house. This is the way all families ought to be run.

　　　–Big Ed in Montgomery, Ala.

Well, bully for you! You trained her right from the beginning, did you? I can believe there are no arguments in your house— just a lot of love, affection, respect, admiration . . . all the good things generated by your compassion and consideration. You should live so long, Mister.

Source: Boston Globe, June 29, 1983.

members by nonconformist ideas or actions. Thus, in the musical *Fiddler on the Roof,* Tevye's third daughter marries outside the Jewish faith. Although he has forgiven his other two daughters for marrying whom they wanted, not whom he wanted, this transgression is considered much more serious. In Tevye's eyes it violates divine law; in the sociologist's terms, it threatens the integrity of the group. His answer to her action is to say "I have no daughter!" and to forbid her from ever entering the family again. Many children have felt the pain of ostracism when their peers have for some reason not allowed them to be "part of the gang." It is because such separation from the group is so difficult to bear psychologically that ostracism is the most feared of negative sanctions and one that will usually be avoided at all costs.

The Symbolic Meaning of Sanctions.   Sanctions are perceived and identified with, not only by those being sanctioned and sanctioning itself, but by all other members of the group as well. As a result, they take on a crucial *symbolic meaning* for the other members: They represent what might happen to *them* if they engage in the same activities. Positive sanctions supply motivation to other group members to work hard to get similar rewards: "Next time, I will get A's and be the one who goes to Florida!" Negative sanctions serve to dissuade not only the offender but also potential future offenders from violating norms or values: "If I go along with that person, I'll be in trouble myself!" It is this symbolic quality of sanctions that helps to maintain, for good or ill, the established order of a culture. All aspects of ideational culture are presented in the diagrammatic summary, Figure 2–3.

THE DYNAMIC NATURE OF SOCIAL INTERACTION

In the preceding discussion of ideational culture it may have seemed at times that guidelines for behavior such as values, norms, and sanctions were unchanging, monolithic things "out there" that people simply encounter and behave in accordance with in their everyday lives. Nothing could be further from the truth.

Although it is absolutely true that society exists to a certain extent "out there," in the minds and behaviors of others, it also is equally true that it exists "in here," in our *own* minds. This fact means that guidelines for behavior are *always* subject to the human process of interpretation that we talked about at the beginning of this chapter. Indeed, guidelines for behavior continue to hold sway in our lives only because in our daily interactions we constantly encounter them, decide to follow them to the letter, to

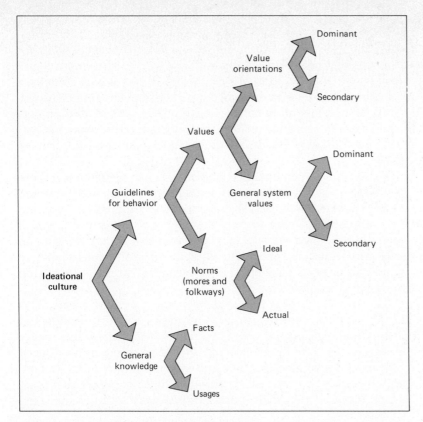

Figure 2–3 Components of Ideational Culture

renegotiate them with others in the group, or to disobey them. Human beings thus dynamically create, maintain, or destroy their social reality to a degree each day of their lives.

Sociologist Peter Berger (1967) suggests there are three continually recurring steps within the dynamic nature of social interaction. First, in encountering other people, we *externalize* ideas about the situation. For example, let us assume we have met our roommate at college for the very first time and now have to decide how to share the room's facilities. Both of us externalize ideas about who will get which bed, which closet, which desk, and the like. Through a process of dialogue, we finally reach an agreement: I will have this bed, closet, and desk, and you will have the other bed, closet, and desk.

At this point, Berger would say we have reached the second stage of dynamic interaction: *objectification* of our discussion. That is, our discussion has led us to set up some guidelines for appropriate behavior, some norms, for our room. The social reality is said to be "objectified" because it is no longer merely in one of our heads or undergoing tentative discussion; we *both* agree that this is an appropriate way to act. This is a very important step, for it means that neither of us can now change the agreement legitimately without consultation with the *other*. This is how guidelines for behavior take on an existence separate from any single individual: They, as does all of culture, become shared and all members who share or experience them, not just ourselves, expect others who share them to have a tendency to think and act in terms of them.

Once our agreements are objectified, we reencounter them every time we enter the room or meet our roommate there and have to decide how to act. We say, in effect, "This is my closet and I'm supposed to hang my clothes here." After a few times of repeating this, we *internalize* our agreement in our minds, and afterward usually act automatically in social interactions where we know this norm is in effect. This internalization is the third step in dynamic interaction.

The important thing to realize here is that we have *created* this social reality dynamically through a process of interpretation and negotiation. Although it now has a reality "out there," this reality is always subject to modification if we but go through the steps of externalization, objectification, and internalization again. In fact, imperceptibly, we are going through these steps all the time, which is one of the main sources of everyday social change (see Chapter 8).

Human beings, therefore, through the process of interpretation, may *always* alter their social world if they choose to do so. However, this may be difficult at times because the agreements the group has made are shared by so many people. With this in mind, we now turn to a consideration of major patterns of cultural variation.

PATTERNS OF CULTURAL VARIATION

We have already described how all group members learn and share some part of an ideational culture. In large groups, such as whole societies, it is not uncommon that relatively large numbers of people come to share the same, or very similar, ideas. Similarly, because of various factors, such as being born in a different historical period or having a different ethnic or racial background, it is not uncommon that, within the same society, there may exist relatively large groups of people who share different ideas from those of the first group. When this happens we may speak of patterns of *cultural variation*.

Dominant Culture

Patterns of cultural variations within any group must be examined in relation to the **dominant culture,** that set of ideas and actions that is shared by the majority of people in that group, the most powerful people in that group, or both. The dominant culture refers to the way of life of individuals who are in the cultural mainstream of a group, who subscribe more or less fully to the ideas that generate action in the group, and who strive toward group goals. For example, in regard to general system values, it has been suggested that the majority of Americans subscribe primarily to the instrumental pattern and secondarily to democratic-humanitarian values. If this is indeed the case, the people who subscribe to this pattern would be considered members of America's dominant culture. To take another example, in areas of the Mississippi Delta only 25 percent of the population is white, whereas 75 percent is black. Yet, in most of the towns in this region, the dominant culture is that subscribed to by the white population. Clearly, this is an example of a dominant culture being maintained not by a majority of the population but by the most powerful members of the community. (We shall have more to say about the whole phenomenon of power differentials in society in Chapter 5, "Social Stratification.")

dominant culture Ideas and actions shared by the majority of people in a group, the most powerful people in that group, or both.

Subcultures

Any group that accepts some of the components of the dominant culture while also sharing values or norms peculiar to itself is known as a **subculture.** There are two principal types of subcultures: normative and valuational.

subculture People who accept only some of the aspects of the dominant culture while also sharing values or norms peculiar to itself.

Normative Subculture.   A **normative subculture** is a group within a dominant culture that focuses at least part of its existence around a set of norms different from those accepted by members of the dominant culture. An example of a normative subculture is provided by Italian-Americans who live together in large metropolitan areas of the United States. This group of people share a single, important cultural input in their lives that other Americans do not —their cultural heritage. As a result, many Italian-Americans may behave differently from members of the dominant culture in specific situations. For example, they may speak in Italian, use different gestures when speaking, use different types of eye contact with others, eat different foods, wear different clothing on occasion, celebrate weddings differently, and so on.

normative subculture A group within the dominant culture that focuses at least part of its existence around a set of norms different from those of the dominant culture.

In certain social situations, then, Italian-Americans may have distinctive norms that set them apart from most other Americans.

This does not mean, however, that Italian-Americans reject the values of American culture as a whole, as well as most of its day-to-day norms. On the contrary, most Italian-Americans probably hold similar value orientations and general system values and have the same general knowledge as other Americans. The distinguishing characteristic of a normative subculture is its focus on a relatively limited set of distinctive norms that guide behavior differently from the norms of the dominant culture in a restricted set of activities. Value agreement is not at issue.

Valuational Subculture.   In the other major type of subculture, however, value agreement *is* at issue. The distinguishing characteristic of a **valuational subculture** is that the members of the group disagree with the emphasis or priority given to certain values within the dominant culture. Usually the disagreement focuses on the priority given to general system values. For example, members of the "New Left," a political group comprised mostly of young people that existed in the early 1960s basically agreed that instrumental and democratic-humanitarian values were appropriate for American society to pursue. They disagreed only on their priority. More specifically, members of the New Left claimed that a primary emphasis on instrumental rather than on democratic-humanitarian values created oppression and injustice. They proposed to reverse the priorities of American values, establishing the democratic-humanitarian complex as primary. They felt such a change in emphasis would result in a more equitable distribution of national wealth and privilege among all members of society.

valuational subculture A group within the dominant culture that disagrees with the priority given to certain values by the dominant culture.

Counterculture

Members of valuational subcultures disagree with the priorities of the dominant group's values, but they do not reject the basic legitimacy of these values. When a group *totally* rejects the values of the dominant culture, it is no longer considered a subculture, but a **counterculture.**

Countercultures are rarer than either type of subculture. They also present a much more serious threat to the dominant culture within which they coexist (Yinger, 1960). Such groups not only reject the important values of the dominant culture, but they attempt to develop an alternative set of values by which to guide their lives. Countercultural adherents see the way of life dictated by the dominant culture's values as faulty, oppressive, and dehumanizing.

The best example of a counterculture to appear in recent years is the hip-radical group that developed in American society during

counterculture A group whose members totally reject the values of the dominant culture and develop an alternative set of values by which to guide their lives.

In the late 1960s, a counterculture comprised mostly of young people sprang up in American society. Ex-Harvard Professor Timothy Leary urged young people everywhere to "turn on, tune in, and drop out." Many did and, as a result, hippie and radical communities, such as that depicted in the top photograph, appeared across America. Despite massive publicity and seemingly hundreds of thousands of participants, however, the hip counterculture was defunct by the mid-1970s. Later in the decade, London's punk phenomenon began to spread to the youth of other European countries and the United States. By the early 1980s, the American version of punk had been incorporated into "new wave" music, art, film, literature, dress, and philosophy. See Box 2.8: "Is the Punk Phenomenon a Counterculture?"

the late 1960s and lasted into the early 1970s. This group consisted predominantly of young people between the ages of 16 and 25, most of whom came from middle- and upper-middle-class backgrounds (Yablonsky, 1968). Within the movement there were essentially two subgroups: the hippie contingent, perhaps best exemplified by Ken Kesey and his group of Merry Pranksters (Wolfe, 1968) and the radicals, perhaps best exemplified by such people as Abbie Hoffman, Rennie Davis, Mark Rudd, and James S. Kunen (Hoffman, 1968; Kunen, 1969; Libarle and Seligson, 1970).

The counterculture was based on the idea that, because of American society's overwhelming emphasis on instrumental values and instrumental activity, it was producing extremely neurotic, unhappy, and basically unfulfilled human beings who were geared primarily to exploitation of others. The following two quotations are typical of attitudes of movement participants:

> [A 23-year-old hippie] We [America] have reached a high level of material development. Many people have become hypnotized and obsessed with a desire for material goods. . . . This is a negative part of contemporary American life and is blocking people from seeing the essence of one another. (Yablonsky, 1968, p. 365)
>
> [David Romano, an 18-year-old, self-proclaimed high school radical] I believe [American] society has created a condition that human nature will just inherently revolt against. . . . People think it's strange that middle class kids like myself become radicals. What, they often ask, do these products of affluent homes have to be angry about? They've never wanted for anything, they've always been provided with the best money could buy, and still they complain and condemn the system that provided all the benefits they have enjoyed. Well, you see, it's because this life is basically unhealthy that we take to the streets as we do. . . . The emphasis on complacency and normalcy, the lack of individuality, the emphasis on keeping people in boxes and slots and defining them one-dimensionally [i.e., as instrumental] . . . all adds up to something that human nature in general and we in particular find intolerable. . . . Some change must be made. (Libarle and Seligson, 1970, p. 11)

To replace the traditional instrumental pattern, the hip-radical movement proposed that Americans enjoy life now and live life for its own sake, not for any potential reward to be received at an old age. In short, Americans should be "expressive."

The hip-radical movement stirred up an enormous amount of controversy in American society. In support of the young people there arose a significant number of American intellectuals who felt that the hip movement was about to revolutionize Western society by changing its predominantly instrumental focus into a predominantly expressive (hence more humane) one. Some of these people wrote influential books stating their support of the movement, for example, Theodore Roszak's *The Making of a Counterculture* (1968), Charles Reich's *The Greening of America* (1969), Philip Slater's *The Pursuit of Loneliness* (1970), and Richard Flack's *Youth and Social Change* (1971).

When the counterculture was at its peak, from 1967 to 1970, it attracted large numbers of American youth. It seemed as though a mass defection from the dominant culture was underway. Suddenly, everywhere (or so it seemed if one watched television or lived in cities) there were huge numbers of American young people who looked hip (long hair, "psychedelic" clothes), talked hip ("man," "Can you dig it?" "flower power," "groovy," "outta sight,") and, to some degree, acted hip (took part in demonstrations, smoked marijuana, went to rock festivals). For many it seemed that the revolution was imminent.

The fundamentally subversive nature of a counterculture makes it a much more serious threat to a dominant culture than either of the two subcultural types. By definition, a counterculture attempts to discredit and replace the fundamental values by which members of the dominant culture live. The counterculture also threatens the size of the dominant culture, since it draws its membership from the ranks of that dominant culture. If defection went unchecked, it is possible that the population base of the dominant culture would be decimated, resulting in collapse. Because most of the members of the late 1960s counterculture were young, it was especially threatening.

For this reason countercultures have historically received harsher treatment from dominant culture members than have their subcultural counterparts. Members of normative subcultures opt to follow only a limited number of unconventional norms, usually determined by ethnic or racial heritage. In most cases the presence of a normative subculture in no way prevents the dominant culture from proceeding with its activity as usual. Although valuational subcultures disagree more seriously with the dominant culture, they still do not demand rejection of the dominant culture's way of life, only a shift in priorities. Thus, although dominant cultures treat valuational subcultures somewhat more harshly than normative subcultures, they generally do not try to suppress them, particularly in democratic countries.

Such is not the case with countercultures. Since most members of the dominant culture have strong commitments to the status quo, the counterculture is often the subject of some type of counterattack, either verbal discreditation or physical violence. For instance, from its initial appearance in the mass media around 1967, the hip-radical counterculture was the target of scathing

verbal attacks from almost every official quarter. By 1968, however, the counterculture still seemed to be gaining momentum
and more young people seemed to be dropping out. Consequently, the actions taken against the counterculture began to
take on a more physical, violent character. There was the "battle
of Chicago" in August of 1968 at the Democratic National Convention, followed by the Berkeley People's Park violence of 1969
—both cases in which police attacked counterculture members
ferociously. Then there were the shootings at Kent State University and Jackson State University in 1970, where four white and
two black students respectively, were killed by National Guardsmen. As the 1970s wore on and the counterculture began to lose
adherents, the violence began to subside. The hip-radical counterculture was no longer seen as posing a major threat to dominant
culture existence.

THE INFLUENCE OF OTHER FACTORS ON CULTURE

Thus far in this chapter we have emphasized the importance of
culture, particularly ideational culture, in shaping social life. Most
sociologists would argue that, until a full understanding of the
culture of a group is obtained, it would be very difficult to provide
an adequate explanation for the social behavior of that group. Yet
culture is not the whole story, for whatever its importance, culture
always interrelates with other factors that affect human life. Often
these factors must be understood as well if we are to explain the
social phenomenon in question.

One of these factors is *environment* (including geography and
climate as well as material resources and food-producing potential). Imagine, for example, trying to explain why San Francisco is
continually named as the favorite city of Americans without taking
into account the fact that it is situated on a peninsula surrounded
on three sides by spectacular ocean and bay views, that the temperature hardly ever goes above 75 degrees or below 40 degrees,
and that its many hills make for a quite unique and extremely
exciting experience (see Box 2–8).

Often, however, environment is not a crucial factor in supple-
menting a cultural analysis, but other factors, such as *population*
and *specific historical events* are. To see the influence of these
factors in a single case, let us return to our example of the hip
counterculture introduced in the last section.

That discussion, you will remember, was able to describe the
stance of each countercultural subgroup—the hippies and the
radicals—and the reaction of the dominant culture to them by
examining ideational cultural factors alone. Yet this analysis did

Box 2–8 SAN FRANCISCO: A UNIQUE URBAN ENVIRONMENT

The well-known American novelist, John Dos Passos, occasionally wrote journalistic articles. One of these was written about the excitement of being in San Francisco. The passage which follows indicates the important interrelationship between material culture (the city itself), ideational culture (the social thoughts in Dos Passos' mind), and environment (geography and climate) in this city.

If you happen to be endowed with topographical curiosity the hills of San Francisco fill you with an irresistible desire to walk to the top of each one of them. Whoever laid the town out took the conventional checkerboard pattern of streets and without the slightest regard for the laws of gravity planked it down blind on an irregular peninsula that was a confusion of steep slopes and sandhills. The result is exhilarating. Wherever you step out on the street there's a hilltop in one direction or the other. From the top of each hill you get a view and the sight of more hills to the right and left and ahead that offer the

prospect of still broader views. The process goes on indefinitely. You can't help making your way painfully to the top of each hill just to see what you can see. . . . This particular morning was a windy morning, half sun and blue sky and half pearly tatters of fog blowing in from the Pacific. . . . (Although it was time for me to get to work) I found I had turned and was resolutely walking up the nearest hill.

This one is Nob Hill, I know that. . . . Ahead of me the hill rises higher and breaks into a bit of blue sky. Sun shines on a block of white houses at the top. Shiny as a toy fresh from a Christmas tree, a little cable car is crawling up it. Back of me under an indigo blur of mist are shadowed roofs and streets and tall buildings with wisps of fog about them, and beyond, fading off into the foggy sky, stretches the long horizontal of the Bay Bridge.

Better go back now and start about my business. The trouble is that down the hill to the right I've caught sight of accented green roofs and curved gables painted jade green and vermillion. That must be in Chinatown. Of course the thing to do is take a turn through Chinatown on the way down toward the business district. . . .

Source: John Dos Passos, "San Francisco Looks West." In Oscar Shoenfeld and Helene Machean (eds.), *City Life* (New York: Grossman, 1969), pp. 484–485.

not, indeed could not, explain why the counterculture arose when it did, and why it disappeared so suddenly (at its peak it looked like it might last for decades). For answers to these questions, let us look more carefully at the effects of population and specific historical events.

The Rise of the Counterculture and Population. Everyone knows there was a baby boom of unprecedented proportions in American society after World War II. Yet when thinking about the hip counterculture, it is often overlooked that the babies from this boom reached the stage of the life cycle known as adolescence in huge numbers in the 1960s. For example, in 1957 the 14-to 24-year-old group in American society comprised 14.9 percent of the total population. But by 1970 this percentage had risen to 19.8 percent. Translated into actual numbers, this was an increase of almost *six million* adolescents in the American population in little more than a decade!

What were the consequences of this increase? On the one hand, despite massive increases in jobs for youth, in enrollments in higher education, and in enlistments in the military, the three traditional "slots" for American adolescents, there were still nearly a million more young Americans "on the streets" in the 1960s than in the previous decade. On the other hand, even for those with jobs, in higher education, and in the military, the future did not look very rosy—for when those six million extra persons tried to get a fixed number of adult jobs, competition was expected to be fierce. It is not hard to see how both these consequences may have contributed to countercultural attitudes; there is nothing so frustrating for a group of people than to see that they have no place in their society.

The Rise of the Counterculture and Specific Historical Events.

In addition to the population pressures, two unique historical events of the 1960s contributed mightily to the development of the youth movement. First, the 1960s were years of tremendous affluence in American society. Even when controlled for inflation, the Gross National Product of the United States saw a jump of over 107 billion dollars between 1965 and 1970 (the peak counterculture period) as compared to well under 100 billion between 1960 and 1965. This meant that all sectors of American society had more money than ever before. In the case of middle-class young people, it meant that adolescent life was not continually pressured by concern over "survival" factors (food, shelter, clothing) even if they were living on the streets. Many hippies got regular checks from home. Others made excellent livings panhandling and by taking part-time jobs. This relative affluence meant that 1960s young people could literally afford to "play around" much more than their predecessors. So many of them turned to the bohemian alternative of the time, being hip.

Second, this group of American young people was deeply affected by the Vietnam War of the 1960s. From one perspective, their concern was moral: There was great concern throughout the country whether the United States was acting to "preserve democracy" in South Vietnam, as the government said it was, or attempting to crush a small nation that had chosen to favor communism over democracy. From another perspective, the young people's concern was personal: Many young men were being drafted to fight in this war. Both aspects contributed to the formation of the radical contingent of the counterculture.

The Decline of the Counterculture, Population, and Specific Historical Events.   By the mid-1970s, the counterculture was dead. The original hippie communities, such as those in San Francisco's Haight-Ashbury district and in New York's East Village had disappeared and college and university campuses across the nation, the residence of many radicals, had returned to relatively peaceful existence. Why?

Let us look at population factors first. By the mid-1970s the children of the baby boom of the post-World War II period were rapidly leaving adolescence and moving into the period traditionally known as adulthood. Despite the competition for jobs so feared in the 1960s, it appears that most of these young people attempted to assume adult responsibilities rather than continue their countercultural life-styles. This movement of the baby-boom population bulge out of adolescence has left that stage of life to an increasingly *smaller* group of young people that the traditional youth alternatives of temporary jobs, higher education, and the military can more easily absorb, leaving few middle-class adolescents "on the streets."

Considering the special historical events that so affected the youth of the sixties, both have changed. On the one hand, economic recession set in about 1971, depriving many Americans, including youth, of the surplus affluence of the previous decade. This made it very difficult to live a countercultural life-style for many. The "spare change" of passersby and the odd jobs at the post office dried up. On the other hand, the Vietnam War ended in 1973, depriving committed radicals of a major focus of their attention and of a lever by which to recruit others. Consequently, for adolescents today, aware as they are of the potential difficulty in getting jobs when they become adults, there is little time to "goof off." Moreover, for present-day adolescents the Vietnam War is simply not an omnipresent, threatening reality; it is, at most, a vague impression of something that happened to others. The result of all this has been, for good or ill, a return to "business as usual."

However, the question of whether the counterculture is *completely* dead is still open. Recently, there has been a "new wave" of rock music, much of it from England, and many of its proponents live what appear to be countercultural life-styles, subscribing to countercultural values. Rennie Davis (Box 2–10) may have

Box 2–9   IS THE PUNK PHENOMENON A COUNTERCULTURE?

According to Lamy (1983), "punk" contains many elements of what sociologists refer to as counterculture. The origins of the punk phenomenon are to be found in youth of the seventies—British punks aged 13 to 19 who donned the costumes of Zombie-like, X-rated cartoon characters. During the summer of 1976 angry mobs of London's "disaffected" young people from inner-city working-class backgrounds protesting economic recession and urban blight created a life-style in mock defiance of that which was generally associated with British formalism and conservatism. Assuming the identity of England's alienated outcasts, punkers were the antithesis of all that they felt their society symbolized.

The punk look was a curious mixture of fifties revivalism, and paramilitary imagery, coupled with safety pins, razor blades, and "angry shades," zippers, and spiked jewelry. Hair was worn closely cropped, teased, feathered, and often dyed bright shocking colors. Faces were made up in the "gaudy and grim starkness of death."

In contrast to their British counterparts, American punkers were primarily middle class and in their mid-twenties. Yet both the British and American versions of punk had their roots in feelings of alienation; both mocked conservative, capitalist big business that they felt dictated what was fashionable, what was stylish, and what music was popular. Both in England and the United States, punkers were cynical about the mass media and the police, indeed, about the entire society for which no one wanted to assume responsibility.

Many of the tamer, more socially acceptable and therefore marketable elements of the punk phenomenon have been incorporated into "new wave" music, art, film, literature, dress, and philosophy: In fashion, short hair, skinny ties, thin dark glasses, and fingerless gloves; in music, The Police, The Clash, The Jam, Culture Club, and Eurythmics, and in cinema, *Diva, The Road Warrior,* and *The Rocky Horror Picture Show,* to mention only a few.

"sold out," but "The Clash" and "Boy George" (Culture Club) may not have, as Box 2–9 attests.

SUMMARY

Much of animal behavior can be characterized as instinctual; that is, animals react to certain conditions in the environment by using inborn, automatic, and unvarying response. In contrast, human beings do not possess instincts but must rely instead on their intelligence for making effective decisions. The complex mental process employed by human beings in the absence of instincts is known as interpretation. Human beings must think about the stimuli that reach their brains, organize their thoughts about the stimuli, and evaluate these thoughts in order to choose a course of action.

Box 2–10 SIXTIES YOUTH AS ADULTS

In the example that follows, the transition to adulthood of sixties youth is depicted. Rennie Davis, the subject of the news story, was once a key radical in the counterculture.

> DENVER (AP)—Rennie Davis, the one time antiwar activist, is now selling insurance in this city. . . . Davis, 37, a defendant in the Chicago Seven conspiracy trial who became a follower of Guru Maharai Ji in 1973, now works for the John Hancock Mutual Life Insurance Co . . .
>
> Davis told the Denver Post he entered the business world to assist companies which "make service their primary goal.
>
> "I found that I needed training in business procedures. I came here basically to learn about business and estate planning."
>
> Davis told the Post that John Hancock officials were aware of his background and were "very kind" to hire him. Davis says he is seeking a new way to live.
>
> "A lot of people in their mid-30s are finding themselves working in major institutions, feeling not so much betrayal of their own philosophy but finding a way to give people an alternative way to live their lives," he said.
>
> Asked if he would feel comfortable selling a policy to cover the nearby nuclear plant at Rocky Flats, he replied: "Well, I wouldn't want to limit where my experience might take me, even to the people who all their lives made war, or into the home of Richard Nixon."

Source: The Morning Union, Springfield, Mass., July 11, 1977, p. 2.

The absence of instincts means that humans have the capacity for exhibiting a variety in their behavior not observed among other animals. Nevertheless, human life is marked by a tremendous amount of consistency and order. The basis for the consistent and orderly patterns found in human behavior is a result of the invention of culture. This important sociological idea informs us that human beings have the capacity to learn and share a way of life that endures across generations. These two factors, the process of interpretation and the invention of culture, are what distinguish humans from all other species.

Culture has two major dimensions. Material culture consists of the observable and tangible products of human activity that do not occur naturally in the physical environment; it provides solutions to the problems of living and coping with reality. Ideational culture consists of a set of ideas learned and shared by the members of a group in the form of general knowledge about the world and guidelines for social behavior.

General knowledge, whether in the form of facts or usages, represents the basic data with which individuals are able to con-

duct their everyday affairs. General knowledge is a kind of background for social situations. Guidelines for behavior suggest how
group members should or should not act in their social encounters.

There are three varieties of guidelines for behavior: values,
norms, and sanctions. Values are concepts of the desirable and
indicate the proper orientation and goal of social situations. Value
orientations provide answers to existential questions of human life:
How does one relate to time, to the physical environment, to other
people? What are the essential qualities of human nature? What
are the most valued activities? General system values identify the
desirable goals of the group. In American society the dominant
pattern of general system values is the instrumental complex that
stresses achievement, rationality, and economic endeavor. There
is also a secondary value pattern known as the democratic-
humanitarian complex, a series of values historically legitimized
by the Constitution and the Bill of Rights.

Another important type of behavioral guideline are norms.
These are ideas about behavior that inform members of a group
what is right and proper to do in a specific situation. Thus there
are norms for how to ride the subway, how to conduct war, how
to eat food, and so on. Sets of norms cluster around human activities, such as parenthood, a classroom, or a family dinner.

Either ideal or actual norms may apply in any given social
situation. Ideal norms specify the exact behavior expected of a
group member in good standing. When associated with a formal
organization, such rules of behavior are often encoded in written
form. By contrast, actual norms are generally learned informally.
They indicate the degree of latitude a person may take with the
ideal norms without incurring the disapproval of other group
members.

Norms may also be categorized as mores or folkways. Mores are
rules of behavior that group members regard as essential. Their
violation is strongly disapproved. Folkways are guidelines for the
ordinary, routine activities of everyday life. They deal with appropriate but not essential standards of behavior. For example, "Thou
shalt not kill" is a mos (singular of mores), whereas "Thou shalt eat
with a fork" is a folkway.

In order to minimize deviant behavior, groups employ sanctions. Positive sanctions such as tangible rewards, praise, and affection are bestowed on members who conform to cultural rules:
Negative sanctions such as criticism, threats, violence, and ostracism are used to punish members who violate cultural rules.

Despite the reality of culture as a force outside human beings,
it is not unchanging or monolithic. It must also be understood as
arising from an on-going, dynamic process of interaction. In this
process people are continually externalizing, objectifying, and in-

Culture determines the most important differences between human beings. To take a very common example: In all societies people have to devise ways to greet one another. *How* they decide to do so, however, is a product of cultural ideas, rather than an inevitable response to biological instinct. In the top photograph, two white Americans greet one another by shaking hands (note position of hands). In the middle photograph, two black Americans greet one another (again note position of hands). In the bottom photograph, two men from other parts of the world embrace upon meeting one another (here handshaking is not the agreed-upon format— embracing is). To fully understand human behavior, most sociologists would argue that we *must* study social interaction and the most important product of that interaction, culture.

ternalizing guidelines for behavior such as values, norms, and sanctions. They always can, and often do, choose to interpret these guidelines differently. The power of culture is *real,* but it is not a reality etched in stone.

All group members learn and share some aspects of the ideational culture. The dominant culture is the way of life accepted by the majority of the group. However, often some members of a group do not fully share or accept the dominant culture. Any set of people who accept only some of the components of the dominant culture while also sharing values or norms peculiar to itself is known as a subculture. A normative subculture (e.g., Italian-Americans living together in metropolitan areas) focuses some part of its existence around a set of norms different from those of the dominant culture. A valuational subculture (e.g., the political group called the "New Left" that emerged in the 1960s) disagrees with the priorities given to certain values by the dominant culture. They seek to change these value priorities while continuing to accept their basic legitimacy. When a group totally rejects the values of the dominant culture, we can say that a counterculture has emerged. Since countercultures are a serious threat to the dominant culture, they generally receive harsher treatment from dominant culture members than do their subcultural counterparts. The experiences of the hip-radical counterculture of the late 1960s are illustrative in this regard.

Finally, as helpful as the concept of culture is in interpreting human social behavior, it is often not sufficient by itself in explaining all aspects of that behavior. Other factors that often need to be included for a full explanation are the effects of environment, population, and specific historical events. The effects of environment were illustrated by looking at the unique qualities of the city of San Francisco. The effects of population and specific historical events were illustrated by an examination of the decline of the hip counterculture in the early 1970s.

QUESTIONS, EXERCISES, PROJECTS

1. Contrast the process that produces action in response to aggression (behavior intended to inflict injury) in animals and human beings.
2. How would you explain the fact that human life is marked by great consistency and order, despite an absence of instincts?
3. "Material culture is a survival package for human beings." Discuss.

4. Discuss ethnocentrism as an expression of the "binding aspect of culture."
5. Summarize the major elements of ideational culture.
6. Using Kluckhohn and Strodtbeck's framework, describe the dominant value orientations of American business.
7. Describe the general system values to which most Americans seem to be committed. Are these *your* values? If so, how have you learned them? If not, what other values do you hold in highest priority and how did you learn *them*?
8. Distinguish between (a) norms and values, (b) ideal norms and actual norms, (c) mores and folkways, (d) normative subcultures and valuational subcultures, and (e) subcultures and countercultures.
9. What is one major way in which a group ensures that its members will conform to cultural rules? Give three examples.
10. Is the women's movement in the United States (a) a normative subculture, (b) a valuational subculture, or (c) a counterculture? Why?
11. Examine a number of children's stories, such as Three Little Pigs, Jack and the Beanstalk, Cinderella, and Peter Pan, to determine the values to which their young readers are being socialized. Identify the central value theme or moral lesson for each story. Do you see any overall similarities? Are many concerned with instrumental or democratic-humanitarian values?
12. Identify several norms of behavior commonly associated with riding on an elevator. Once you have identified these norms, violate them by behaving in an inappropriate manner on an elevator (nothing illegal or harmful, please). Briefly describe the reactions of other passengers as well as your own feelings in response to your deviant behavior. How would you explain these reactions?

SOCIALIZATION

Culture persists across generations of individuals. The basic elements of most of the roles that we play existed long before any of us were born and will likely survive our deaths. Similarly, most of the values associated with our society have persisted for centuries.

How is the persistence of such complex cultural patterns possible? How can we explain the fact that the majority of people who grow up in America conform to group standards and eventually fill the roles defined for them by society? How is it, in other words, that most people become "good Americans"—individuals who believe in "the American way"? Clearly, the question of how culture is effectively transmitted to individuals is one of the most crucial in sociology.

THE FUNCTION OF CONFORMITY

To many of us words such as *conformity* and *obedience* have bad connotations. They suggest nightmarish images of life under the rule of an absolute dictatorship. Yet *all* societies, *regardless of their political institutions*, must depend on gaining a certain amount of obedience and conformity from their members. Let us, then, briefly look at how such qualities are evoked in the social setting.

Sherif (1936) investigated the influence of group norms on decision making. He devised an experimental situation that used the fact that a stationary pinpoint of light appears to move when

viewed in a completely darkened room. Sherif first asked his subjects individually to view the pinpoint of light and report its direction and range of movement (actually, of course, the light only seemed to move and was entirely stationary). He then placed them in groups of three or four. He found that the estimates of movement given by individuals in a group situation tended to converge around an overall group judgment. For example, perhaps individual A initially saw the light as moving 3.5 inches, whereas individual B saw it moving 6.5 inches, and individual C saw it moving 2 inches. But when they later viewed the light *together as a group,* they came to a compromise agreement that the light was "actually moving" 4 or 5 inches!

Sherif also found that the power of the group endured over a long period of time. A year after the first testing, the subjects were again exposed individually to the same experimental situation. Although they were viewing the light alone, they tended to give the same judgment of direction and movement that their group had developed a year earlier.

Asch (1952) carried out a series of studies that further demonstrated the influence of group pressure to conform. In the first of his studies a group of eight individuals were asked to match the length of a line with one of three comparison lines (see Figure 3–1). All judgments were made out loud and in order of seating in the room.

Actually only one participant in the Asch study was a naive subject, that is, the others were confederates of Asch who had been instructed to respond incorrectly when asked to match the length of the lines. Over a number of trials with different groups, approximately one third of the naive subjects made incorrect estimates in the direction of the inaccurate majority.

Follow-up interviews with the naive subjects who responded incorrectly were revealing. Some subjects actually misperceived the length of the lines. Some identified the correct lines but doubted their own judgment. Others conformed in order to avoid appearing different from the other group members.

Just as it operates in experimental studies, so conformity operates in social interaction. *If a group is to persist, its members must conform at least minimally to cultural values and norms.* In large part this means that values, norms, and sanctions must be trans-

---

People in all groups conform to one degree or another—in dress, in speech, in likes and dislikes. Despite the fact that conformity is often thought to be a negative aspect of social life, the truth is that it has numerous very necessary and positive aspects as well. For example, it helps group members identify one another, it makes the job of the group easier to accomplish, and it gives group members a solid sense of "belonging."

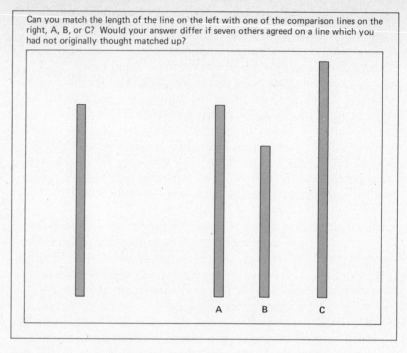

Can you match the length of the line on the left with one of the comparison lines on the right, A, B, or C? Would your answer differ if seven others agreed on a line which you had not originally thought matched up?

Figure 3–1

personality The configuration of habits, expectations, and attitudes that
is both enduring and characteristic of an individual.

ferred into the **personality** of the individual—that configuration of habits, expectations, and attitudes that is both enduring and characteristic of an individual's overall orientation to life.

Such a transference of culture into personal attitudes occurs to some degree in every human being. For example, American values that emphasize achievement are often expressed within an individual personality as a compulsive desire for hard work. Similarly, our cultural emphasis on individualism can frequently be observed as an intensely negative attitude toward any type of collective solutions to political problems. Somehow, such solutions are seen as "socialistic" or "communistic." On a group level, the antiblack norms of many white groups are represented at the individual level as a rigid, emotionally charged, negative attitude toward black Americans. Blacks are condemned automatically whether or not those condemning them have any reason for feeling the way they do.

EARLY SOCIALIZATION

The complex process whereby the norms, values, and sanctions of a group are transferred to, and internalized by, individual per-

It's contagious. It started (left) with the bespectacled lad in the front row of the choir of Boston's Cathedral Church of St. Paul. "Yawn syndrome" then spread to his neighbor (center) and finally to a third boy. The choir sang at a recent session of the International Conference on Faith, Science and the Future at Massachusetts Institute of Technology.

sonalities is called **socialization.** Although this process occurs continually throughout life, there is little doubt that many basic cultural ideas are internalized early in an individual's life experience.

Most observers of society agree that childhood is the period during which much socialization occurs. There is disagreement, however, as to exactly what the most important mechanisms of childhood socialization are. Some theorists believe such socialization involves mainly **unconscious processes** —emotions and urges in the child of which he or she is either totally or partially unaware. The most important theory of this type is that of Sigmund Freud and his followers. In sharp contrast to the Freudian approach, theorists in the tradition of George Herbert Mead have emphasized the key role of **consciousness,** the individual's awareness of his or her "self" as influenced by language and social interaction. Let us look at each of these explanations in turn.

Freud's Concept of the Superego

Few concepts do more to explain the vital link between culture and the individual than does the Freudian notion of the superego. In Freud's (1920; 1922; 1930) theory the personality has three components, the id, the ego, and the superego. The **superego** is the internal representative of cultural norms, values, and sanctions; it is the element of personality concerned with questions of right and wrong, good and evil, moral and immoral, and the like.

At birth the infant lacks any conception of morality and has no

socialization The process whereby culture is transferred to, and internalized by, individual personalities.

unconscious processes Emotions and urges of which an individual is unaware.

consciousness The individual's awareness of self.

superego The internal representative of cultural norms, values, and sanctions.

Sigmund Freud (1856–1939), undoubtedly one of the most important psychologists of all time, spent a great deal of his time theorizing about the nature of the relationship between the individual and society.
Fundamentally, he saw human beings driven by instinctual energy which resided in the id (see text). While from the point of view of the individual this energy was satisfaction seeking, from the point of view of society, it was potentially dangerous because one person's desires might come into conflict with another's and serious conflict might ensue. Consequently, Freud saw society and the individual as being at odds with one another. Most sociologists now reject the notion of instincts in the sense that Freud meant them. Nonetheless, Freud's concepts of the ego and, particularly, of the superego as society's "representative" in each individual's personality still retain great usefulness. Even if individuals are not driven by id-based instincts, the knowledge of the "do's and don't's" of social life still become part of the personality.

superego. Freud argued that the personality of the infant consists merely of the **id,** a reservoir of psychic energy based on inborn needs and drives. The primary aim of the id is to reduce pain and heighten pleasure. But the id is ill-equipped to meet its goal, since it can do little more than form mental images of desired objects (e.g., dream about food or drink) or operate by reflex.

id A reservoir of psychic energy, whose primary aim is to reduce pain and heighten pleasure.

Because human needs can be satisfied only in relation to the external world, the child must learn to act in an intelligent, rather than impulsive, manner. A process is needed that enables the child to devise and evaluate possible plans of action in the search for objects in the external world that will satisfy his or her needs. This process Freud calls the development of the **ego.** During the second year of life the differentiating ego enables the child to deal with the objective world in a more rational manner than is possible when he or she is guided by raw impulse (id).

ego The element of personality that enables the individual to devise and evaluate possible plans of action.

Despite this significant advance, however, the child may still have problems coping with the outside world. Even given a newly formed ego, inexperience may lead the child to attempt things that are dangerous (e.g., crossing the street to chase a ball) and individual desires may often come into conflict with the desires of others (e.g., wanting to play with the same toy as a sibling). In short, beyond immediate wants and desires, the child still has no internalized conception of what he or she should or should not be doing. Social rules of behavior to guide actions have not yet become a part of the personality. It is at this point that the third major component of personality, the superego, begins to develop.

The superego arises in the child's mind during the fourth or fifth year as a direct result of the rewards and punishments imposed by the child's parents on actual or intended behavior. In order to maximize these rewards (i.e., to gain pleasure) and minimize these punishments (i.e., to avoid pain), the child gradually learns to behave in conformity with the social norms and values that his or her parents transmit. During this process the child internalizes a complex set of cultural guidelines for behavior and learns to be "responsible."

As the child internalizes a sense of morality from encounters with his parents, the superego develops two sides, conscience and ego ideal. The **conscience** is the negative side of the superego; it is the result of parental proscriptions about behavior (the "shouldn'ts" of behavior). Before the superego is fully formed, these proscriptions come from actual punishments (such as spanking) or implied punishments ("If you do that, you won't get any dessert."). However, when the proscriptions have been fully internalized in the personality, the actual punishment or threat of punishment *no longer needs to be expressed* by another person. When faced with behavioral alternatives, the child feels guilty if he engages in a proscribed act. Indeed, *guilt* is one of the prime

conscience The negative side of the superego, resulting from parental proscriptions about behavior, the source of feelings of guilt.

ego ideal The positive side of the superego, resulting from parental prescriptions about behavior; the source of feelings of pride.

Oedipus complex A sexual desire for the parent of the opposite sex, coupled with a feeling of hostility for the parent of the same sex.

mechanisms of social control (devices for making sure that the dictates of the group are carried out) and its presence in most individuals is a sure sign that socialization has taken place.

The **ego ideal** is the positive side of the superego; it is the result of parental prescriptions about behavior (the "shoulds" of behavior). It tells the child what is "good to be" and what is "worthwhile" to strive for. Prior to the formation of the superego, the parental prescriptions take the form of direct rewards ("If you help me, I'll give you a quarter for a video game."). As the superego develops and the prescriptions become internalized, the child begins to feel a sense of internal *pride* when he does what he is supposed to ("I am a good boy."). Like guilt, *pride* is a mechanism of social control; it helps ensure that the individual, even in the absence of outside control, will attempt to pursue the ideals of the group (see Box 3–1).

According to Freud, the development of the superego is affected by the way the child experiences the **Oedipus complex,** which arises in all children between the ages of 3 and 5. During this stage the child harbors a sexual desire for the parent of the opposite sex and feels hostility for the parent of the same sex. Thus boys feel themselves in a competitive struggle with their father for the love of their mother, whereas girls feel themselves in a competitive struggle with their mother for the love of their father. When the child realizes the futility of the rivalry and comes to fear

---

Box 3–1 THE SENSE OF HONOR

Closely related to pride is the sense of *honor,* of feeling good when one does what the group believes is right. Many societies make honor a cornerstone of their social organization. For hundreds of years Japanese society had a strict honor code, particularly for its military class, the *samurai.* Not to follow the code exactly led to feelings of guilt, often severe enough that they could be assuaged only by ritual suicide. In our own society we see honor at work in our desire to "uphold the family name," or in attempts to "act as God would wish," and so on. Yet honor is, like most social codes, a somewhat arbitrary invention. Sometimes we catch a glimpse of this. In the following passage from

Shakespeare's *Henry the Fourth, Part I,* Falstaff finds himself trying to uphold this sense of honor and then wonders why he's doing it.

Honor pricks me on . . . Can honor set a leg? No. Or an arm? No. Or take away the grief of a wound? No. Honor hath no skill in surgery then. What is honor? A word. What is that word honor? Air. A trim reckoning! What hatch it? He that died o'-Wednesday! Doth he feel it? No. Doth he hear it? No. 'Tis insensible then? Yea, to the dead. . . . Therefore I'll none of it. Honor is a mere scutcheon, and so ends my catechism.

the response the competitive parent might make to his or her hostile behavior, the stage is set for a major change in the orientation of the child regarding his or her parents. **Identification** becomes the means by which the oedipal conflict can be resolved; a boy seeks to become like his father in order to gain the affection of his mother; similarly, a girl seeks to become like her mother in order to gain the affection of her father. Identification reduces the feelings of hostility toward the parent of the same sex and also reduces the fear of a hostile response by that parent. In terms of social consequences, identification assures socially appropriate sexual identification and, more generally, acceptance of the parents' cultural standards in the superego.

identification A child's attempt to become like the parent of the same sex in order to gain the affection of the parent of the opposite sex.

In summary, the superego is culture's *internal* representative. It asks only whether behavior is morally right or wrong, not whether the behavior actually satisfies the basic needs of the individual, and thus it is basically at odds with both the id (the repository of needs) as well as the ego (the means to satisfy them). Freud conceived of the personality as a kind of battlefield for conflicts between the requirements of society as represented by the superego and the needs of the individual as represented by the id and ego. The very act of living among other human beings, according to Freud (1930), creates tremendous unrest and discontent in the individual; he or she is asked to inhibit desires of the id that society has condemned (e.g., completely unregulated sex) and to substitute socially approved goals (e.g., sex with "approved" others: a spouse).

There are elements of Freudian theory (e.g., the universality of the oedipal conflict) that most contemporary sociologists no longer accept. Yet Freud's theory of personality provides the basis for many of our modern views of the socialization process. His concept of the superego continues to be one of the most important ideas to explain the relationship between culture and personality.

Role-taking and the Development of Self

Freud's theory of socialization emphasizes unconscious processes in the personality of the child. By contrast, George Herbert Mead (1934) emphasizes the **self**—that unique capacity of human beings for self-awareness and self-evaluation. According to Mead, the development of the self depends on the distinctly human ability for taking the role of the other or, more simply, **role-taking,** whereby an individual can determine the intention of others based on their actions.

self The individual's capacity for self-awareness and self-evaluation.

role-taking The mental process whereby an individual determines the standpoint of others based on their actions.

Role-taking and Significant Symbols. As suggested earlier, much of the behavior of human beings comes about as a result of

interpretation and choice rather than from instinctually pro-
grammed responses. Consider this situation: Individual A sees Individual B coming rapidly toward him, fists clenched and arms
raised. On the basis of B's gestures, A *imagines* the intended
actions of B (e.g., to engage him in a fist fight) and *decides* whether
to stay and fight, run, or cower in fear. In other words, by *taking
the role* of B, A is able to evaluate the possibilities for action.

According to Mead, the basis for human action, cooperation,
and order is an elaborate set of **significant symbols,** especially
language. People in a given culture agree that certain symbols
mean the same things. These significant symbols, shared by the
members of a language community, permit the members to share
a common definition of the situation and to anticipate the behavior of one another. Only through the development of such common definitions is social life possible. For instance, a clenched fist
and a raised arm are understood by large numbers of individuals
as gestures of anger and hostility. The word *dog* suggests a similar
image to most members of society (e.g., a four-legged animal that
can be domesticated).

Another characteristic of significant symbols is that they are
arbitrary; that is, the particular form and content of significant
symbols are not predetermined in any way by the physiology of
their users. In displaying anger, dogs are limited to instinctual
responses such as growling and baring teeth. Human beings expressing anger employ significant symbols; they can growl or snarl,
but they can also employ any number of words and physical gestures understood by an enemy. The sole criterion is that the
enemy shares their definition of the situation and will therefore
understand what is being communicated.

Significant Other and Generalized Other. Through the process
of role-taking aided by the use of significant symbols, the individual comes to define and evaluate the events or objects in his or her
world. Mead argues that an individual regularly takes the role of
both significant others and generalized others. The **significant
other** for any individual is any person with whom the individual
interacts frequently and emotionally. The prototypical significant
other is a parent, but the person may also be a close relative,
intimate friend, lover, husband, wife, and so forth. Those who
comprise a person's significant others play a large part in determining consciousness. For instance, in taking the role of his father
as a significant other, a boy might come to believe deeply in the
desirability of regular exercise in daily life. Similarly, in taking the
role of a particular teacher as a significant other, a girl might come
to regard reading as an important activity and become an avid
reader in later life.

significant symbols A set
of symbols that are shared
by the members of a lan-
guage community.

significant others The
people with whom an indi-
vidual interacts frequently
and emotionally.

As role-taking abilities grow, the individual also learns to take the role of the **generalized other,** that is, the viewpoint of a group or community as a whole rather than of particular significant others. By so doing, the child, over a period of time, comes to internalize the norms and values of society. To put it another way, the internalization of the generalized other is Mead's concept which parallels Freud's concept of the superego. The central difference is that, whereas Freud saw the internal representative of society developing unconsciously, Mead saw it as developing from a conscious process.

generalized other The viewpoint of a group or community as a whole.

Taking the role of the generalized other is an extremely important precondition for the development of the self, since the individual must learn to define and evaluate the self as others define her. An individual must be able to "get outside of herself" and "view herself as an object," if she is ever to be able to evaluate her own behavior as or as not appropriate. We now turn to a consideration of how this development of the self occurs.

George Herbert Mead (1863–1931) saw the relationship between the individual and society as a fundamentally positive, mutually-supportive one, as opposed to Freud's theories. People, he felt, basically became human only by their dynamic interactions with others and their reflections on those interactions. Whereas Freud often seemed to imply that people would be happier as individuals without society, Mead believed the opposite. It is in social life that we develop our full human potential. It is through our individual interpretations of society as we encounter it that we, as individuals, and society, as a whole, develop.

I The spontaneous, impulsive, and innovative aspects of the self.

me That aspect of the self that is the internal agent of conformity and social control.

Stages in the Development of the Self.   Mead regarded the self as a dynamic process within the individual having two phases called the *I* and the *Me*. The **I** represents the spontaneous, impulsive, and innovative dispositions of the individual, those dispositions that have not yet come under the control of society. As a result, the I is responsible for instances of both individuality and nonconformity on the part of a member of society. The **Me** aspect of the self is the agent of conformity and social control within the individual, that phase of the self that can develop only when the individual has taken the role of the generalized other. Every action of the individual begins with the I and ends with the Me; the individual's initial behavior (the I phase) comes under the control of society and is evaluated by its internal representative (the Me phase).

The self emerges in the individual to the extent that role-taking abilities have developed. Before role-taking occurs, an infant can engage merely in imitation of the behavior of others. The infant smiles, grabs, holds, waves, and repeats words, all without having any understanding of the meaning of these actions. However, in the first real stage of self-development, which Mead calls **play,** the child begins role-taking on a very basic level, by taking the roles of the significant others in his or her life—mother and father, sisters and brothers, playmates, and the like. Around the age of 2, the child begins to "play at" certain connected activities—roles—for the first time.

play Mead's first stage of self-development, in which the child begins role-taking.

To illustrate, take the behavior of a young child, Billy, who uses his doll in order to begin to look at himself from his father's standpoint. Billy pretends that he is daddy and that his doll is Billy. Looking down at his doll, Billy angrily scolds, "Billy, you are a bad boy. You know better than to break your brother's airplane and to lie about it!" In this process Billy has taken an early step in the development of his self. He is beginning to see himself as his father sees him in certain situations. He is beginning to understand what certain roles like "bad boy" and "good boy" mean and how an individual playing them is supposed to act.

During the stage of play the child has no single standpoint from which to view the self and hence no unified self-conception. Instead, the child passes from one role to another depending on the nature of the situation at the time (e.g., from playing mother to sister to father).

game Mead's second stage of self-development, in which the child learns to take a number of roles simultaneously and achieves a unified self-conception.

By the age of 4 or 5, however, the child enters the second stage in the development of the self, the **game.** In the game stage the child for the first time learns to take a number of roles simultaneously and thereby begins to achieve a unified self-conception.

The complexity of the game makes higher level demands on its participants. The whole interaction process depends on each person's playing his or her part correctly. Consider a baseball game in which each player is expected to take the role of all the other players. For example, a catcher must simultaneously be aware of the specialized expectations of other players, being prepared to throw to the second baseman in an attempted steal, giving and receiving signals from the pitcher, and so forth.

In order to be a part of the game, a child must take the role of the entire group; the child must be able to view events and objects related to the game (including the self and others) from the standpoint common to the group as a whole. In time, from experiences in various games, the individual comes to take the role of the generalized other, the community as a whole, enabling him or her to behave in a consistent, organized manner and to develop unified self-awareness. In other words, the roles we play in the games of childhood become part of our consciousness. They become the content of our self and determine the major guidelines within which we think and act. To see this process more clearly, let us examine in more detail one form of game most children play.

Street Games: An Example of Role-taking and Socialization. As they are growing up, children want very much to know how to act properly in social situations (in order to attain their goals, to receive praise, and to avoid disapproval). As a result, they often invent ways of practicing together major roles they will play in later life.

Street games, some forms of which are found in virtually every society, are just such a voluntary invention. They are particularly useful as agents of socialization not only because they teach children appropriate ways to think and act, but because they are also fun. Consequently, unlike other forms of socialization such as formal schooling, which may often become tedious or just plain hard work, street games are eagerly participated in by children and require virtually no adult supervision. Let us look at a few examples.

We have already seen that American society favors achievement as a major value. One of the ways Americans symbolize the amount of their achievement is by being recognized as "the best" at what they do. Thus it is not surprising that we find in most American street games a decided emphasis on "winning," which means being the best in a game. This focus on winning as the central objective of the game ranges all the way from the small children's games of hide and seek, kick the can, king of the mountain, and hopscotch to the more organized games of older children such as roller hockey, stick ball, and so on.

In addition to teaching children what it feels like to play both the winner and loser roles, street games teach children other important roles that they will have to play as adults. For example, in some games children learn to be followers and leaders. These roles are often predominant in such games as follow the leader, capture the flag, and organized team games such as sandlot football. Organized team games in particular are also good at teaching children other social requirements that are useful in living in an industrialized, corporate society, for example, the need for specialized roles ("Well, somebody has to play defense if we are going to play at all!") and the need for submission of individual desires to group goals ("The team can never win if everybody is trying to be a 'showoff' all the time!").

In other words, few major types of activity are wasted in a society. Almost all—even those that may superficially appear not to be—are tightly woven into the social fabric of the whole social order and help it to re-create itself in its own image. Street games are no exception to this rule. Our society prides itself on individual achievement, so street games reflect this emphasis. Similarly, our society on occasion positively sanctions aggressive behavior of one individual toward another and acquisition of material goods. Therefore it is not surprising to find street games that allow children to practice these types of behavior. As exercises in aggression there are games like keep away, flinch, and many team sports such as football, hockey, and the like. To practice acquisition of material goods, another emphasis of our society, there are games like marbles, flipping trading cards, and having the "best collection" of something before anyone else on your block.

Truly, the selves that are formed, even partially, as a result of the participation of children in street games, are selves that are consistent with the overarching patterns of human behavior in that society.

AGENTS OF SOCIALIZATION

Family and Peer Group as Agents of Socialization

Much of the socialization process occurs through the persons and groups to which an individual turns for normative guidance. The most influential agents of socialization in the early life of the child are typically located in the context of the family unit. Many observers of contemporary American society contend that the middle-class American family, once responsible for a wide range of

By playing with others outside the home, we learn a great deal about society and social roles that we will be taking in later life. George Herbert Mead (see text) talks about games being very important aspects of each child's socialization, and street games are excellent examples. The children playing "tug-of-war" (top) learn about team play, strength, and competition. The girls playing hopscotch (middle) learn agility, numbers, and competition. The boys playing stickball (bottom) learn complex skills, intricate role relationships, team play and, again, competition. The fact that so often American street games have to do with competition should tell us something important about our society.

economic and socialization functions, has become a highly specialized institution whose activities center on socialization during the period of early childhood (Parsons, 1955).

However, as the middle-class American child grows beyond the first few years of life, she or he also grows beyond the exclusive control of family members (see cartoon). The school soon becomes a focal point for social interaction and hence for important socialization influences. What is more, the intense pressures in our society for an individual to leave the original family unit at marriage make it difficult for that individual to maintain a close family tie at home. Instead, the individual turns increasingly to nonfamily members for normative guidance. To put it in more formal terms, by the time they have become adults, most Americans have left their original family unit, known as the **family of orientation,** and established a new family unit based on marriage, known as the **family of procreation.**

family of orientation The individual's original family unit in which early socialization occurs.

family of procreation The new family unit established by the individual at marriage.

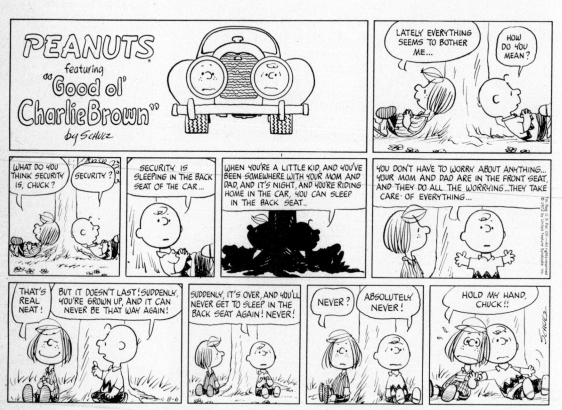

The isolated nature of the American family—typically composed of two parents and their biological offspring living in a separate dwelling—explains a good deal about the emergence of the importance of the peer group in contemporary American society. The **peer group** is that group of people who are similar to an individual in such characteristics as age, sex, economic, political, and religious background. Although all individuals throughout life will have peers with whom to associate, the key thing in American society is the peer group's extra importance as an agent of socialization. It fills the gap in the socialization process that occurs during later childhood and adolescence after the family of orientation has lost much of its influence and before the family of procreation has begun. In the absence of the peer group as a source of normative support the American adolescent would either be left without a source of orientation or would be forced to continue a reliance on the family of orientation, making independence difficult to achieve.

peer group People who are similar to an individual in age, sex, economic, political, and religious background.

The importance of the peer group may also be related to a broader trend in American society that David Riesman (1950) has characterized as a shift from inner- to other-directedness. During the period of tremendous industrial and technological expansion in the nineteenth and early twentieth centuries, Americans typically internalized the norms and values of their culture during early childhood through the agency of their parents. As adults, such persons were **inner-directed,** that is, they possessed an internal source of normative guidance (a superego) to which they could refer throughout their lives.

inner-directed Riesman's term to characterize an individual who has an internal source of normative guidance.

But as the birthrate began to follow the death rate in its downward trend, social life became more bureaucratized. "Other people," not the material environment, became the focus of activity and concern. As a way of adjusting to this change in society, modern Americans, especially those who operate within bureaucratic organizational contexts, became increasingly **other-directed.** Rather than possessing internalized normative standards, they turned to their peers as a source of guidance for the socially appropriate forms of behavior. This process occurred not only during adolescence but also continued into adult life.

other-directed Riesman's term to characterize an individual whose source of guidance is his or her peer group.

The main factor influencing the other-directed individual's decisions of appropriateness of behavior is *gaining the approval of others.* The other-directed person is constantly searching for what is acceptable in each situation; attitudes and actions depend on the demands of those involved in a particular situation at a particular moment. Thus, in Arthur Miller's famous play about American society, *Death of a Salesman,* the lead character, Willy Loman, teaches his sons that the most important thing in life is to be "well liked." In a sense, then, the other-directed person lacks morality, having no firmly entrenched sense of what is right and wrong, except for a generalized disposition to gain the approval of others by conforming to *their* expectations. (see Box 3–2).

Reference Groups as Agents of Socialization

reference group A group that influences an individual but in which he or she does not necessarily hold membership.

Agents of socialization are frequently located in the groups to which an individual actually belongs, such as the family unit or peer group (see Box 3–3). Yet socialization also occurs through **reference groups**—those groups in which an individual does not necessarily hold membership. Consider, for example, one of the factors that enters into patterns of marijuana usage among high school students in many regions of the United States. It has been reported that college-oriented high school students are more likely to use marijuana than students who do not plan to attend college. It turns out that an important reference group for mari-

---

Box 3–2 OTHER-DIRECTED YOUTH AND THEIR FADS

Adolescence is a period of extreme other-directedness: teenagers are especially sensitive to changes in fads and fashions which might impress their peers. Conformity often means acceptance, whether indicated by wearing the "right" brand of sneakers and sweater, having the "right" haircut, listening to the "right" music, or owning the "right" stereo equipment.

Adolescent fads are nothing new. In the 1920s, teenagers rushed to crossword puzzles, yo-yos, roller skates, and Hi-Li. Everywhere they engaged in endurance contests such as around-the-clock dance marathons, flagpole sitting, cross-country races, and gum-chewing or peanut-pushing contests.

In 1939, a new round of fads was established when goldfish swallowing invaded the nation's college campuses. At St.

Mary's University, a sophomore set a record by eating some 210.

In the fifties, young people stuffed themselves into anything and everything from Volkswagen bugs to phonebooths. At Colorado State University, 53 students squeezed themselves into a hearse.

Fads of the sixties included skateboards and Frisbees, and, later in the decade, psychedelic posters and T-shirts. In 1974, college students took off their clothing in order to "streak" through public libraries, police stations, football stadiums, and parties. Fifteen hundred University of Georgia students participated in the largest mass streak in history!

Many of the teen fads of the eighties are a reflection of the new electronic era: portable headset stereos, digital watches, video games, MTV, and personal computers; but new-fangled preppie hairstyles and new wave fashions and music are anything but new, except, of course, to those too young to remember the fads of the forties and fifties.

Source: Ernie Anastos with Jack Levin, *Twixt: Teens Yesterday and Today* (New York: Franklin Watts, 1983).

Box 3–3 PRESENTATION OF SELF IN EVERYDAY LIFE

In our society the importance of group influence in everyday interaction can be partially accounted for by the desire on the part of participants to control the images they project, to gain the approval of others, and to avoid social embarrassment. Individuals frequently guard against such a *loss of face* even when it becomes extremely costly to do so. They engage in *face-saving* behavior, whereby individuals develop tactics and strategies designed to prevent social embarrassment before it happens. For example, a man who seeks to befriend a woman might remain aloof and make a false show of indifference until he receives some signal from her of acceptance and desire to develop a relationship. Persons who have experienced embarrassment or disapproval attempt to control the image they present and to reestablish the appearance of their capability or strength by engaging in *face-restoration* behavior. For example, a waiter who accidentally spills a glass of water over a customer might pretend that he missed wetting anyone, in the hope that the incident will be ignored by those who witnessed it.

As the well-known sociologist Erving Goffman (1959) points out, face-saving frequently depends on the cooperation of others, on the ability of a witness to, or participant in, a social encounter to employ protective practices or tact. For example, a clumsy waiter might avoid social embarrassment if a customer pretends that he didn't really get wet; a patient might tactfully ignore the growling stomach of the dental hygienist who works on his teeth; or the people in a quiet room might overlook an individual who has belched uncontrollably.

Failure to fulfill the requirements of an "assigned part" can generate tremendous loss of face as well as efforts at restoring it. Consider the plight of Stanley Milgram, a social psychologist, who asked his students to commit the inappropriate yet seemingly insignificant act of going up to someone on the subway and asking for his seat. Then, Milgram tried it himself.

I approached a seated passenger and was about to utter the magical phrase. But the words seemed lodged in my trachea and would simply not emerge. I stood there frozen, then retreated, the mission unfulfilled. My student observer urged me to try again, but I was overwhelmed by paralyzing inhibition. I argued to myself: "What kind of craven coward are you? You told your class to do it. How can you go back to them without carrying out your own assignment?" Finally, after several unsuccessful tries, I went up to a passenger and choked out the request, "Excuse me, sir, may I have your seat?" A moment of stark anomic panic overcame me. But the man got right up and gave me his seat. A second blow was yet to come. Taking the man's seat, I was overwhelmed by the need to behave in a way that would justify my request. My head sank between my knees, and I could feel my face blanching. I was not role-playing. I actually felt as if I were going to perish. Then the third discovery: as soon as I got off the train, at the next station, all of the tension disappeared (Tavris, 1974, p. 72).

juana usage is the college population, as a group that many high school students aspire to join. As a result, norms regarding marijuana usage are often accepted by high school students based on their presence in an important reference group (Mauss, 1969).

This phenomenon is referred to by sociologists as **anticipatory socialization,** whereby an individual acts in accord with the norms and values of a group that he or she aspires to enter. Thus high school students may adopt the norms of college students, medical students may adopt the norms of practicing physicians, and immigrants may adopt the norms of the native group.

On the other hand, individuals are also affected by the reference groups they have left. The influence of groups in which individuals previously held membership but to which they no longer belong is known as **retrospective socialization.** This phenomenon occurs when an individual comes to value what has been lost. The operation of retrospective socialization can be found in the behavior and attitudes of some downwardly mobile persons, for example, middle-class individuals who have taken less prestigious or lower-paying jobs and have moved downward in socioeconomic status. Such "skidders" may continue to think and behave in accord with middle-class norms and values, while experiencing a working-class life-style. For instance, they are more likely than working-class persons whose status has remained constant to accept conservative political ideology and to strive toward middle-class success goals (Wilensky, 1961).

Television has become an important source of reference in the process of socialization. On prime-time dramatic series, for example, violence is typically depicted as an effective means to achieve goals—a means employed by star TV heros in the course of saving the life of an innocent victim, searching a suspect, or bringing a villain to justice. Children are provided with an array of models to imitate (see Boxes 3–4 and 3–5).

In addition to supplying socialization models, television also defines social reality for the millions of children who spend at least several hours daily "glued to the tube." Gerbner et al. (1978) have demonstrated that heavy TV viewers develop a "mean world view." That is, they become excessively concerned about their personal safety, crime and law enforcement, and trusting other people. Heavy viewers have a distorted perception of social reality. Based on TV images seen every day, they tend to overestimate the proportion of Americans in the world population, the proportion of white males, the amount of wealth in our society, and the amount of violence they are likely to encounter.

anticipatory socialization The influence on an individual of the norms and values of a group that the individual aspires to join.

retrospective socialization The influence on an individual of the norms and values of a group in which the individual no longer holds membership.

Does television ever have a profound impact on human behavior? On Sunday evening, November 20, 1983, an estimated 70 million people gathered before television sets across the nation to see the $7 million movie "The Day After," in which a nuclear war destroyed Kansas City and much of the rest of the United States. Responses varied from candlelight vigils, town meetings, discussion groups, and talk shows, where psychiatrists counseled viewers who suffered from the televised depiction of doom. Rev. Jerry Falwell, head of the Moral Majority, labeled the film a "blatant political statement in favor of disarmament" and threatened to boycott the sponsors of the program.

SOCIALIZATION AND HUMAN NATURE

Most human beings spend much of their daily lives in interaction with other human beings. While interacting they are deeply influenced by the behavioral guidelines of culture. But even when people do not directly participate in social interaction (as we have seen from a consideration of Freud's concept of the superego and

Box 3–4 PRIZEFIGHTS AND HOMICIDE

What is the effect of mass media violence in the real world? Are serious, even fatal, acts of aggression such as murder actually triggered by what is shown on TV?

To find out, sociologist David P. Phillips (1983) examined the homicide rates immediately after televised publicity was given to heavyweight championship prizefights, 1973 to 1978. He found a brief but sharp increase in U.S. homicides—overall, an increase of almost 13 percent.

This effect peaked on the third day following the prizefights and especially after heavily publicized events. For example, the largest third-day peak occurred after the most publicized prizefight studied: after Muhammad Ali and Joe Frazier's "thrilla in Manilla."

Results obtained by Phillips suggest that prize fights trigger homicides through modeling of aggression. Some members of society apparently imitate the violence of heavyweight fighters which is usually depicted as highly rewarding, exciting, and justified.

Mead's concept of the Me), they still tend to act in socially prescribed ways. For example, literally millions of Americans of both sexes exhibit highly predictable behavior five days a week prior to entering their major social encounters of the day. At night they set their alarm to get up at an appropriate time. Once it goes off, they get out of bed, wash up, put on their work clothes, eat something, get in the car or go to public transportation, travel to work, and then engage in their job for 8 hours.

Now, what is singularly remarkable about much of the behavior just described is that it does not involve any contact with another person; that is, it can take place completely outside social interaction. Yet the behavior exhibited is clearly *social* in that it is performed by millions of people in almost identical fashion. It is not a series of random psychological acts; it is a highly predictable pattern of acts that have social learning as their origin and social life as their objective.

All this is another way of saying again, of course, that we are socialized creatures; we carry in our heads the demands of our culture. Thus the culture of society not only regulates our behavior when we are participating in group activities, but it also provides us with a whole series of ideas about appropriate behavior that we carry around with us and apply in situations when we are apart from the group.

By this time a whole series of questions may have arisen in your mind. For example, you may wonder just what it is about human nature that makes human beings so social. Is there nothing that human beings do that is *not* influenced by socialization? Is there no behavior determined by inherent characteristics? Now that we have considered the socialization process in some detail, we are in a position to provide meaningful answers to such questions.

Two Cases of Social Isolation

One way to begin to answer these questions is to see what human beings are like who have had no opportunities for social interaction, no contact with society whatsoever. Studying such subjects would control for the influence of socialization so that we could assume that whatever qualities exist in such people would be the consequence of their inherited biological or psychological nature.

Box 3–5 ANN LANDERS

Teach kids by example

Dear **Ann Landers:**

Am I a lone nut, or are there others who feel as I do? Last week my husband and I and our three kids had supper at my in-laws'. They are lovely people and we get along fine.

As usual, the TV was on. After a few words of polite conversation, my husband switched channels to a boxing match. The two fighters were beating each other senseless. One had blood all over his face and his lip was swollen to three times its natural size. The other looked as if he might lose an eye. There sat our two young boys, seven and 17, transfixed. Our 11-year-old daughter became disgusted and went to the other room to read. My husband and his father were enjoying every minute of the human massacre.

As we were leaving, my mother-in-law expressed her disappointment. "We hardly spoke a word to each other." Well,

Source: Boston Sunday Globe, January 25, 1981, p. B6.

how could we with the TV four feet from the dining room table?

I confess, at home it is no better. My husband is crazy about sports on TV. Last week he and the boys sat glued to the set watching a barbaric hockey game. The players hit each other with their sticks, and finally the doctor was called on the ice to see "how bad it is."

I've rambled a lot, but I hope you can make some sense of this. Please tell me, Ann, is the rest of the world crazy or am I?
—Connecticut Yankee

You're just fine, lady. It's those folks who love to see someone get killed in the ring or burn up in a car or get carried off the field on a stretcher. They are the sickies. And they've been around since the Christians were fed to the lions.

Your best hope is to teach your sons, by example, the importance of gentleness and nonviolence and hope they can achieve some sort of balance in their conflicted lives.

But to find such a sample of unsocialized humans is a difficult task indeed. First of all, with extremely few exceptions, human beings everywhere live out most of their lives in a group of some type. Second, almost all those extremely few individuals who do exist in isolation have left their group *after* having been socialized in it for a period of time. Most of these "deserters" are adults (monks, hermits). The few children in this category are those who have had human, hence social, care for at least the first 3 to 5 years of life.* That is, it is impossible to know that behaviors are exclusively a product of biological or psychological inheritance and are not due to social contact.

Although it has not been possible to find any case where an individual's earliest life has been totally devoid of human socialization, there are a few well-documented cases in which a minimum of interaction has transpired between a child and other human beings and therefore little socialization, at least in the "normal" sense, has taken place. It is to an examination of two such cases of extreme isolation that we now turn for evidence bearing on our question of inherited human nature.

Both these cases, reported by Kingsley Davis (1947), received much less than the normal amount of human interaction during the first 6 years of life. The first case is that of Anna (a pseudonym used by Davis to protect her real identity).

According to Davis, the reason Anna was so deprived of human contact was directly linked to her status as an illegitimate child. Anna's mother lived with her own father. When she had Anna, her second illegitimate child, her father was incensed and demanded the child live elsewhere. However, the fact that Anna was a sickly child, in addition to her socially defined illegitimacy, made her somewhat unattractive for adoption or placement in a foster home. Consequently, she was shuttled around at least six times to both public and private residences during the first 5½ months of her life. Finally, when it became evident that Anna was unwanted everywhere, she was returned to her mother. Anna's grandfather, of course, protested her return vigorously.

To placate her father, Anna's mother sequestered Anna in the attic. She remained secluded there for the next 5½ years. During this time Anna received an absolute minimum of human atten-

---

*There supposedly remain a small number of children who have been abandoned or isolated from other human contact very early in life and have survived. Unfortunately, however, most such cases are legendary, fictitious, or blatantly fraudulent. This is particularly true of so-called feral children—children who have been abandoned by other human beings and brought up by animals. Classic actional examples are Edgar Rice Burrough's *Tarzan* and Rudyard Kipling's *Mowgli*. None of these cases has ever established beyond question that any human being has *ever* survived without minimal human care in the early weeks, months, or years of life.

Despite huge popularity in the last 50 years, the character created by Edgar Rice Burroughs known as Tarzan appears to be nothing more than a romantic myth. Social scientists have been completely unable to substantiate *any* story of a human infant raised from birth by other animals (Tarzan was supposedly raised by apes). Nonetheless, such stories continue to spark public imagination, despite evidence, ironically provided here in a scene from the film, "Tarzan's Secret Treasure," that children derive most of their socialization from interaction with, or imitation of, other human beings. (Here "Boy," Tarzan's son, learns how to make an "ape-call" by imitating his father.)

tion. She was given food, a little clothing, and little else. Certainly, she received extremely little affection of any kind.

When at last Anna was discovered by the authorities, removed from her attic room, and placed in a private home, she was suffering from various physical maladies, particularly malnutrition, and she showed *almost none* of the qualities that we generally assume all human beings have. She crawled on all fours and made animal like, unintelligible sounds. She could not walk, talk, or do any type of concentrated activity that showed anything but the bare minimum of intelligence. She could not understand what was said to her and could take only minimal care of herself. In short, she was much closer to being in a state that we would associate with animals rather than with a 6-year-old child.

Isabelle (also a pseudonym) was "raised" under conditions remarkably similar to Anna's. Also an illegitimate child, Isabelle was born to a deaf-mute mother and was sequestered for 6½ years until her discovery. Unlike Anna, however, Isabelle had the benefit of continuing (if somewhat unusual) human encounter, for her mother spent much time with her alone in the room. Nevertheless, when Isabelle was discovered, it was found that she, like Anna, was almost totally lacking in the "normal" human attributes. She could not talk, walk properly, or do much of anything that showed intelligence beyond that of a 6-month-old child. She had, however, learned to communicate with her mother with gestures. "Her behavior toward strangers," Davis writes, "especially men, was almost that of a wild animal, manifesting much fear and hostility."

What happened to Anna and Isabelle after they were discovered in their isolated states? Both girls, when placed in appropriate facilities where a great deal of human attention was given to them, changed radically in a short period of time. Both learned how to walk properly and to talk somewhat effectively. They also began to think more intelligently about solving problems and dealing with new situations. In other words, their uniquely human *potentialities* began to manifest themselves only *after* intensive *social* experiences where such abilities were encouraged to develop.

On a scale of normal human development Isabelle far exceeded Anna. Despite the great care given her, Anna reached a point beyond which she did not seem to be able to develop. Three years after her discovery, when she was actually 9, she had reached a mental age of approximately 2 years. She made no further progress until she died 2 years later. Her inability to develop further was attributed to possible congenital feeblemindedness. It is, however, quite possible that the severity of her early social deprivation contributed greatly to her lack of response to further social treatment. In the other case, after 2 years of intensive social care, Isabelle reached a mental age equivalent to her chronological age, then 8½, and thereafter was like a normal child in virtually every respect. It is possible that her progress can be related to the fact that she received her mother's attention much of the time, even though it was socially incomplete due to her mother's physical disabilities.

Examining the evidence of both these cases (and they are representative of the other well-documented cases in the literature) we come to one inescapable conclusion: *without socialization there is no element of human nature that automatically ensures that human beings will develop the characteristics we generally associate with them,* such as the ability to walk upright, to talk, to think abstractly, to make choices. To the contrary, all these traits appear to be the products of *social* exchanges. Apparently, the individual gradually picks up a certain amount and quality of information from those exchanges. This becomes *internal* information that guides the individual's action, not only when in groups, but also when no one else is around. Thus the cases of Anna and Isabelle indicate that whatever a distinctly *human* nature may be, it must be developed in a social context. In short, we need society to become human. To put it slightly differently, we need each other, and by helping one another in interaction, we encourage our own fuller development.

Are There General Human Tendencies?

Although social interaction develops our uniquely human characteristics, most of these characteristics are still subject to the limits imposed by our biological makeup. For example, human speech is limited in its development by size of the larynx, shape of the tongue, and so forth. It is physiologically impossible to utter sounds above or below a certain frequency. But within those very general boundaries immense variation is possible. In this respect one can hardly think of two more different languages in terms of pronunciation, word formulation, and the like than Chinese and English. In fact, the possibilities for variation are so great that it hardly makes sense to speak of any general human tendency regarding language. We can say that human beings have the biological potentiality to speak, but to predict on a biological basis how any given group of human beings will develop this potentiality is impossible.

The same may be said for many other human characteristics. Although general limits are determined by physical structure, the great variety of behaviors observed within these limits indicates that there are few natural tendencies. To give an important example, the physical differences between men and women are distinct and are determined genetically. However, beyond these purely physical differences there is little evidence indicating any important inherited behavioral differences between the sexes other than those associated with reproduction. Thinking of our own society, there is no biological characteristic that ensures that women will be primarily emotional, passive, and intuitive or that men will be unemotional, aggressive, and intellectual. Yet literally millions of men and women in this country, and throughout much of the world, display these characteristics. Surely there must be something "natural" or "inevitable" in all this if so many people are doing it; surely all this behavior cannot be completely the product of socialization—the learning of conventions by women and men.

But this is exactly what we are claiming. Perhaps the best way to provide evidence for this point would be to turn to other societies and see how they have dealt with the question of gender. If we find that women and men invariably act according to the characteristics just described (women being passive, etc., men being aggressive, etc.), then we would have a case for a general human tendency that appears to be biologically linked to inherited traits. If, on the other hand, we do not find such a predictable tendency, then we may conclude that the question of human nature is very much a sociological question. We may conclude that an observer must look carefully at socialization in any given society to determine how that society has "invented" human nature.

Although there are a number of excellent studies on the subject of inherited versus social sexual gender traits, none has surpassed the elegant simplicity and profundity of Margaret Mead's *Sex and Temperment in Three Primitive Societies* (1939). In this book Mead describes three native societies in New Guinea and the manner in which each molds the broad potentialities of human biology to suit its own social needs.

The Arapesh, the first of these groups, live in a rugged, mountainous terrain and have to work hard to survive. They have little level land to cultivate, few trees for firewood or shelter, and few other materials from which to make much more than the basic necessities of life. One might expect that in such a physical environment the Arapesh would have developed into a warlike, self-centered group of people, where each person is out for his or her own good and unwilling to sacrifice for others. Indeed, other societies with similar adverse environmental conditions, such as the Ik of Uganda in Africa, have turned out much that way (Turnbull, 1972).

Instead of being aggressive and hostile, however, the Arapesh are peace-loving and cooperative. The central focus of life, moreover, is more than just mutual cooperation. In this society the adults of both sexes devote much of their energy to bringing up a new generation of children in this cooperative ideal. Although women must bear the children physically, the care of them is equally a concern of both sexes. As Mead put it,

> Arapesh life is organized about [a] central [idea wherein] men and women, physiologically different and possessed of differing potencies, unite in a common adventure that is primarily maternal, cherishing, and oriented away from the self towards the needs of the next generation. . . . Men are as wholly committed to this cherishing adventure as are women. It may be said that the role of men, like the role of women, is maternal. (1939, pp. 14, 15)

In other words, the Arapesh have developed in *both* sexes the characteristics that many Westerners would consider inherently "feminine." Moreover, they have done very well by this arrangement, as they appear to be a happy, peaceful, and untroubled group.

Their neighbors to the south, the Mundugumor, have a totally different life-style. This society lives on a treacherous river about a hundred miles from the Arapesh, but the focal point of their social order is cannibalism. Although their land is highly fertile in comparison to the Arapesh's mountainous terrain, the Mundugumor do not cultivate much of it. Rather, they obtain many of their material needs by bartering with neighboring tribes. They satisfy most of their other needs, including food, by living off the land, that is, by merely taking from the plentiful supplies around them (fish in the river, tobacco in the fields, coconuts, etc.) whatever they need.

One might expect that, given such a plentiful physical environment, the Mundugumor would see no necessity for aggressive, warlike behavior. However, Mundugumor society is riddled with anger, hostility, aversion, greed, and exploitation for self-benefit. Clearly, physical environment has little predictive value for the social scientist.

Like the Arapesh, both sexes in Mundugumor society exhibit the same behavior pattern. However, the pattern exhibited is the *opposite* of that found in Arapesh society. As Mead explains it, in Mundugumor, "both men and women are expected (and actually are) to be violent, competitive, aggressive [in sexual encounter], jealous, and ready to see and avenge insult, delighting in display, in action, in fighting" (Mead, 1939, p. 225). What the Mundugumor see as natural for both sexes is akin (although admittedly somewhat more extreme) to what many in our society would consider to be inherently "masculine" characteristics.

The Tchambuli, the third group, live in a lush river area much like that of the Mundugumor, but they developed still another special pattern of behavior for the sexes. In Tchambuli society the sexes exhibit different behaviors, a pattern not unlike our Western one. The primary responsibilities of the women center around bringing in the food and caring for it, whereas the primary responsibilities of the men involve organizing the major ceremonies around which much of life centers. Most of the social activity of the community is similarly divided into specific sex responsibilities and one sex does not infringe on the rights and duties of the other. To put it in the vernacular, each sex has its place, knows its place, and stays there.

In Tchambuli society most of the controlling power of the social order is held by the females. However, unlike the Western image of the aggressive male who controls the social life, the typical Tchambuli female is generally loving and jovial and devoted to the care of her children and her man with a sort of patronizing air. Tchambuli men are relatively unsure of themselves in many social situations, are dominated and act it, and are eternally squabbling over various issues. In short, in some respects, the Tchambuli women exhibit what many members of our society would consider "masculine" traits, whereas the Tchambuli men exhibit what are often considered "feminine" traits.

Taking evidence from these three societies then, we can see that *no* behavioral pattern emerges with regard to gender. In none of the societies does what we Americans might consider a "natural" pattern present itself (women passive, etc., men aggressive, etc.) nor does any of these societies seem to be even aware of such an alternative. What they perceive for each sex is as *natural* to them as our pattern appears to us. But the pattern, as we can see, is obviously the result of social selection from a range of possibilities rather than of biological determination.

From these data we are forced to an inescapable conclusion regarding human nature. As Mead herself put it,

> [Human nature] is almost unbelievably malleable, responding accurately and contrastingly to contrasting cultural conditions. The differences between individuals who are members of different cultures like the differences between individuals within a culture, are almost entirely to be laid to differences in conditioning, especially during childhood, and the form of this conditioning is culturally determined. (1939, p. 250)

Thus Mead's three societies indicate that within extremely wide physiological boundaries, "human nature is what you make it." How human nature develops in any particular social setting depends on the socialization practices of that group at any given time.

Such evidence suggests that we can regard the specific behaviors of any society as relative and as a product of the dynamic process of interpretation and interaction discussed in the last chapter. Regarding sex role behavior in our own society, it allows us to see the arbitrary nature of these sex roles, to decide what their consequences are, either individually or on the society as a whole, and if we so choose, to change those roles (see Box 3–6). One group that has been involved in such a redefinition of sex role behavior in recent years is the Women's Liberation movement. Fundamentally, this group argues that traditional American sex roles are highly limiting of the development of full human potentialities and particularly oppressive of women. We shall return to a more complete discussion of the women's movement in Chapter 8.

Finally, regarding the issue of socialization and human nature, let us note that not all sociologists agree with our conclusions. A few argue that there truly are biological instincts or predispositions that shape specific social behaviors. These arguments run

The following newspaper article suggests that socialization of sex role behavior may begin very early in the life of a child.

Box 3–6   BABIES IN PINK ARE SO GIRLISH

If there's one place you can't tell the players without the scoreboard it's the hospital nursery.

To the non-parent, all newborns look alike, which is why they kept getting switched in 19th-Century comedies and Scarlet Pimpernel novels. Same round mushy faces, same soft bodies and same chicken legs and arms.

You can't even tell if they're boys or girls without a diaper check.

Nevertheless, it's here, right here in the hospital nursery, in the first 24 hours of life, that sex typing begins, according to the research recently completed by Tuft University's Frank Provenzano under the supervisoin of Drs. Jeffrey Rubin and Zella Luria.

From last April to August, Provenzano, a 23-year-old graduate student, lived like an obstetrician, dashing out in the middle of the night to be on hand for the delivery of 32 infants at the Lawrence Hospital in Medford.

With pad, pen and questionnaire he talked to the proud fathers who had just seen their first-born through the glass window. He asked them what the babies looked like and whom they looked like. (The boys were generally reported to look like daddy and the girls like mommy.)

Scale includes opposites
Then they were given a sheet of contrasting characteristics on which to scale their newborns. The bi-polar scale included opposites like "firm-soft, big-little, hardy-delicate, large featured-small featured."

The next day the mothers were given the same questionnaire.

There were no objective physical differences between the 16 baby boys and the 16 baby girls in terms of birth size, weight . . . muscle tone, heart rate, respiratory system, color and irritability.

But nevertheless, the parents labeled male infants as hardier, firmer, bigger, more alert and more large featured than their female infants. The girls conversely were scaled as softer, smaller, finer featured, etc.

"The fathers were much stronger sex typers than the mothers," says Provenzano, and his figures back him up.

Fathers rated their sons as quite significantly firmer than their daughters, while mothers rated them only slightly firmer. Fathers rated their sons as much hardier, while mothers again narrowed the sex gap. The researchers thought that the mother's perceptions might have been less stereotyped because they had held the real babies.

There was one interesting conflict though. While fathers thought their daughters were more cuddly, mothers thought their sons were more cuddly. This they described as the Oedipal effect.

The most obvious result of the study was proving that parents labelled their first-born more by cultural stereotype of their sex than by individual reality—before they were a day old.

Source: Ellen Goodman, "Babies in Pink Are So Girlish," *Boston Globe,* February 23, 1972, p. 16. Reprinted by courtesy of the Boston Globe.

The real question is what it means. If parents perceive of baby boy as hardier, do they treat him differently? Is he more likely to be tossed in the air, treated roughly, etc.? If they expect him to be alert, easy going and active do they accept and encourage different characteristics? How do attitudes affect behavior?

Professor Zella Luria cautions against concluding from this study how parents will actually handle their children. That is something they will study next, she says.

The handling is different
Other studies in the Boston area have dealt with the different ways parents handle boy babies and girl babies.

A study at the New England Medical Center showed that fathers were more apprehensive over the well-being of their daughters and more likely to rough-house with their sons.

A BU study showed that fathers verbalize more to their infant daughters than their infant sons because they see them as needing nurturing, and conversely mothers verbalize more to their infant sons because they are considered "more irritable." (At about 3 months, mothers start talking more to girl babies.)

These different behaviors originally suggested to Provenzano that parents were viewing male and female infants differently right from delivery. Or right from cultural stereotypes.

Thirty-two deliveries later he is satisfied that he has proved it.

The only thing he can't figure out is why he only got one cigar out of the deal.

all the way from building a case for male domination as a biologically conditioned surity—*The Inevitability of Patriarchy* (Goldberg, 1974)—to a case for inherited aggressive tendencies (Lorenz, 1966; van den Berghe, 1974; Wilson, 1975). We shall return to a detailed consideration of this argument in Chapter 9.

Individualism—Myth or Reality?

Throughout this chapter we have portrayed the human being as a social being, as a unit in a larger order that generally moves in accordance with socially prescribed rules for behavior. The social aspects of human behavior are easily seen in the many cases of conformity to cultural norms and values we have previously cited. Even more interestingly, when human beings *deviate* from prescribed rules, they frequently do so in patterns that are themselves socially "expected." To take a simple example, a person who commits a robbery often does so in a manner similar to the way in which others have committed robbery before—at a time when they are not likely to be caught, using expected weapons (guns, knives, and the like), and using expected vocabulary ("This is a stickup. Everyone up against the wall. Any noise and you're dead."). In short, as we have mentioned, much of human behavior is in some manner socially prescribed; that is, it is structured by the guidelines for appropriate behavior in a society.

Certain questions naturally arise from such statements. If behavior is socially prescribed, is there any such thing as true individuality? If we act in a socially prescribed manner, even when we deviate, does the unique self in which we put so much stock exist at all?

A partial answer to the question of individuality can be found in our earlier discussion of G. H. Mead's conception of the I—the phase of the self in which the impulsive, spontaneous, innovative aspects of human behavior originate. Mead's concept of I prevents us from having an oversocialized view of human behavior. It reminds us that not all human behavior is under the control of cultural norms and values. It informs us, as does our earlier discussion on the dynamic nature of interaction (Chapter 2), that the *potential* always exists in human beings for change, innovation, and spontaneity and that no two humans interpret experience exactly alike in all circumstances.

Another part of the answer can be found in the complexity and number of social interactions in which human beings become involved. For example, most members of Western society are socialized in a family. Many are also brought up as members of other groups, such as ethnic and religious subcultures, and are educated at various schools. All such experiences ensure that in most major respects we shall be shaped in ways quite similar to many other human beings. It is this commonality that makes us essentially predictable in most social situations: Thus people who are brought up as political Democrats tend to vote as Democrats as adults; people who are brought up in a nuclear family tend to raise their children similarly.

Yet within these commonalities of human experience there are still very important social differences. No matter how similar the social experiences of individuals may be, they are never *exactly* the same. Hence all of us have been shaped differently from others. Let us consider growing up in a family as an example.

Assume that we are considering three children, two of whom live in the same nuclear family, one of whom lives in another. The first two children belong to a family of Italian ancestry. This heritage means that many of the social interactions among members of that family are characterized by some version of Italian cultural traits, for example, certain gestures, voice inflections, eating habits, beliefs about family unity, attitudes toward relatives, and the like. Clearly, the two children brought up in this family cannot help but learn certain of these Italian cultural traits that they take with them to subsequent social interactions.

Now, let us assume that the third child's family is of Scottish ancestry. Again, certain characteristics can be expected to exist in the family's social interaction, but they will differ from those of the Italian family. The gestures, inflections, eating habits, beliefs, and attitudes all have a Scottish cultural origin. Just as the Italian children are shaped by the "Italianness" of their social interactions, so the child of the Scottish family is shaped by the "Scottishness" of these interactions.

When the children of these families meet outside their respective homes, there are fundamental differences between them as individuals. It must be understood that these differences are social in origin and nature. The Italian children are different from the Scottish child because of different social emphases and experiences, not biological or psychological inheritances.

To take the example one step further, let us return to the Italian family. Let us assume that the older child is male and the younger is female. These simple biological differences in birth order and sex are likely to produce tremendous differences between the children as individuals because of their social importance to the family. For example, the firstborn will experience various types of social encounters that his sister is not likely to experience as intensely. He is likely to be indulged more, "shown off" to relatives and friends more, encouraged to do certain things with his life because of his firstborn status (perhaps take over the family business). A second child in the same family, even if he is male would not have the same experiences. The firstborn is shaped differently by his specific social encounters than any subsequent child. Thus this shaping process means that the firstborn child will carry with him certain characteristics that very few other people have: characteristics associated with a firstborn Italian son.

The second child in our example is a female. Quite apart from her birth-order status, the sexual difference has important implications for the variety of social encounters that she will experience. Girls are talked to differently from how boys are talked to, they are regarded by relatives and friends differently, they are taught to gesture differently, to use certain words and not others, to sit differently, and so on. Females will thus bring to their outside social interactions a whole set of social characteristics that are different from those of males.

The main point of the foregoing example should be obvious: No human being ever develops in exactly the same way as any other human being, even on the social level. We all experience our social encounters somewhat differently, and these encounters serve to give us our uniquely individual characteristics. The first child in our example is male, firstborn, of Italian ancestry with particular parents and siblings, residing on W Street in X town in Y state in Z country, at a particular time in history. All these characteristics together make this person different from any other human being on the face of the earth, either now or in the past. No other human being shares exactly these social characteristics.

But it can also be seen that these differences are all simultaneously a direct product of social interactions and prescriptions (e.g., the selections people make in different treatment of male and female children). Thus we may conclude that individuality does exist for human beings; each individual represents a unique configuration of social influences that characterizes no other person. However, most of the differences among people that contribute to their individuality have actually been shaped and developed by a lifetime of social input.

Finally, let us return to the question of consciousness. We argued in Chapter 2 that human beings are distinctive for two reasons: their unique ability to form culture and their equally unique ability to interpret the world. This chapter has stressed how deeply culture is inherent in human beings. Nevertheless, culture does not mold us indelibly, like bottles in a mass assembly line; nor does it mold us in the same manner, only because we have different social experiences (i.e., because we play different roles—Irish, woman, etc.). We still can think. Each human being has his or her own form of consciousness and can *choose* to manipulate his or her behavior, thoughts, or roles. True, often we don't do this—we play the role as the social situation dictates; culture *does* run deep—we have a tendency to believe in and not to think carefully about cherished social notions (God, being male, being American, being black, or whatever). Yet, on the most basic level, our lives are of our own making. We either live as we are expected to or don't because we make choices. Sometimes our choices are well informed, sometimes they are not. Nevertheless, they are ours.

That is one of the main reasons for studying sociology: It provides more information about the forces in our lives and our relationship to them; it gives us more ability to choose, to exercise our consciousness, and thus to live our own lives.

SUMMARY

In order to persist, all societies depend to some extent on gaining obedience and conformity from their members. In large part this

means that cultural values, norms, and sanctions must be transferred to the personalities of individuals. The complex process whereby the culture of a group is internalized by individual personalities is known as socialization.

Most observers of society agree that many important influences of socialization occur during childhood. Two of the major theories of early socialization are those of Sigmund Freud and George Herbert Mead.

Freud's theory holds that the superego is the internalized representative of cultural guidelines. The superego develops during the fourth or fifth year of life based on the rewards and punishments imposed by the child's parents or caretakers. As the superego arises, the child begins to operate in a socially acceptable way to gain the pleasure of feeling internal pride (the ego-ideal) and to avoid the pain of feeling guilt (the conscience). When the superego has been fully incorporated into the personality, reward and punishment from external sources are no longer necessary.

According to Freud, whether or not a child develops an effective superego depends on the way she or he experiences the oedipal conflict, a proscribed sexual desire for the parent of the opposite sex and feeling of hostility for the parent of the same sex. The Oedipus complex is resolved only when a child comes to identify with the same-sex parent in order to relieve his or her fear of the response of that parent to his or her hostile behavior. When the resolution occurs, the child reduces the hostility toward the same-sex parent and is satisfied with gaining the affection of the opposite-sex parent.

George Herbert Mead's theory of socialization focuses on the distinctly human capacity for role-taking, the process whereby an individual can determine the intentions of others and anticipate

It is very difficult when studying life not to go overboard in one of two directions: Either we have a reaction "against" the insights of sociology and claim we are nothing but individuals unaffected by social life, or we tend to see human beings as "automatons," as being almost totally shaped by social rules and regulations and possessing virtually no true individuality whatsoever. Both reactions are extreme, and both contain only elements of truth. For example, at first glance this photograph of people waiting for a subway train in Boston may look like an undifferentiated "mass"—everyone is doing the same thing, looking nearly alike. But as we look longer and more carefully at the photograph, the people in it, despite the similarity of their purpose and dress, begin to take on more and more individuality. In how many ways can these people be distinguished from each other? In other words, it appears we are *both* individuals *and* social products simultaneously. Society takes on its character to a large degree from the nature of the human individuals that comprise it and those individuals, in turn, take on their character (personality) to a large degree from the nature of the society. As Charles Horton Cooley put it, society and the individual are "twin-born."

their behavior through the understanding of shared significant symbols such as gestures and language. By means of role-taking abilities, the child comes to define and evaluate events and objects including herself or himself. Initially, this occurs as the child takes the role of significant others (e.g., parents, teachers, etc.). But as role-taking abilities grow, the child learns to take the role of the generalized other, that is, the standpoint of a group as a whole. In this way the child eventually comes to internalize the norms and values of society and to evaluate herself or himself on the basis of group standards.

Thus the self emerges in the individual to the extent that role-taking abilities develop. In the first stage of self-development, play, the child begins taking the roles of significant others (e.g., mother and father). During this stage the child passes from one role to another and therefore has no single standpoint from which to view the self. By the age of 4 or 5, however, the child enters the second stage of self-development, the game. In this stage the child can take a number of roles simultaneously. In order to be a part of the game, a child must take the role of the entire group. In time, from experiences in various games, the individual comes to take the role of the generalized other and develops unified self-awareness. An excellent example of how this process develops is promoted by considering the nature of childhood street games.

The most influential agents of socialization in the early life of the child are typically located in the family. In American society the middle-class child grows beyond the exclusive control of family members after the first few years of life. The school and the peer group soon become centers of social interaction and hence of important socialization influences. The influence of the peer group developed in our society to fill the gap in the socialization process during later childhood and adolescence after the family of orientation has lost much of its influence usually before the family of procreation has begun.

The rise of the importance of the peer group may also be related to a trend in our society from inner- to other-directedness. During the nineteenth and early twentieth centuries, Americans were typically inner-directed; that is, they internalized the norms and values of their culture primarily from their parents. But as social life became more bureaucratized, Americans shifted to other-directedness; they turned more and more to their peers for normative guidance and to peer approval as a criterion for evaluating the appropriateness of behavior.

Agents of socialization such as the family or peer group are located in the groups to which an individual belongs. However, socialization also occurs through reference groups, groups in which a person does not actually hold membership. Reference groups may influence an individual through anticipatory socialization, the effect on behavior of the norms and values of a group that the individual aspires to join, or through retrospective socialization, the continuity effect of the norms and values of groups a person has left.

Is there nothing that human beings do that is not influenced by socialization? Is there nothing inherent about human nature at all? Extreme cases of social isolation suggest that there is no element of human nature that automatically ensures that human beings will develop the characteristics we generally associate with them. On the contrary, all these traits appear to be the products of socialization.

Human nature is extremely malleable. It is capable of generating tremendous variety under contrasting cultural conditions. As suggested by cultural differences in behavioral patterns associated with gender, how human nature develops in any social setting depends on the socialization practices of that group at a particular time.

Throughout this chapter the human being has been characterized as a social being. Given the tremendous influence of social aspects of human behavior, is there any true individuality? The answer is threefold: First, the uniqueness of the individual is assured by the operation of the I, that phase of the self that does not come under the control of cultural norms and values, and the dynamic nature of interaction discussed in Chapter 2. Second, each human being experiences a convergence of a unique combination of social influences; the individual is shaped and developed by a lifetime of social input unlike that experienced by any other human. Finally, whatever the intensity of social input, human beings are conscious beings with the ability to think about and accept or change their lives.

QUESTIONS, EXERCISES, PROJECTS

1. What do Sherif's and Asch's experiments tell us about the nature of conformity? Can you think of examples of similar behavioral patterns in your experience?
2. According to Freud, how does the superego develop in the personality of a child?

3. How accurately can you take the role of the other? From the members of the class choose a partner whose attitudes you feel you might be able to predict from your informal conversations together. Based on what you think you know and without any discussion with your partner, supply the following information about your partner: (a) political party preference (Democrat, Republican, etc.); (b) religiosity (very religious to atheistic); (c) attitude toward college (e.g., loves it for learning's sake, a necessary evil, on the verge of dropping out); (d) expectations for future family life (e.g., marriage and children, marriage without children, remain single). Have your partner list this information about himself or herself and then compare your lists to determine your accuracy with respect to taking the role of the other.

4. Distinguish between significant others and generalized others in G. H. Mead's conception of the self.

5. Identify and describe G. H. Mead's stages in the development of the self.

6. Discuss the key historical factors in the emergence of the peer group as an important agent of socialization in American society.

7. Name at least five reference groups that you believe may have influenced your behavior or attitudes during the last year. Specify in what ways you were influenced by each.

8. Describe what an individual would be like who is socially isolated from birth. Include such characteristics as personal appearance, ability to communicate and reason, and development of motor skills.

9. "How human nature develops in a social setting depends on the socialization practices of that group." Discuss.

10. Based on your reading of Chapter 3, argue in favor of the position that individualism is a possibility for human beings who live in groups.

11. Communication researchers have suggested that the mass media depict a white, male, middle-class world. Examine this hypothesis by conducting a content analysis of 50 full-page advertisements taken from widely circulated magazines. Indicate the percentage of dominant characters in these ads who are (a) black and white, (b) female and male, and (c) upper, middle, working, and lower class (as indicated by occupation). Do most characters portrayed in your sample of advertisements tend to be white, male, and middle class? As a related matter, determine the percentage of women and blacks who are assigned stereotyped occupations. For women, stereo-

typed occupations might include housewife, nurse, and secretary. For blacks, stereotyped occupations include athlete, entertainer, and domestic. How do such patterns influence socialization?

THE STRUCTURE OF SOCIAL INTERACTION

The major concepts of culture and socialization alert us to the unique capacity of human beings to develop, maintain, and internalize a set of guidelines for social interaction, enabling them to orient their actions to one another and to participate in the group experience. Interaction is so basic to the human condition that most people take it entirely for granted as a necessary circumstance of life, never stopping to ask why it develops or how it is maintained. Yet much of the work of sociology focuses squarely on the nature, causes, and consequences of social interaction, on the actual behavior of individuals when they come together and adjust to one another's presence. For instance, a sociologist might investigate the social encounter between a used car salesman and a customer, between strangers who aid one another during a crisis, between black and white community members vying for power, or between a husband and wife who attempt to settle some disagreement.

Given its cultural underpinnings, it is not surprising that social interaction often acquires a patterned and stable character, a long-standing **social structure** of its own. The essential characteristics of interaction repeat themselves over time, making it possible to identify and participate in relatively permanent relationships. We have already seen that norms, values, and sanctions are internalized and influence behavior often in subtle and unnoticed ways. Similarly, social structure provides an often unrecognized model for interaction.

social structure Interaction that acquires a patterned and stable character so that many of its elements are repeated over time and are shared by many members of a society.

Consider eyes for instance: How we use our eyes in encounters with others is both complex and patterned, yet we are usually unaware of this patterning. Sociologist Allan Mazur notes that: (1) In most situations, silent eye contact between individuals who do not know one another well is inappropriate; it is seen as impolite and, if done, produces tension; (2) people walking toward each other often look into each other's eyes until they are 5 to 10 yards apart and then, getting closer, avoid eye contact; (3) eye contact between two people of *equal* social status is entirely appropriate when talking; (4) in a conversation between two people of *unequal* social status the lower-status person is expected to look at the person of higher status, but the individual of higher status looks at the lower-status individual only if he or she chooses to do so. To test some of these observations, Mazur asked some of his students to willfully violate these unconscious patterns by staring at other people in elevators, a place where, after a brief glance, it is usually appropriate to look only at the floor or the walls. He found that such "staring was so anxiety-provoking to both the students and the others in the elevators that we had to discontinue asking students to try it" (Quoted in Collins, 1983, p. D1).

STATUS AND ROLE

status Any social position that involves prescriptions and expectations for behavior.

role A specific set of norms and expected behaviors associated with a status.

As the example of eye contact demonstrates, at the core of much of the structure of interaction is the idea that individuals occupy a particular **status** or social position that involves prescriptions and expectations for behavior. Examples of different statuses are doctor, lawyer, mother, teacher, employee, friend, lover. Moreover, individuals who occupy any given social position are expected to adhere to a **role,** a special set of norms or expected behaviors associated with that position. In a sense, individuals who interact are like actors giving a performance on stage; society is an "audience" that expects its members to play numerous parts and to follow the scripts assigned them (see Box 4–1).

Although status and role can be separated for explanatory purposes, in actual social life they cannot be. Imagine acting outside the appropriate status of "student" by, for example, (1) knocking on a restroom door of the student union, (2) conducting a conversation while standing less than 2 inches from a classmate, or (3) sticking your fingers into the mouth of someone you have just met. Sound bizzare or inconsistent? For the student status and role, yes; but consider that (1) "students" are not supposed to knock on restroom doors, whereas "custodians" frequently can, (2) "classmates" are not supposed to stand less than 2 inches apart while talking, whereas "lovers" can, and (3) "students" are not supposed

Box 4-1 THE ROLE OF SENIOR CITIZEN

Many of the things we expect of elderly Americans can be summarized in "the role of senior citizen." An important aspect of this role is its lack of *prescriptions* for behavior, rules for what ought to be done, and its emphasis instead on rules for what ought not to be done. Thus, elders are *not* expected to have jobs, to engage in sexual activities, or to get married. Unfortunately, the role of senior citizen fails to suggest precisely what elderly Americans are supposed to do instead—except to say very vaguely that they find some new activities for those they have given up and prepare for death. The role of senior citizen is so lacking in alternatives that retired people may become virtually imprisoned in a "roleless role." Members of our society may expect and even encourage them to be asexual, incompetent, unproductive, and disengaged. Mandatory retirement laws are only the "tip of the iceberg." In more subtle ways, perhaps, we indicate to elderly Americans that they are "supposed to stay out of the way, sit in their rocking chairs, and enjoy the Golden Years."

Source: Jack Levin and William C. Levin, *Ageism: Prejudice and Discrimination Against the Elderly* (Belmont, Calif.: Wadsworth, 1980).

to stick fingers in the mouth of another person, whereas "dentists" most assuredly can. Thus, in order to identify the appropriateness of a particular role behavior, it is essential to determine the status of the person exhibiting that behavior. For instance, here are a few common status–role configurations:

STATUS	ROLE
Teacher	Give lectures, assign papers, lead discussions, give exams
Housewife	Cook, feed children, provide clothing and shelter
Shoe salesperson	Measure foot size, assist customers to try shoes, encourage buying
Friend	Converse informally, be supportive, give aid during difficult periods
Physician	Give physical examination, make diagnosis, treat illnesses

Most members of our society would quickly recognize the status–role patterns. However, some might be a little uneasy about the simple and clear-cut way in which they are stated. We live in a rapidly changing, complex society whose members typically play numerous roles and occupy many different positions. What is more, the structure of interaction and the definition of statuses and roles, although basically stable, do undergo change over a period of time. As a familiar and important illustration, consider the manner in which the status and role of women have been modified during the past several decades. Many women would not now accept the traditional definition of the "housewife" status–role previously given. Occupying multiple statuses with changing

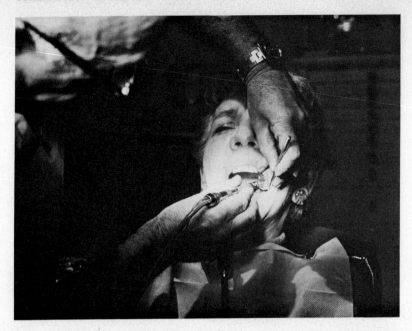

Few people have the *right* to stick their fingers in our mouths, even to the point of causing us discomfort; but people occupying the status of dentist have such a right. We even seek them out to allow them to do their probing!

role conflict A situation in which an individual becomes the recipient of incompatible or contradictory role requirements.

status set The totality of an individual's concurrent statuses.

definitions of roles may create **role conflict.** An individual may become subject to incompatible or contradictory role requirements, that is, may be expected to behave in ways that are inconsistent with one another. Just how nerve-wracking role conflict situations can be is nicely depicted in Box 4–2.

Each individual is involved in a variety of social relationships and occupies a number of statuses. The totality of an individual's concurrent statuses is known as a **status set.** For instance, one person might concurrently be a student, daughter, friend, employee, classmate, and roommate. The behavior expected of the individual at any given time depends on the particular status occupied at that particular time within his or her status set (e.g., even a dentist wouldn't stick her fingers in your mouth if you met her at a party)

One's status set is a potential source of role conflict. To illustrate, we turn to a study of hashers, part-time employees in the kitchens of college sororities, conducted by Zurcher, Sonenschein, and Metzner (1966). Hashers are the bottom of the kitchen hierarchy. They have low prestige and are expected to do the menial labor around the sorority. More importantly, hashers are expected to be subservient to the group of college women whom they are paid to serve. Imagine the role conflict that develops when a male college student takes part-time em-

Boston Globe, September 28, 1983, p. 74.

ployment as a hasher in a sorority house. The role of hasher (low prestige, subordination, lack of sophistication, and menial labor) is at odds with the role of college man (high prestige, superior status, white-collar work, intelligence, and sophisticated taste). In order to tolerate the conflicting expectations for their behavior, hashers frequently work out an elaborate set of defense mechanisms involving rationalization ("This job is only temporary."), denial ("I took this job only to meet girls."), and projection ("These girls are all a bunch of duds.").

Each member of society has a status set in the sense that he or she occupies a number of different statuses at any given time. Correspondingly, the individual also has a **role set** for every status occupied, designating all the role relationships in which he or she is involved by virtue of occupying that particular position. As an employee, for example, an individual maintains one kind of relationship to employers, another to customers, and still another to fellow employees. An individual occupying the position of teacher relates in different ways to students, to the principal, and to other teachers. Role sets for a few statuses follow:

role set All the role relationships in which an individual is involved by virtue of occupying a single status.

STATUS AND ROLE SETS FOR A HYPOTHETICAL INDIVIDUAL

STATUS	ROLE SETS
Teacher	To students, principal, and other teachers
Husband	To wife and children
Son	To mother, father, and siblings
Customer	To employee, employer, and other customers
Patient	To doctor, nurses, receptionist, and other patients
Defendant	To lawyer, judge, and jurors

The presence of role conflict in an individual's role set means that some of the persons to whom this individual relates hold incompatible expectations for his or her behavior. In a classic study, Gross, McEachern, and Mason (1957) interviewed 105

Box 4–2 DOCTORS: FAMILIARITY BREEDS CONTEMPT

By Allan Parachini
Los Angeles Times

LOS ANGELES—Elizabeth Babbott Conant is 53, holds a doctorate and teaches evolutionary and vertebrate biology at Canisius College in Buffalo. She is, as such, not the average doctor's office patient.

A longtime scientist, Conant had not thought much about how she felt about abstractions like the relationship between physicians and patients until recently when, on three occasions over a couple of weeks, her doctors or their employees did something that made her blood boil.

At issue is the way many physicians address their patients, their women patients in particular: The patient is called by a first name and the physician is "Dr. Blank."

What makes Conant's anger important is that her complaint—that doctors and their employees too often treat patients as if they were their children or servants—is one that is being made and heard increasingly.

To Conant and others who have thought about and protested this minor headache of medicine, the question of forms of address may seem frivolous at first, but it is symbolically important to them, if only because of what it may say about a doctor's underlying attitudes toward his or her patients.

For Conant, first it was an X-ray technician young enough to be her daughter who walked into the waiting room at a Buffalo hospital and called out, "Elizabeth?" Then there was the secretary who called from a physician's office and asked her. "Now, Elizabeth, are you free Wednesday morning?"

Finally, there was the doctor who called her himself and opened the conversation with, "Elizabeth, this is Dr. B—."

Taken together, all the interactions bothered her. "It struck me that we call our servants and our students by their first names," she said in a telephone interview. "And our doctors call their patients by their first names. It is being treated like children.

"I have a suspicion that, partly, doctors do it because it's always been that way. But partly, [the practice has] a role in retaining power."

Conant became angry enough about what she perceived as an intentional denigration by physicians and their employees that she fired off a thoughtful but angry letter to the editor of the New England Journal of Medicine. The journal published the letter last month.

But while the experience of being treated like a child by her physicians was new to Conant, it is hardly new to doctors. In fact, her letter is only the latest of a half-dozen letters and articles published in medical journals over the last eight months.

The question of forms of address between doctors and patients has been the subject of debate for years, but while it might have been dismissed previously as inconsequential compared to other things that might be considered annoying or degrading about medicine, the first name-last name issue shows signs of coming into its own now as a festering controversy.

The problem was summed up succinctly last May in a full-page patient protest bearing the heading, "A Piece of My Mind," published by the Journal of the American Medical Assn. (AMA).

The AMA journal article, written by Lucille Natkins of Great Neck, N.Y., struck a familiar chord with many readers. In it, Natkins recalled how she and a doctor she identified by a pseudonym, Dr. James Gold, started off on an equal footing as Dr. Gold and Mrs. Natkins.

When Natkins needed surgery, however, things changed. As she awoke under a postoperative anesthetic haze, she heard Gold greeting her with: "Hi, Lucille, this is Dr. Gold!"

"Stupor turned to rage," wrote Natkins. She said she wanted to scream: "That's not the way it goes! It's 'Hi, Lucille, this is Jim' or 'Hi, Mrs. Natkins, this is Dr. Gold.' "

Some physicians say they do not understand what all the fuss is about.

Dr. Jack E. McCleary, a Sherman Oaks, Calif., dermatologist, contended that he finds that 95 percent of the patients in his office prefer exactly the form of address others find so offensive.

"Very few of my patients call me Jack and I don't invite them to call me Jack," he said. "I think this is just because of the respect they might give to the medical profession and the title of doctor."

school superintendents to determine how they would resolve a problem stemming from incompatible demands from others. The superintendents were directly in charge of setting the salaries of their teachers. The teachers expected them to recommend the highest possible salary increase, politicians generally expected them to recommend the lowest possible salary increase, and members of the parent–teachers' association held both kinds of expectations. In an attempt to resolve this conflict the superintendents sought to balance two factors: (1) their perceptions of the *legitimacy* of the expectations of others, that is, whether or not others had a right to feel that the superintendent was obligated to them, and (2) their perceptions of *sanctions,* the rewards and punishments that others might apply to them. Gross, McEachern, and Mason report that some superintendents gave more weight to the legitimacy of expectations, underplaying the sanctions that could be applied against them; others gave priority to sanctions and were relatively unconcerned with whether or not others had a right to expect a particular course of action. The intricacy of this situation should remind us, once again, of the continuing dynamic nature of social interaction (see Chapter 2).

THE GROUP EXPERIENCE

A **group** is the social context within which interaction takes place and consists of two or more persons who are mutually aware of one another's presence and adjust their actions toward one another. The essential ingredient in the definition of a group is social interaction. Several individuals who share certain social characteristics but who are not interacting are classified as a **social category,** not as a group. Thus the members of a family may constitute a group, but all individuals who are fathers form a social category;

group Two or more persons who are mutually aware of one another's presence and adjust their actions toward one another.

social category Any classification of individuals who share certain characteristics but who are not interacting.

the people who reside on a particular floor of an apartment building may constitute a group, but all people who reside in apartments form a social category.

Primary and Secondary Groups

The vast number and diversity of groups in which human beings participate can be classified with respect to their size, function, form, and purpose. Sociologists have found that certain types of groups share a number of characteristics.

One of the most important classifications is the **primary group.** Charles H. Cooley (1909, p. 23) described primary groups as follows:

primary group A group characterized by relatively small size, cohesion, and intimate, informal, and influential interaction.

> Those characterized by intimate face-to-face association and cooperation. They are primary in several senses, but chiefly in that they are fundamental in forming the social nature and ideals of the individual. The result of intimate association, psychologically, is a certain fusion of individualities in a common whole, so that one's very self, for many purposes at least, is the common life and purpose of the group. Perhaps the simplest way of describing this wholeness is by saying that it is a "we"; it involves the sort of sympathy and mutual identification for which "we" is the natural expression. One lives in the feeling of the whole and finds the chief aims of his will in that feeling.

A primary group, then, is characterized by (1) relatively small size, (2) informality among its members, (3) solidarity or cohesion, (4) profound influence on the personality development of its members, and (5) interaction with the whole person (rather than with specialized aspects). Classic examples of primary groups are the members of a family at dinner and two lovers.

The importance of primary groups can be seen in the functions that they perform for their members. Primary groups tend to provide intangible and generalized benefits for their members. Because of the intangible quality of the benefits, it is frequently forgotten that the primary group is present in the life of the individual from birth on. As noted by Faris (1953), "the primary group is the great socializer," meaning that the humanization of an individual usually takes place within a primary group context, beginning with the family. What is more, primary group participation provides the individual with a sense of belonging and acceptance, without which he or she would surely fall prey to disorders of thought, emotion, and behavior. As Homans (1950) suggests, an individual who is not an accepted member of some primary group —a family, a friendship network, or a work group—may have a great deal of trouble dealing with society, let alone himself or herself.

A **secondary group,** in contrast, is characterized by very different qualities. Rather than being intimate and producing a feeling of "we-ness" among its members, it tends to be formal and produces a feeling of "I" and "you" as distinct entities; rather than having a generalized purpose for being, it has a specialized purpose; rather than having a great influence on personality, it usually has little effect on personality. Classic examples of secondary groups are buyers and sellers in a department store, people at a hockey game, and people belonging to a large trade union. The importance and effects of secondary groups, particularly in modern society, are elaborated on in the remainder of the chapter.

secondary group A group characterized by formal relationships, little influence on personality, and specialized interaction.

A summary of the essential characteristics of both primary and secondary groups is contained in the following table.

The Formal Organization

Many secondary groups that are established in order to serve a specialized set of goals can be regarded as **formal organizations.** The members of American society are extensively involved with formal organizations, having created a wide range of special purpose groups, including schools, unions, corporations, political groups, prisons, hospitals, and churches, to mention only a few.

formal organization A secondary group with a formal structure established to serve a specialized set of goals.

The formal organization is distinguished by its **formal structure,** the complex of norms and objectives defining the roles and procedures with which participants are officially expected to comply. A number of well-defined and widely understood rules oversee an elaborate division of labor and determine the procedures for all activities involved in participating in the organization.

formal structure The set of norms and objectives that define the roles and procedures with which members of a formal organization are officially expected to comply.

PRIMARY AND SECONDARY GROUP CHARACTERISTICS: A SUMMARY

	PRIMARY	SECONDARY
Groups	Family	Trade union
	Playgroup	Church congregation
	Friends	School
	Neighborhood	Baseball team
Relationships	Husband-wife	Employer–employee
	Parent-child	Salesman–customer
	Friends	Officer–subordinate
	Neighbors	Union members
Elements	Informality	Formality
	Much influence on personality	Little influence on personality
	Interaction with whole person	Specialized interaction
	Personal	Impersonal

Source: Adapted from Kingsley Davis, *Human Society* (New York: Macmillan, 1949), p. 306.

Formal structure defines *specialized roles in a division of labor.* In a school, for example, such roles might include teachers of specialized subjects or grade levels, a principal, an assistant principal, tutors, counselors, a school psychologist, a speech therapist, student teachers, a nurse, secretaries, janitors, cafeteria employees, and students. What is more, a school may be part of a larger formal organization (a school system) containing other specialized administrative roles such as superintendent, assistant superintendent, school board member, parent–teachers' association, and the like.

The division of labor created by formal structure produces an *interdependence* of roles, so that the participants must rely on one another for the attainment of organizational goals. For example, teachers send sick students to the nurse; the cafeteria staff prepares food for students and teachers; students with special needs leave their classrooms to see a tutor or counselor; school board members consult with the superintendent regarding budgetary matters.

The specialized roles in a formal organization form a *hierarchy of authority,* in which certain participants are assigned the formal right to give orders to others. In a school system commands flow downward from the office of the superintendent to the principal to the teaching staff. Decision making is also structured; specific levels or positions in the organization are assigned the specialized capacity to make decisions concerning particular types of problems. For example, a teacher may decide whether or not to pass a student in his or her class, but only someone at a higher level of authority (e.g., the superintendent) can determine overall educational goals, criteria, and philosophy for the school system as a whole.

Given a structured, ongoing hierarchy of authority in most formal organizations, it can be readily seen that people at the bottom of this hierarchy usually have little influence on the way the organization runs. Consequently, interaction is conducted under much more rigid conditions than it is between, say, roommates. The question then arises, are formal organizations restrictive? (See Box 4–3.)

Given an affirmative answer to this question, we must remember that *all* social agreements are restrictive (see Chapter 2.). This then raises a second question: Is the restriction of the formal organization worth it? That is, are the benefits it provides really useful to people and is its existence necessary in a complex society? The answers to these questions will not be simple, but we shall begin by considering the nature of bureaucracy.

Bureaucracy as Formal Structure.   One of the most maligned concepts relating to modern society is that of *bureaucracy.* It is

---

Box 4–3   ARE FORMAL ORGANIZATIONS RESTRICTIVE?

Yes, they are! Recall being in elementary school and having to ask permission to get out of your seat? "In most auto assembly plants, a worker must even get permission from his foreman before he can go to the bathroom." And other places we have heard of have time limits for such visits as well as rules that preclude taking reading material along. Why? Because they were needed to curb worker abuse. But persons enacting positions for which they have little respect or self-investment are amazingly creative at finding ways around such rules. . . . What's a supervisor to do?

Most visible are time restrictions; there is a time to be at work, a time for coffee breaks, a time for lunch, and so on. Children in some elementary schools are conditioned early to accept such a day. We have noted schedules in many where ac-

tivities are arranged by the minute and have listened to some teachers who assure us with intensity that they see to it that their class begins reading at 10:06 A.M. and spelling at 10:38 A.M. However, there is another side. Time restrictions are essential if the activities of hundreds are to be considered in the most efficient manner. Telephones must be answered, and teachers need to be present when first graders arrive. The tension is inherent, to a degree at least, so long as we seek to produce less costly goods and services.

Spontaneity of interaction is largely curtailed within any organization. Primary school children learn, eventually, to raise their hands. Once assigned to any position within an organization, you too will learn quickly who you are permitted to talk with and when. You don't wander around the building in a carefree manner; your movements are restricted. You have no business appearing in most offices and such behavior will not be tolerated for very long.

Source: Thomas E. Drabek and J. Eugene Haas, *Understanding Complex Organizations* (New York: Brown, 1973), p. 100.

---

popular to associate bureaucratic organization with the most inefficient and dehumanizing elements of modern life, with "red tape" and unending computer errors, with apathetic bureaucrats who operate on a rigid 9-to-5 schedule (with a long lunch hour).

Yet bureaucracy is generally chosen over other methods of organization because of its unparalleled ability to *increase* organizational efficiency and maximize coordination. The classic sociological understanding of bureaucracy was developed by the great German sociologist Max Weber (1946).

Weber observed that industrial societies tend toward greater **rationalization**, that is, they increasingly emphasize rules and procedures that are designed to maximize efficiency rather than the sentimental and spontaneous activities characteristic of traditional (preindustrial) societies. In this process of rationalization it is likely that industrial societies will also adopt the type of formal organization that is most rational and efficient: the bureaucracy.

In order to describe the central elements that make up a bureaucracy, Weber developed what he called an **ideal type**, an

rationalization An emphasis on rules and procedures for maximizing efficiency.

ideal type An abstract model of a social phenomenon.

abstract model of a bureaucracy designed to summarize the key features found in all bureaucracies. The interesting thing about an ideal type is that, being an abstract model, it may never *completely* correspond to anything in social reality; that is, it may not totally categorize any actual phenomenon because any actual phenomenon has many individualized elements that the model does not take into account. For example, the ideal type of bureaucracy may not describe in complete accuracy the complexities of interaction at the Xerox plant in Rochester, New York. Nonetheless, if Weber has done his job correctly, the ideal type of bureaucracy will point to all the *essential* features of the Xerox plant. In a similar fashion, an ideal type is a marvelous sociological tool for comparative puposes; it allows researchers to get quickly to the essential features of any similar social phenomenon anywhere. In order to understand the use of the ideal type more fully, we turn to the specifics of Weber's ideal type of bureaucracy.

bureaucracy A type of formal structure that contains well-defined roles, is ruled by a few, has written rules and goals, and evaluates its members based on their specialized role performance.

Bureaucracy can be defined in terms of several characteristics. Like other forms of formal organization, it contains a number of roles having specialized privileges and obligations. Bureaucratic organization is hierarchical; it is typically overseen by a few persons who make major decisions and pass directives to those at lower levels. The members of a bureaucracy tend to be evaluated on the basis of their specialized role performance rather than on any other criteria; that is, members are assigned to their specialized roles on the basis of their expected competence rather than on the basis of some other role relationship such as kinship. For example, the person in charge of electronic data processing for a particular corporation would probably be hired on the basis of previous work experience and advanced training rather than because he is the president's nephew. Moreover, once in a position, the participant's ability to secure raises, promotions, vacations, offices, and other benefits also depends on role performance.

Finally, bureaucracy usually has a set of written rules and goals, representing the official objectives and requirements of the organization. Since these rules are written, members of the bureaucracy can determine the privileges and obligations of their assigned role. Thus most universities publish a faculty handbook that specifies the obligations and rights of the faculty role, including eligibility for insurance, tenure, sabbatical leave, and teaching responsibilities.

A clear-cut example of bureaucratic organization is the large business corporation. It contains a number of specialized roles such as accountant, sales manager, salesperson, computer analyst, marketing director, public relations director, president, treasurer, and so on. The authority structure of a large business organization is hierarchical, so that a small number of persons, usually a board of directors, makes major policy decisions influencing the organization at all levels. Promotions and salary raises are determined in large part by the contributions made by members toward the corporation's goal of profit. For example, raises to salespeople often depend on their sales figures over a period of time. Regarding organizational rules and goals, the large business corporation typically issues an annual report of business transactions and files a summary statement of its official purpose and procedures.

Informal Structure of a Formal Organization.   No matter what its effectiveness, the formal structure of an organization cannot eliminate all sources of conflict or achieve perfect coordination of its specialized organizational functions. Lapses in communication and conflicts between specialists inevitably occur, despite the presence of official procedures for recruiting personnel and an authority system for overseeing the division of labor.

The **informal structure** of a formal organization—the unofficial norms and unwritten procedures that arise from informal, primary ties in the dynamics of day-to-day interaction—frequently has much to do with heightening or diminishing the level of conflicts in the organization, especially those that cannot be handled by (or are created by) its formal structure. Take the situation of a large work organization whose minute division of labor has restricted its workers to their specialized functions. A net result may be to reduce possibilities for workers to cross lines of specialization and to assist fellow workers outside their designated areas of responsibility.

informal structure The unofficial norms that arise in a formal organization from informal, primary ties.

The informal structure of the organization can intervene in the form of informal groups in which individuals meet one another as whole personalities and that cut across a wide range of organizational roles. In other words, the actual norms may come to predominate over the ideal norms (see Chapter 2). In his study of formal work organizations, Gross (1953, p. 63) reports that cliques of workers meeting during overlapping leisure periods crossed specialty lines within the organization and served an important integrative function.

> It was discovered that the eleven cliques that were found in the office tended to cut across work sections, and thus brought together, on an informal basis, persons from various segments of the structure. Within these groups, horizontal communication was easy, persons volunteered assistance to one another, and, by being able to compare their specializations with one another, gained some conception of the relation of their work to the whole. At the same time, isolates proved to be peculiarly vulnerable to the inadequacies of the institutional controls.

In this example the informal structure supported the effectiveness of the formal organization with respect to fulfilling its official goals. In other cases, however, the informal structure may be at odds with the official goals of the organization. For example, small work groups may slow down the rate of productivity by establishing informal norms of worker output significantly lower than those specified by the rules of the formal structure.

Bureaucracy and the Poor: An Example of Bureaucratic Ineffectiveness.   Sociologists Sjoberg, Brymer, and Farris (1966) have offered the following rather remarkable general proposition: In order to maintain itself, the client-centered bureaucracy tends to neglect those in greatest need of its services—those, in fact, whom the organization was established to assist. For example, lower-class clients in child guidance clinics generally are neglected in favor of middle-class clients who seem to respond better to therapy (Hunt, Gurrslin, and Roach, 1958). Scott (1967) similarly reports that agencies servicing the blind concentrate their programs on clients who seem to have the greatest likelihood of success. In public housing socially handicapped tenants (particularly blacks on welfare or women) are less likely to obtain adequate housing-related services than are other project tenants (Levin and Taube, 1970).

One of the reasons disadvantaged clients tend to be mistreated or passed over by organizations designed to serve them may be found in the very nature of bureaucracy itself. Bureaucratic organizations keep written reports of their objectives and their performance. For instance, many profit-making corporations issue an annual report of earnings to their stockholders. Second, client-centered bureaucracies are frequently expected to justify themselves by some quantitative measure of their achievements (the number of clients serviced, treated, cured). Clients with difficult problems may require a large amount of time and effort, while success in such cases cannot be predicted with confidence. As a result, bureaucracy may select for processing those clients whom it perceives as *most likely* to have success. Thirdly, there is some question whether client-centered bureaucracies are really "client-centered" at all. Like all bureaucracies, they are structured hierarchically. As a consequence, the jobs of all workers depend on the good opinion of their work by their superiors. In actuality, then, all bureaucracies may be "superior-centered" and may pay little attention to the formal definition of their job if it is not also the central interest of their boss! To put it in terms already discussed, the reference group of bureaucratic workers may not be their clients but their superiors. All these factors combined may help to make many client-centered bureaucracies extremely insensitive organizations.

Let us now briefly return to the questions posed before we considered bureaucracy as a type of formal organization: Are the benefits of formal organizations worth their restrictiveness? On the one hand, as Weber suggests, bureaucracies, despite the stories about their inadequacies (some of which are true, to be sure), are the most efficient means that human beings have yet devised for handling complex and massive problems. Imagine, for example, whether the education you and hundreds of thousands of others are receiving now could have been possible without massive formal educational organizations throughout this country. Imagine whether the standard of living we enjoy would be possible without bureaucratic organizations bringing us food (the supermarket), clothing, housing, plumbing facilities, and so forth. On the other hand, if Sjoberg, Brymer, and Farris are right, bureaucracies, in addition to being restrictive, may also be terribly poor at doing their job at peak efficiency.

There is, in other words, no simple answer to the question of the "worth" of bureaucracies. We are not trying to "get off the hook" in taking this position. In fact, the reason that we raised the question in the first place was because we felt many readers would raise it themselves. Rather than leave it at that and allow the question to be given the easy answer—"If formal organizations are restrictive of human choices, they probably aren't worth it"—we choose to present the other side of the story—the fact that formal organizations provide most of the supposed benefits of our life-style from food to films, from buses to books. Hopefully, this presentation will suggest how truly intricate and complex the structure of social interaction is in all its aspects and take us further away from easy answers. To illustrate this point further, we shall return to the paradoxes of society in the section "Mass Society" later in this chapter.

The concept of society. To this point we have examined groups that satisfy specialized needs and goals. **Society** can be defined as the largest group that attempts to provide the means for satisfying all the needs of its members. Smaller groups generally can meet only some of the needs of their members and usually depend for their survival on some larger network of relationships. For example, two lovers may be able to satisfy most of their emotional needs together, but it is unlikely that they will be able to satisfy other basic needs, such as the need for food, without entering into other groups. Although a business corporation may help to meet the economic needs of its employees, the employees must look else-

society The largest group that seeks to provide the means for satisfying all the needs of its members.

where for other groups to satisfy their emotional, religious, educational, and political needs. These other groups are all part of society.

social system A group whose parts are interdependent.

Society can be regarded as a **social system,** as a group whose parts are interdependent. This means that the parts of society affect one another. If one part changes, then the other parts may change as well. Other kinds of systems operate in a similar way. For instance, changing a worn battery will likely improve the operation of the entire engine of an automobile. Removing an inoperative kidney will cause some changes in the functioning of the human body.

How are the parts of a society interdependent? As a humorous example we can consider the last episode of the smash TV series "M*A*S*H" which was aired on February 28, 1983. In New York City, immediately after the show, water consumption rose by an incredible amount, so much so that water mains all over the city threatened to burst. The reason? While the show was on viewers stayed glued to their sets, not wanting to miss a moment. But when it was over, they dashed to their bathrooms. Consequently, the flow rates in the city's water mains went up by a total of 320 million gallons in a little over 2 minutes! According to Andrew McCarthy of the city's Department of Environmental Protection: "Our engineers say you would have to have 1 million people flushing their toilets at the same time to achieve that rate. The readings went through the ceiling. There was never a jump like this before" (*Finger Lakes Times,* March 15, 1983, p. 1).

As a more serious example of how a social system operates, let us discuss a recent change originating in the educational institution of our society: a marked rise in the proportion of college-educated women. The effects of this change have been far-reaching. A larger number of women now hold elected office, thus changing the political institution. A significant increase in the number of working women has changed the economic institution and is influencing the growth of day-care services and restricting the family institution. (see Box 4–4). The women's movement has met with strong resistance of various kinds, so that women continue to be excluded from leadership positions in education, business, and politics. But the overall pattern is clear enough. The effects of a modification in the status of women within one institution have been felt throughout the institutional structure of our society.

The interdependence of parts of the social system applies at the individual level as well as at the group level. The input of each individual is sometimes capable of influencing society as a whole, although this is difficult to see in a large, complex society such as the United States where some people are constantly wondering

---

Box 4–4 HOUSEWORK AND WAGE INEQUALITY BETWEEN THE SEXES

If the parts of society are interrelated, then a change in one area of society might produce change in other areas as well. What changes in the role of woman might occur from changing the distribution of housework by sex? Would working women continue to earn much less than their male counterparts if men did more of the housework and child rearing?

To find out, Coverman (1983) studied a national probability sample of 1,515 men and women who were working for pay at least 20 hours a week. She found that much of the male–female income gap can be explained by the sexual division of labor in the home. Whether or not they also work outside, wives tend to be primarily responsible for housework and child care. Thus their time devoted to daily household tasks

places women at a disadvantage on the job relative to men who are freed from such responsibilities. Specifically, men have more time and energy to expend on the job; they are more adaptable to long and relatively inflexible working hours; and they benefit from support services provided by their wives (e.g., volunteer work and entertaining) which may be useful for furthering career goals.

Coverman's study may help explain why social policy has had so little effect on reducing wage inequality by sex. Policymakers have not adequately emphasized solutions to the unequal distribution of housework—solutions such as flexible work hours, homemaker payments, and child-care facilities sponsored by employers or government.

"What can one person do?" For example, let us assume that you become convinced that the automobiles being manufactured are unsafe. You write letters of complaint to your congressional representatives and automobile manufacturers and begin to convince your friends to do the same. Then you decide to speak publicly on the issue. Shortly you find that you have inspired a whole group of people to write and protest automobile safety standards. Your group attracts the attention of the local press and a story is published in a newspaper with a large readership. The story reaches other disgruntled automobile consumers and they either join your ranks or talk about the issue to others who eventually join. In this manner the whole affair snowballs and you find yourself writing a book for mass publication on the subject of automobile safety, as well as being interviewed on television and radio. All this engenders massive support for your position. Then the automobile manufacturers, silent to this point, feel they must take action. They begin to issue rebuttals to your accusations. You retort and a nationwide controversy involving the federal government develops. Finally, the public support for your position becomes so strong that the automobile manufacturers agree to make certain safety changes in their product. You and your legion of followers push for congressional support so that the changes promised by the manufacturers will be enacted into law. After this battle is over and automobiles have been made much safer than they were, you find yourself interested in protecting the consumer in other ways and so you undertake to form a consumer advocate's bureau that produces other positive changes in consumer products. In retrospect, it can easily be seen that one person has been responsible for all this change in society.

Sound farfetched? Perhaps, but the story just recounted is that of Ralph Nader, a man who got the idea that he would like to see safer automobiles made and wound up head of one of the most effective consumer protection organizations in American society. Similarly, small groups of people all over America and Europe are banding together in an attempt to stop the nuclear arms race.

MASS SOCIETY

Things have certainly changed! Contemporary America is a far cry from the America of the past. And those having a nostalgic preference for a former time—those who long for a return to strong primary group ties, craftsmanship, local politics, and a simple life —frequently use an image of what they call "mass society" to identify a long-standing trend in American society that they deplore. The image of mass society is painfully clear:

- Waiting lines a mile long
- Traffic jams at 5 o'clock
- A 9-to-5 work schedule that lacks meaning
- Individuals who don't help one another
- Prime-time television on Saturday night
- Distant, omnipotent, and corrupt leadership
- People who feel very much alone
- City dwellers and suburbanites living in "boxes"
- No parking places
- And so on. . . .

America as a Mass Society

mass society A society characterized by large-scale urbanization, bureaucratization, and industrialization.

Sociologists also employ the term **mass society** and use it to refer to any social order characterized by large-scale urbanization, bureaucratization, and industrialization. Not unlike the popular usage, the sociological conception of mass society generally views modern relationships as being superficial, temporary, and secondary, providing individuals with little protection from the large-scale forces that play on them. From this viewpoint the emergence of mass society has meant (1) the eclipse of community, (2) social isolation, (3) alienation from work, (4) anomie, and (5) political apathy. Let us consider each of these aspects in turn.

The Eclipse of Community.   The trend toward mass society has meant that local communities have lost much of their autonomy or independence to distant centers of control (Stein, 1960). For instance, the employment structure of an entire town may well depend on a single giant corporation whose central office is located a thousand miles away; most television programs reaching millions of families throughout the United States originate in New York or Los Angeles; large apartment complexes have absentee owners who are minimally concerned with the day-to-day problems of their tenants.

Social Isolation.   Closely related to the eclipse of community, there is a widespread decline in the incidence of primary group ties based on territory or neighborhood, a condition that has resulted in a reduced sense of identification with particular localities.

Isolation is also encouraged by another trend, namely, that mass society thrives on mobility. Business executives frequently move from one city to another in order to find employment, even if they must leave family, friends, and a sense of belonging. In a similar way, college professors often move across country for the sake of another position.

A third factor contributing to isolation is the continued residential restriction of most members of racial minority groups to ghettos. In the blackout of August 1977, in New York City, for example, this isolation and the pent-up hostility it produces, were vented in large-scale looting of business establishments. Obviously, the situation of racial minorities, nearly two decades after the urban upheavals of the 1960s, has not improved all that much.

Alienation from Work.   Some sociologists argue that work in mass society has become far too segmented and specialized as a result of the nature of bureaucratic organization and mass production. For example, work assignments that originate in one department are passed on to another department and are finally completed in yet another department. Any given bureaucrat sees merely a single phase of the process and as a result cannot envisage the entire task. What frequently happens is that the operation appears to be chaotic (Bensman and Rosenberg, 1960).

Mass production, on the other hand, is generally organized on the basis of economic efficiency in such a way that the performance of any given operation can be divided and subdivided to a maximum extent. Unfortunately, this aspect of mass production may also create a degrading and meaningless work situation. As Swados (1957, p. 202) argues, "It is degrading to any man who ever dreams of doing something worthwhile with his life; and it is about time we faced the fact."

According to Neumann (1960, p. 270), alienation from work (the feeling that one's employment has no important relation to one's life) is so basic to the nature of mass society that it affects every aspect of the lives of its members: "Modern society produces a fragmentation not only of social functions but of man himself who, as it were, keeps his different faculties in different pigeon-holes—love, labor, leisure, culture—that are somehow held together by an externally operating mechanism that is neither comprehended nor comprehensible."

Anomie.   It will be remembered from our discussion of anomic suicide in Chapter 1 that Durkehim's concept **anomie** refers to a state of normlessness in which individuals are confused about which standards of conduct are acceptable. For example, our society has created an anomic condition for the relationship between the aged and youth, so that responsibilities, obligations, and rights concerning the aged continue to be ill-defined. Should young marrieds take their parents into their own home if the parents can no longer care for themselves or should they put their parents in a retirement community or nursing home? Should older people be forced to retire before 65 in order to make room for younger people? As a result of unanswered questions such as these, many young people feel confused, if not guilty, about any position they take relative to the aged. Recent social changes have created similar uncertainties in the relationship between men and women as well as between blacks and whites. Should men open doors for women? Should women refuse such gestures if they are made? Should blacks receive special consideration because of past oppression? Should blacks demand or reject such special consideration from whites? Again, we have no set answers to these questions.

anomie A state of normlessness in which an individual experiences confusion regarding acceptable standards of conduct.

Political Apathy.   As Riesman and Glazer (1971, p. 399) have suggested, millions of Americans are unattached to local, national, and international political events; millions of others pay only minimal attention to political happenings, and millions more merely watch the course of politics "as they would a horse race." In most major polls taken since President Nixon's resignation in 1973 the American public has shown deep distrust of and cynicism toward politicians (see Box 4–5).

The detachment of the individual from the political institutions of his or her society is directly related to a lack of attachment to primary or intermediate associations in which ideals and loyalties arise. The individual feels minimal allegience to national political institutions and does not internalize their political norms.

In summary, then, there is some evidence for the critique of

Many of those who claim we live in a mass society argue that because we must interact in such huge, secondary settings as the subway (top), we have had an eclipse of community, a heightening of social isolation in the midst of many (bottom, left), and an increase in our feelings of alienation from work (bottom, right).

Box 4–5   POST-WATERGATE, POST-ABSCAM CYNICISM?

How would you rate the honesty and ethical standards of clergymen, congressmen, car salesmen, and other occupational groups? Pollster George Gallup (1981) asked this question of a national probability sample of American adults, with the following results: Clergymen were ranked highest among all occupational fields—some 63 percent of the sample reported believing that the ethical standards of the clergy were either "high" or "very high." By contrast, car salesmen ranked lowest: only 6 percent placed the honesty of this group in the high or very high category. Sadly, perhaps, congressmen didn't score much better than car salesmen. Only 15 percent thought highly of their ethics and honesty.

mass society. Paradoxically, it seems, the same forces that have freed the individual from reliance on external authorities and binding tradition and have provided the opportunity to develop, for most of the society, mental, emotional, and life-style capabilities that were impossible only a few decades ago, have also created the eclipse of community and widespread social isolation, alienation from work, anomie, and political apathy. But is this the whole picture?

The Rediscovery of the Primary Group

More recently, sociologists have modified their conceptions of mass society in line with research that has unexpectedly uncovered the presence of important primary group ties in modern society. According to Katz and Lazarsfeld (1955), the "rediscovery of the primary group" has occurred independently in several different areas of research. We shall review three of them here. The key thing to note in each case is that the primary group experience was *always* present in these groups; sociologists and journalists alike, in their effort to describe (and often condemn) the trends of a mass society, simply *overlooked* or *ignored* the continuing importance of such groups.

Mass Media Research.   Although the mass media (and especially television) were generally regarded as having an immediate and direct impact on their audience members, research into the nature of mass communication did not support this view. Instead, communication researchers uncovered a two-step flow of communication impact. Specifically, they found that a message from the mass media must first travel to **opinion leaders**—key persons in the

opinion leaders Key persons in primary groups.

primary groups of an ultimate audience—who decide whether or not to pass its content to other members. (See Figure 4–1.)

Military Research. A large survey of soldiers during World War II (first discussed in Chapter 1) determined that combat motivation (the willingness to fight) was directly related to a soldier's desire to "avoid letting the other fellows down," to protect his friends in combat rather than to express any sense of patriotism, hatred of the enemy, or fear of discipline from above. Although the acceptance of general goals of combat depended on patriotism and an acceptance of official commands, the specific efforts to achieve military goals relied much more on the strength of a soldier's primary group ties to his buddies in his own unit (Stouffer, 1949).

Industrial Research. The Hawthorne studies at the Western Electric Company are classic examples of the importance of human relations in an industrial setting. The original intent of the Hawthorne studies was to examine the influence of working conditions and incentives on workers' productivity (Roethlisberger and Dickson, 1939). However, the impact of informal work groups in the factory setting became the focus of inquiry when it was discovered that productivity was more a function of the actual norms that developed within informal groups of coworkers than of the physical setting or incentive schemes (the ideal norms) passed down by management.

In the bank wiring room of the Western Electric Company, for example, Roethlisberger and Dickson report that the workers shared a rigorously enforced idea of what constituted a proper day's work, so that the average output tended to remain constant at 825 connections an hour. According to the informal norm of the group, a "good guy" worked at a pace neither so slow that others had to "carry him" nor so fast that management would have lowered the rate for piecework.

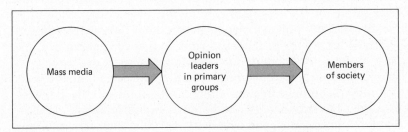

Figure 4–1 The Two-Step Flow of Mass Communication Impact

Counteracting Forces in Mass Society

Needless to say, mass society undoubtedly does contain fewer of the primary ties once associated with social interaction—forms such as the neighborhood, the rural village, and the extended family. Yet we must be careful lest we exaggerate. As Arnold Rose (1962, p. 316) notes about the city, supposedly the *non pareil* of social isolation, alienation, anomie, and apathy:

> A sense of identity with the local community does seem to arise in the modern city, even if not to the same extent as in the folk society. Friendship groups do develop in the city, if not always on a residential basis. A good many friendly primary relationships develop in the large city, and one can gain a sense of personal identity with an urban neighborhood and even with a city as a whole. And this may be increasing as the urban population is more likely to be urban-born rather than migrants displaced from rural and village backgrounds.

In other words, at the same time that older forms of social interaction have abated, a number of new institutions and structures have arisen, institutions and structures that may help to compensate for the loss of traditional primary ties in mass society. Such newer types of social interaction are important for their capacity to counteract feelings of loneliness and isolation among the members of a mass society. By way of illustration, we shall now examine the impact of technological innovations, the voluntary association, and community and friendship networks.

Technological Innovations. Numerous social critics have deplored the decline of the neighborhood unit, arguing that it once served as a crucial focus of warm and intimate primary interaction. What is too frequently overlooked, however, is that an individual's network of primary group relations need no longer be confined to a physical area of residence. Technological innovations in transportation, especially the automobile, although partially responsible for the eclipse of community, have also provided the means whereby millions of persons are able to visit friends and relatives despite the distances separating them. What is more, the basis of social interaction, once dependent almost exclusively on shared residence, has become increasingly related to the interests that individuals have in common regardless of where they choose to reside. For instance, two individuals from *different* neighborhoods might become good friends as a result of their mutual interest in tennis or photography.

Too little recognition as well has been accorded the widespread presence of the telephone which has helped individuals to establish and maintain friendship networks beyond narrow territorial boundaries. Recent innovations have greatly expanded the role of the telephone in the form of the citizen's band radio and computer mail. As Aronson asserts (1974), it is highly doubtful that individuals could sustain primary contacts of any importance whatsoever while physically scattered throughout a metropolitan region were it not for the cohesion provided by the telephone. The telephone then can be regarded as a counteracting force in mass society, a mechanism employed by numerous persons who might otherwise be largely deprived of the means for having intimate and informal social interaction of substance.

The Voluntary Association. Another counteracting force against the loss of traditional forms of primary group interaction is the **voluntary association,** a formal organization consisting of persons who come together on a part-time basis to focus on some common interest, need, or problem. As early as the 1950s sociologists generally recognized the importance of the voluntary association in everyday life when they characterized American society as a nation of joiners. Bell (1956) observed that the voluntary communal activity in the United States had reached an unprecedented level with thousands of voluntary associations, organizations, clubs, societies, lodges, and fraternities whose memberships were close to 80 million individuals. Axelrod (1956) similarly reported that nearly two thirds of the population of a large urban center were members of some formal organizations, although fewer held active membership. In recent years there has been an immense proliferation of voluntary associations; for example, singles bars, health and natural food stores, health gyms, karate clubs, meditation and yoga centers, "stop smoking" groups, encounter groups, and the like. In addition, from 1970 to 1981, there has been a 50 percent increase in national associations, including those related to business, science, education, public affairs, and hobbies. (Fraternities have returned to the college campus—see Box 4–6).

voluntary association
People who come together on a part-time basis to focus on some common interest, need, or problem.

It must be emphasized that the voluntary association is a secondary group that is specialized with respect to its activities and objectives and rarely involves the whole personality of its members. At the same time, the nucleus of a voluntary association (e.g., its executive board and active members) often constitutes a primary group of some significance. What is more, the specialized concern of a voluntary association provides a reason for meeting not only formally but informally between meetings as well. Consider, for example, the case of the tenants' association in public housing, whose members have typically banded together in order

to improve the quality of services relating to their shared tenancy. Regardless of its effectiveness in achieving formally stated goals, tenants' associations may perform a latent or unintended function by providing the focus for informal interaction to occur, thereby counteracting feelings of loneliness and despair. It is interesting to note in this connection that members of such tenants' associations sometimes turn out to be the residents who are most satisfied with the public housing project in which they live (Levin and Taube, 1970).

Community and Friendship Networks.   Our consideration of the influence of technological innovations such as the telephone and the rise of voluntary associations in recent years suggests that some primary group ties are maintained in less visible and untraditional ways: What other evidence is there that this may be the case?

Herbert Gans (1962) attempted to examine the veracity of the mass society thesis by looking at the community and friendship networks among the five main groups that comprise today's cities:

The stereotypic view of what life "used to be like" before the coming of mass society and what it is like now, after the arrival of mass society, is depicted by these two cartoons. Although there is obviously some truth in the "situations" created by each cartoon, recent sociological research has indicated that the image of modern society created by the cartoon on p. 156 is a good deal more complicated than this stereotypic vision would suggest (see text). Moreover, the "idyllic" vision of rural society recreated in the cartoon (above) is also less than completely accurate, as anyone who has seen re-runs of films like *High Noon* or *Shane* or virtually any John Wayne Western can attest.

(1) the "cosmopolites" ("students, artists, writers, musicians, and entertainers, as well as other intellectuals and professionals" p. 629); (2) the unmarried and childless; (3) the "ethnic villagers" ("ethnic groups . . . found in each inner city neighborhoods as New York's Lower East Side, living in some ways as they did when they were peasants in European or Puerto Rican villages" p. 630); (4) the "deprived" (the poor, the emotionally or otherwise handicapped and, particularly, the nonwhite population); and (5) the "trapped" ("the people who stay behind when a neighborhood is invaded by non-residential land uses or lower status immigrants, because they cannot afford to move" p. 630). A good example of

Box 4–6   FRATERNITIES—A COUNTERACTING FORCE ON THE CAMPUS?

In their study of a national sample of 161 colleges and universities, Fox and Levin (1983) report that membership in college fraternities and sororities declined dramatically during the early 1970s. In 1966 some 30 percent of all college students belonged to Greek-letter societies; by 1976, however, this figure had dropped to only 19 percent nationwide. In fact, fully two thirds of these colleges had experienced declining fraternity enrollments. On some campuses they completely disappeared.

Apparently, many college students of the early seventies regarded fraternity membership as inconsistent with their interests in civil rights, student rights, antiwar activism, feminism, equality, and independence. On those campuses where dormitory rules were relaxed or abolished and students demonstrated in a number of causes, fraternities were especially likely to be associated with elitism and "establishment" politics.

According to Fox and Levin, we are now experiencing a major resurgence of interest in college fraternities across the country—a resurgence that is likely to continue for years to come. By 1981, almost one half of all colleges and universities had already reported seeing growth in fraternity enrollments.

The seventies' emphasis on "doing your own thing" left many students in a state of confusion. Thus the fraternity began a comeback for the same reason that junior proms came back: More and more students desire *structured* opportunities to meet other students, date, and develop friendships. In a mass society independence can be very lonely!

this latter group are the people currently living in abandoned tenements in New York City's South Bronx area.

After a consideration of each of these groups, Gans concluded that all of them except the "ethnic villagers" were detached from the type of traditional neighborhood life that still exists in small towns and used to be more prevalent in urban areas. However, *only* the "deprived" and the "trapped" seemed to be highly characterized by the supposed negative effects of mass society: an excessive amount of secondary group experiences and impersonal, segmented, transitory, and predatory life-styles (pp. 632–633). More specifically, the "cosmopolites" and the unmarried and childless have numerous primary group ties that are not visible in traditional neighborhood forms. They may not, for example, know anyone in their building or even on their street because their friends live in other parts of the city. On the other hand, the "ethnic villagers" do have a visible primary group network based on neighborhood.

Furthermore, more recent participant observation studies (see the discussion of this technique in Chapter 1) by Elliot Liebow (1967), Gerald Suttles (1968), Joseph Howell (1973), and Carol

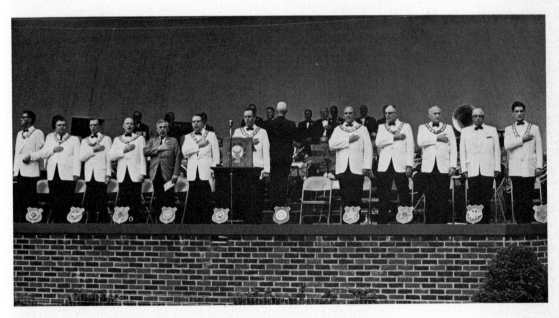

Despite the claims of alienation, social isolation, apathy, and so on, which are made concerning mass society, the fact remains that many people maintain or develop primary group relationships. For example, the technological innovation of the telephone and its more recent version in the computer terminal (top) has made it possible for people to communicate with one another over long distances. In addition, voluntary associations, such as the Elks (bottom) have done much to develop meaningful associations for people in our modern world.

Stack (1974) have all indicated a deep-rooted social order among "deprived" and "trapped" urban groups. This "social order of the slum" (to use Suttles' phrase) includes numerous primary group ties and other meaningful relationships. Although these latter authors are not very sanguine about the prejudicial social stratification system (see Chapter 5 for more on this topic) that has produced "deprived" and "trapped" groups in the first place, they do indicate that there still exist many positive and human elements in the life-styles of these groups, which have been maintained in the face of great adversity.

To conclude this section, then, we would suggest that although claims for the negative effects of mass society are not ungrounded, to take them to extremes is also unwarranted. Once again, we see that modern social structure has evolved various complex forms that often modify one another. As one final example of this phenomenon, we turn to the intriguing problem of bystander apathy.

Bystander Apathy in a Mass Society

Social scientists have long sought to discover why witnesses to emergency situations do not always come to the rescue of those in trouble. At first glance this phenomenon seemed to be just another horrible manifestation of mass society: Individuals are being assaulted, even murdered, in view of numerous witnesses who neither help to fight off an attacker nor even bother to call the police.

Is such apparent apathy just another sign that the members of a mass society are indifferent to the plight of others? Quite the contrary, recent research has made clear that witnesses to a crisis who fail to help tend to be profoundly upset, distressed, and emotionally involved, even if they are unwilling to come to the rescue.

An important factor in willingness to act is the presence of a crowd. Several studies have shown that witnesses to an emergency are less likely to help if the crisis occurs in the presence of many people. In other words, an individual would tend to receive aid more quickly on an uncrowded road than on a busy thoroughfare.

Informal Norms in Public Places.   Imagine that someone is having a heart attack on 34th Street, New York City, during the weekday lunch hour. The victim clutches his chest in pain, staggers for half a block, and collapses onto the sidewalk. Will anyone come to his aid? As demonstrated by Darley and Latane (1968), before offering help, a passerby must first notice that something is happening and, second, decide that the event constitutes an emergency.

One reason that a passerby may not attend to an apparent emergency is that one of the most pervasive norms regarding behavior in public places is "Do not invade the privacy of strangers." Americans consider it to be bad manners to observe others' behavior; in our society it is a breach of etiquette to invade the privacy of strangers by prying, staring, or listening intently. Thus a person walking on 34th Street may simply not notice the victim or, registering that his behavior is unusual, may quickly turn away.

Secondly, once a passerby has noticed that something is happening, he or she must still interpret that event. Offering help will not be considered if the event is not interpreted as an emergency. For instance, someone lying on the sidewalk may be experiencing a heart attack, but he may also be sleeping off a drunken spree. Before reacting to such an ambiguous scene, the passerby is likely to look to others in order to determine how they are reacting to the same scene. If others appear to be upset, concerned, or excited, the passerby too is likely to become upset, concerned, or excited. If others seem to be calm and unconcerned, the passerby is more likely to ignore the situation.

Here again subsequent action may be influenced by informal norms of behavior. Thus it is a violation of an informal norm associated with interaction in public places to react with intense emotion among strangers. Consequently, individuals in public places are careful not to overreact. As a result, they frequently appear to be less concerned, less excited, less scared, or less angry than they actually feel. Consider the behavior of patients in a dentist's waiting room or the reactions of airplane passengers awaiting departure. Can you imagine a more "relaxed" group of persons? Who would guess from their behavior that most of them actually feel nervous, anxious, scared, or fearful? Witnesses to public emergencies similarly may be likely to try to react as little as possible.

The presence of others who do not notice the event or who seem to be unconcerned and emotionally detached from it may falsely suggest that the situation at hand is actually not an emergency at all and that help would be unnecessary, if not inappropriate, to offer. Individual witnesses to such an event may fear social embarrassment by intervening alone in the face of such apparent indifference. As a result, many will proceed with their own affairs, even though feeling a profound sense of unresolved conflict.

The first response to this explanation may not be positive because there is a tendency to dismiss seeking information on the basis of social comparison as a negative aspect of our society. Yet all of us gain much useful information by observing others who are experiencing the same events as we. For instance, have you even chosen a restaurant on the highway by the number of cars or trucks in its parking lot or have you ever examined a consumer report magazine before making an important purchase? The same phenomenon is at work in interpreting a strange occurrence on a crowded street.

The preceding responses are as likely an explanation of bystander apathy as the standard argument that "people are alienated from one another in mass society and unconcerned with each other's fate." Moreover, response of bystanders, even in cities, is nowhere near as low as might be expected. Response seems clearly to be influenced by the social structure of the place where the emergency situation occurs, with town people exhibiting more primary group behavior and city people more secondary group behavior. In other words, it may well be that the special informal norms for behavior in public urban places that people share are the causal factor of bystander apathy rather than any widespread lack of concern for the welfare of others in modern society (see Box 4–7).

The news isn't *all* bad. One can find numerous examples of individuals who have made the newspapers by risking embarrassment and personal safety to come to the aid of strangers. In July 1983, two passengers on a flight to Miami overpowered a Florida man who was in the process of hijacking the Northwest airliner to Havana. In September 1981, 19-year-old Kay Pope subdued a bank robber in Cornwall, England; as a result, she sustained gunshot wounds and other injuries. In May 1983, a group of Duxbury, Mass., teenagers saved a 17-year-old girl from drowning after her car veered off a bridge and overturned in 6 feet of water. In December 1980, three members of the Northeastern University hockey team chased and caught the man responsible for knocking down and robbing an elderly woman as she walked near the campus. In October 1983, after a nationally televised movie about a kidnapped boy, an agency in New Paltz, New York, got more than 2,000 phone calls from concerned viewers across the country who offered information about lost children.

SUMMARY

Given its cultural underpinnings, it is not surprising that social interaction acquires a long-standing structure of its own. At the core of this social structure is the idea that individuals occupy statuses (particular positions in society) and are expected to adhere to roles, the norms or expected behaviors associated with a status. In order to judge the appropriateness of a particular behavior, we must first know the status of a person and the exact nature of the expected role for that status. Since statuses and roles experience some degree of change over time, individuals may undergo role

Bystander apathy is often taken as a sign of the near-total anonymity and lack of concern for others produced by mass society. For example, the woman (top), who had purposefully tied herself to a telephone pole to see what would happen, had to wait for 110 cars to pass before someone stopped and asked if she was all right. As the text indicates, however, there may sometimes be mitigating social circumstances that keep people from "interfering" in the problems of others. Moreover, many people are in fact quite willing to help: Lenny Skutnik (bottom) was honored by first lady Nancy Reagan after he dived into the Potomac River to rescue a survivor of the Air Florida jet crash on January 13, 1982.

Box 4–7 "WHO WOULDN'T HELP A LOST CHILD? YOU, MAYBE."

Takooshian, Haber, and Lucido (1977) conducted a new test of bystander apathy. They had a young child stand on a busy street in 4 large cities (New York, Boston, Philadelphia, and Chicago) and in 12 smaller towns surrounding these cities. The child simply said to passersby, "I'm lost. Can you call my house?" During the experiment (see the discussion of this technique in Chapter 1), 184 people, 127 in the cities and 57 in the towns, were approached by the 14 children employed.

The results established clear response differences between urban and town environments. In the cities 46 percent of those approached offered help; in the towns fully 72 percent did so. Moreover, response patterns among people in each environ-ment differed. In the towns all people approached, even those who didn't help (who usually offered excuses), were sympathetic. In the city great sympathy was expressed only by a few respondents, even among those who did help. One "helper" solved the problem of aiding the child by saying, "Here's a dime. Try the call yourself." Another responded, "Go into that restaurant. Your mother's waiting there." Of the people who did not respond at all to the child's plea in the city, many just walked by quickly, others gave the child a curt "no," and others just put money into the child's hand. One even responded by snapping, "So what's your problem, kid? I'm lost too."

conflict; that is, they may become the recipients of incompatible role requirements.

The totality of an individual's concurrent statuses, known as a status set, is a potential source of role conflict. The role associated with one status may be at odds with the role associated with another. The several role relationships involved with one particular status, known as a role set, may also be a source of conflict. Persons in the different relationships may hold incompatible expectations for the individual's behavior.

A group, the social context within which interaction takes place, consists of two or more persons who are mutually aware of one another's presence and adjust their action toward one another. Sociologists have found that certain types of groups have a number of characteristics in common.

One of the most important classifications is the distinction between primary and secondary groups. Primary groups are characterized by personal intimacy, informality, and have great influence on personality, whereas secondary groups are characterized by distance, formality, and have little influence on personality.

Many secondary groups are formal organizations—groups characterized by a formal structure that defines the roles and procedures with which participants are officially expected to comply, specialized roles in a division of labor, and a hierarchy of authority.

As conceptualized by Max Weber, bureaucracy is a type of formal organization that characterizes many of the secondary groups found in our society. It contains a number of roles having specialized privileges and obligations. Bureaucratic organization is hierarchical and ruled by a few persons. Members of a bureaucracy tend to be evaluated on the basis of their specialized role performance. Finally, bureaucracy has a set of written rules and goals, representing the official objectives and requirements of the organization.

The informal structure of a formal organization represents the unofficial norms and unwritten procedures that arise from informal, primary ties. The informal structure of an organization can intervene in the form of informal groups in which individuals meet one another as whole personalities. These informal groups may support official organizational goals, but they may also work against them.

Society is the largest group that attempts to provide the means for satisfying all the needs of its members. It can be regarded as a social system in that it is a group consisting of interdependent parts. Modification of one part is likely to have effects throughout the whole institutional structure.

Sociologists employ the term mass society to refer to any social order characterized by large-scale urbanization, bureaucracy, and industrialization. The sociological conception of mass society has emphasized the eclipse of community, social isolation, alienation from work, anomie, and political apathy.

More recently, however, sociologists have modified this conception in line with research that has uncovered the presence of important primary group ties in modern interaction. The "rediscovery of the primary group" has occurred in research in mass media, the military, and industrial relations. A number of new institutions and structures have arisen in mass society which may help to compensate for the loss of traditional primary ties. Such new structures include technological innovations, voluntary associations, and reformulated community and friendship networks.

"Bystander apathy" at first appeared to be just another manifestation of the indifference associated with mass society, but careful research has indicated that witnesses to a crisis tend to be profoundly upset and emotionally involved. Several studies have shown that witnesses to an emergency are less likely to help if the crisis occurs in the presence of many people. Informal norms concerning behavior in public places often prevent individuals from recognizing that something is happening and from deciding that the event constitutes an emergency.

Social interaction is an extremely complex and intricate process. All enduring encounters between two or more people become *structured*—that is, they develop regular routines of behavior (roles) and "positions" for participants (statuses)—whether they are on the primary or secondary group level. Even an expressive activity such as dancing has a very detailed, social structural aspect to it. Even modern dancing, on the surface so much more "spontaneous" than the Mexican dance pictured here, is highly structured—as anyone who has been to a disco or seen the film "Flashdance" can attest.

QUESTIONS, EXERCISES, PROJECTS

1. Specify the role traditionally associated with each of the following statuses: (a) student, (b) physician, (c) mother, and (d) teacher. Indicate how these roles may have changed in recent years.

2. From your own experience (or the experience of someone whom you know well), give an example of role conflict in (a) a status set and (b) a role set. How were these conflicts resolved?

3. List five primary groups and five secondary groups in which you have been involved during the last year.
4. Analyze your college or university as a formal organization. In particular, indicate the most important characteristics of its formal and informal structure.
5. What characteristics make military life an excellent example of bureaucratic organization?
6. If society is a social system, then changing one of its parts might influence changes in its other parts as well. The Supreme Court decision of 1954 ruled racial segregation illegal. Indicate the impact, if any, that this change in the legal institution may have had on other institutions in our society.
7. From a sociological viewpoint, what has the emergence of mass society meant for its members?
8. What are the counteracting forces in a mass society?
9. "Witnesses to a crisis who fail to help may actually be profoundly upset, distressed, and emotionally involved." Discuss.

SOCIAL STRATIFICATION

As we saw in Chapter 4, interaction frequently acquires a definite and long-standing social structure. One of the most important characteristics of that structure is **social stratification** —a ranked set of strata or social classes that reflect inequality in the possession of the things (such as wealth and material goods) and qualities (such as prestige and power) that society's members consider valuable. Is social stratification an inevitable part of social life? Or, is it a manifestation of certain types of cultural organization—that is, essentially "invented" like rituals of eating and sex role behavior have been invented differently in different cultures?

Certainly before this century most people thought stratification inevitable. Take wealth, for example. The Bible contains the famous verse, "The poor ye always have with thee," and such sentiments were echoed by a famous Church of England hymn:

The rich man in his castle
The poor man at his gate
God made them, high or lowly
And ordered their estate.

Moreover, the facts bear out such notions. There are rich countries and poor countries. For example, in 1979, the average income per person in Switzerland was $14,034; in the United States it was $9,869; and in Japan, $8,901. In contrast, per person income in Nigeria was $831; in the Philippines, $546; and in India, $169! Furthermore, it is no secret that there are rich people and poor

social stratification A ranked set of strata or social classes that reflect inequality in the things that society's members consider valuable.

169

people in the United States. Thus in 1981, 19.3 percent of all American families made $35,000 or more a year. Comparatively, 23.1 percent made less than $5,000 per year. And the figures get even more intriguing when one considers race. Taking into account all the white families in the United States in 1981, 21.6 percent made over $35,000, but only 11.4 percent of Hispanic and 8 percent of black families were as wealthy. Considering the poorest families—those earning $5,000 or less—9 percent of all white families were in this category, whereas 12.5 percent of the Hispanic and 22.9 percent of the black families were as poor. Rather remarkable differences.

How do we explain them? Fortunately, we now have some relatively sophisticated sociological theories that provide a helpful beginning.

THEORIES OF STRATIFICATION

Marx

The influential nineteenth-century social theorist Karl Marx (1818–1883) argued that social stratification was essentially an outgrowth of economic processes. He felt that in an effort to meet their needs people are likely to become competitive with one another for scarce material resources. Once this happens, it is also likely that one group will eventually gain the upper hand in this competition: This is the beginning of social stratification.

social class An aggregate of persons who perform essentially the same activities in daily life.

As soon as social stratification appears, each group becomes a true **social class,** an aggregate of persons who perform essentially the same activities in daily life. Moreover, each social class is characterized by a distinctive **class consciousness,** an awareness among its members of their place in the social stratification system. However, as Marx and his coauthor, Frederick Engels, point out, the separate individuals who comprise a class are "a class only in so far as they have to carry on battle against another class; otherwise they are on hostile terms with one another as competitors" (Marx and Engels, 1930, p. 49). As an illustration, let us examine Marx's classic description of the rise and supposed fall of capitalism.

class consciousness An awareness among the members of a social class of their place in the social stratification system.

bourgeoisie The capitalist class, those individuals who own property and the machinery of production.

In a capitalist economy (for more on the rise of modern capitalism see the discussion of the economic institution in Chapter 6) two distinct classes emerge: the **bourgeoisie,** those who own property and the machinery of production, and the **proletariat,** those who sell their labor in working the machinery of production, but do not own it. There is no question of the inequality of these two classes. Because of their control over the economic forces of soci-

proletariat The worker class, those individuals who sell their labor.

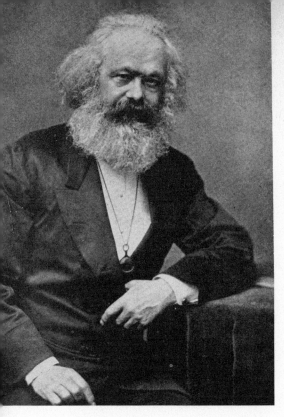

Karl Marx (1818–1883) was, of all social analysts, probably the one who has had the greatest influence on social life world-wide. Unfortunately, because his theories formed the ideological basis for various communist revolutions in the Twentieth Century—most notably those in Russia and China—and because much of the Western world is at political odds with these nations, Marx is often depicted as a man committed to totalitarian control of the individual by the state. Actually, the exact opposite is the case. Marx was deeply concerned with the quality of human life and the welfare of the individual. His animus against the capitalist economic system developed during the nineteenth century when capitalism was in full sway in many European nations. Observing this situation, Marx felt that capitalism was, more often than not, advantageous only to the few people who controlled the economic apparatus and highly disadvantageous to everyone else. He thus proposed the eventual overthrow of those in power by those not in power and the establishment of a common ownership of the economic apparatus as a means of correcting the imbalances of capitalism. In his proposed communist system the state would not *dominate* the individual, rather it would provide for the individual's various needs, while the individual developed his or her potential to the fullest as he or she saw fit.

ety, members of the bourgeoisie are more or less in control of their own lives. They can live where they want, eat what they like, and so on. Because of their *lack* of control over the economic forces that shape their lives, members of the proletariat are more or less at the mercy of the more powerful bourgeoisie. They must live where there is enough work for them to stay alive and support their families, eat what they can afford, and so forth.

Marx theorized that as capitalism developed, the gap between the two classes would widen: The bourgeoisie would become more exclusively the "haves" and the proletariat the "have nots." Eventually, this would result in such massive exploitation of the proletariat by the bourgeoisie that the workers would come to realize their common plight, at which point, class consciousness would be transformed. Previously, the workers had been aware of each other only as people sharing the same life-style and often as being in competition with one another. Now they would become aware that they had deep interests in common and that their station in life was the direct product of their exploitation by the bourgeoisie. In other words, the workers' consciousness would change from being a class *in itself* to being a class *for itself*. As this happened, they would come to realize that the only way to solve their predicament would be to work collectively to overthrow those who control the machinery of production. This spontaneous "revolt of the proletariat," Marx argued, was assured of victory by the sheer weight of numbers (see Box 5–1). Furthermore, it would result in a classless society in which conflict and exploitation would be totally absent. In this utopian state of **communism** the proletariat would both work and own all property and machinery of production, and everyone would be equal and assured of personal and social dignity.

communism A classless society in which everyone works and owns the means of production.

We shall examine the Marxian theory in greater detail in Chapter 8. For now, however, it is important to emphasize that Marx tended to think of stratification in economic terms alone. He felt the development and persistence of social classes to be primarily dependent on the economic forces in society. Although he recognized that differences in power and prestige also existed, he felt that such differences were always a result of economic position. For him the key variable in determining social class was the relationship of any group to the ownership of property and the machinery of production.

Box 5–1   MARX AND ENGELS ON THE REVOLT OF THE PROLETARIAT

In this excerpt from "The Communist Manifesto," Marx and Engels indicate the ten most important measures that will have to be taken after the successful revolt of the proletariat to ensure the rapid and permanent establishment of the communist state. How many of these measures have been implemented, even partially, in our society since the appearance of the "Manifesto" in 1847? What does this suggest?

1. Abolition of property in land and application of all rents of land to public purposes.
2. A heavy progressive or graduated income tax.
3. Abolition of all rights of inheritance.
4. Confiscation of the property of all emigrants and rebels.
5. Centralization of credit in the hands of the state, by means of a national bank with state capital and an exclusive monopoly.
6. Centralization of the means of communication and transport in the hands of the state.
7. Extension of factories and instruments of production owned by the state; the bringing of cultivation of wastelands, and the improvement of the soil generally in accordance with the common plan.
8. Equal liability of all to labor. Establishment of industrial armies, especially for agriculture.
9. Combination of an agriculture with manufacturing industries; gradual abolition of the distinction between town and country, by a more equitable distribution of the population over the country.
10. Free education for all children in public schools. Abolition of children's factory labor in its present form. Combination of education with industrial production, etc.

Source: Lewis Feuer, ed., *Marx and Engels: Basic Writing on Politics and Philosophy:* (New York: Anchor, 1959).

Weber

Following Marx, the German sociologist Max Weber (1864–1930) also recognized the importance of economic forces in producing social stratification. Unlike Marx, however, Weber contended that other forces in society exist independently of economic forces that shape one's social position. He argued that individuals can be located in a system of social stratification with respect to their possession of any of three social characteristics: **wealth,*** **social honor** or **prestige** (the amount of positive social recognition accorded an individual by other members of the group) and **power** (the ability of an individual to make decisions that affect the lives of other individuals). (See Box 5–2.)

The expansion of Marxian theory contained in Weber's analysis of stratification is important to realize. First, since Weber recognized that social rank is not tied *exclusively* to the individual's role in economic production, his scheme allowed for the possibility that there can be more than two social strata. In the Marxian scheme you either owned property and the machinery of produc-

wealth The possession of material goods.

social honor (prestige) The amount of social recognition accorded an individual by other members of society.

power The ability of an individual to make decisions affecting the lives of other members of society.

Box 5–2   STUDY: HISPANICS' POWER IS GROWING

NEW YORK—Hispanic Americans see large corporations and the federal government as unresponsive to their needs, and they are very much aware of their growing economic and political clout, Coca-Cola USA said yesterday.

The firm interviewed Mexicans, Cubans, Puerto Ricans and other Latin American groups in the five largest markets in the United States—New York, Chicago, Los Angeles, San Antonio and Miami—which represent 50 percent of all Hispanic consumers.

"Coca-Cola took a good look and is not

about to forget what it saw," Brian G. Dyson, president of Coca-Cola USA, said. "The fact that Hispanics make up 28 percent of Los Angeles or 20 percent of New York City is indication enough that no corporation or government body can afford to ignore."

Coca-Cola also announced that it is contributing $100,000 to Hispanic community groups in each of the metropolitan cities in the study.

Major corporations and the federal government fared about equally in the eyes of Hispanics, getting a 39.6 percent and 38.8 percent negative reading, respectively, for their responsiveness to needs of the Latin American community.

Source: Boston Globe, November 16, 1983; p. 49.

---

*Weber actually used the term "class" to indicate the concept of possession of material wealth. Although that term is consistent with his conceptual scheme, it was felt that to use Weber's original term here might result in confusion with the usage of the same term in the previous discussion. For this reason we have decided to use the easily distinguishable term "wealth" which was the basis of Weber's definition of class.

tion or you didn't. The inevitable process of the accumulation of control of economic forces in the hands of the bourgeoisie combined with the removal of this control from the hands of the proletariat essentially eliminated the possibility of any stable "middle class." Weber's scheme, on the other hand, recognized that other factors may come to bear on a person's position in the social stratification system of a society, for example, people may be classified as middle class simply because of their level of educational attainment, their racial background, and the like.

Second, Weber recognized that any of the three characteristics of stratification may affect any of the others. Thus the amount of social honor a woman has, for example, can affect the amount of power or wealth she has or both. For instance, because of his central role in quarterbacking the victorious New York Jets in the Super Bowl in 1968, Joe Namath was accorded great social honor among sports fans throughout the country. Realizing this, many major firms and merchandisers asked Namath to advertise their products on national television, thereby greatly increasing his wealth. In another case, General Dwight David Eisenhower, chief architect of the allied victory in Europe during World War II, was accorded such prestige for this feat that he was subsequently elected President of the United States, despite the fact that he had virtually no professional political experience. Needless to say, not only was his power greatly enhanced, but his wealth as well; besides receiving the salary of a president, Eisenhower was beseiged by mass media companies (newspapers, radio, television, books) to publish his memoirs at substantial royalty figures. More recently, former President Gerald Ford, not a wealthy man before his term in the White House, was paid $1 million for the exclusive rights to publish his memoirs.

Third, Weber recognized that the three characteristics of position in the stratification system need not necessarily coincide (although they often do: the Kennedy family is a good example). In other words, Weber allowed for the possibility that **status inconsistency** may exist. Thus someone might enjoy a good deal of prestige, but little wealth, tremendous power but little prestige, and so on. Familiar examples of status inconsistency are the highly respected teacher who has little wealth and the wealthy gangster, such as those depicted in the film *The Godfather*, who has great power but little prestige outside a small circle (see Box 5–3).

status inconsistency A lack of coincidence or overlap among the three characteristics of stratification, wealth, prestige, and power.

Mills

However, despite status inconsistencies, there is also a tendency in modern societies (as intimated by the Kennedy example), for wealth, prestige, and power to coalesce. One contemporary sociologist who has argued this very strongly is C. Wright Mills (1956).

Fundamentally, Mills suggests that there is a **power elite** in most modern societies that essentially runs the society. The power elite is comprised of the highest status members of three groups: the military (e.g., the Joint Chiefs of Staff), industry (e.g., the presidents of the automobile and steel industries), and politics (e.g., the president, high officials in the administration, senators, and congressional representatives.) These people, Mills argues, all tend to come from similar backgrounds (upper-middle or upper class) and have similar interests, not the least of which is maintaining or increasing their own wealth, prestige, and power. Consequently, given the opportunity to meet on matters of national policy, they can be expected to develop policies that are as often self-serving as they are nation-serving (Recall our discussion of instrumental and democratic-humanitarian values in Chapter 2).

power elite A group of high status members of the military, industry, and politics, who make policy decisions.

Riesman

Other contemporary sociologists, notably David Riesman (1950), argue for a more *pluralist* conception of the interrelationship of wealth, prestige, and power—suggesting that monolithic deci-

Max Weber (1864–1930), along with Marx and Durkheim, is usually considered to be one of the greatest sociological theorists. Convinced, like Durkheim and Comte, that the study of social action could be scientific, he argued that human social behavior could be understood by employing the method of *Verstehen,* or sympathetic empathy. By this, Weber meant that the social researcher could come to understand the actions of others by carefully considering their situations, the past influences on their present situation, and their present predispositions given those circumstances. Given this orientation, it was inevitable that Weber put great emphasis on historical research as part of the sociological enterprise. His work, as a result, was particularly wide-ranging. He not only considered carefully the elements of stratification described in this chapter, but the structure of bureaucracies (see Chapter 4), the sociology of religion and social change (see Chapter 8), and the sociology of law, of politics, and of music.

sions, such as those presumably made by a power elite, are hardly ever made in modern societies. Rather, the whole process of decision making is one of complex exchange, modification, and compromise among groups at all levels. Although leaders have more power than average members of their groups, they can only make decisions that are, ultimately, in accordance with the beliefs of the group's members. If leaders go too far astray from group norms and values, they are not likely to remain leaders for long. (President Nixon's fate may serve as an example here. Recall, also, our discussion of the two-step flow of communication, Chapter 4.)

SOCIAL MOBILITY

social mobility The dynamic aspects of stratification.

The concept of **social mobility** summarizes the dynamic aspects of social stratification. There are two types of social mobility, vertical and horizontal.

Box 5–3 STATUS INCONSISTENCY: A PHD'S LAMENT

by Bob MacDonald
Globe Staff

Mike Halberstram is having big problems with his *dharma. Dharma,* he explains, is a philosophical concept from India. Your *dharma* is what you were meant to be. Some are destined to be plumbers, others are meant to be poets.

Halberstram is said to have been the smartest kid ever to come out of Malone, N.Y. They had to send him out of town to a more challenging high school. He holds three master's degrees and a doctorate in English literature from Yale. A published article derived from his doctoral dissertation on Thomas Wolfe caused such an uproar in the academic world that he has been the subject of lengthy stories in the New York Times and Village Voice.

What's wrong with Halberstram's *dharma* is that his most recent job, the best he could find, was as a bagel bagger at Freedman's Bakery in Quincy Market.

While Halberstram acknowledges it is possible that his *dharma* was to be a bagel bagger all along, that all this academic stuff was just a digression, Indian philosophy does offer another explanation.

"The age that we're living in is said to be a time of *adharma,"* he notes, "that is, a time in which the whole structure of *dharma* of allotted duties, is in decay, and it's a real mess."

At the root of Halberstram's decaying *dharma* is the lack of jobs in the academic community. And where else do you go with a doctorate in English lit? Halberstram did have a teaching position at Northeastern, but he knew that was only temporary.

Going from the posthumous works of Thomas Wolfe to mixing lox and cream cheese is a tricky transition, and Halberstram's job is not without its problems. Halberstram may know all about Beowulf, but he knew nothing about bearclaws and some of the other more esoteric pastries sold at Freedman's.

"I don't think the boss thinks I learn fast enough," says the man with three master's and a PhD. "He told me to get a list. I've got a list, but I don't know what to look for. When somebody asks me for bearclaws, I don't know what they are. Not only that, I don't know *where* to look for them. I can't picture them. I never *heard* of them!"

Still, Halberstram is happy in the job he's overqualified for. "I actually enjoy it," he says. "I only wish the salary were higher. It's a very relaxing job. There's no politics. There's no infighting. You sell bagels and Whoopee Pies and so on, and that's all that's expected of you, and there's a certain pleasure in that. There's no faculty meetings, no controversy, no envy among employees."

And all of us can take heart, for the same Indian philosophy that deals with *dharma* states that we are living in an Age of Enlightenment, and how much more enlightened can we be than having a man entitled to put "Dr." in front of his name dishing out our Whoopee Pie?

The future is brighter for Mike Halberstram, too. When we last talked to him he was giving up the bakery and had begun a training program at the Holiday Inn in Cambridge to become a desk clerk. What sort of educaitonal background is needed to become a hotel desk clerk?

"Absolutely none," said Halberstram.

Source: Boston Globe, pp 1, 16.

Vertical Mobility

vertical mobility Any upward or downward change in social rank.

Vertical mobility refers to any upward or downward change in the social rank of an individual or group and can be said to occur whenever there is a major shift in wealth, prestige, or power. For instance, an individual might achieve upward vertical mobility through a change in level of wealth by receiving a sizeable increase in salary. The change in social position may be symbolized by moving to a more prestigious neighborhood, getting a more expensive car, and wearing more expensive clothes. An individual might experience downward vertical mobility by having to take a sizable cut in pay. Such a change in position might also be symbolized by alterations in the person's relationship to material goods—moving to a less highly regarded neighborhood, trading in the "big car" for a more efficient model, and wearing clothes until they are threadbare.

Similarly, upward mobility through a shift in prestige might be attained by an actor who successfully undertakes difficult Shakespearean roles after having acted mostly in low-quality television programs. On the other hand, when an actor no longer plays such difficult roles and returns to low-quality television or even no work at all, he or she becomes a "has-been," and can be said to be downwardly mobile in regard to prestige.

career mobility Changes in an individual's occupational status.

generational mobility Changes in social rank between parents and their children.

Both the preceding examples are representative of a subtype of vertical mobility that sociologists have called **career mobility**—changes in an individual's occupational position. Another subtype of vertical mobility recognized by sociologists is **generational mobility**— changes in social strata between parents and their children. Probably the best examples of continuing upward generational mobility in this country have been provided by the waves of immigrant groups that came to the United States around the turn of the twentieth century. Typically, first-generation immigrants were impoverished, unskilled, and relatively uneducated; as a result, most were forced to assume lower-class positions in the stratification system and lower-class employment such as low-paid factory work, menial labor, and domestic work. Many of these immigrants were able to gain enough wealth so that their children were allowed the privilege of attending school and obtaining the necessary education to get positions higher in the stratification system. Many of *these* second-generation immigrant children moved from the lower-class positions their parents held to lower-middle- or middle-class strata. This upward generational mobility in turn provided even more opportunities for *their* children, the third generation, to advance higher in social position. It was not unusual for the third-generation children to move solidly into the middle levels of the middle class or even into upper-middle-class and upper-class positions, becoming owners of businesses, skilled technicians, college-educated professionals, and the like.

Horizontal Mobility

The second major type of position change that sociologists recognize is **horizontal mobility.** This type of shift does not involve a change in social rank, but, rather, a change in position at the same level of power, prestige, or wealth. For instance, an employee of a company might be transferred to a similar position in the same organization, having no greater or less authority, salary, or prestige. This type of mobility is often found within large corporations where vertical mobility is blocked by the existence of only one position at the highest level of hierarchical structure. Since only one person can be president of the company, as young executives get better at what they do and need some form of upward mobility, a proliferation of vice-presidents occurs. The person or persons who were vice-presidents before cannot move up, but they are not "moved out" by the vertically mobile younger people. They are simply given a horizontal shift in position, say, from executive vice-president in charge of sales to executive vice-president in charge of purchasing. In a similar way, an employee may attain horizontal mobility by shifting from a job in one company to an identical job in another company.

horizontal mobility Any change in position that does not involve a change in social rank.

STATUS TYPES

Closely associated with social stratification is the concept of status that we introduced in Chapter 4. Usually, sociologists focus on two major types of status with regard to social positioning: ascribed status and achieved status.

Ascribed status

Ascribed status is positioning in the social stratification system by virtue of characteristics that an individual has at birth or acquires through the process of biological maturation. Such characteristics are sex, age, race, family background, and the like. For example, historically, certain positions in our society have been reserved for males or females only. The classic case is that the male must become the "breadwinner" and the female must become the "housewife."

In a society where ascribed status is the major determining factor in social positions, little vertical social mobility can be expected to occur. People are inherently locked into positions that limit their actions and their actions can have little, if any, affect on

ascribed status A position based on hereditary or developmental characteristics.

The relative impact of ascribed and achieved status was a key element in the popular film, "Trading Places." In the lead role, Eddie Murphy played a destitute and uneducated young black man who, on a bet, was placed in complete charge of a multi-million dollar industrial empire. His ultimate acceptance by the "upper-crust" of corporate America "proved" that social position is determined not merely by who a person is, but by what a person does.

Boston Globe, March 17, 1983, p. 75.

caste A closed system of stratification in which vertical mobility is not permitted.

their status. A completely closed system of stratification in which there is no possibility of mobility is known as a **caste** system. The most familiar example of caste is the Indian stratification system that existed before modernization (and still persists to some extent). This system was based on a complex hierarchy of strata sanctioned by the Hindu religion and rigidly maintained by norms of interaction governing marriage, ritual, occupation, and all aspects of life. For example, members of the lowest ranking group, the untouchables, were isolated from the higher castes in every major respect, including places of worship, schools, residences, places to walk, and use of well water. The problem visited upon South African blacks because of their negatively defined ascribed status is poignantly described in Box 5–4.

Achieved status

In principle, stratification in American society is based on the second major type of status, **achieved status** (although it is not difficult to find important exceptions). In this case, social position is determined not by who or what a person *is*, that is, not by ascriptive characteristics, but by what a person *does*. This principle is illustrated by the American maxim: "The best person gets the job" and is reflected in the bureaucratic evaluation in terms of specialized job performance.

achieved status A position based on role competence rather than on ascribed characteristics.

The two main issues in achieving status are: (1) how to do it and (2) how to maintain it once it has been attained. Consider educa-

---

Box 5–4 ASCRIBED STATUS AND PERSONAL IDENTITY

A few years ago, the newspapers reported the story of a 44-year-old South African woman whose skin had turned progressively darker because of the drugs she was taking to counteract a brain tumor. The darkening of her skin had a profound effect all its own: people treated her differently. Specifically, she was ordered off "whites only" buses, was shunned by friends, couldn't get a steady job, and was deserted by her husband. In addition, the woman's 16-year-old daughter whose skin hadn't darkened at all was also kicked off a whites only bus when a driver recognized her from the times she had accompanied her mother.

In July 1983, a month old South African infant girl with light skin and no clearly definable racial physiognomy was found abandoned in a field. The authorities in Johannesburg later decided she was "colored" rather than white, based on laboratory tests of a snippet of the infant girl's hair.

This decision will determine where she is permitted to live, who can adopt her, whom she is permitted to marry or have sexual relationships with.

In South Africa, classification as white, colored, or black doesn't always have much to do with genetics or appearance. For example, the Japanese are classified as honorary whites essentially so that Japanese business people can use white facilities without being harassed.

The question, "Who am I?" is at least in part a psychological question. That is to say, it is partially a matter of how we *feel* about ourselves, what we *think* of ourselves, how much *confidence* we have in our abilities, and how *highly* we evaluate our behavior. At the same time, however, there is a sociological reality to the question of personal identity—a sociological reality based on ascribed status. As the South African experience suggests, *we are in part what other people define us to be, no matter what we think of ourselves.* If the people who define us have more power than we, then they might also choose to determine what bus we take, where we live, what jobs we are eligible to fill, and even whether we live or die.

Source: "White Woman's Apartheid Story," *Boston Globe,* January 22, 1978, p. 18. "Abandoned Baby's Race Becomes an Issue in S. Africa," *Boston Globe,* July 28, 1983, p. 3.

tion. Why are *you* in school? Clearly, to get an education. But, if one is honest, one may admit that there is a little more to it than that. Getting an education is one of the most important mechanisms for achieving higher status in American society. Regarding income-generating power, recent figures indicate that the average college graduate earns about 45 percent more salary *per year* than the average high school graduate. Moreover, only 20 percent of American households are headed by a college graduate. Thus *merely having the degree* ensures a higher (achieved) status than four fifths of the rest of society (Current Population Survey, *American Demographics 1982*).

There's still more: As journalist Tom Wolfe sardonically observed in a recent public lecture, the job of most middle-class Americans is to find a way to "pass the BA line," that is, to get a college degree so that they will be seen by themselves and their peers as elites. Wolfe also notes that passing the BA line gives people the requisite "cocktail party info," that is, the generalized knowledge about the world and "high sounding ideas" that show one is an "educated person." For example, after taking a sociology course, one learns about Marx, Weber, and even Freud. How useful this general knowledge might be in discussing world events or the latest books!

Such advantages of higher education are hardly lost on most students and their parents, and although there is nothing inherently "wrong" with these advantages, focusing on them exclusively can make the other purpose of education—getting truly useful information about how to live one's life—decidedly secondary. For many, alas, the primary interest is in getting the "piece of paper" that admits them to a job and the cocktail party circuit.

Maintaining status once it has been achieved can also be difficult. For example, if parents have attended college and received degrees, their children are most likely "required" to attend at least as good a college to maintain the social standing of the family. If upward mobility is desired, the children have to attend a better college and/or get a higher degree—for example, a PhD instead of "merely" a BA. Or take the issue of grades: To maintain status "it isn't enough to get an A this term, you have to get one *next* term, too!" Otherwise, you become a "backslider," a "flash in the pan." The same issues are frequently at work in residential areas. A key phrase of the late 1950s and early 1960s was the desire of many to "keep up with the Joneses,"—to have the latest gadgetry that one's neighbors had and to keep one's home in as good condition as or better than others'. Such an orientation, of course, is exactly what David Riesman (1950) meant by modern Americans being "other-directed" (see Chapter 4). And, although Riesman's theory is now seen by many sociologists to be a bit passé, appar-

Weber recognized that wealth, prestige, and power are often intimately related, and that wealth alone could not always account for the position of people in the hierarchy of society's stratification system. Corporate executives (top), being directly connected to the economic system, usually develop both wealth and power simultaneously, with prestige as an adjunct characteristic. Bruce Jenner (bottom left), by contrast, first attained prestige for being an outstanding olympic athlete; wealth and a modest amount of power came later. Sometimes, however, gaining prestige can provide the opportunity for gaining relatively important power. Winners of beauty pageants, such as that depicted (bottom right), get prestige automatically and, if they are talented or fortunate, wealth and power may follow, as well. Consider the case of Anita Bryant, a runner-up in the Miss America Beauty Pageant. Bryant, as a result of this early national exposure, later became the sales representative for Florida's orange juice industry. This, in turn, afforded her an opportunity to mount strong public opposition to homosexual rights laws in Florida. When that campaign was successful, Bryant became the champion of antihomosexual rights groups across the country.

ently the old other-directed zeal has not disappeared entirely as a recent newspaper article attests: To maintain one's achieved status in a suburban neighborhood, apparently the lawn still cannot be ignored (see Box 5–5).

STUDYING SOCIAL STRATIFICATION: THREE APPROACHES

Most attempts by sociologists to study the characteristics of social ranking in a particular group or society fall into three general categories: (1) reputational, (2) subjective, and (3) objective.

The Reputational Approach

Using the reputational approach, a sociologist asks the people in a community to evaluate one another's power or prestige. For

---

Box 5–5 "LAWN IS KING"

"The [summer is the] time of year," said [George Walsh, a worker for Gardner's Village Lawn Center in West Hempstead, Long Island], "when you really find out how much lawns mean to people. Some people are hysterical." Suburban symbols come and go—patios giving way to redwood decks, plastic flamingos to home computers—but it seems that the suburban lawn has never been more important.

"People spend more and more time and money on their lawns every year, most all of it on front lawns," said Bob White, the owner of Gardner's Village. "That tells you something.

These are trying times, when homeowners battle against the browning of suburbia caused by the awful combination of searing sun and watering restrictions and the onslaught of all sorts of lawn fungi and bugs. . . . Water-use restrictions have been instituted this summer (1982) in many su-

burbs, including Ho-Ho-Kus, N.J. John Shuart, the borough administrator said that police cars with loudspeakers had patrolled the streets informing residents of the restrictions, sometimes awakening them at 3 to turn off their sprinklers.

Suburban police issue summonses for illicit lawn watering, and residents have been known to be put on probation for an offense. In Ho-Ho-Kus one woman was openly violating the restriction on a recent day, and explained, "I will not let my lawn die."

"The importance of the lawn cannot be overestimated," said Jack Bienstock, a suburban area manager for Lawn-A-Mat, one of the many franchise lawn-care services that have become popular in recent years. The services charge between $100 and $350 a year to spread seed, fertilizer, and chemicals that control weeds, insects and disease.

"Lawns reflect how a person keeps his house inside," Mr. Bienstock said. "If he has a lousy lawn it indicates he doesn't care, or maybe that he can't afford the neighborhood."

Source: William E. Geist, "For Suburbia, Lawn Is King," *New York Times,* August 2, 1982, pp. B1, B16.

example, in his study of the power structure of Regional City (Atlanta), Floyd Hunter (1953) asked authoritative persons in the community, such as members of the chamber of commerce and the League of Women Voters, for the names of community leaders. Using the 175 names given as a basis, he then asked a set of judges within government, business, civic organizations, and "high society," to rank the most powerful leaders from each of several fields. The top 40 persons—from the fields of industry, finance, the professions, government, labor, and recreation—were regarded by Hunter as the top leadership of Regional City, those persons who ruled the policy making in their community.

Another example of the reputational approach to social stratification is Warner and Lunt's (1941) study of Yankee City (Newburyport, Mass.), a relatively small New England community. These investigators placed individuals into social strata "by the evaluations of the members of Yankee City itself, e.g., by such explicit statements as 'she does not belong' or 'they belong to our club.' By this method Warner and Lunt discovered that the members of Yankee City were distributed among six social strata, ranging from upper-upper class to lower-lower class.

The Subjective Approach

Despite the obvious advantage of obtaining people's impressions of each other's position in the stratification system, the reputational approach is by no means foolproof. It assumes that members of a community can *accurately* perceive one another's wealth, power, or prestige, an assumption that may be only partially warranted in many cases. The subjective approach, in contrast, asks the members of a community to place themselves (not one another) in a system of stratification. A sociologist using this method typically asks the respondent a question such as "In what social class do you belong?" In most cases the investigator supplies several choices of social classes from which the respondent selects one. For instance, Richard Centers (1949) asked a national sample of white adults to respond to the following question in 1945: "If you were asked to use one of these four names for your social class, which would you say you belonged in: the middle class, the lower class, working class, or upper class?" Centers obtained the following results in his study:

- Upper class 3%
- Middle class 43%
- Working class 51%
- Lower class 1%
- Don't know 2%

Studies such as Centers' have consistently suggested that the majority of Americans seem to be aware of social ranking. At least three fourths of the adult Americans approached in such studies have been willing to assign themselves to a social class, even when they were not given a list of names (as in Centers' study) and had to select one of their own.

However, studies using the subjective approach have also demonstrated the great extent to which Americans are *unwilling* to identify themselves with either the upper or the lower class. As pointed out by Centers, 51 percent of his sample indicated that they belonged to the working class. When the working-class alternative is excluded from a subjective study, however, and respondents are asked to choose from among only upper, middle, and lower class, as many as 90 percent assign themselves to the middle class.

The reluctance of many respondents to select an upper-class designation for themselves, even when their wealth, power, and prestige levels suggest that they might do so, may reflect the democratic-humanitarian values of American society (see Chapter 2). In our ideal picture of ourselves as a nation we believe that everyone is supposed to be equal. To assign ourselves to an upper-class position may carry subjective connotations of superiority, of being better than other people, a characteristic that most Americans may not wish to acknowledge they feel, even if they do.

On the other end of the social scale, the reluctance of so many people to choose a lower-class designation may reflect the instrumental value pattern of our society. On the one hand, since the instrumental pattern stresses achievement and hard work, it is always more respectable to work than not to work. The middle-class designation indicates that one is doing enough to be respectable. The working-class alternative has the same positive connotations, even if it indicates a rank somewhat lower than the middle-class alternative. On the other hand, the lower-class designation has negative connotations. Choosing the alternative may appear to be an admission to the pejorative characteristics such as laziness and immorality associated with the lower class.

The Objective Approach

Both the reputational and the subjective approaches require awareness on the part of respondents regarding the social stratification of their community or group. Both methods collect information about stratification by asking individuals how they see the power, prestige, or wealth of members of their society. An investigator using the objective approach, in contrast, preselects certain criteria for stratification of a population. Respondents are not

Social class can be detected in many ways, including how people of different classes live or dress (by choice or necessity). Upper class is depicted here (top) in a restaurant; middle class is shown (middle) in front of a private home; lower class is seen (bottom) in the setting of slum apartment buildings.

asked to evaluate or rank themselves or others, but rather to supply information concerning the selected criteria. The sociologist then makes all the decisions concerning the placement of society's members based on the accumulated data. Many different criteria have been applied to indicate social rank, such as income level, occupation, location of residence, type and condition of living room furniture, style and quality of clothing, and language and speech patterns (Barber, 1957).

Occupation seems to be one of the best indicators of position in a system of stratification (Kahl and Davis, 1955). For example, in an early attempt to specify occupational status, Edwards (1940) developed a set of categories that he claimed combined the social, economic, and political forms of stratification into a single occupational index. With his index, Edwards tried to represent "not only a major segment of the nation's labor force, but, also, a large population group with a somewhat distinct standard of life, economically, and, to a considerable extent, intellectually and socially" (p. 179). Edwards' occupational groupings are as follows:

1. Professional
2. Proprietors, managers, and officials
   a. Farmers
   b. Wholesale and retail dealers
   c. Other proprietors, managers, and officials
3. Clerks and kindred workers
4. Skilled workers and foremen
5. Semiskilled workers
6. Unskilled workers
   a. Farm laborers
   b. Laborers, except farm
   c. Servant classes

The National Opinion Research Center (NORC), beginning in 1946, asked representative samples of Americans to rank 90 occupations on a 5-point scale from "excellent standing" to "poor standing." These ratings were scored so that any occupation that received the excellent rank from all respondents would be given 100 points. Notice that NORC did not ask respondents to rank the members of their community (reputational approach) or themselves (subjective approach), but to evaluate the prestige of occupations, so that sociologists might subsequently apply these evaluations to members of society.

The most recent objective occupational prestige studies were undertaken by Coleman and Rainwater (1978). Using essentially the same approach as the NORC studies, Coleman and Rainwater asked a sample of 600 Bostonians and 300 citizens of Kansas City to rank a list of occupations. The sample was drawn to reflect a broad range of ages, both sexes, all races, and different economic positions. The results are contained in Table 5–1.

As the table shows, Coleman and Rainwater made a distinction between blue-collar and white-collar jobs. Their results indicate that some blue-collar positions in modern America have higher occupational prestige than many white-collar jobs—a finding that would not likely have appeared had the study been conducted in 1900. Nevertheless, the very highest prestige rankings are reserved for white-collar jobs and the very lowest for blue-collar ones.

Coleman and Rainwater also claim that their results reflect the *magnitude* of prestige accorded each occupation—a distinct advance over earlier studies. Thus they would argue that the highest-ranked job—that of president of a billion dollar corporation—has about twice the prestige of a senior partnership in a Wall Street firm, almost 6 times the prestige of the job of machinist or new car salesperson, and nearly 20 times the prestige of the lowest-ranked job—that of the unemployed person who does the occasional odd job. Clearly, all jobs are *not* equal. (Remember the old adage: "Stay in school and get your degree." Or, in Tom Wolfe's phrase: "Make sure you cross the BA line!")

The NORC and Coleman/Rainwater Occupational Prestige Scales, despite their interesting representation of social honor rankings, are limited in that they do not *directly* examine the wealth or power dimensions of ranking. Nonetheless, it can easily be seen by examining Table 5–1 that the characteristics of wealth and power are usually associated with those occupations ranked as having high prestige and are not so likely to be present in those occupations ranked as having low prestige. A full-scale objective measure of stratification would have to include these characteristics and their interrelationships directly.

Needless to say, measuring social stratification in all its dimensions is an extremely difficult task. In the objective approach the sociologist may overlook important information of which only the people themselves may be aware. The limitations of the reputational and subjective approaches have already been noted. The best solution to this problem would be to develop a study using all three approaches to social stratification.

SOCIAL CLASS IN AMERICA: THE BREAKDOWN

Social class in America is a complex affair. Americans do not seem to regard class lines as rigidly drawn and often pay little attention to class differences that in other societies would raise the hackles

Table 5–1 OCCUPATIONAL PRESTIGE IN AMERICA

"BLUE-COLLAR" OCCUPATIONS	SCORE	"WHITE-COLLAR" OCCUPATIONS
	583	President of a billion-dollar corporation
	438	Chairman of the board of an aerospace company
	324	Physician
	289	Senior partner of a Wall Street law firm
	264	College professor
	252	Owner of a factory that employs 100 persons
	212	Department head in state government
	194	Manager of a large factory
	185	Sales engineer
	178	Chemist
	165	Civil engineer
	156	Clothing store owner
	154	Optical technician
	149	Salesman for an electrical manufacturing company
	135	Owner of a dry-cleaning store
	134	Accountant
	132	Insurance salesman
	131	High school teacher
Construction foreman	127	
Brickmason	127	
Electrician	125	
	123	Traveling salesman for a wholesale company
Airplane mechanic	119	
Plumber	114	
	113	Assistant manager of an office supply company
	112	Office manager of a moving company
Factory foreman	111	
Bulldozer operator	110	
Tool and die maker	108	
Plasterer	108	
Fireman	104	
	104	Bank teller
Welder	104	
Carpenter	103	
Machinist	103	
	100	New car salesman
	100	Manager of a small store in a city
Glasscutter in a factory	98	
	97	Accounting clerk in a government office
	97	Bookkeeper
Machine repairman in a factory	96	
Radio/TV repairman	95	
Truckdriver	94	
Automobile repairman	90	
Barber	88	
Printing press operator	88	
	88	Mailcarrier
Railroad freight inspector	88	

Table 5–1 *(Continued)*

"BLUE-COLLAR" OCCUPATIONS	SCORE	"WHITE-COLLAR" OCCUPATIONS
Concrete finisher	88	
Housepainter	82	
	81	Expediter
Machine operator in a truck factory	80	
Metal grinder	80	
Dockworker	78	
	78	Ordertaker in a wholesale house
Spraypainter	77	
	76	Stockclerk
Restaurant cook	74	
Taxicab driver	74	
Punchpress operator	74	
Gardener for a large institution	73	
Coal miner	72	
Assembly line worker	69	
Hospital attendant	69	
Restaurant waiter	68	
	66	Shipping clerk
	66	Salesclerk in a hardware store
Laborer in a furniture factory	65	
Airport baggage machine operator	63	
Filling station attendant	63	
Loom operator in a knitting mill	61	
Janitor	58	
Laborer in a bottling company	57	
Clothes presser	55	
	53	Downtown newsdealer
	52	Grocery clerk
Parts checker in a factory	52	
Shoe repairman	50	
Garbageman	47	
Ditchdigger	46	
Shoe shiner	31	
Unemployed man who does odd jobs sometimes	30	

Source: Richard P. Coleman and Lee Rainwater, *Social Standing in America* (New York: Basic Books, 1978), Table 3–1.

of different class members. For example, as depicted in the television series, "Upstairs, Downstairs," before World War I, British upper-middle class homeowners would simply *never* have hobnobbed with members of the servant class who attended them— a sentiment that was returned by the "downstairs" staff: It was simply not their place to be social with those "upstairs." But, from the beginning of our nation, Americans of different classes have "rubbed elbows" more frequently.

Despite the uncertainties in creating totally accurate classifications for all Americans, sociologists now think they have a fairly accurate picture of the class structure that exists within our society. This understanding comes mainly from Warner and Lunt's Newburyport studies and Coleman and Rainwater's Boston/Kansas City studies, discussed in the previous section. Together, these analyses suggest there are *seven* main social divisions in the United States.

The Upper-Upper Class

These are the true "bluebloods." Probably less than 2 percent of the population, this group is usually considered (and considers itself!) members of "high society" and is characterized by inherited wealth and a gracious way of life that reflects generations of affluence. These people have typically attended private schools and prestigious colleges and universities, are members of "well thought of" churches and associations and usually exert great influence over an area's social life. They tend to cluster in specific areas —on Hill Street in Newburyport, on Ward Parkway in Kansas City, on Nob Hill in San Francisco, on Beacon Hill in Boston, or on Park Avenue or Central Park West in New York. Many have extensive suburban or exurban estates. Linked by blood, marriage, shared schools and clubs, this stratum comes the closest to being a self-conscious group (a class "for itself," in Marx's terms). Their exclusivity is captured well by the joke about Boston's "Brahmins": "In Boston, the Lodges speak only to Cabots and the Cabots speak only to God."

The Lower-Upper Class

Although this group also appears at the very top of an area's social hierarchy, it shows important differences from the upper-upper class. Composed of very successful executives or professionals and making up another 1 to 2 percent of the population, it represents those who have *achieved* elite status. That is, their wealth and power have been *earned* rather than *inherited*. Consequently, even when members of this group have *more* money or live in more prestigious places than some members of the upper-upper class, they are seen as somewhat lower in prestige—as "nouveau riche." They do not usually have the exclusive club contacts of the blueblood class and cannot "automatically" get their children into the most well-thought-of school. Nevertheless, most make in excess of $60,000 a year and also tend to live in well-defined areas —such as Manhattan's upper East Side, Detroit's exclusive Grosse

Pointe Shores suburb, or in exurban developments like Pittsford, near Rochester, N.Y.

The Upper-Middle Class

This third level contains professionals and managers who are quite comfortable financially but who lack the greatest wealth. They typically earn between $35,000 and $60,000 a year. A larger group than the upper class—roughly 10 percent of the population—this group exerts considerable influence in community organizations. Likely to be graduates of colleges and holders of advanced degrees, people in this category commonly reside in "better," but not truly "exclusive," suburban areas (Devon, near Philadelphia, for example) or relatively high-prestige inner-city neighborhoods (Cambridge, near downtown Boston, for instance). Coleman and Rainwater (1978) suggest that there is a "marginal" group within this class—people who don't earn all that much (perhaps $20,000 to $40,000) but who are seen as essentially upper-middle class because of their education or relatively prestigious jobs. Examples include "engineers, college teachers, middle-level civil servants, or researchers" (1978, p. 128).

The Middle-Middle Class

These are what people usually mean when they talk of "average Americans." Some are "people who didn't finish college but are making good money—maybe certain kinds of small businessmen, craftsmen getting top pay, and salesmen of all sorts" (Coleman and Rainwater, 1978, p. 128). Others are slightly less prestigeful but are nevertheless secure and respected. On the white-collar side, they are high school or elementary teachers, accountants, or bank tellers; on the blue-collar side, they tend to be construction foremen, electricians, plumbers, or factory shift supervisors. They tend to earn between $15,000 and $30,000 and live in "respectable," but hardly opulent neighborhoods—such as San Francisco's Richmond District or parts of New York's Borough of Queens.

The Lower-Middle Class

This group is composed of lower-level white-collar workers—clerks, bookkeepers, mailcarriers—and rank-and-file blue-collar employees—factory workers, truckdrivers, automobile mechanics, dockworkers. Although incomes vary (a few very successful truck drivers make well over $30,000, for example), the typical salary ranges between $12,000 and $20,000. Depending on how many children are in the family, these people "get by," but with not much left over. Satirized in the "Archie Bunker" television series, this group often lives in moderately priced neighborhoods in center cities—the South Side of Kansas City or East Boston—or in working-class suburbs like Mipitas, Calif. Many of their neighborhoods are ethnically based—Boston's Irish "Southie" is an example.

The Upper-Lower Class

Whereas the lower-middle class "gets by," this group constantly struggles. They are distinguished from the group above them by possessing fewer skills and less education. They earn roughly between $8,000 and $12,000 and tend to hold jobs like waiter, factory worker in a nonunion plant, hospital attendant, airport baggage operator, janitor, or sales clerk in a hardware store. They live in more tattered neighborhoods than the lower-middle class. Frequently, such neighborhoods are composed of ethnic or racial minorities. The black suburb of Glenarden, near Washington is one example. Nevertheless, as Coleman and Rainwater (1978, p. 129) suggest, despite their low income, this group is working and proud of it (even if they don't love the job). They are usually indignant about those on welfare.

This group, and the lower-middle class, are the American "working class," a group of "forgotten Americans," those who tend to go unnoticed because of all the publicity given to the very wealthy and the very poor. The whites in this group are profiled by sociologist Peter Schrag in Box 5–6.

The Lower-Lower Class

The outstanding characteristic of this group is that the people in it lack regular employment. Such people are likely to live in the poorest or most segregated housing areas, not only because their lack of resources prohibits living in better districts, but because they often are shunned by other groups or are kept out of other areas by active discrimination. Examples of lower-lower class neighborhoods include Chicago's South Side, Los Angeles' Watts, and New York's South Bronx. Most people in this group are poorly educated, a large percentage receive public assistance (welfare), and a great many are black, Puerto Rican, or Hispanic. In terms of life-style, they are the "deprived," the "trapped," and the "disaffiliated" as Herbert Gans (1962) termed them (see Chapter 4). Most make a clear distinction within their ranks between a more prestigious group—"people who are on welfare but keep themselves clean"—and others who are "just dirty—they don't have any pride at all" (Coleman and Rainwater, 1978, p. 130). Frequently, the areas in which these people live are "crime-riddled." The plight of this group is poignantly portrayed in Box 5–7

Box 5–6   AMERICA'S WORKING CLASS: THE "FORGOTTEN AMERICANS"

There is hardly a language to describe him, or even a set of social statistics. Just names: racist-bigot-redneck-ethnic-Irish-Italian-Pole-Honkie-Yahoo. . . . The man . . . who watches the tube, plays the horses, and keeps the niggers out of his union and his neighborhood . . . who cheers when the cops beat up on demonstrators. Who is free, white and twenty-one, has a job, a home, a family, and is up to his eyeballs in credit. In the guise of the working class—or the American yeoman or John Smith—he was once the hero of the civics book, the man that Andrew Jackson called "the bone and sinew of the country." Now he is "the forgotten man," perhaps the most alienated person in America. . . .

Between the slums and suburbs there are South Boston and South San Francisco, Bell and Parma, Astoria and Bay Ridge, Newark, Cicero, Downey, Daly City, Charlestown, Flatbush. Union halls, American legion posts, neighborhood bars and bowling leagues, the Ukrainian Club and the Holy Name. . . . If you look for it, you find it everywhere: the rows of frame houses overlooking the belching steel mills in Bethlehem, Pennsylvania, two-family brick houses in Canarsie (where the most common slogan, even in the middle of a political campaign, is "curb your dog"); the Fords and Chevies with a decal American flag on the rear window (usually a cut-out from the *Reader's Digest,* and displayed in counter-protest against peaceniks and "those bastards who carry Vietcong flags in demonstrations"); the bunting on the porch rail with the inscription, "Welcome Home, Pete." The gold star in the window.

When he was Under Secretary of Housing and Urban Development [in the 1960s], Robert C. Wood tried a definition. It is not good, but it's the best we have:

He is a white employed male . . . earning between $5,000 and $10,-000 [now, more likely double that]. He works regularly, steadily, dependably, wearing a blue collar or white collar. Yet the frontiers of his career expectations have been fixed since he reached the age of thirty-five, when he found that he has too many obligations, too much family, and too few skills to match opportunities with aspirations. . . .

He does all the right things, obeys the law, goes to church, insists—usually—that his kids get a better education than he had. But the right things don't seem to be paying off. While he is making more than he ever made—perhaps more than he'd ever dreamed—he's still struggling while a lot of others—"them" (on welfare, in deomonstrations, in the ghettos)—are getting most of the attention. "I'm working my ass off," a guy tells you on a stoop in South Boston. "My kids don't have a place to swim, my parks are full of glass, and I'm supposed to bleed for a bunch of people on relief." In New York a man who drives a Post Office trailer truck at night (4:00 P.M. to midnight) and a cab during the day (7:00 A.M. to 2:00 P.M.), and who hustles radios for his Post Office buddies on the side, is ready, as he says, to "knock somebody's ass. . . .

Whatever law and order means, for example, to a man who feels his wife is unsafe on the street after dark or in the park at any tine, or whose kids get shaken down in the school yard, it also means something like normality—the demand that everybody play it by the book, that cultural

Source: Peter Schrag, *Out of Place in America* (New York: Random House, 1969), pp. 14–16, 18, 22, 24, 25.

and social standards be somehow re-stored to their civics-book simplicity, that things shouldn't be as they are but as they were supposed to be.

Somewhere in his gut the man in those communities knows that mobility and choice in this society are limited. He cannot imagine any major change for the better; but he can imagine change for the worse. And yet for a decade he is the one who has been asked to carry the burden of social reform, to integrate his schools and his neighborhood, has been asked by comfortable people to pay the social debts due to the poor and the black. In Boston, in San Francisco, in Chicago (not to mention Newark or Oakland) he has been telling the reformers to go to hell. The Jewish school teachers of New York and the Irish parents of Dorchester have asked the same question: "What the hell did [New York Mayor] John Lindsay (or the Beacon Hill Establishment) ever do for us?" . . .

Some men leave their sons money (wrote a union member to the *New York Times*), and some investments, some business connections, and some a profession. I have only one worthwhile thing to give: my trade. I hope to follow a centuries-old tradition and sponsor my sons for an apprenticeship. For this simple father's wish it is said that I discriminate against Negroes. Don't all of us discriminate? Which of us . . . will not choose a son over all others? . . .

The conditions of trauma and frustration in the middle. What does it take to be a good American? . . .

Some of the poorest people in America are white, native, and have lived all of their lives in the same place as their fathers and grandfathers. The problems that were presumably solved in some distant past, in that era before the textbooks were written —problems of assimilation, of upward mobility—now turn out to be very much unsolved. The melting pot and all: millions made it, millions moved to the affluent suburbs; several million—no one knows how many—did not.

which describes Lutie Johnson's Harlem, an area of New York that is almost exclusively black. Although written nearly four decades ago, the passages accurately describe the contemporary situation of many of America's poorest, particularly those of minority status.

IS SOCIAL STRATIFICATION INEVITABLE?

We began this chapter with a series of observations and statistics that suggested the all-pervasiveness of social stratification. In all societies that we could easily think of, society's members are distinguished by differing amounts of wealth, power, and prestige, and the amenities of life that accompany these attributes. This statement is as true of communist societies, such as the Soviet Union and the People's Republic of China, as it is of capitalist societies, such as the United States. Although communist societies have made some clear progress at redistributing wealth among members of their population, they have been less successful at redistributing power and prestige. Moreover, anthropologists, in

Box 5–7 "THE STREETS OF HARLEM" LUTIE JOHNSON'S AMERICA

A man came suddenly out of a hallway just ahead of her—a furtive, darting figure that disappeared rapidly in the darkness of the street. As she reached the doorway from which he had emerged, a woman lurched out, screaming, "Got my pocketbook! The bastard's got my pocketbook!"

Windows were flung open all up and down the street. Heads appeared at the window—silent, watching heads that formed dark blobs against the dark spaces that were the windows. The woman remained in the middle of the street, bellowing at the top of her voice.

Lutie got a good look at her as she went past her. She had a man's felt hat pulled down almost over her eyes and men's shoes on her feet. Her coat was fastened together with safety pins. She was shaking her fists as she shouted curses after the man who had long since vanished up the street.

Ribald advice issued from the windows:

"Aw, shut up! Folks got to sleep."

"What the hell'd you have in it, your rent money?"

"Go on home, old woman, fore I throw somp'n special down on your rusty head."

As the woman's voice died away to a mumble and a mutter, the heads withdrew and the windows were slammed shut. The street was quiet again. And Lutie thought, no one could live on a street like this and stay decent. It would get them sooner or later, for it sucked the humanity out of people—slowly, surely, inevitably.

She glanced up at the gloomy apartments where the heads had been. There were row after row of narrow windows—floor after floor packed tight with people. She looked at the street itself. It was bordered by garbage cans. Half-starved cats prowled through the cans—rustling paper, gnawing on bones. Again she thought that it wasn't just this one block, this particular street. It was like this all over Harlem wherever the rents were low. . . .

Streets like the one she lived on were no accident. They were the North's lynch mobs, she thought bitterly; the method the big cities used to keep Negroes in their place. And she began thinking of Pop unable to get a job; of Jim slowly disintegrating because he, too, couldn't get a job, and of the subsequent wreck of their marriage; of Bub left to his own devices after school. From the time she was born, she had been hemmed into an ever-narrowing space, until now she was very nearly walled in and the wall had been built up brick by brick by eager white hands.

Source: Ann Petry, *The Street* (Boston: Houghton Mifflin, 1946), pp. 228–229, 324–325.

their myriad studies of societies, large and small worldwide, have not given us much reason for thinking that some unequal distribution of wealth, power, and prestige does not exist in *all* societies.

The conclusion seems clear, then: Some form of social stratification appears to take place in *all* human societies. But, in addition, something else should be emphasized. Although social stratification of some sort may be inevitable, the detrimental and dehumanizing effects of distinguishing people in terms of wealth, power, and prestige *are almost entirely a product of the particular culture of a society and the values and practices of its members.*

Giving power to different qualified individuals is often reasonable: It allows the group to attain its goals more easily. But to use power to *dominate* another human being, or to keep that person from getting enough to eat or living in a particular neighborhood is not so reasonable. It is self-serving in the worst sense and destructive of the lives of others.

In other words, we frequently use our wealth, power, and prestige to advance ourselves at the expense of others. Recall, in the statistics given at the beginning of this chapter, that, in terms of percentages, more American blacks were poor when compared with American whites. Consider as well that most blacks, despite progress in the past two decades, still live in segregated neighborhoods. Why? Don't blacks have as much of a chance to make money and live where they want as whites? After all, these are the 1980s, not the 1880s. Perhaps the basic problems still remain. As Box 5–8 indicates, in the late mid-1970s racial discrimination in housing was "alive and well" in America. Do you think it has disappeared by now?

Considering income, an even more interesting situation emerges. President Reagan's administration, in an attempt to balance the budget and finance other priorities (e.g., the military), has cut various domestic programs in recent years. Although probably not consciously designed to hurt the poor, elderly, and minorities the most, this is exactly what such cutbacks have done. Thus a report made public by the Congressional Budget Office indicated

---

Box 5–8   RACIAL DISCRIMINATION IN HOUSING

Segregation practices . . . are subtle but no less effective than those of former years. Sociologist Diana Pearce investigated real estate practices in a 1974–1975 study of the Detroit area. Pearce sent black and white couples posing as buyers to a random sample of about one hundred real estate firms, 87 percent of them in Detroit suburbs. Although the couples gave nearly identical income and family information to the real estate brokers, Pearce found that the salespersons showed homes to three of four white couples, but only one of four black couples. Further, when blacks and whites were taken to see houses, they were taken to different areas. This is known as "racial steering." . . .

I know this from personal experience. In 1963, after completing my Ph.D. and receiving a faculty appointment at Michigan State University, I attempted to buy a home in East Lansing. Although I had a job and an adequate income, I was not able to find anyone willing to sell a home to a black family. It was not until I had filed suit against three realty firms and had received indifferent to hostile treatment from many East Lansing residents that I was finally able to purchase a home.

Source: Robert L. Green, *The Urban Challenge: Poverty and Race* (Chicago: Follett, 1977), pp. 164–165.

that program cutbacks in 1984 would reduce benefits for those in the "below $10,000" income range by $430 per person. In the $10,000 to $20,000 range the reduction would be $300 per person; and in the "above $20,000" range, the reduction would only be $140 to $170. More specifically, the budget cuts sliced income security programs such as food stamps and housing assistance by about 10 percent, reduced education and social service programs by 18 percent, and cut employment programs by 60 percent (*Finger Lakes Times*, August 22, 1983, p. 1). To put it another way, although the rich didn't get directly richer by such budget cuts, the poor certainly got poorer, aggravating further their already disadvantageous position in society. In addition, since a greater proportion of the black population are recipients of such programs, the cuts hurt America's blacks more than America's whites.

The key fact here is the result of such actions. Whether or not intended, they have augmented the inequities of social class in America. It *doesn't* have to be this way, unless we *want* it to be. Social stratification may be to some degree inevitable in human societies, but the manipulation of its central variables (wealth, power, and prestige) to the advantage of some and the disadvantage of others is, more often than not, up to the members of society themselves.

SUMMARY

One of the most important characteristics of social structure is the widespread presence of social stratification. Stratification refers to a ranked set of categories reflecting inequality in the things that society considers valuable.

Karl Marx gave early direction to the study of social stratification, arguing that social ranking was an outgrowth of economic forces and the relationship of the individual or group to ownership of property and the means of production. For Marx, social classes were defined as aggregates of persons who performed essentially the same activities in daily life. Furthermore, each class was characterized by a distinct class consciousness, an awareness among its members of their place in the social stratification system. In capitalist societies, for example, there existed two classes fundamentally in competition with one another: the bourgeoisie, whose members owned most of the property and means of production in the society, and the proletariat, whose members owned neither of these things.

Max Weber advanced on Marx's system by contending that there are three characteristics that determine stratification: wealth, social honor (or prestige), and power. Weber's conception of social ranking recognized that several social strata might exist and also took into account that any of the three characteristics may affect one another and may not coincide.

Two conflicting perspectives of the effects of wealth, prestige, and power in modern society are those of C. Wright Mills and David Riesman. Mills argued that these characteristics coalesced in a special high status group of military, industrial, and political leaders that he called the power elite. This group essentially controlled all the major decisions of the society because of their influential position. Riesman, on the other hand, argued for a more pluralistic vision of decision making in American society. He suggested that decisions were made in a continuing series of negotiations and compromises between leaders and their constituencies at all levels of modern society.

The concept of social mobility summarizes the dynamic aspects of stratification. Vertical mobility refers to any upward or downward change in the rank of an individual or group along the lines of wealth, prestige, or power. Horizontal mobility refers to a change in position at the same level of wealth, power, or prestige.

Closely associated with social stratification is the concept of status. The two main types are ascribed status, position determined by inherited or developmental characteristics; and achieved status, position determined by behavior. All societies make use of ascribed status in determining social position to some extent and some put a great deal of emphasis on achieved status as well.

The three main approaches to the study of stratification are the reputational, the subjective, and the objective. The reputational method asks respondents to evaluate the members of their community in terms of wealth, power, or prestige. The subjective approach asks the community members to rank themselves on dimensions of stratification. The objective method requires that the investigator make all decisions concerning the placement of individuals based on criteria that presumably measure the amount of wealth, power, and prestige held by a person or group.

Modern sociological research indicates that there are seven main social class divisions in America, ranging from the upper-upper class (the true "blueblood aristocracy") to the lower-lower class (people living in this country's worst slums). Members of each of these groups are characterized by varying amounts of wealth, power, and prestige, although the possession of such characteristics does not always ensure an "absolute" position in society. Thus some truckdrivers may have a fair amount of wealth but still belong to the lower-middle class, whereas some rabbis or priests may have little wealth but still may be considered as members of the upper-middle class.

Is social stratification inevitable? After a consideration of our own and other societies, we concluded that, to a certain degree, it was. However, we also concluded that the excesses of stratification—the instances where wealth, power, and prestige are utilized to dominate and dehumanize other people—were *not* inevitable but, rather, were a product of a given culture and discriminatory practices by some of society's members against others.

QUESTIONS, EXERCISES, PROJECTS

1. Briefly summarize the Marxian view of social stratification.
2. Identify Weber's three dimensions of social ranking and indicate the implications of Weber's analysis for stratification.
3. Define and illustrate the two types of social mobility.
4. Identify the ascribed-status and the achieved-status characteristics in the following resume:

   Name: Martin Spinelli
   Age: 62
   Sex: Male
   Education: Parsons University (B.S. in Economics)
   Work Experience: Bank Teller and Assistant Manager
                       Personnel Manager
                       Director of Marketing

5. Does social ranking influence how a person is eulogized after death? Using any of the schemes suggested in this chapter, categorize the occupational prestige of individuals in their obituaries. For this exercise use the obituary column of any local newspaper. Do your results suggest that certain social class positions are better represented than others, or are all social rankings equally represented?
6. In what ways does ascribed status influence your way of life now and your future opportunities?
7. Define and illustrate the three approaches to the study of social stratification.
8. Using your hometown as an example, classify its various social classes. Use the model provided in the chapter—ranging from upper-upper class to lower-lower class—as a guide. Are all classes represented? If not, why not? Are wealth, power, and prestige always "high" with the uppermost classes and "low" with the lowermost?
9. Is social stratification inevitable? Discuss, once again using your hometown as an example.

SOCIAL INSTITUTIONS

In Chapter 4 we indicated that there are some extremely important characteristics of social structure that would demand more detailed treatment because of their widespread influence in the everyday life of most societies. Social stratification, which we dealt with in Chapter 5, was one such characteristic. Yet another is represented in the phenomena known as social institutions— which include the economy, the family, education, religion, the political system, the military, health services, and the media.

We may define **social institutions** as the representative ways that any of society's members have developed to solve certain core human problems. **Core human problems,** in turn, are those problems that demand social answers for the continued existence of any society. The answers provided by each society to each of these problems result in a social institution.

THE ECONOMY

How do we get the material resources—food, water, and shelter —to ensure our physical survival? This *basic needs problem* cannot be avoided if the members of a society are to stay alive. Consequently, the people of a society must establish some pattern of behavior that leads to the procurement of the material necessities of life. Exactly what means each society will use to procure these necessities, however, can vary widely, depending on such factors

social institutions The representative ways that society's members have developed to solve certain core human problems.

core human problems Those problems that demand social answers for the continued existence of any society.

as climate, physical environment, type of plant and animal life available, as well as the social preferences of the members of the society.

For example, one society may decide that the most efficient way of procuring food and clothing is to be nomadic, following game as it moves from place to place seasonally. Another society in the same type of environment might decide instead to stay by a single water source, build permanent shelters, and procure the necessary food and clothing by agriculture and herding.

Once a decision has been made about the proper way to procure material necessities, however, it is likely to become a norm for most (if not all) members of the society, and it is likely to be taught to new generations. As soon as this normative aspect of the solution to the basic needs problem develops, we have the beginnings of the social institution we call **the economy.**

the economy The social institution that provides the answer to the basic needs problem by developing ways of procuring the material necessities of life.

However, institutions are usually more complex than our example indicates. For instance, not only does a society have to decide on a general "how-to" orientation regarding the procurement of the material necessities of life (such as the decision to be nomadic or sedentary), it also has to provide answers to other questions as well: For example, will the people of a society compete or cooperate with one another? When is the best time to procure the material necessities—each day, once a week, or only during certain seasons? Which people in society will procure the basic material necessities—all of them, the men only, the women only, the upper-class people, the lower-class people? And, what is the best set of techniques and artifacts to be used in procuring the basic necessities?

As each of the additional aspects of the basic needs problem is resolved for any given society, the economic institution gets more complex and is likely to touch on all other aspects of social structure—the roles of the sexes, the expectations for different social classes, the way people organize their daily routines, and so on. To make the institution even more complicated, most societies produce at least some members who take on certain economic activities as their life's work—people, for example, who become herders exclusively, or the makers of the tools used in agriculture. Or, if the society is large and complex enough, there may be people who obtain medical training and care only for others who have physiological brain disorders (neurosurgeons), people who teach the young about the science of social interaction (sociologists and anthropologists), or people who make other peoples' "time off" from economic pursuits more enjoyable by providing them with entertainment (dramatists, film and television personnel), and so on.

This whole process of the development and assignment of different specialized activities to different groups of people in society is called a **division of labor.** Societies may be studied comparatively according to the degree of specialization they have attained in their division of labor. The United States, for example, would rate very high on a specialization of economic activities scale, whereas the three societies described in Chapter 3, the Arapesh, the Mundugumor, and the Tchambuli would rate relatively low.

division of labor The assignment of different specialized activities to different groups of people in society.

The Development of a Growth Economy and the Market System in Modern Society

Perhaps the most important distinction that can be made for an understanding of the modern economic order of Western societies is that between a **subsistence economy** and a **growth economy.** The former can be defined as an economy where people work as hard as is necessary to produce the materials necessary for satisfying their basic needs and then devote the rest of their activity to other pursuits with a similar degree of interest—such as religious, familial, or political activities. In other words, as Robert Heilbroner has put it in speaking of medieval society, "economics [is] a subordinate and not a dominant aspect of life" (1968, p. 36).

subsistence economy An economy where people work as hard as is necessary to produce the material resources of life and then devote the rest of their time to other pursuits.

growth economy An economy where people work harder in procuring the material resources of life than is necessary for mere subsistence.

In a growth economy, on the other hand, the economic activities of a population become the dominant role that people play in their day-to-day lives, with other activities assuming a lesser part of their commitments and energy. Beginning toward the end of the Middle Ages, this crucial change from a subsistence economy to a growth economy began to develop in Western society. Let us briefly examine how this crucial change developed.

From the fall of the Roman Empire in the fifth century, European society had been characterized by an economic "arrangement" known as feudalism. As Elbert Bowden describes it:

> Feudalism really isn't an economic system. It's a situation in which there isn't any "nationwide" economic system. There isn't any "nation," really—just a lot of little independent political-economic units . . . each operating almost entirely on its own. . . . Almost all of the production and distribution choices were determined by the rules of the society, but as interpreted, enforced, and sometimes modified by the lord of the manor. People were bound to the manor where they were born. They produced the things they were supposed to produce—usually the things their fathers before them had produced—and they received their traditionally established just shares of the food and other things. (1974, pp. 13–14)

As can be readily grasped from this description, feudalism is an economic order grounded in tradition, nonchange, and subsistence pure and simple. Although it dominated the European landscape for close to a thousand years, various forces eventually began to coalesce that would undermine its viability as an economic arrangement. Heilbroner (1968, Chapter 3) suggests some of these forces. First, a group of itinerant merchants began to make important economic and cultural connections between feudal estates and towns beginning in the eighth and ninth centuries. Not only did these merchants entice their clients with wares from far-off places, they began to structure a tight web of permanent trade relations across the continent. Second, as new goods poured into the feudal estates, more people were attracted to the estates as places to live. This population growth resulted in towns developing into cities—the process of **urbanization**—and brought a veritable "explosion" of new ideas and interests into medieval life. Third, this burgeoning social life was stimulated greatly by the returning Crusaders who, in their travels to the Holy Land, had encountered the vital, open market cities of the Middle East with all their riches.

urbanization The process of increasing population and trade that transforms villages and towns into cities.

Fourth, to the merchants in the changing medieval cities, it became obvious that their goal of a better economic system could be furthered greatly if they were in alliance with other political districts. Hence a gradual tendency developed for centralized political units to form—the process of **nationalization**—with the corresponding breakdown of the autonomy of the previous feudal estates. This, of course, made large-scale trading easier and affected many more people than had previously been the case.

nationalization The process that transformed previously scattered political units into centralized political units.

Fifth, as nationalization progressed, so did the desire of each nation to provide the greatest economic benefits for itself. This led to a process of national exploration, settlement, and annexation of foreign lands—the process of **colonization**. Sixth, this great increment in economic activity meant that the traditional means of exchange, trade, was rendered more and more inefficient. In its place a reliance developed on a more generalized medium of exchange, money, which afforded economic actors much more freedom in purchasing power and in debt payment than had previously been possible. Finally, and perhaps most importantly from a sociological point of view, a set of religious ideas developed —specifically, those of Protestantism—which provided the moral legitimation for people to engage in an enterprising economic life. (We shall develop in greater detail the important connection between the modern economic order and Protestantism when we deal with specific theories of social change in Chapter 8.)

colonization The process of exploration, settlement, and annexation of foreign lands to a parent nation.

As all these processes fused, the transition to a growth economy was effected. Its hallmark was the **market system,** which was organized around a rather different set of economic relationships than

market system An economic arrangement characterized by individual initiative, the profit motive, competition, and a focus on the general wants of consumers.

those of the previous feudal system. In the first place, individual workers were no longer bound to lords and manors as they had been. Rather, they were able to sell their labor skills to whomever would pay the highest wages. Second, as a result of this incentive, the profit motive came into being—the attempt by each person engaged in economic activity to be paid enough so that not only could the basic material necessities of life be afforded, but other items of a comfortable life—stylish clothes or religious artifacts, for example—could be purchased. Third, under these conditions, economic activities became increasingly competitive. That is, because people were now striving for profits, it was inevitable that the better paying positions went to the more skilled individuals; hence individual workers had to outdo each other in some way to get the greatest economic benefits. Finally, the market system was characterized by a shift from a "necessities only" orientation to an economic orientation stressing "wants"—that is, an orientation toward producing the myriad different commodities or services that people may develop a desire for when their basic needs are satisfied.

The key fact about the development of the market system is that, over time, it affected more and more people, resulting in a rising standard of living relative to basic needs for a greater proportion of the population than had previously been the case. This mechanism set the stage for the Industrial Revolution and the development of our modern economic order, a topic to which we now turn.

The Industrial Revolution and the Modern Economic Order.

Although **industrialism** —the process of manufacturing similar goods, such as clothing, machinery, dishes, in large quantities for consumption—had existed in Western society to a very limited degree before the eighteenth century, it was only after the market system had been adopted on a large scale that it began to grow in influence. For all intents and purposes, large-scale industrialism— and, consequently, the Industrial Revolution—began in England about 1750.

Heilbroner (1968, pp. 74–75) suggests that one important reason that English society proved so amenable to industrialism was the English penchant, particularly evident in the upper-middle classes, for engineering and guiding economic activities by the most scientific methods available. Even more importantly, if efficient methods were not available, many innovative Englishmen invented them.

Perhaps the most famous and important example of an invention that changed the economic order was James Watt's invention

industrialism The process of manufacturing goods, such as clothing, dishes, etc., in large quantities for consumption.

of the steam engine. This machine, perfected by 1775, had literally hundreds of applications—from textile manufacturing to flour mills to the mass production of the common pin. Its ability to save hand labor and to contribute to the mass production of items was nothing short of remarkable; it took very little time for entrepreneurs to put it into widespread use. By 1781, for example, Matthew Boulton, Watt's partner in a steam engine manufacturing company was claiming that "the people of London, Birmingham, and Manchester [are] all 'steam mill mad' " (Heilbroner, 1968, pp. 76–77). From then on, the Industrial Revolution was in full force. Other inventions, such as Arkwright's spinning jenny and Maudslay's automatic screw machine, revolutionized areas of production. "The Revolution . . . fed upon itself. The new techniques . . . simply destroyed their handicraft competition around the world and thus enormously increased their own markets" (Heilbroner, 1968, p. 75). Throughout the nineteenth and twentieth centuries industrialism has spread enormously in most Western societies (see Box 6–1).

There is no doubt that industrialism has brought more adequate satisfaction of the basic needs problem to more people in Western society than any other economic arrangement of the past. For example, in the latter half of the twentieth century, most members of American society have better quality and quantity of food,

---

Box 6–1 GROWTH OF THE AUTOMOBILE INDUSTRY

Here is just one example of how massive the growth of one contemporary industry has been and how it has deeply affected the functioning of our entire society.

[In] 1905 there were 121 establishments making automobiles [in the United States], and 10,000 wage earners were employed in the industry. By 1923 the number of plants had risen to 2,471, making the industry the largest in the country. In 1960 its annual payroll was as large as the national income of the United States in 1890. Not only that, but the automobile industry had become the single greatest customer for sheet metal, zinc, lead, rubber, leather. It was the buyer of one out of every three radios produced in the nation. It absorbed twenty-five billion pounds of chemicals a year. It was the second largest user of engineering talent in the country, bowing only to national defense. It was the source of one-sixth of all patents issued in the nation and the object of one-tenth of all consumer spending in the country. In fact, it has been estimated that no less than one job out of every seven and one business out of every six owed their existences directly or indirectly to the car. . . . [Moreover] because of the existence of the car, some fifty thousand towns managed to flourish without rail or water connections. . . . (Heilbroner, 1968, p. 97)

water, clothing, and shelter and have better medical and dental care than was the case even a few decades ago. The result has been that many of us live longer and healthier lives.

This generally high and continuing level of economic prosperity is reflected in the following statistics. For example, in 1960 the average per capita "disposable" (i.e., what's left after taxes) income of all Americans was $1,947. Comparatively, in 1970, it was $3,390, and in 1980 it was $8,012. Although this growth is not so great as it seems because of the effects of inflation, the same pattern emerges when we consider disposable personal income in "constant" dollars, that is, dollar figures controlled for inflation by picking one year's dollar worth as the constant referent point. Thus when 1972 dollars were used as the reference point, disposable personal income per capita in the United States was $2,709 in 1960, $3,665 in 1970, and $4,472 in 1980 (*Statistical Abstract of the United States, 1982–83,* p. 421).

Problems with the Modern Economic Order: Some Examples.

Despite widespread economic prosperity, however, industrialism has not brought with it uniformly positive benefits. One clearly evident drawback, for example, that may in the long run threaten the existence of the entire planet, has been the massive depletion and waste of the earth's natural resources. Another is the increasing pollution of much of the environment to levels that threaten the health produced by the Industrial Revolution. Whether our national awareness of the severity of these problems, or our desire to do something about them, is sufficiently developed to curtail the continuing rape of the planet by industry is not clear at the present time.

It is not at all difficult to see why we might "drag our feet" on environmental issues. For example, one of the great depleters of our resources and pollutors of our environment is the automotive industry (see Box 6–1). Yet, because the automotive industry has a tremendous influence on our entire economic order, to make major changes in that industry would upset the many relationships that industry has with all its related industries and customers to some degree. Clearly, this would involve jobs changing, profits being redistributed, massive inconvenience and increased costs for those relying on the automobile for fast transportation, and perhaps the elimination of certain industries altogether (e.g., if we changed to a steam engine for automobiles, still a possibility, what would happen to the massive oil industry?). Consequently, out-and-out resistance, delay tactics, or total lack of interest are the attitudes many Americans assume toward forcing the automotive industry to change its relationship to the environment.

Other problems associated with the industrial order affect

The steam engine (top) invented by James Watt in the late Eighteenth Century, revolutionized the economy of most Western nations. The power it provided at very cheap cost made the mass production of goods a reality rather than a dream. Our entire modern economy is based on the mass-production ability of machines (bottom).

human interaction more directly. Factory life, from the beginning, has been fraught with many disadvantageous conditions,
from excessive work weeks to the exploitation of child labor to, in
the contemporary context, the sheer boredom that results from
doing the same repetitive job day-in-and-day-out many years running.

To some extent, these problems have been lessened by the
development of trade unions which have real bargaining power
with management. Over the years, trade unions, with their ability
to effect work slowdowns or even work stoppage by striking have
been able to provide greater benefits in pay, work hours, and
illness and retirement compensation for their members. However,
although these solutions are helpful in the short run, they themselves feed into an ever-spiraling inflation rate. Management,
forced to meet demands of industry, is in turn forced to raise
prices to consumers. In time, this means that consumers must
make more money to purchase the same amount of goods, and
hence more demands develop for increased wages, and so on—ad
infinitum it seems.

A third problem affects middle- and upper-middle-class populations. In recent decades, because of the spread of industrialism to
many new areas of the world, American industry has had to face
stiff competition—the competition with Japanese radios, TVs, and
stereo equipment is one example. Such competition has meant
that American industries could be more competitive if they controlled all the supply industries for their products. Thus a widespread tendency has developed for amalgamation with other industries, the result being the development of massive
corporations.

Because these corporations pursue goals and produce end products that are often far removed from the direct interests or jobs
of people working within the industry at various levels, a vision has
arisen of many modern employees being highly alienated from
their work. This image of a contemporary "organization man,"
first developed by William Whyte in the 1950s, suggests an employee working without interest in a job and with no ability to
change the conditions of that job. This image persists into the
present as shown in Box 6–2.

Finally, there is a problem that refuses to go away, even in the
most affluent times—namely, the fact that widespread poverty
exists in American society despite the plenty. We saw some of the
evidence concerning American poverty in Chapter 5, in our consideration of social stratification. To examine the existence of poverty another way, consider total income of the country. In 1980
the wealthiest 60 percent of American families—those making
$17,390 and above—accounted for 83.4 percent of all income

Box 6–2   CORPORATE ALIENATION

The following excerpt from Joseph Heller's novel, *Something Happened,* illustrates the alienation felt by many corporation executives from the whole process of the corporation:

> All these twelve men (who run the corporation) are elderly now and drained by time and success of energy and ambition. Many have spent their whole lives here. They seem friendly, slow, and content when I come upon them in the halls (they seem dead) and are always courteous and mute when they ride with others in the public elevators. They no longer work hard. They hold meetings, make promotions, and allow their names to be used on announcements that are prepared and issued by somebody else. Nobody is sure anymore who really runs the company (not even the people who are credited with running it), but the company does run . . .
>
> Every two weeks we are paid with machine-processed checks manufactured out of stiff paper (they are not thick enough to be called cardboard) that are patterned precisely with neat, rectangular holes and words of formal, official warning in small, black, block letters that the checks must not be spindled, torn, defaced, stapled, or mutilated in any other way. (They must only be cashed.) If not for these words, it would never occur to me to do anything else with my check but deposit it. Now, though, I am occasionally intrigued. What would happen, I speculate gloomily every two weeks or so as I tear open the blank, buff pay envelope and stare dully at the holes and numbers and words on my punched-card paycheck as though hoping disappointedly for some large, unrectifiable mistake in my favor, if I did spindle, fold, tear, deface, staple, and mutilate it? (It's my paycheck, isn't it? or is it?) What would happen if, deliberately, calmly, and with malice aforethought and obvious premeditation, I disobeyed?
>
> I know what would happen: nothing. Nothing would happen. And the knowledge depresses me. Some girl downstairs I never saw before . . . would simply touch a few keys on some kind of steel key punch that would set things right again, and it would be as though I had not disobeyed at all. My act of rebellion would be absorbed like rain on an ocean and leave no trace. I would not cause a ripple.

Source: Joseph Heller, *Something Happened* (New York: Knopf, 1974) pp. 13, 18–19. Copyright © 1966, 1974 by Scapegoat Productions, Inc. Reprinted by permission of Alfred A. Knopf, Inc.

earned in that year. That left the bottom 40 percent of America's families to share only 16.6 percent of the remaining available income. Even more distressing, the bottom 20 percent of the population—those families earning less than $10,286—had to make do with only 5.1 percent of the country's income! (Hacker, 1983, p. 144).

A full examination of the reasons for such widespread poverty in our society is impossible here. However, whatever factors are at work, the division of modern society into the "haves" and the "have nots" has to be clearly linked to the tendency of capital to accumulate more rapidly in the hands of those who have it than in the hands of those who do not. As noted by Hacker (1983) 42 percent of the national income was earned by only 20 percent of the families. To make the point even more strongly, the *Statistical Abstract of the United States, 1982–83* (p. 449) indicates that 20.7 percent of the total national *wealth* (income plus savings plus property holdings) is controlled by only 1 percent of the population!

This tendency of capital to accumulate in the hands of a few has long been of theoretical and practical concern. Karl Marx, for example, spent most of his life working out a detailed critique of, and solution to the problem (see Chapters 5 and 8). More recently, our own government has introduced various measures designed to keep this "accumulation factor" under control. For instance, to keep corporations from controlling an entire market—which would allow the corporations to set prices at any level they wish —antitrust legislation has been introduced. On another front, the graduated income tax has attempted to take a greater proportion of annual income from those who make more profit than from those who make less profit, and the welfare system—a true attempt to redistribute income—has tried to provide monies for the disadvantaged poor. Yet, to a greater or lesser degree, all these attempts have failed? Why?

The reason, suggests Herbert Gans (1973), is because, at bottom, we really both need and want an impoverished class to keep our society going in the manner to which we have become accustomed. More bluntly, Gans argues that in a highly stratified society based on economic competition, someone always has to be "at the bottom" (see Box 6–3). As long as the majority is not, society feels that it is a small price to pay for continued economic prosperity.

In support of his thesis Gans lists what he considers to be the *positive* functions of poverty: positive for the majority of society's members, that is; certainly not for the poor. Here we consider only a few: First, the existence of a poor class of people, with no economic independence, ensures that the "dirty work" of society— such things as garbage collection, manual labor, servant jobs—will be filled by someone. Poor people, if they wish to work at all, literally cannot afford to say "no" to such jobs.

Second, by taking such jobs at extremely low pay, the poor actually subsidize their employers. By paying the lowest wages possible, employers can take the money "saved" and reinvest it in

Box 6–3   THE FUNCTIONS OF POVERTY—IN POETRY

The great English author William Blake, in this excerpt from his poem, "The Human Abstract," goes right to the core of what Herbert Gans was to call the "positive functions of poverty." The stanza is all the more remarkable in that it was written almost two centuries ago; in the 1790s at the beginning of the English industrial revolution:

Pity would be no more
If we did not make somebody poor;
And mercy no more could be
If all were as happy as we.

their business (thus solidifying their hold on their share of the market) or use it for personal enjoyment. As a French writer put it at the beginning of the Industrial Revolution: "To assure and maintain the prosperities of our industries, *it is necessary that the workers should never acquire wealth*" (quoted in Gans, 1972, p. 279; italics our emphasis).

Third, many people in our society make their livings directly from the poor. Various organizations and individuals, such as welfare agencies, the inner-city police, the Salvation Army, pentecostal ministers, prostitutes, and drug dealers "serve" the poor in one way or another. The elimination of poverty would substantially reduce *their* income.

Fourth, poor areas serve as a place where less-qualified members of certain professions can practice—doctors, lawyers, and teachers who are unable to "make it" in the more competitive higher echelons of society. In the same way, the poor are more or less forced "to buy goods which others do not want and thus prolong their economic usefulness, such as day-old bread, fruit and vegetables which would otherwise have to be thrown out, second-hand clothes, and deteriorating automobiles and buildings" (Gans, 1972, p. 279).

Finally, the poor serve a "referencing" function, both for social norms and for positioning within the prestige hierarchy. "The defenders of hard work, thrift, honesty, and monogamy need people who can be accused of being lazy, spendthrift, dishonest, and promiscuous to justify these norms" (Gans, 1972, p. 280). Moreover, claims concerning the poor's supposed "lack of ambition" continue to be made even when all available research contradicts the assertion. Thus sophisticated sociological studies of the poor in Baltimore (Goodwin, 1971), Houston (Davidson and Gates, 1974), and New Orleans (Reissman, 1969) have *all* shown that poorer members of our society—blacks, whites, His-

Gans (see text) argues that poverty has positive functions for some members of society—specifically, those people who are higher up in the status hierarchy than the poor. For example, the rich (bottom) can ride in Cadillacs driven by hired chauffeurs, while the poor (top) must take public transportation or walk. By riding in such luxury, the rich can demonstrate to themselves as well as others how much more "successful" they are than those who must use less auspicious means of transportation.

panics, and Indians alike—have as much of a desire to succeed and work as any other group of Americans. The key differences are: (1) They have fewer jobs for which they are "qualified." (2) The jobs they do have available, as Gans notes, are usually menial and low-paying. (3) They are actively discriminated against in some job markets.

Gans' analysis also gives us additional insight into why so many of the poor (see Chapter 5) are of minority status (black, Hispanic, Indians). They are all groups that have noticeably different racial characteristics from those of white America. If economic discrimination is to be practiced, it is much "easier" to carry it out against people who are noticeably different from oneself. Whatever else blacks and other racial groups do, they cannot change the color of their skin. They can always be singled out. In contrast, by eradicating many of their ethnic, religious and linguistic differences over the years, groups of *white* Americans—Irish, Italians, Jews, Poles, Russians—have been able to assimilate into the mainstream of society and attain many of the benefits of American affluence. The same opportunity is not afforded those with ineradicable racial characteristics, as indicated by the distressing case reported in Box 6–4.

If Gans is right in his analysis, the monetary benefits of our modern economic order are unlikely to be shared equally throughout the population as long as that economic order remains competitive and within a highly stratified society. His conclusions about the existence of poverty in the midst of plenty are: "phenomena like poverty can be eliminated only when they either become sufficiently [problematical] for the affluent (e.g., by high crime rates making their lives miserable even in the suburbs), or when the poor can obtain enough power to change the system of social stratification" (1973, p. 120).

THE FAMILY

Turning from the core human problem of obtaining the material necessities of life, we come to another set of concerns of great magnitude. How can we ensure the reproduction of enough members so that the society can survive? How can we control sexual behavior so that adults will have a moral responsibility for the adequate socialization of children?

Quite obviously, these complex issues, which may be called the love, marriage, and children problems, are capable of equally complex answers. Despite their complexity, however, almost every human society has worked out what, to its members, is a useful set of behaviors related to these problems in the institution known as **the family.**

the family The social institution that provides the answer to the love, marriage, and children problems; usually characterized by a group sharing a common residence and working in economic cooperation.

Box 6-4   RACIAL EPITHETS PAINTED ON MALDEN CHURCH

By Wendy Fox
Contributing Reporter

The three white letters glare from the dark shingled roof of the Imani Temple in Malden.

"KKK."

They're repeated on the doors and windows of the stone and stucco church and they share an outside wall with words like "nigger" and "hell."

Inside the building yesterday, Rev. Thaddeus Wheeler marveled at the gall of the Monday morning vandals—who, he said, must have used a ladder to get to the roof—and said the 25 members of his black Pentecostal congregation are more shocked than angry.

"The Bible teaches there will come times like this and you have to pray for people," he said. "We're not angry. We have to try not to become sick like that."

Sometime Monday between about 2 A.M. and dawn, Malden police said, vandals painted the racial epithets and initials of the Ku Klux Klan on the church. Sgt. Robert Barthelmess said yesterday it's a first for Malden, where the city's 998 blacks constitute about 1.9 percent of the city's 53,386 population.

"We've never had anything racial here," he said. Police found a can of paint and a plastic bag full of paint in the neighborhood near the church, but have no suspects.

Barthelmess and Rev. Wheeler and several neighborhood residents think the painting was done by neighborhood teenagers upset that they haven't been able to use the church lot as a hangout since the Imani Temple rented it last August.

"I think the kids don't want to be moved," Barthelmess said.

"We figure they may resent us being here," Rev. Wheeler said. "At one time, before we opened the church, they had the freedom of sitting on the steps and smoking and drinking."

A resident of the Salem Towers apartment building for the elderly across the street said she was appalled by the vandalism.

"I hope they catch them," said the woman, who is white and didn't want her name used. "It was probably done by kids, but this is awful."

And Julian Corin, a white pharmacist at Faulkner Pharmacy also across from the church said: "It's always been a mixed neighborhood here. They've always gotten along fine as far as I know and I've been here 25 years."

Paul McCarthy walked around the church yesterday, surveying the damage talking to Wheeler. Malden officials have started a one-person vandalism awareness program, and as of last Thursday, McCarthy has been running it.

"It's basically going to be stuff like vandalism in the parks," he said. "Then all of a sudden I got this and I thought oh, boy, it's going to be a hot summer.

"But the problem probably is the kids have nothing to do, this has been their hangout, and who knows if it's racially motivated?"

Rev. Wheeler said the congregation hasn't decided yet how best to remove or paint over the damage, but he's certain the church will stay where it is.

"We're not going to pack up and leave," he said. "This is not against us. It speaks against the people who did it."

Source: Boston Globe, July 7, 1982, p. 24

Murdock's Conception of Family.   Exactly what do we mean by "the family"? In 1949 anthropologist George Murdock studied the family forms of 250 different societies. Based on his observations, Murdock defined the family as ". . . a social group characterized by common residence, economic cooperation, and reproduction. It includes adults of both sexes, at least two of whom maintain a socially approved sexual relationship, and one or more children, own or adopted, of the sexually cohabiting adults" (Murdock, 1949, p. 1).

Murdock argued that the family in some form was universal; that is to say, it could be found in every human society, and it always performed the following functions:

1. Reproduction. In every society the family is responsible for giving birth to children, thereby reproducing the population.
2. Socialization. In every society the family is expected to train and care for the children, so that they might ultimately take their places as "adult members in good standing" of society.
3. Control of sexual relations. In every society the sexual drive is regulated so that sexual relationships between husband and wife are approved and encouraged.
4. Economic cooperation. In all known societies family members engage in a division of labor involving a specialization of economic tasks by sex and age.

Close scrutiny of family arrangements throughout the world, however, has revealed the presence of at least a few family forms that may not fit Murdock's definition. Consider the Nayar of the Malabar Coast of India. Prior to 1792, Nayar men served as mercenary soldiers who frequently left their villages in order to wage war against neighboring peoples. As a result, family life among the Nayar failed to include the maintenance of a common residence or sustained sexual relations between husband and wife. For all practical purposes, the Nayar family system lacked a father as a continuing member. Instead, Nayar men were required to reside with their wives for only a few days during their marriage ceremony, after which time there were no further obligations for shared living arrangements or sexual relations. Married Nayar women legitimately engaged in sexual relations with "visiting husbands." Biological fathers had no economic, social, legal, or ritual obligations to their children (Adams, 1971; Gough, 1974).

Another possible exception to Murdock's conception of family forms is the case of the Israeli kibbutzim, where many of the functions usually identified with the family institution are performed instead by the community as a whole. According to Spiro (1956), husband and wife do not have primary responsibility for the care and the socialization of the children of the kibbutz; such tasks are performed instead by specialized teachers and nurses in communal child-care centers and schools. Also at variance with Murdock's conception of family life is Spiro's observation that the entire kibbutz community rather than the family is the basic economic unit. All economic activities are carried out on behalf of the community as a whole: Women take their turns cooking for all members of the kibbutz and not just for their husbands; men work to produce goods and services for the kibbutz community and not exclusively for their wives.

Finally, consider our own society today. In the last 20 years the divorce rate in the United States has skyrocketed. In 1960 that rate was 2.2 per 1,000 (i.e., "2.2" Americans per 1,000 in the population were divorced); in 1970 it was 3.5 per 1,000; and in 1980 it was 5.2 per 1,000 (Hacker, 1983, p. 106). This means that more and more Americans with children are living without a member of the opposite sex present. Although Murdock would certainly not see this as problematical according to his definition, such changes have certainly altered the way *we* define "family" in this country (See Box 6–5.) Consider as well that the number of homosexual couples with children is also increasing. Typically, what happens is that one person in a marriage gets divorced, takes the children, and starts living with a member of the *same* sex. Certainly, in this person's eyes they have a family, but Murdock's definition would not accord them such a status.

Variations in Family Structure. Whether or not it is universal, the family is undoubtedly an important institution in most societies. Very clearly, family life varies in many respects from culture to culture. In our own society, for example, the predominant family unit is the **nuclear family** consisting of wife, husband, and their children. In many other societies, however, the nuclear family is merely a part of a larger **extended family** unit consisting of "blood" relatives and their nuclear families. In the extended family organization three or more generations are involved. For example, an extended family might include grandparents, parents, and children, all living together in the same household or neighborhood.

The acceptable forms of marriage also vary widely from society to society. In American society **monogamy** is the rule, meaning that men and women are permitted to have only one marriage partner at a time. By contrast, many societies practice some form of **polygamy**, where marriage involves more than one man or woman. There are two types of polygamy: **polygyny** where one man may have more than one wife, and **polyandry** where one woman may have more than one husband.

nuclear family A family unit consisting of a husband and a wife and their children.

extended family A family unit consisting of numerous blood relatives and their nuclear families.

monogamy A form of marriage where the man and woman are permitted only one marriage partner at a time.

polygamy A form of marriage where one or both partners are permitted other marriage partners.

polygyny A form of marriage where the man is permitted more than one wife.

polyandry A form of marriage where the woman is permitted more than one husband.

neolocal A family residence pattern where the married couple does not live with either set of parents but resides alone in an independent household.

patrilocal A family residence pattern where the married couple resides with the husband's family.

matrilocal A family residence pattern where the married couple resides with the wife's parents.

patrilineal A descent system where descent is recognized through the father's family line.

matrilineal A descent system where descent is recognized through the mother's family line.

bilateral A descent system where descent is recognized through both the mother's and the father's family line.

Family forms also vary with respect to the place of residence of the married couple. In American society the pattern is typically **neolocal** —husband and wife do not live with either set of parents but reside by themselves in an independent household. In many other societies the pattern of residence is **patrilocal**, where husband and wife reside with the husband's parents, or **matrilocal**, where husband and wife reside with the wife's parents.

Finally, in a similar manner, family forms may also vary by society depending on how they recognize legitimate descent lines. For example, many societies recognize descent only through the father's family line. This is a **patrilineal** descent system. In such a society children would be likely to be named after a member of their father's family, to know many if not all the father's near relatives well, and to inherit the wealth, prestige, and power of the father's family line. In such a system the mother's family names, relatives, and symbols of social achievement would be likely to be deemphasized in the child's upbringing.

On the other hand, many other societies recognize descent as legitimate only when it is considered through the mother's family line. This is a **matrilineal** descent system and in such a system the reverse of the situation just described as being characteristic of the patrilineal system would apply.

The third major descent alternative is a **bilateral** descent system. As the name implies, this type of descent reckoning sees both

Marriage ceremonies in different cultures vary even more than family structure. Note the different styles of dress and the different degrees of solemnity in the above photographs. The one on the left depicts a marriage in the United States, the one on the right a marriage in Southeast Asia.

the mother's and father's family lines as important heritages for children. Such a system is characteristic of most modern Western societies, our own included. Offspring of a family in a bilateral system would be likely in the normal case to know both sets of relatives fairly well and to inherit symbols (or lack thereof) of social achievement from both sides of the family. Normally as well, children of such families bear first and middle names that may be linked to either side of the family tree. Moreover, with the spread of the women's movement (see Chapter 7), there is an increasing tendency for women to keep their original family name after marriage or acknowledge it by a hyphenated last name. Children of such marriages often carry hyphenated last names as well, emphasizing more concretely their bilateral descent.

Nevertheless, worldwide there is no doubt that marital arrangements tend to give the males of society more prestige, power, and wealth. Just why this inequitable state of affairs might exist is discussed in Box 6–6.

Changes in the American Family. At about the same time that large-scale industrialization was taking hold in American life in

Box 6-5 ANN LANDERS

The Modern Wedding Party

Dear Ann Landers:

First, let me say I sent away for your "New Bride's Guide" the very day you mentioned it in your column and it is well worth the $2. A few weeks later I clipped a cartoon by Signe Wilkinson of the San Jose Mercury News that put me in stitches. That cartoon made it clear why a person needs a "New Bride's Guide."

The cartoon depicted the modern wedding party. Each person had a number and the identification appeared in a "key" below. It's difficult to explain in words what a cartoon looks like, but I'll do my best. The drawing showed (1) Bride, (2) bridegroom, (3) bridegroom's daughter from

first marriage, (4) Bride's mother, (5) Bride's mother's current lover, (6) Bride's sperm donor father, (7 & 8) Sperm donor's parents who sued for visitation rights, (9) Bride's mother's lover at time of bride's birth, (10) bridegroom's mother, (11) bridegroom's mother's boyfriend, (12), bridegroom's father, (13) bridegroom's stepmother, (14) bridegroom's father's third wife, (15) bridegroom's grandfather, (16) bridegroom's grandfather's lover, (17) bridegroom's first wife.

Couldn't you just die, Ann?
                         —Planet Earth 1983

While that cartoon is hilarious, it says a great deal about what is happening in today's society. Don't sneer, you skeptics out there. You could be in a similar photo yourself one of these days.

Source: Boston Globe, December 15, 1983.

the late nineteenth century, the American family began to change both in structure and function. Prior to the Industrial Revolution, the extended family was the most important family unit. Large families were highly valued, since they provided more people to work the fields, cook the meals, and care for the children. It was not unusual to find grandparents, parents, and children all working together as a cooperative unit to fulfill most of life's needs.

With the onset of industrialization, the need for large, three-generation families declined and there was a sharply increasing incidence of the nuclear family form. Goode (1963) has attributed the rise of the small nuclear unit consisting of husband, wife, and children to the particular demands imposed by industrial society. Based on his analysis of family change in several major societies (e.g., in Japan, China, India, Europe, and the United States), Goode argued that the nuclear family freed the individual from kin obligations that, in the context of the extended family, would not have permitted geographic and social mobility to occur. What is more, industrialization gave rise to specialized formal organizations to deal with many of the problems formerly handled by the members of the extended family unit. Schools teach skills; political systems punish deviants; child-care centers "baby-sit"; corporations pro-

Box 6–6   WHY MEN DOMINATE WOMEN

Despite the possibility of any given society adopting any of the major forms of marriage, residence, or recognition of descent, the fact is that such forms are not adopted randomly. The available data indicate that, worldwide, polygynous societies occur over 100 times more frequently than polyandrous societies; patrilocal residential patterns occur in three quarters of all known societies, with matrilocal patterns appearing in only 10 percent of societies (the remaining 15 percent being neolocal); and that patrilineal descent systems are 5 times more prevalent than matrilineal descent systems (Harris, 1977). Overall, this adds up to an overwhelming proportion of human families and, consequently, societies being dominated by males.

Why is this the case? Is it because it is somehow "natural"—that is, innate—for men to control women? Or is it because of some social or environmental conditions that historically, led the majority of societies to adopt these male-dominated patterns? Anthropologist Marvin Harris argues from new evidence for the latter interpretation.

Fundamentally, Harris' argument goes like this: Early human societies, and quite a few contemporary ones, were at a distinct disadvantage. Getting an adequate living from the land (the basic needs problem) was difficult and became more difficult the greater the population was. Because such societies did not have the complex technology and knowledge that make the solving of the basic needs problem easier in the modern world, increases in population threatened to deplete their scarce resources. To make matters worse, because of the scarce resources problem, many of these societies were necessarily engaged in warfare with other societies over the lands where the resources were located.

In warfare, the principal combatants were almost always male. The reason for this can be linked to the technological situation as well. In societies with little technology, battles tended to be fought with spears, clubs, bows and arrows, and other muscle-powered items. "Under these conditions" Harris suggests, "the greater average strength and height of the human male . . . became critically important." (1977, p. 116) Consequently, physically brawny and psychologically "tough" men became preferred offspring. To make men risk their lives in combat, two sanctions (see Chapter 2) were invented: on the negative side there was ostracism; on the positive side there were offers of sexual access to numerous and preferred women and the "possession" of women as wives, concubines, and drudge workers. These two social orientations—the "macho" image and women as sexual objects and drudge workers—are the key elements in the male chauvinist ideology that runs through so many societies. Moreover, Harris argues, the preference for macho men and the necessity of being ready for war, led to the organization of most societies around male figures—thus the high incidence of polygyny, patrilocality, and patrilineal descent systems.

Male dominance in social life, however, led to an important population problem. If men were to be given relatively unrestrained sexual access to appropriate females as reward for their success in war, what was to keep these females from becoming pregnant continually and increasing the population beyond the ability of the environment to sustain it? To be sure, warfare might help this problem somewhat by killing off some of the males. But this would only reduce the male population below the normal biological ratio of males to females (105 males to 100 females) and would provide no respite whatsoever from later population problems because of the ability of a few males to keep many females pregnant.

Indeed when Harris and his colleague William DiVale looked at male-female ratios in low technology-high warfare societies, they found some very puzzling data. Rather than finding a lower male-higher female ratio than the biological norm (105 :100), they found the opposite. The average in these societies was 128 males under 14 years of age to 100 females under 14 years and some societies even showed a ratio of 200:100 favoring the males. Since there was no reason to assume reproductive irregularities in so many societies, Harris and DiVale were left with one—social—conclusion: These societies had practiced a high degree of female infanticide—the killing of female children. (This is not to say that male infanticide was not practiced as well. Harris says that the data clearly suggest that it was. It was, rather, that female infanticide was practiced more frequently.)

Female infanticide, then, according to Harris' theory, horrible as it may sound, was the worldwide socially invented mechanism of population control. With biologically fertile females in short supply, no matter the number of biologically fertile males, population growth could be maintained at an "acceptable" level given the resources of the environment. Female in-

fanticide also had the added function of reinforcing the social preference of giving birth to sons—a preference that continues throughout much of the world even today.

Today, of course, the type of warfare and environmental pressures experienced by low technology societies is fast disappearing. Why then does male chauvinism persist if there is no biological, or environmental, reason for it? One reason, Harris maintains, is because of the power of "tradition" (norms and values, see Chapter 2) in our lives. So much of our daily life is centered around the male dominant patterns—for example; who goes to work and who stays home. Another reason is because it is advantageous to those in power to keep that power. Power, as we saw in Chapter 5, is the ability to control situations along the lines of one's desires. Many men, realizing they have this advantage in much of social life, are loath to relinquish it.

On the more positive side, not everyone feels this way. The recent women's movement (see Chapter 7) and many men and women not specifically associated with the movement have begun to recognize the prejudicial aspects of a society organized around male chauvinist principles. Consequently, change toward more equal treatment of the sexes is occurring. Whether full equality is going to be a reality soon, however, is less than clear at the present time.

vide jobs and money; and nursing homes care for the aged. (See the discussion of specialization in Chapter 8.)

The Role of the Aged in the American Family.   Just as industrialization has been linked to the decline of the extended family, so it has been associated with deterioration in the status of the aged (Cowgill and Holmes, 1972). It is clear, for instance, that most businesses in our industrialized society have instituted an unprecedented system of compulsory retirement, whereby persons over 65 are forced into unemployment regardless of their health or productivity. There seem to be two reasons for this retirement system. On the one hand, there is the widespread belief (not always accurate in individual cases) that younger, rather than older, people are more productive on the job. On the other hand, there is the reality of increasing population. In a society that finds it has more and more workers to find occupations for (which has been the case in our own society since its inception), there are only two main options: to expand occupations (an alternative that can only be pushed to certain limits if the demand for a certain product is limited) and to open up already existing occupations by retiring older workers.

In the past 30 years particularly, all of this has worked to create a "roleless role" for the aged. Many, because of loss of income and reliance on meager social security benefits, must give up their homes of long-standing; some are forced into unwanted dependent relationships with their children or grandchildren, and most are left with virtually nothing meaningful to do. When all else fails, many have to take up residence in "retirement communities" or "homes for the aged" which carry, at best, mixed blessings. Perhaps worse, the rest of society has evolved a normative definition that sees the old as useless and impaired. In a classic British rock song by the group, "The Who," there is the line: "Hope I die before I get old!" Our own society is not very different in its negative degradation of age (see Box 6–7).

In sharp contrast, aged Americans who lived 200 years ago usually commanded respect, power, and privilege. As a result, early Americans actually made themselves out to be *older* (not younger) than they were with respect to dress and hairstyles. Men would hide their natural hair beneath a wig or would powder their hair to give it the white color associated with aging. (Remember all the portraits of George Washington?) Within a Puritan society old age was regarded as a sign of election and as a special gift from God (Fischer, 1977).

It should be emphasized that industrialization—although viewed by many as a contributing factor—does not *necessarily* bring about decline in the status of the aged. As shown by Palmore (1975), the Japanese tradition of respect for elders has maintained itself in the face of advanced levels of industrialization. The Japanese elderly continue to be well integrated into their families, most of them holding household functions and living with their children. What is more, Japanese elderly continue to be employed until they stop for health reasons.

The difference between the Japanese system and our own may be linked to the values of each society. As already seen (Chapter 2), American society has a deep commitment to instrumental values, among which are practicality, efficiency, and individuality. There is some doubt in our society about both the practicality and

How each society treats its aging members is a result of the interplay between cultural values and historical circumstances. In American society, for example, the values of efficiency and individuality coupled with the evolution of the nuclear family structure have led to the creation of homes for the unemployed aged, where many older Americans must spend their last years (top). A contrasting case is contemporary Chinese society, where the values of communalism and respect for the aged have merged with an extended family network of long historical duration to produce a continuing and meaningful role for the aged (bottom). How modern China's push towards becoming a major industrialized society will affect the role of the family in general and the aged in particular will not be known for some time.

Box 6–7 IMAGES OF OLD AGE

The following segment from the 1970s hit TV series, "Mary Hartman, Mary Hartman," indicates what seems to be the typical American belief about the capacities of the aged. Mary's grandfather has entered the kitchen. Mary turns to him and literally yells, "GOOD MORNING, GRANDFATHER! HOW ARE YOU?" The grandfather looks a bit irritated and says, in a normal voice, "Fine," then sits down. Then Mary's husband Tom enters and issues a similar, extremely loud greeting: "GOOD MORNING, GRANDFATHER! HOW ARE YOU?" Once again appearing a bit agitated, Mary's Grandfather says "Fine," in a normal voice and goes about his business. Finally, Mary's daughter enters and goes through the same high decibel greeting. This time, Mary's grandfather jumps up from his chair and says in some anger, "For gosh sake, doesn't anybody realize I'm just *old,* not *deaf?*"

efficiency of keeping the aged fully employed or in positions of high power and prestige. For us, the mature adult years, roughly ages 35 to 60 are regarded as the prime of life. With our view of individuality, we believe it is each person's responsibility to care for himself or herself throughout life. Thus when older people retire, most Americans do not regard it as their duty to care for their aged relatives. In contrast, although the industrially successful Japanese place premiums on practicality and efficiency as we do, there is a belief in their society that one's last years of life are most valuable assets to the society at large in terms of wisdom, remembrance of the past, and the like. Moreover, as distinct from our own tradition, the Japanese have a strong belief in communal familial relationships—the responsibility of all members of a family for one another's well-being. These two normative differences mean that Japanese elders are treated differently from American elders. Does one system seem better to you than the other? Why?

The Future of the American Family.   Is the American family a "dying" institution? Judging by divorce statistics alone, as we have previously seen, we might easily conclude that it is. The number of divorces per 1,000 persons (the crude divorce rate) has steadily increased from 0.7 in 1900 to 2.6 in 1950 to 5.2 in 1980. To use another measure, as recently as 1955, the divorce rate by couples in American society was 1 of 4. By the early 1970s, however, the national average had risen to 1 of 3, and in some specific areas of the country was much higher. For example, in California the rate was a rather remarkable 2 of 3, and in the Los Angeles area it was a nearly unbelievable 1 of 1 (See, 1975).* What is more, almost one

*Remember this is a *ratio.* It does *not* mean that everyone who marries in Los Angeles gets divorced. Many do not. Many others, of course, get married and divorced many times, thus bringing about the ratio of 1 to 1.

million unwed couples are currently living together in the United States. Most such cohabitations do not lead to marriage (Clayton and Voss, 1977).

A more optimistic view of the future of the American family can also be found in marriage data. First of all, the divorce rate is high, but so is the marriage rate. Although the marriage rate has declined sharply in recent years—from 148.0 per 1,000 in 1960 to 107.9 in 1979 (Hacker, 1983, pp. 101–102), it is clear that most young persons continue to look forward to getting married and having children. In a recent survey of 1,190 college students, only 12 expressed their approval of having children outside marriage (Bower and Christopherson, 1977). Secondly, most divorced persons in our society eventually remarry. So strong is this tendency that "serial monogamy", long fashionable in Hollywood, is fast becoming a socially acceptable norm. Finally, there is no evidence that cohabitation is replacing marriage. On the contrary, those couples who live together tend to do so for short periods of time. And they, like their contemporaries who do not cohabitate, usually look forward to eventually establishing a permanent relationship via marriage (Bower and Christopherson, 1977).

EDUCATION

In simple, relatively stable societies, the family unit takes major responsibility for seeing that ideational culture—a society's general knowledge and guidelines for behavior—is effectively transmitted from one generation to another. More by example than instruction, agents of socialization such as grandparents, parents, and siblings hand down a repertoire of facts, usages, norms, and values as accumulating over many generations and continuing to have legitimacy for generations to come.

However, as societies become more complex (a good example is our description of the rise of industrialism earlier in this chapter), the division of labor also becomes more complex, with people specializing in different occupational roles. As this occurs, the knowledge and training needed to perform these specialized roles are ever more difficult to obtain. Indeed, in time, it becomes *impossible* for the family unit—historically the main agent of socialization as we have just seen—to provide this specialized knowledge.

To this situation, particularly in modern societies, is added another complicating factor: namely, that the members of these societies believe that their children should have not only the specialized knowledge that will provide them with economic success in adult life, but generalized knowledge as well that will make them well-informed citizens. This knowledge, which traditionally includes the three 'r's—readin', writin', and 'rithmetic—now also includes some knowledge of national history and of political processes, not to mention some knowledge of international affairs and of scientific discoveries. Quite obviously, the average family unit will be quite ill-equipped to provide all this information.

The core human problem in modern society thus is twofold: How do we provide the young with the specialized knowledge necessary to perform the complex tasks of society? And how do we provide the young with the generalized knowledge necessary to make them well-informed citizens as adults? The answer, of course, has been for modern societies to develop a separate institution, **education,** to handle these problems of formal socialization.

In American society, for example, virtually thousands of educational programs—colleges, universities, junior colleges, graduate schools, business schools, high schools, intermediate schools, elementary schools, kindergartens, nursery programs—involve millions of individuals from age 3 through young adulthood and longer. In 1850 less than 2 out of every 100 school-aged Americans were actually enrolled in school; by 1975 the school enrollment rate had increased to include more than 90 out of every 100 school-aged Americans. In 1870 only 2 percent of persons 18-years-old were high school graduates; by 1975 this figure had increased to 74 percent.

education The social institution in modern societies that provides the answers to the problems of formal socialization—specialized occupational knowledge and generalized citizen knowledge.

The Functions of Education

Many people associate education with innovation and change. They tend to think of scientific and technological knowledge as originating in the research facilities of major colleges and universities. They tend to emphasize the historical fact that "getting an education" was frequently an avenue of upward mobility for disadvantaged members of society.

In our rapidly changing technological society it is indeed true that many important innovations and discoveries have occurred within the confines of the educational institution. It is equally true, however, that the central function of education is frequently not change at all, but the *maintenance of the status quo.*

This happens in several different ways. First, as noted earlier, education prepares individuals to play the specialized roles existing in our society. In the occupational realm this means that children must acquire information about the availability and desirability of various occupational positions and receive formal training in the specialized skills required to occupy such positions. All these occupations, of course, are deeply integrated into the overall structure of the society.

Education also reinforces the basic values of our society. In American society this means that individuals representing diverse social classes and ethnic groups receive a *common* educational background with respect to content (but not always to quality). The very structure of the American educational experience—its highly competitive and achievement-oriented character—prepares students to become highly competitive and achievement-oriented adults, qualities highly prized in our instrumentally dominated value system (see Chapter 2). Several studies support this "teaching of value priorities" function. Hoge (1971) and Morris and Small (1971) report that student values and views of "the good life" are essentially unchanged in the last three decades and Eve (1975) and Kandel and Lesser (1972) report a basic similarity between adolescent and adult outlooks on all major dimensions.

Another important way in which education maintains the status quo is by means of educational tracking. In the method known as **ability grouping** students are sorted into homogeneous groups on the basis of "their ability to perform classroom tasks" such as reading or arithmetic. With respect to higher education, ability grouping may determine whether or not a child can enter college or, if he does extend his education, whether or not he is able to attend a prestigious school. Howe and Lauter (1972) argue that ability grouping helps ensure that white, middle-class children

ability grouping The sorting of students into homogeneous groups on the basis of their ability to perform classroom tasks such as reading or arithmetic.

Box 6–8   ABILITY GROUPING IN AMERICAN SCHOOLS

Ability grouping has been operating effectively to limit competition with the children of white, middle-class parents who, on the whole, have controlled the schools. In New York City in 1967, for example, nonwhites, the vast majority of the poor, made up 40 percent of the high school population; they constituted about 36 percent of students in the "academic" high schools and about 60 percent of those tracked into "vocational" high schools. In the Bronx High School of Science and in Brooklyn Tech, elite institutions for which students must qualify by examination, "nonwhites" totaled only 7 and 12 percent of the students, respectively.

But the real effects of tracking can better be seen in the statistics of students in the academic high schools. A majority of blacks and Puerto Ricans fill lower tracks, which lead them—if they stay at all—to "general" rather than "academic" diplomas. Only 18 percent of academic high school graduates were black or Puerto Rican (although they were, as we said, 36 percent of the academic student population); and only one fifth of that 19 percent went on to college, as compared with 63 percent of whites who graduated. In other words, only 7 percent of the graduates of New York's academic high schools who went on to college were black or Puerto Rican. The rest, for the most part tracked into non-college-preparatory programs, left school with what amounted to a ticket into the army. (Howe and Lauter, 1972, 232–233)

continue to fill the technological and professional roles of our society, whereas low-paying and unpleasant occupations are supplied with lower-class and minority manpower.

This process works in the following way: By and large, middle- and upper-middle-class children, the great majority of whom are white, are raised in a familial environment that stresses the "three 'r's" from the beginning. This is possible largely because of the economic stability of these families. That is, because of the occupations held by the adult members of the family, it is possible for the children to get continuing, adult-supervised educationally oriented attention most of the time. This supervision is usually provided by the mother of the children or some other adult (e.g., the teacher of a nursery school) who is likely to have a background of relatively lengthy formal socialization.

Lower-class children, on the other hand, the majority of whom are nonwhite in American society, are raised in a familial environment that is much more likely to be less economically stable than the familial environments of middle- and upper-class children. For example, one parent may be missing, laid off, untrained for anything more than manual labor, or make so little money that the other parent is forced to work as well just to provide the basic necessities of life. Furthermore, parents of lower-class children are less likely to have been so extensively educated as their middle- and upper-class counterparts. As a result, *regardless of the desires of the parents for adequate preschool training for their children,* these children are much less likely to receive the continuing, adult-supervised, educationally oriented attention that children of higher classes receive.

Consequently, when children around 5 or 6 years of age enter formal educational facilities, middle- and upper-class children already have a distinct advantage over lower-class children because of the type of preschool training they received as opposed to the preschool background of the lower-class children. Almost inevitably then, when ability grouping occurs, white, middle- and upper-class children make up the bulk of the "college-oriented" tracks, whereas nonwhite, lower-class children are disproportionately represented in "vocational" tracks (see Box 6–8).

It should be clearly noted here that this disadvantage in education comes from the *social* condition of unequal social classes and not from any inherent biological differences between races. Further, remember Gans' argument on the positive functions of poverty earlier in this chapter on how this unequal tracking system maintains the status quo. Gans stated that a hierarchical, competitive society always needed an "underclass" to make its hierarchical definition of the situation "work." Unequal educational opportunity is one more way of ensuring that the poor will always be part of our society. It was this understanding that motivated the nation-wide attempt to desegregate American schools in the 1950s and 1960s and to bus children from one school to another to compensate for unequal school environments. Both programs have had limited success.

Education as a Mechanism of Social Control. Although it is true that the primary reason for the existence of the formal education system in modern societies is for the transmission of generalized and specialized knowledge deemed vital by the society, it is also true that such an institution is a mechanism of social control as well.

Compulsory education serves as a "baby-sitter" or custodian for children and adolescents who would be problematical if they were not cared for. For example, a highly industrialized society such as ours requires that at least one, and often two, parents in the family unit be away from home at work for large portions of the day. Given this situation, who is going to take care of young children? The answer, for at least a good part of the day, is the school.

Of course, as children grow older and become better able to take care of themselves, this baby-sitting function may become less important. But without adequate adult supervision, who is going to keep young people out of mischief which they might get into by being alone or in groups on the streets? The answer, once again, is the school. David Bakan (1971) argues that it is absolutely no coincidence that *compulsory* education in America developed at exactly the same time that juvenile delinquency was becoming a major problem in many industrialized American cities (between 1910 and 1930).

Finally, in this respect, education serves as a protective mechanism for the labor market from a deluge of adolescents. High school and college attendance occupies the time of millions of young people whose presence in the labor market would otherwise create massive unemployment for adult Americans.

Structural Aspects of American Education

The educational institution in American society has often been criticized for having an excessively rigid and authoritarian formal structure (Farber, 1969). Most observers would in fact agree that schools generally ask their personnel to adhere to a rigid schedule containing numerous rules for almost every activity. In addition, students are generally required to occupy subordinate and dependent positions in relation to teachers who occupy positions of great authority (Havighurst and Neugarten, 1962).

So profound is the authoritarianism of formal education that some have likened the school to a prison in which students are the passive inmates and adult personnel are the wardens and guards. In the 1960s Fred Wiseman's film *High School* documented the emphasis on obedience to authority and conformity as found in a typical suburban high school. Even the emergence of open classrooms and forms of alternative education—a trend of short-lived duration—has done little to change the basic structure of American education.

Once again, it is instructive to see why this authoritarian structure would be so prevalent in the educational institution. As already seen, most modern societies are highly bureaucratized (see Chapter 4) and industrialized. These characteristics mean that most people's occupational roles, whether executive, white collar, or blue collar, have to be performed in a highly routinized, regulated way if they are to be performed successfully. Most American children will wind up filling these routinized, regulated occupational roles. It would therefore be easier if, when they come to them, they already had experience and knew how to function under such a system. Seen in this light, the underlying authoritarian structure of most of American formal education becomes more understandable.

The Possibilities of Education: A Balance?

That's the bad news. Most readers of this book are clearly aware that there *are* problems with American education. Yet, on another level, education in the United States has been a resounding success. It *does* provide most people with the information or skills they need to exist in society; it *does* make us more knowledgeable about national and world affairs, history, or the role of society in our lives; and it continues to allow status advancement for many people. In general, the more education people obtain, the more prestige and power, even wealth, they achieve.

Moreover, the educational institution is not impervious to positive change. Although desegregation and busing did not have the tremendous positive effects expected of them in the past few decades, the *attempt* to introduce these effects *was* made. In addition, in recent years, education has been opened to more equal participation by women. Thus in 1972 women (who comprise slightly over 51 percent of the population), received 43.7 percent of the undergraduate degrees awarded in this country. By 1980 that percentage had risen almost to parity, to 49.2 percent. It was the same for professional degrees: in 1972 women got only 7.2 percent of the degrees awarded; in 1980 they obtained 30.2 percent. In medicine, in 1972 women received 9.0 percent of the degrees; in 1980 they got 23.4 percent (Hacker, 1983, pp. 243–

244). Although such figures clearly leave room for further improvement (i.e., continuing equalization), they do indicate that some progress has been made.

Finally, it should be noted that not all school or classroom situations are as bleak as those previously portrayed. Many good teachers still exist in American schools and numerous dedicated, critical students abound. The key seems to be to establish some kind of balance—between education's formal status quo supporting function and its equally important education-for-its-own-sake function. Education *can* still be a truly liberating and joyous experience, as suggested in Box 6–9.

RELIGION

One of the unique aspects of human beings, as we discussed in Chapter 2, is their ability to ask questions and to wonder about the world. If it is the purpose of the family and educational institutions to provide answers to many questions human beings ask, who or what aspect of society provides the answers to the *ultimate* questions of human life? For example, what is the nature and meaning of life? What is the most moral way for human beings to act and who has decreed such behavior? Because of the pressing nature of such questions as a core human problem in social life, it is not surprising that human beings have invented an institution whose purpose it is to address and resolve such questions—the institution of **religion**.

religion The social institution that provides the answers to the ultimate questions of human life; a unified system of beliefs and practices relative to sacred things.

Following Durkheim, we may define religion as "a unified system of beliefs and practices relative to sacred things" (1965, p. 62). Although all culture consists of various sets of beliefs and behaviors associated with them, Durkheim sees in religious beliefs and practices a unique quality—the quality that can be captured by the distinction between the **sacred** and the **profane**. Sacred things, Durkheim argues, are "things set apart and forbidden" (1965, p. 62), things somehow special, divine, not of this world. Profane things, on the other hand, are everyday and mundane things. Because of their sacred quality, religious beliefs or practices assume a "transcendental" quality, a unique moral legitimation that goes beyond (transcends) everyday beliefs and objects (1965, pp. 52–57). Consequently, because of their sacred quality, it is in religious beliefs and objects that the ultimate answers about human life and the ultimate moral legitimation for human behavior in any society rest.

sacred A set of beliefs, practices, or objects set apart or forbidden because of their special, divine, or other-worldly nature.

profane In contrast to the sacred, the designation of beliefs, practices, or objects as being everyday, mundane, and of this world.

From society to society, or religious group to religious group, the nature of the sacred may vary considerably. Regarding religious beliefs, for example, both Jews and Christians recognize the sacred origin of the Ten Commandments. In contrast, Jews and

Box 6–9 EDUCATION AND ECSTASY

The previous sections have all suggested that the educational institution is frequently a reflector of, and preparer for, the status quo. Years of sociological research have indicated this to be true of all societies that have formal socialization systems. Unfortunately, this has, more often than not, led to an educational system that has taken the excitement and sheer delight out of learning. This is unnecessary, argues educator George B. Leonard (1968). He suggests that the purpose of human life is self-education and that that process in its pure state is ecstatic—an eager, delighted "Yes!" or "Wow!" or "How can I find out more?" He says we know this by how most young children react to learning before they have entered the formal educational system and by those "breakthrough" days that still occasionally occur in formal educational settings.

> "Some days its different," the . . . teacher continued. "The whole thing's different. I don't know why."
>
> How many of those times do you remember? SOMETHING HAPPENS. A delicate warmth slides into parts of your being you didn't even realize were cold. The marrow of your bones begins to thaw. You feel a little lurch as your own consciousness, the teacher's voice, the entire web of sound and silence that holds the class together, the room itself, the very flow of time all shift to a different level. And suddenly it is Christmas morning, with students and teacher exchanging delightful gifts

while bells silently chime; the old furniture around the room reflects a holiday gleam; your classmates' eyes sparkle and snap like confetti and you realize with the certainty of music how rare and valuable each inhabitant of that room has become, has always been. Or you find yourself trembling slightly with the terror and joy of knowledge, the immensity of existence and pattern and change. And when it ends and you must go, you reel from the room with flushed face, knowing you will never be quite the same. You have learned.

> How many . . . days [like this]? One out of a hundred? Then you are of the favored. (Leonard 1968, pp. 8–9).

How do we make the occasional days more frequent? Leonard realizes it is not easy, given our society's vested interest in rationality and order and in making sure people fill certain narrowly defined occupational roles. Yet, he argues, ecstasy is not opposed to these factors. People should be free in their education to do what they like, to follow the threads that interest them. Only if they are given this freedom can education be personally relevant and continually ecstatic. He concludes as follows:

> Every child, every person can delight in learning. A new education is already here, thrusting up in spite of every barrier we have been able to build. Why not help it happen? (1968, p. 237)

Christians disagree about the coming of the divine Messiah. Christians have believed that such a person did come to Earth nearly 2,000 years ago and have named their religion to emphasize their belief in his divinity. Jews, on the other hand, feel the Messiah is yet to come. Regarding religious practices, Jews observe Passover and Rosh Hashanah as high religious holidays, whereas Christians observe Christmas and Easter. Even within the same religion differences appear. Many Catholics, for example, recognize papal infallibility and have canonized the great religious leaders of their history in the institution of sainthood. Protestants, on the other hand, have neither pope nor any single religious authority to whom they look for religious guidance and have no procedure for making saints.

Theories of Religion

It is easier to see the contrasting ideas that have developed concerning the functions of religion in society if we look at the major theories of religion.

Marx.   In 1844 Marx coined what was to become a classic phrase, that religion "is the opium of the people" (1964, p. 42). By this, Marx meant that whatever else religion did in society, it was a mechanism that helped keep the economically destitute "in their place." It had a "drugging" effect because in religious services certain ideas were emphasized. People were told that suffering was natural to life; that their impoverished state was inevitable, somehow a consequence of their past actions, and that little could be done about it; and finally, that if only they would be patient, there would be reward in the next life. Whatever the purpose of its leaders, then, Marx argued that the real function of religion was to defuse the proletariat's natural anger at the bourgeoisie (see Chapter 5) and create a passive underclass, accepting of its impoverished state. Consequently, he argued that the only way people could truly be free and happy was to give up such religious views and, by revolution, improve their real situation (1964, p. 42).

Durkheim.   Durkheim's theory was quite different. If you recall from Chapter 1, Durkheim believed that society has a reality *external* to the individual. It was a collective representation of human sentiments about the world. No wonder, then, Durkheim argues in his examination of religion in tribal and premodern societies, that people often felt as though an "outside" force was causing them to do things. There was such a force—the collective moral force of society—that suggested that stealing, the anger one felt against one's neighbor, and so on were to be avoided.

However, not realizing that this force was social in origin, tribal and premodern societies assumed, not unreasonably, that the force must come from *beyond* this world, from the divine world. From this assumption, religious beliefs and practices emerged as did the entire complex institution of religion.

For Durkheim, then, religion is nothing more than the worship of social forces. As he puts it, religious forces are "human forces, moral forces. . . . Thus religion, far from ignoring the real society and making an abstraction of it, is in its image; it reflects all its aspects . . ." (1965, pp. 466, 468). In religion, Durkheim feels, are all the important aspects of social life, good and bad, practical and impractical, writ large. To make the key aspects of social life sacred, therefore, even if they are not recognized as such, is extremely important. It not only continually reminds people of the central concerns of their social life, but it unites the group around an overriding set of sacred moral beliefs and practices and thereby holds the community together. Whereas Marx wanted religion abandoned in all societies, Durkheim would argue that, if society did not have some equally strong cohering force to replace it, the abandonment of religion would be the highest folly: It would create anomie (see Chapter 1) to an unbearable degree.

Freud. Some elements of both the Marxian and Durkheimian theories can be found in Sigmund Freud's (1961) theory of religion. On the Marxian side, Freud sees religion as an illusion, as a set of answers that speak to each individual's deepest fears, anxieties, and hopes and that keep each person from seeing the world as it really is and working to overcome those fears, anxieties, and illusory hopes. On the Durkheimian side, Freud sees religious beliefs as the strongest internalized aspect of the superego, itself society's representative in the individual's psychology (see Chapter 3). As such, it helps assure moral behavior in its adherents. People who believe in religion's moral dictates act morally because they feel that such behavior is unquestionably "right" and because they feel terribly guilty if they do not.

Weber. Max Weber's (1963) emphasis on the evolutionary role of religion in complementing social change is different from all preceding theories. For Weber, religious beliefs, because of their special nature as sacred ideas, are the most important ideas for legitimating various types of social behavior. Consequently, when changes in belief occur, as they are likely to do from time to time, originating from any social sphere—economic, political, and so on —they can only become lasting and important changes in society if they are somehow incorporated into or legitimized by the religious order.

The process by which this incorporation and legitimation of change occurs is called **rationalization**—the "classification, specification and systematization of ideas" (Parsons, 1963, p. xxxii) and is a key function of religion. More specifically, rationalization of social change is begun by a religious prophet, a person who is in some way related to the changes that are occurring and who,

rationalization The process of classification, specification, and systematization of ideas that occurs historically in a society.

charisma A special, magnetic quality that a person has by virtue of natural endowment or because of some extraordinary means.

above all, has **charisma**. Charisma, one of Weber's key concepts, is a special magnetic quality "that inheres in [a] person simply by virtue of natural endowment [or by] some extraordinary means" —such as communication with God (Weber, 1963, p. 2). The prophet (Moses, Christ, Luther, Mohammed, are examples) comes to some new religious understanding of the world that incorporates the social changes of the times (e.g., the exodus of the Jews from Egypt in Moses' case, the defection from the Catholic Church in Luther's) and explains—rationalizes—to his or her followers why it is crucial to follow this understanding. The explanation is followed because of the religious nature of the ideas being presented and the charismatic leadership of the prophet. If, over time, more and more people are won to the fold, the social change spreads in society and the direction of the social order is forever altered. It is Weber's contention that much of the development of modern society can be explained only when this "support of social change" function of religion is taken into account. (We shall return to a specific example of Weber's thesis of the role of religious ideas in producing social change in Chapter 8.)

The Organization of Religion

Religious associations take the form of cult, sect, or church, depending on their degree of institutionalization and level of formality. At one end of the continuum, **cults** represent the most loosely structured and unconventional forms of religious organization. They consist of small numbers of persons who band together in order to express a revolutionary religious cause—a cause that is at great variance from that of established religious orders. In Roman times the Christians were members of a cult. Today the adherents of the Reverend Moon's Unification Church—the "Moonies"— could be considered a cult.

cult A small number of people banded together to express a revolutionary religious cause.

Most cults dissipate after a short period of time. They are held together only as long as their charismatic religious leaders are able to mobilize the continued loyalty and passion of their followers. In order to survive and remain viable, religious institutions must take the form of either sect or church.

sect A small religious association that generally appeals to poor propertyless, or otherwise marginal members of society.

A **sect** is a small religious association that generally appeals to poor, propertyless, or otherwise marginal members of society. As in the case of a cult, the sect frequently expresses a cause that places its membership in a position at odds with the established religious organization to some degree. Unlike cults that develop independently of the conventional church, sects usually emerge out of established religious orders and represent some departure from them. Also unlike cults, sects perpetuate themselves over time by developing a loose structure usually consisting of a part-time ministry from the congregation who leads a highly involved membership in a number of emotionally charged services. The recent "born-again" movement in Protestantism often begins as a sect within local churches.

The most highly structured and conventional religious organization is known as the **church.** Unlike a sect, the church draws its membership from those who represent the cultural and economic mainstream of a society—those in possession of wealth and property. Thus the religious beliefs and rituals of the church generally reflect an acceptance of the prevailing social order. Also unlike the loosely structured sect, the church typically engages a specialized and full-time ministry who leads the congregation and socializes new members (e.g., children) in religious beliefs and rituals.

Sects may occur as an organized rebellion among some members of an established church who reject a traditional religious position and seek to break away from the church. A religious association that begins as a cult or a sect may also become a church, if its membership grows in size and its organizational structure grows in complexity.

church The most highly structured and conventional form of religious organization whose membership is drawn from the mainstream of society.

The Religious Factor in Modern American Life

The secularization of American society in the twentieth century is no illusion (see Box 6–10). Indeed, the wane of the influence of religion on American life had apparently gone so far in the early 1960s that *Time* magazine ran a cover story that proclaimed and seriously considered arguments that "God is dead."

Does religious affiliation continue to play a part in the lives of the members of American society? To find out, Lenski (1961) interviewed a sample of 656 Detroiters, most of whom were Protestants, Catholics, or Jews. His findings indicated clearly that " . . . religion in various ways is constantly influencing the daily lives of the masses of men and women in the modern American metropolis" (p. 320). More specifically, Lenski reported that an individual's religious preference will help determine whether or not he or she votes Republican, prefers a welfare state, has many children, continues his or her education beyond high school or college, maintains ties with the family, is upwardly mobile, enjoys his or her job, buys "on time," or saves money.

All this, however, only indicates the influence religious background will have on social behavior. Do people still think religiously and act religiously? Andrew Greeley (1972), analyzing a Gallup poll reported the following: In a nationwide sample of Americans conducted in 1965, 99 percent of the Protestants, 100 percent of the Catholics, and 79 percent of the Jews interviewed indicated a belief in God; 94 percent of the Protestants, 99 percent

Box 6-10   AMERICAN CIVIL RELIGION

Historically, the direct influence of specific religious groups on American society has waned. We began as a Protestant nation fundamentally and, for over 100 years, Protestantism was the national religion. With the massive waves of European immigration to this country beginning in the latter half of the nineteenth century and continuing until the early 1900s, however, great numbers of Catholics and Jews arrived. Since our Constitution provided freedom of expression for all religious groups, it became progressively harder to identify Protestantism with the nation as a whole. As a result, the twentieth century has seen a progressive withering away of most specific religious identifications in American society. What is left, argues sociologist Robert Bellah (1967) is a uniquely American civil religion—a highly generalized set of beliefs recognizing God as the ultimate guide and "the Kingdom of God on Earth" as the ultimate material goal, but without specific relation to *any* religious creed. Moreover, the focus of this American civil religion is on the moral, almost sacred, mission of the nation itself; a belief in American society and its progressive development as an ultimate concern.

As analogies with the Judeo-Christian tradition, Bellah suggests the following: American society has always been seen by its people as "the promised land" in much the same way that the Jews have historically regarded Israel. The Revolutionary War can be likened to the Exodus from Egypt, a breakaway from an oppressive external control; the Constitution and the Bill of Rights are our Ten Commandments. The Civil War is analogous to the Christian breakaway from Roman rule, a return to moral principles in the face of the antihuman forces of slavery. Moreover, we have important days of "worship" like all religions: Memorial Day, growing out of the Civil War, and the Fourth of July, growing out of the signing of the Declaration of Independence, are annual days of rededication to the American Dream. Every election is like communion, a recommitment to the democratic process.

Moreover, we have historically invoked American civil religion in our foreign adventures. In the nineteenth century we had "Manifest Destiny," an almost God-given duty to colonize and civilize the North American continent. Our entry into all the wars of the twentieth century was always argued as a moral responsibility—to "end all wars" or to "make the world safe for democracy." Our intervention in other countries (e.g., Haiti, the Dominican Republic, Vietnam) has always carried with it a similar rhetoric of a religious kind.

Currently, however, Bellah argues American civil religion is in trouble. Because of its very abstract level, people can vehemently disagree with statements of the civil religion. For example, all the above mentioned interventionist or expansionist activities (with the possible exceptions of World Wars I and II) were roundly denounced by many as immoral acts. Unless those who interpret American civil religion can find a way of expressing it that satisfies the fundamental beliefs of most Americans, it undermines the legitimacy of the state as a whole. He suggests that the best alternative would be a transition to a world civil religion that would take into account a cross-cultural recognition of our moral responsibilities for all human beings and nations while at the same time recognizing their rights to self-determination.

Sociologist Robert N. Bellah (see Box 6-10) has suggested that, as the direct influence of traditional religion has waned in everyday American life, we have substituted for it a "civil religion"—that is, a deep belief in the ultimate morality of and necessity for American values and "the American way of life." Similar to any other religious belief system, the American civil religion has its rituals and rededication ceremonies. The July 4th ceremonies across the country are an excellent example. At these affairs, there are usually large parades resplendent with the high-school marching band and the local fireman's association (with its members all decked out in their finest uniforms) among other notaries. For speeches there are the town or city officials telling of their area's great resources and of the improvements made or likely to be made in years to come. Finally, in the evening, after a meal of hot dogs, cola, apple pie, and ice cream, there are the fireworks displays, with booming rockets—symbolically recreating "the rockets' red glare" phrase from the national anthem—and, at the end, a huge glowing American flag done in fireworks.

of the Catholics, and 70 percent of the Jews interviewed believed in the effectiveness of prayer; 75 percent of the Protestants, 80 percent of the Catholics, and 62 percent of the Jews interviewed indicated that religion was an important factor in their own lives (p. 11). As a consequence of considering this and other data, such as the tremendous growth in recent years of traditional and non-traditional religious groups among the young (the Jesus movement is an example of the former; the Hare Krishna of the latter), Greeley concludes that although religion has changed in recent years —no longer being acceptable on a "self-evident" basis and no longer being limited to the established religions—it still is very much alive and well in our society.

The Reality of Religious Experience

All the theorists considered in this section have tended to regard religion as having very distinct "this worldly" functions—an institution of social oppression (Marx), an institution of social cohesion (Durkheim), an institution for salving psychological doubts and ensuring moral behavior (Freud), and an institution for augmenting social change (Weber). There seems little doubt that, to some degree, the institution of religion performs all these social functions.

Recently, however, sociologists have turned to a reexamination of the possibility that religion is actually performing the "other-worldly" function it and its adherents have always claimed for it. As early as 1902, William James in his classic study of *The Varieties of Religious Experience* examined what people throughout history and from many different cultures claimed they experienced psychologically when they had religious experiences. He found, amazingly enough, that although many of these people had never had contact with each other or with other people who might have told them what to expect, their experiences, even though often triggered by very different phenomena (depression, sexual orgasm, epileptic fit, communing with nature), were remarkably similar. All felt that (1) "the visible world is part of a more spiritual universe from which it draws its chief significance"; (2) "union or harmonious relation with that higher universe is our true end"; (3) prayer is an effective way to communicate with that world; (4) these experiences added a great zest to life; and (5) these experiences produced individual assurance that unending safety, peace, and love were the ultimate nature of the universe and the self (James, 1958, p. 367). See Box 6–11 for two of these experiences.

James's study, until recently, had had little systematic evidence to support it. In 1975, however, Greeley and McCready conducted a nationwide study of 1500 Americans which asked them the following question about a religious-type of experience: "Have you ever had the feeling of being very close to a powerful spiritual force that seemed to lift you out of yourself?" (Greeley and McCready, 1975, p. 15). Forty percent of the respondents said they had such an experience at least once, 20 percent had it

Box 6–11 TWO RELIGIOUS EXPERIENCES

The great Russian novelist, Fyodor Dostoevsky, had frequent epileptic fits. Occasionally, these fits were preceded by an intense religious experience. Prince Mishkin, the protagonist of *The Idiot* also has these fits. Dostoevsky's description of one of Mishkin's experiences (which we can assume is largely autobiographical) is quoted. In most respects this description matches the second experience described by British educator F. C. Happold.

> (Dostoevsky) [T]here was a moment or two in his epileptic condition, almost before the fit itself . . . when suddenly . . . his brain seemed to catch fire at brief moments, and with an extraordinary momentum his vital forces were strained to the utmost all at once. His sensation of being alive and his awareness increased tenfold at those moments which flashed by like lightning. His mind and heart were flooded by a dazzling light. All his agitation, all his doubts and worries, seemed composed in a twinkling, culminating in a great calm, full of serene and harmonious joy and hope, full of understanding and the knowledge of the final cause. . . . Reflecting about that moment afterwards, when he was well again, he often said to himself that all those gleams and flashes of the highest awareness and, hence, also of "the highest mode of existence," were nothing but a disease, a departure from the normal condition. . . . And yet he arrived at last at the paradoxical conclusion: "What if it is a disease?" he decided at last. "What does it matter that it is an abnormal tension, if the result, if the moment of sensation, remembered and analyzed in a state of health, turns out to be harmony and beauty brought to their highest point of perfection, and gives a feeling, undivined and undreamt of till then, of completeness, proportion, reconciliation, and an ecstatic and prayerful fusion in the highest synthesis of life?" . . . But that it really was "beauty and prayer," that it really was "the highest synthesis of life," he could not doubt, nor even admit the possibility of doubt. . . . What indeed was he to make of this reality? . . . He *had* had time to say to himself at the particular second that, for the infinite happiness he felt in it, it might well be worth the whole of his life. "At that moment," he once told Rogozhin in Moscow during their meetings there, "at that moment the extraordinary saying that *there shall be time no longer* becomes, somehow, comprehensible to me."

> (Happold) It happened in my room in Peterhouse on the evening of 1 February, 1913, when I was an undergraduate at Cambridge. If I say that Christ came to me I should be using conventional words which would carry no precise meaning; for Christ comes to men and women in different ways. When I tried to record the experience at the time I used the imagery of the vision of the Holy Grail; it seemed to me to be like that. There was, however, no sensible vision. There was just the room, with its shabby furniture and the fire burning in the grate and the red-shaded lamp on the table. But the room was filled

Source: Fyodor Dostoevsky, *The Idiot* (London: The Folio Society, 1972), pp. 262–263; F. C. Happold, *Adventure in Search of a creed* (London: Faber and Faber, 1955).

> with a Presence, which in a strange way was both about me and within me, like light or warmth. I was overwhelmingly possessed by Someone who was not myself, and yet I felt I was more myself than I had ever been before. I was filled with an intense happiness, and almost unbearable joy, such as I had never known before ... And over all was a deep sense of peace and security and certainty.

several times; and 5 percent had it often. Furthermore, two thirds of those indicating such an experience placed it at the top of a 7-point intensity scale. Interviewing some of these respondents, Greeley and McCready found that most of them clearly indicated the same feelings that James' study had uncovered almost three quarters of a century before. They conclude that whatever other functions religion performs, it also, for many, does seem to provide a very real other-worldly experience, wherein "the total personality of a person is absorbed in an intimate though transient relationship with the basic forces, cycles, and mechanisms at work in the universe and in his own [life]," an experience that has always been "at the core of all religion" (1975, pp. 24–25).

OTHER INSTITUTIONS

There are other core human problems raised in human societies that also lead to the formation of institutions. In concluding this chapter, we shall briefly mention a few.

First, how do we attain the goals of the society? How do we make sure that the central rules of the society will be followed and ensure that deviants from these rules will be punished? These questions have always been answered by the development of a **political system.** All communities of any size and all nations have a **government,** a legitimately recognized set of statuses and procedures for implementing and obtaining the goals of the group by using socially approved patterns. In our own society the goals we wish to attain are officially interpreted by the occupants of the statuses of president and members of the House and Senate. As a convenience, all these statuses have evolved additional substatuses—for example, press secretary, foreign affairs advisor to the president—to make their functioning easier in a complex society.

In addition, most modern societies have a well-established **political process** that establishes and carries out the procedures for getting people to fill the various vacancies in government as they occur. We, for example, have two major political parties, the candidates of which try, every few years, to convince the electorate of their ability to fill a vacant governmental status more adequately than "the other guy." (Happily, now "the other person" more frequently.) Before the twentieth century, on the other

political system The social institution that provides the answers to the problems of goal attainment and rule enforcement in a society.

government A legitimately recognized set of statuses and procedures for implementing and obtaining the goals of the group.

political process The procedures which exist for filling vacancies in government when they occur.

hand, the English employed the political system of royalty, where descendants of previous national leaders automatically assumed vacant governmental statuses.

To make sure that the rules of the society are carried out, most societies and communities have some type of police force that is specifically charged with apprehending certain types of deviants. In the United States, we have, at the national level, such agencies as the FBI and the National Guard. On the local level there are community police forces.

To interpret the rules of society, most societies employ a rather intricate **legal system.** This subinstitution usually also has the right to punish deviants. At the national level the federal district courts and the Supreme Court perform these functions. In some societies aspects of the legal system also make legal decisions that affect the society as a whole. In the famous Miranda case of the 1960s, for example, the Supreme Court ruled on the right of accused criminals to be informed of their Constitutional rights before being questioned by authorities. After this decision, police and other law-enforcement agencies, having made an arrest, were required to inform alleged criminals that anything they said might be held against them, that they had a right to contact a lawyer, and so on.

legal system A subinstitution charged with interpreting the rules of society and with the right to punish deviants.

Second, how do we protect ourselves from external threats to our national security? How do we gain the materials necessary for our survival if these are possessed by other societies unwilling to part with them? These are obviously the questions of defense and offense that lead to the establishment of the **military** as a social institution. Once again, virtually all human societies have either an established ongoing military establishment or had one in the past. In the modern West most societies have subdivided the military institutions into key subinstitutions on the basis of their primary deployment—navies (sea), armies (land), air force (sky).

the military The social institution that provides the answers to the problems of national security and procurement of scarce resources from other societies that do not wish to part with such resources.

Third, how do we take care of the ill in the society? This problem has obviously led to the establishment of an institution primarily associated with **health.** In our own society involvement in this profession is regarded as particularly prestigeful given its humanistic orientation. Medicine and dentistry are its two main subdivisions, although other areas, notably psychiatry, are important.

health The social institution that provides the answer to the problem of how to care for the ill of society.

Fourth, how, in a modern society, do we communicate information to the population at large? This problem has become of greater significance in human societies as population and the amount of knowledge to be shared have increased. The resulting institution is **the media.** As this problem became more acute historically, the written word had to replace word of mouth. Books, flyers, and pamphlets became items of widespread use. Later, newspapers appeared. In the nineteenth century the telegraph made its appearance, and in the twentieth century, the telegram,

the media The social institution in a modern society that provides the answers to the problem of how to communicate with the population at large.

the telephone, radio, television, recordings, and film. All these inventions, obviously only possible at a certain level of technological development, increased the ability of people to communicate with one another.

SUMMARY

Social institutions such as the economy, the family, education, and religion are representative ways that society's members have developed to solve certain core human problems.

The economy deals with the basic needs problem—that of procuring the material necessities of life. To understand the modern economic order of the West, it is essential to examine the movement from a subsistence economy in the Middle Ages, where economics was seen as only one of many aspects of life, to the development of a growth economy in which economic activities predominate—from the late 1700s to the present. The development of a growth economy and the market system set the stage for the growth of industrialism—the process of manufacturing similar goods for mass consumption. Industrialism brought more adequate satisfaction of the basic needs problem to more people in Western society than any other economic arrangement of the past.

However, it has created problems as well. First, there has been increasing pollution of the environment and massive depletion of natural resources. Second, factory life has contributed to boredom, exploitation, and lengthy work weeks. Third, industrialism has created "organization men" who work in the context of huge corporations and lack interest in their jobs. Finally, there is the presence of widespread poverty in the midst of economic prosperity.

Almost everywhere, the family is responsible for dealing with the core human problems of regulating sexuality, reproducing new members, and socializing the children. Murdock argued that the family was universal and that everywhere it performed the functions of reproduction, socialization, control of sexual relations, and economic cooperation. However, a few family forms such as those found among the Nayar of India, on Israeli kibbutzim, and in present-day American society (e.g., the ever-growing single-parent family), may not fit Murdock's conception.

Whether or not it is universal, family life varies from culture to culture with respect to type of family unit (nuclear and extended families being the most prominent subtypes), form of marriage (monogamy, polygyny, polyandry), place of residence of the married couple (neolocal, patrilocal, matrilocal), and type of descent system (patrilineal, matrilineal, bilateral).

Industrialization has been associated with the decline of the large three-generation family—the extended family—and an increase in the nuclear family form. Industrialization has also been implicated in the declining status of the aged. Data suggest that the American family, rather than being in a state of decline, is actually experiencing changes while still maintaining sustained commitment from most members of society.

The educational institution in modern societies deals with the core human problem of providing the young with the specialized knowledge necessary to perform the complex tasks of society and the generalized knowledge necessary to be well-informed citizens. Many people associate education with innovation and change. However, a central function of education is the maintenance of the status quo. More specifically, education both routes people into acceptable status quo jobs and reinforces the basic values. Moreover, it "tracks" students so that white, middle-class children will continue to fill the desirable occupational roles, whereas low-paying and unpleasant jobs are being supplied with lower-class and minority manpower. Less obviously, education serves as a mechanism of social control, baby-sitting for very young children (thereby allowing adults more occupational freedom), and acting as a custodian for older children, keeping them both off the streets for a good portion of the day and out of the labor market where they would likely create massive unemployment for many adult members of society. Moreover, the structure of American education was seen to be essentially authoritarian in character. This condition was linked to the necessity for a bureaucratized, industrialized society to produce adults capable and willing to work within a highly regulated and routinized occupational system. Contrarily, the educational institution has been responsive to attempts to make it more equitable in recent years (desegregation and busing) and has continued to provide advancement to more particular groups—most notably, women in the period from 1970 to 1980.

The religious institution answers questions about the ultimate meaning in life. Its key feature is its focus on what are recognized as sacred beliefs, practices, or objects. Different theories argue for different functions of religion. Marx saw it as an institution that continued the oppression of the poor. Durkheim viewed it as the symbolic worship of society and as a prime means of ensuring social integration. Freud saw it as a means of satisfying the individual's deepest anxieties and hopes as well as a way of ensuring psychological internalization of society's most important rules. Weber viewed religion as a prime ingredient in the legitimation of important social change.

Religious associations take the form of cult, sect, or church, depending on their degree of institutionalization and level of formality. Cults and sects are loosely structured and unconventional; churches are highly organized and usually draw their memberships from the cultural and economic mainstream of a society.

Finally, recent evidence has indicated the widespread prevalence of religious experience among modern Americans, suggesting that religion may truly have an "other worldly" function as well as the "this worldly" functions previously mentioned.

Other important institutions were briefly considered. The political system is the institution that solves the core human problem of attaining group goals and enforcing obedience to social rules. Key subareas are political process, the government, the police force, and the legal system.

The military is the social institution that provides the answers to the core human problems of national security and procurement of scarce resources that other societies have but are unwilling to give up. Health is the social institution that provides the answers to the core human problem of how to care for the ill of society. And, finally, the media is the institution in a modern society that provides the answer to the problem of how to communicate with the population at large.

QUESTIONS, EXERCISES, PROJECTS

1. Define an institution and list three characteristics that clearly distinguish an institution from other aspects of social structure (e.g., "social class").
2. Briefly outline the development of the modern economic system.
3. Recalling your hometown, write a short paper indicating whether poverty was a social problem. If it was, to the best of your knowledge, does Gans' theory of the positive functions of poverty help explain the existence of poverty in your town. If poverty was not a problem, indicate why it wasn't and describe the social class structure of your town (refer back to Chapter 5 if you wish).
4. List and define the different types of family structure, residential pattern, descent system, and marriage relationships.
5. In Box 6–6 Marvin Harris argues that men continue to dominate women because of men's desire to maintain power in a

society. Outline Harris' theory and, taking examples from your own experience, give examples of male domination. Make specific suggestions regarding how this system of domination might be changed.

6. Do the aged have a crucial role in modern America? Give examples from your own experience.

7. How has your own education provided the generalized and specialized knowledge necessary to live the "good life" in our society?

8. Is education a mechanism of social control? If you answer "yes," describe how, in your experience, this mechanism has worked; if you answer "no" describe how, in your experience, you have been free to choose your own educational direction.

9. Has your education been frequently "ecstatic" as this experience is described by George Leonard? If it has been, what social circumstances have contributed to these experiences; if it hasn't been, what social circumstances have contributed to the lack of these experiences?

10. Define religion and give three examples of different religious groups from your experience.

11. What are the four main sociological theories of the function of religion in society? Which of these seems to you to describe the function of religion most accurately?

12. Distinguish among cults, sects, and churches and give two examples of each.

13. Give five examples of American civil religion from your experience.

14. How has the political institution shaped your life as a member of this society?

15. The media is all-pervasive in modern life. Write an essay describing how the media serves as a mechanism of socialization (refer to Chapter 3 if you wish).

COLLECTIVE BEHAVIOR

In Chapters 4, 5, and 6 we focused on aspects of social life that are, in one form or another, relatively permanent features of all modern societies—status and role, primary and secondary groups, formal organizations, social stratification, and social institutions. Just because these aspects of social structure are relatively permanent, however, does not mean that they are static and unchanging. Indeed, in many of our examples we tried to show how certain aspects of social structure—the American family, for example—have been remarkably sensitive to the dynamics of social interaction over the years.

In Chapters 7 and 8 we focus more directly on these dynamics as they occur in many modern societies. In this chapter we are concerned with the form of less-structured interaction that sociologists call collective behavior; in the next, we shall look at the processes of social change in general.

Collective behavior occurs whenever human beings come together in a relatively spontaneous manner in a situation in which their actions are not fully controlled by conventional norms, values, and sanctions. In this chapter we examine forms of collective behavior known as crowds, mass hysteria, rumor, public opinion, and social movements. Sociologists generally approach the study of collective behavior by focusing on three phenomena: contagion, convergence of attitudes, and emergent norms/alienation.

collective behavior The behavior of groups of people who come together in a relatively spontaneous manner. Their actions are not fully controlled by conventional norms, values, and sanctions.

CONTAGION

contagion A process whereby emotions, attitudes, and actions spread quickly from one participant to another, transforming the separate individuals into a uniform mass that thinks and acts in concert.

When collective behavior arises, people may act quite differently from how they would in everyday situations. For example, they may uncritically accept attitudes that would otherwise be distasteful to them and may say and do things that they would normally find repulsive, such as ridiculing another person or committing murder and mayhem. Some forms of collective behavior can temporarily transform many people rapidly and intensively into a uniform mass that thinks and acts in concert. Such a transformation process is known as **contagion** and is one of the most important elements of collective behavior (Turner and Killian, 1957).

The contagion approach to the study of collective behavior focuses on the social and psychological conditions that allow people temporarily to act differently from how they would act under everyday circumstances. We examine these conditions in the context of the major types of contagious collective behavior: crowds, mass hysteria, and rumors.

Crowds

crowd A temporary cluster of people who react together to a common stimulus while in close physical contact.

A **crowd** is a temporary cluster of people who react together to a common stimulus while in close physical contact with one another. Sociologists distinguish between two types of crowds: expressive and active.

expressive crowd A crowd that exists to provide a release of tension for its members through their reaction to an observed event.

Expressive Crowd. One of the most easily recognized crowd types is the **expressive crowd.** Common examples of the expressive crowd are people at revivalist religious services, people gathered together to observe some happening in a public place, and members of an audience to a concert, film, or sporting event. As suggested by its name, the central focus of an expressive crowd is that its members express themselves in some way about the thing they are observing together. Typical forms of self-expression are laughing, screaming, crying, singing, applauding, whistling, cheering, and so on. An example is behavior at a rock concert.

On the psychological level, the primary goal of the expressive crowd is to allow its members some type of continuing tension release. Although tension release such as screaming or laughing is occasionally permitted in normal, everyday interaction, it is not normatively sanctioned as the primary purpose of that interaction. For this reason forms of tension release are generally not continued over long periods of time. (Imagine, for example, what the other people in a classroom may think of two students who come to class and giggle incessantly throughout the period.)

Expressive crowds provide a release from everyday tensions and routine. Rock concerts—here one given by Michael Jackson—have served as a focus of tension release for American young people since the early 1950s with the advent of Elvis Presley. They serve also as a means of subcultural identification.

Expressive crowds are special social situations outside everyday norms where continuing tension release is permissible. For example, a Marx Brothers movie provides a 2-hour time slot during which laughter—from incessant giggling to outright guffawing—is allowed free rein; a sporting event allows a period of time during which people may scream, jump up and down, and holler obscenities in public. In expressive crowds people may act out their psychological frustrations and tensions without becoming the object of negative social sanctions (as they surely would if they indulged excessively in these practices in everyday situations).

A factor that allows tension release full flow in expressive crowds is the *anonymity* of the situation. Gustave LeBon, (1895) in his early analysis of crowds, argued that when individuals come together in a crowd, they in a sense "lose" their individuality. No longer can their actions be easily identified by others. Rather, they are acting in concert with many other people, many or all of whom they may not know. Such anonymity of action LeBon saw as lessening the controls on behavior that usually exist in everyday life. People feel they can engage in all sorts of behavior that they could not elsewhere. Thus, it is not unusual to find that people who normally fill passive roles in everyday interaction become very aggressive if the crowd does. Often, in fact, people will actually seek out expressive crowds to release their tensions; for example, after a hard week's work men may go to hockey games on the weekend. In other words, the focus of the expressive crowd members is primarily *internal*. The outside event (the revival meeting, the championship game) often is merely an "excuse" for such social behavior to occur.

Because of this internal focus of the expressive crowd and the lack of its participants' focus on the structure of social interaction itself, it is the most predictable of collective behavior forms. Its participants usually follow a clearly worked out set of norms. They gather at an assigned time, cluster about as expected, express themselves when appropriate, and so on. Of course, the intensity of an expressive crowd's reaction is not *completely* predictable—the rock star may give a lackluster performance; the home team may never score. (For more on the relationship of the expressive crowd to the audience, see Box 7–1). Similarly, there are times when expressive crowds unpredictably transform themselves into active crowds; and when this happens, the norms that controlled the crowd may be dispensed with altogether. A perfect example is the rock performance that so inflames the audience that people are hurt and property is damaged.

Active Crowd.   The second major type of crowd behavior is known as the **active crowd.** In this type of collective gathering people come together to attempt some change in the world around them. Thus, in contrast to the expressive crowd, the focus of an active crowd is primarily *external*. Its members wish to change their relationship to some outside agency, such as the police, college administration, employers, or some other group. Tension release may still be an important function of active crowds, but it is decidedly secondary to the goal of change.

active crowd A crowd that forms in order to act out a shared feeling toward persons or events and to attempt to change some situation or relationship.

Because of its focus on changing the situation, the active crowd does not have a coherent set of special norms with which its members can identify; rather, it is the main function of the active crowd to work out such new relationships. Thus members of an active crowd are much more ambivalent about how to act than those in an expressive crowd. This ambivalence makes active crowds unpredictable and potentially dangerous. In speaking about this characteristic, the noted social psychologist Roger Brown (1965, p. 736) says that the people in the crowd

Box 7–1   THE HOME ADVANTAGE IN SPORTS: THE EFFECT OF THE EXPRESSIVE CROWD

Players, coaches, and fans have known for years that there is a distinct advantage to playing sporting events before a home audience. Many reasons have been given for this advantage: team quality (better teams win more often at home), knowledge of the home playing ground, visitor fatigue from travel, and, not least, the contagion element—the encouragement to superior performance felt by a player when being exhorted by the expressive home audience. Until recently, however, little evidence about this whole phenomenon of the home advantage existed.

Consequently, in order to determine the magnitude and importance of what they called "the invigorating influence of supportive social congregation," Schwartz and Barsky (1977) examined five types of sport. More specifically, they looked at the results of (1) 1,880 major league baseball games played in 1971; (b) 182 professional football games played in the National Football League in 1971; (c) 910 college football games played in 1971; (d) 542 professional hockey games played in the National Hockey League in the 1971 to 1972 season; and (e) 1,485 college basketball games played in the Philadelphia area between 1952 and 1966.

Interestingly, Schwartz and Barsky not only found that the home advantage was a very real factor in all these sports, but they also discovered that the magnitude of the home advantage varied by sport. Baseball teams won 53 percent of their home games; professional football teams won 58 percent; college football teams, 60 percent; hockey teams, 64 percent; and college basketball teams; a rather remarkable 82 percent. Since this variation was quite striking, as well as unexpected, Schwartz and Barsky attempted to develop an explanation for the variation by examining the variables previously thought to be at work.

First, they examined the variable of team quality. Although they found, as might be expected, that better quality teams enjoyed a larger home advantage when playing lower quality teams (e.g., higher quality baseball teams won 60 percent of the home games played against low quality teams), they also found that higher quality teams still *kept* their home advantage when playing teams of equally good caliber (higher quality baseball teams won 52 percent of their home games against equally high quality opponents). The same results were found when the data for lower quality teams were examined: Although lower quality teams lost some of their home advantage playing high quality visitors, they did not lose as much as they would have when playing a high quality team on *its* home ground, and they enjoyed the "normal" home advantage (in baseball, about 52 percent of the time) when playing teams of equally low quality. These findings suggested to Schwartz and Barsky that the home advantage was *not* attributable to team quality.

Next, the researchers examined the possible contribution of knowledge of the home field to the home advantage. They reasoned that knowledge of the home field would be most important in sports where standardization of playing area was least prevalent. Whereas rather pronounced field variation exists in baseball (turf, distance to fence, angle of fence, etc.), less exists in football (type of turf and weather conditions primarily), and very little exists in hockey and basketball. Consequently, if home advantage was affected significantly by this variable, one would expect baseball to enjoy a greater home advantage than the other sports, particularly over hockey and basketball. However, Schwartz and Barsky's data indicated exactly the opposite pattern. This suggested that knowledge of playing field is not a major variable contributing to the home advantage.

Third, they turned to the issue of visitor fatigue. Although they had no way to assess whether, in any *individual* game, visitor fatigue would have made the visitors play worse, they reasoned that the effects of this variable could be seen if the home advantage statistics were examined over a whole season. If the season were divided into first and second halves and visitor fatigue was a factor, they felt that the home advantage would be greater in the second half of the season when the visitors were more worn out from so much prior travel. They found no difference in home advantage between season halves in baseball, college football, and college basketball and only minimal differences in professional football and hockey (e.g., the home advantage increased from 55 percent in the first half of the season in professional football to only 57 percent in the second half). Thus they concluded that visitor fatigue had, at best, a minimal effect on home advantage.

At this point, only one variable remained that might significantly account for the home advantage: the contagious effect of the expressive audience itself. In examining this variable Schwartz and Barsky found that the home advantage clearly increases with crowd size. Using baseball as an example again, they discovered that home teams won only 48 percent of their games when attendance was low (less than 20 percent of stadium full), increased their winning percentage to 55 when crowd size was medium (20 to 39 percent of arena capacity), and peaked at a 57 percent winning advantage when attendance was high (over 40 percent of capacity).

Moreover, they argue that the reason why some sports have greater home advantage percentages over others can be explained by looking at two other factors: the nearness of the crowd to the playing area and the frequency and intensity of the crowd's reaction to the game's plays. Thus, baseball, the sport with the smallest home advantage, is a game where the audience is generally at some distance from the playing field and in which crowd reaction is slowly paced in accordance with the game. Football, the sport with the next highest home advantage, increases both these factors: the crowd, although still at some distance from the field usually *surrounds* the field (this is only possible in a few baseball parks) and the pace of the game is quicker and, literally, more hard hitting. Finally, hockey and basketball, the sports enjoying the largest home advantage, are games where the crowd is usually very close to the playing field and in which play and contact are very intense and frequent. Both these factors serve to increase the direct, continuing concentration of the audience on the game and the transference of emotion contagiously to the home players. Here is a quote from a Rutgers basketball promotion:

> At every bounce of the ball, a Rutgers cry erupts. Scarlet fans virtually surround the playing area and seem an extension of the action. Up above, there's no heaven for opponents, only a frenzy of support for the homesters. The fans cheer appreciably at every Scarlet effort and even the near-misses are given favor. Time-outs provide no comfort as the Rutgers band takes over and adds further support for the Scarlet. (cited in Schwartz and Barsky, 1977, p. 652)

In other words, Schwartz and Barsky conclude "that the home advantage is attributable in the main to audience support" (1977, p. 656). Howard Cosell, take note.

must have two opposing impulses, the same two impulses for every one. One of the impulses, the one initially dominant, is in conformity with a recognized norm or value, the other is not. The opposed impulses are such things as: to rush to an exit in a theater, to take one's turn in reaching the exit; to attempt to lynch someone, to let the law take its course; to try to push one's way to the teller's cage in a bank, to take one's turn; to make a confession and to be converted at a revival meeting, to remain a quiet member of the audience. [Furthermore, the] situation must be such that it is physically possible to take the non-normative action; i.e., there must be a theater exit or a person to be lynched or a teller's cage or a revival meeting.

What are the triggering mechanisms that induce active crowd behavior to go in one direction or another? One way of getting a partial answer to this question is to take a look at solutions to the problem of ambivalence experienced by active crowd members.

Members of active crowds are likely to be in a state of anomie (see the discussion of this term in Chapter 1) and their thoughts dominated by confusion, nervousness, and anxiety. Since the primary goal is change of some kind, established norms cannot be applied to give meaningful order. And, since a new relationship to the social world has not yet been worked out by the crowd, other norms of behavior are not readily available either. Consequently, members of such groups become highly susceptible to any solutions presented to resolve their predicament.

Imitation is one example of a solution to the ambivalence problem. Imagine yourself in an active crowd that is in a particularly ambivalent situation, say, protesting governmental policies concerning a war and facing a regiment of armed National Guardsmen. (This situation, of course, occurred often for members of the peace movement during the late 1960s.) Suppose you don't know what you are supposed to be doing. Suddenly, you see someone running. You start running, too. Others in the crowd think *you* must know what you are doing and start imitating you. Pretty soon everyone is running. Where? Why? Perhaps no one knows for sure, but any action seems to relieve the anxiety generated by ambivalence. This is contagion in its true sense.

imitation A radical solution to the ambivalence felt by active crowd members. They unthinkingly copy the actions of one another.

Suggestibility is another radical aspect that is often present in active crowds. One person in the crowd, often a leader, gets an idea and voices it aloud. If the suggestion purports to offer some solution to the anxiety of crowd members, they may immediately and uncritically agree with it. In the classic western movie, after the bank has been robbed and the outlaws have escaped, the sheriff says, "Let's go get 'em, boys!" and the crowd roars its ap-

suggestibility A radical solution to the ambivalence felt by active crowd members. Suggestions are uncritically accepted.

Gustave Le Bon (1841–1931) felt that the crowd represented humanity at its most volatile. In his principal works, *The Crowd* (1896) and *The Psychology of Revolution* (1913), Le Bon argued that modern times were becoming increasingly subject to the influences of crowds in everyday affairs. This situation he attributed to the supposed destruction of old institutional forms, such as the family, religion, and politics, by the advancing industrial age. Moreover, given the essentially irrational and unpredictable nature of crowd behavior, Le Bon worried that they would undermine the very fabric of civilization. Consequently, he felt strongly that those in power should resist, with force if necessary, mob behavior for the good of the society as a whole. Most sociologists today would not share Le Bon's extreme concerns about the inevitably destructive nature of crowds. Nevertheless, his theories regarding the role of anonymity, irrationality, and suggestibility of crowds are still useful.

proval. Everyone gets his gun and horse and rides off into the sunrise. Of course, if crowd members stopped and thought about what they were doing, they might act differently. Let's say one man's wife is due to have a baby any day and the posse is sure to keep him away for weeks. Or they might stop to consider the possibility that the outlaws are leading them into a trap. It is not crucial whether a suggestion actually will lead to a solution of the problem faced by the active crowd. What is important is whether it alleviates the ambivalence the crowd is feeling at the time.

A third radical solution to the problem of ambivalence is **emotional contagion,** whereby some emotional expression spreads rapidly throughout a crowd. The emotional level of an active crowd

emotional contagion A radical solution to the ambivalence felt by active crowd members. Emotional expression quickly spreads throughout a crowd.

is most often quite high; the members are assembled in the first place usually because of a strong desire for change; hence the ambivalence of the crowd situation adds tension. This emotional tension in active crowds is commonly released in the form of fear or anger.

Fear often becomes contagious when one or more members of a crowd suddenly feel a threat to personal safety or to the safety of the group and express this fear to others. The entire crowd may become convinced that they are being threatened and that desperate measures are necessary to preserve their well-being. When fear spreads through a crowd, panic may occur and crowd behavior may take a dangerous form. For example, in the Vietnam War, threatened by the Viet Cong, some retreating South Vietnamese soldiers trampled women and children in order to escape their pursuers.

Anger may spread in much the same way. In 1966 at a soccer game in Lima, Peru, a decision of the referee against the favorite

Active crowds, unlike their expressive counterparts, are always oriented toward some change in their relationship to the outside world. These New York transit workers are demonstrating for higher wages.

team quickly changed an expressive crowd into a raging active crowd. People trying to injure the offending official, then began getting mad at one another. The result was a major riot in which scores of people lost their lives and thousands more were injured.

Of course, the actions of active crowds need not always be so irrational. In criticizing what they regarded as the excessive emphasis of LeBon on the irrational nature of crowd behavior, Turner and Killian (1957) have argued that the behavior of an active crowd may not be random and haphazard at all; it may actually help to resolve a problem with which the crowd is faced.

In the area of racial disturbances, for example, southern lynchings of blacks may have accomplished just what they were intended to accomplish—to reinforce white supremacy in the eyes of both white and black communities and to deter those who might dare to challenge it in the future. Similarly, in the civil rights riots of the 1960s much of the destruction to property was not done randomly at all, but, rather, was focused on white-operated or white-controlled establishments that were known in the black community for exploiting its members.

A more recent example of an active crowd is provided by the Women's Peace Encampment in upstate New York. In the summer of 1983 women from all over the country came to a small camp near the Seneca army depot in the Finger Lakes region in order to protest the alleged storage of nuclear weapons at the army depot. To that end, the women staged a series of carefully planned, summer-long "crowd actions"—marching from the National Women's Historical Site in the town of Seneca Falls to the depot, confronting depot soldiers at the gates, allowing themselves to be arrested for "disturbing the peace," and so on. These actions brought much local and national attention to their cause. By the end of the summer the women's encampment had attained many of its goals—had helped stimulate a continuing national debate about the horrors of nuclear weapons, called attention to the fact that it was a camp run *entirely* by and for women, and underscored their political opposition to a male-dominated society (symbolized by the military). Clearly, such examples suggest that active crowds may have their ultimate objectives very much in view even in the presence of immediate tensions and anxieties.

To put it another way, not everyone involved in an active crowd is necessarily unconsciously susceptible to imitation, suggestibility, or emotional contagion. In fact, some people even use these mechanisms to manipulate crowds to achieve their own ends. Public speakers, politicians, sports coaches, and military personnel throughout history have been all aware of the characteristics of active crowds and have known how to move them in the direction they wished. Some manipulators have even gone so far as to plant associates in active crowds to start the contagious reactions. On the positive side, public speakers such as St. Paul have been able to motivate their listeners to undertake and accomplish great personal improvements in their lives. More negatively, Adolf Hitler was able to engulf the world in war partly because of his ability to manipulate active crowds.

Our discussion thus far indicates that the expressive crowd is usually based around a stable pattern of interaction and is quite predictable. On the other hand, the active crowd has many fewer elements of stability and predictability. In our next case, these elements disappear completely, with virtually *any* reaction becoming possible.

Mass Hysteria

Mass hysteria refers to a form of contagious collective behavior in which the same fear motivates a large number of individuals to react whether or not they are all physically together. It is usually initiated through the mechanism of suggestibility. Some idea is communicated to people which produces great fear in them. They spread their terror by passing on the information to others nearby, producing rapidly proliferating emotional contagion. Then, usually while this process is continuing, someone acts—for example, flees—and others start to imitate the behavior. In medieval Europe, for example, word of the plague was often enough to produce mass hysteria with the characteristics just described. Sometimes the actions taken by the frightened people helped solve the problem they faced; sometimes they did not. More recently, there are the tragic examples of someone yelling "fire" in a crowded restaurant, night spot, or theater. In mass hysteria, as in the panic that may overtake an active crowd, the immediate release of almost unbearable tension is the objective of the action.

Perhaps the best modern example of mass hysteria was initiated by Orson Welles's 1938 radio dramatization of H. G. Wells' novel *The War of the Worlds.* Welles presented the subject of the novel, an invasion of earth by hostile Martians, in the form of a news broadcast. Millions of listeners failed to realize that the program was merely a dramatic adaptation and believed that the radio station was actually reporting the landing of the Martian spaceships in New Jersey.

The result was mass hysteria. In short order, large-scale panic and terror spread throughout New York, New Jersey, the South, and even as far west as San Francisco. Thousands fled their homes to escape the reported "gas raids from Mars." Phone calls swamped police departments. As reported by Howard Koch (1970, p. 96), the following was typical of reactions to the broadcast.

mass hysteria A form of collective behavior in which the same fear motivates a large number of people to react, whether or not they are physically together.

Riots may not be as "irrational" as early social thinkers such as Le Bon thought. For example, the 1980 uprising in Miami's Liberty City left 16 dead and 400 injured; but most of the violence was directed at white members of the community who were seen as responsible for alleged police brutality and economic discrimination.

My girl friend and I were at a party in the village. Someone turned on the radio. It was just when the Martians were spraying the people at Grovers Mill with the heat ray. At first we couldn't believe it was happening but it was so real we stayed glued to the radio getting more scared every minute. My girl began to cry. She wanted to be with her family. The party broke up in a hurry, our friends scattering in all directions. I drove like crazy up Sixth Avenue. I don't know how fast—fifty, maybe sixty miles an hour. The traffic cops at the street crossings just stared at us, they couldn't believe their eyes, whizzing right past them going through the red lights. I didn't care if I got a ticket. It was all over anyway. Funny thing, none of the cops chased us. I guess they were too flabbergasted. My apartment was on the way so I stopped just long enough to rush in and shout up to my father that the Martians had landed and we were all going to be killed and I was taking my girl home. When we got to her place, her parents were waiting for us. My father had called them. Told them to hold me there until he could send a doctor as I'd gone out of my mind.

The day after the broadcast, newspaper headlines read, "Fake 'War' on Radio Spreads Panic over U.S.," "Radio Listeners in Panic, Taking War Drama as Fact," and "Fake Radio 'War' Stirs Terror through U.S." Reactions to Welles' broadcast point up how susceptible most of us are to believing even the most bizarre stories if they are made to sound at least minimally plausible and tap a deep fear within us. If you believe this type of hysteria couldn't happen today, see Box 7–2).

Rumor

From a sociological point of view **rumor** can also be regarded as a form of contagious collective behavior. We can define it as face-to-face communication that develops in response to some extraordinary circumstance among individuals who "pool their intellectual resources in an effort to orient themselves" (Shibutani, 1966). In other words, rumor usually arises in order to provide a satisfactory definition of some ambiguous situation. Like imitation, suggestibility, and emotional contagion in crowds, rumor serves to relieve tensions by explaining circumstances that have not been previously understood and resolved.

Rosnow (1974, p. 27) describes rumor as "(a) a communication process (or pattern) as well as a product, (b) one that is easily started and disseminated but which may be difficult to stop, and (c) one that is constructed around unauthenticated information."

These characteristics are well represented in a rumor that circulated in 1969 to the effect that Paul McCartney of the Beatles had been killed in an automobile accident and replaced by a double. Despite numerous denials *by McCartney himself* and an overwhelming lack of hard evidence, the story of McCartney's death continued to gain momentum as well as credibility. As the process unfolded, Beatles fans discovered a number of "clues" to support their unfounded suspicions. The following have been taken from a study by Rosnow and Fine (1974) and show just how bizarre the rumor process may become.

rumor Face-to-face communication of information that develops in order to provide a definition of an ambiguous situation.

- Clue 1. In the Beatles album *Revolution* the voice saying "Number Nine, Number Nine, Number Nine" becomes "Turn me on, dead man" when played backward.
- Clue 2. In "Strawberry Fields" from the *Magical Mystery Tour* album someone is heard to say "I buried Paul" when the background noise is minimized.
- Clue 3. The *Sgt. Pepper* album depicts a part of a grave containing flowers in the shape of Paul's bass guitar.
- Clue 4. In a photograph inside the cover of the *Sgt. Pepper*

Box 7–2   MYSTERIOUS ILLNESS. ALL IN THE MIND?

Outbreaks seem to strike groups under pressure

By Linda Matchan
Globe Staff

The auditorium was packed with youngsters rehearsing for the spring concert when the first of nine East Templeton grade schoolers swooned and fell to the floor. In a matter of minutes, scores of children were rushed outside into the fresh air, about 40 of them beset by nausea and dizziness. Six were taken to the hospital.

Because the children recovered quickly, the concert went on as scheduled that May night in 1981. It quickly became a disaster. After a girl in the front row collapsed, 30 more were stricken. Willard Chiasson, the school superintendent, recalls the pandemonium as "lemmings going off a cliff."

In the weeks and months of investigation that followed, public health officials could find no organic cause for the mysterious outbreak in the small Western Massachusetts school's water supply, ventilation system, food, or buses.

Today, more than two years later, many medical experts have concluded that while the children felt genuinely sick, the illness originated in their minds and not their bodies.

Dr. Gary W. Small, a Massachusetts General Hospital psychiatric resident who studied the incident on his own along with state investigators, says he was soon convinced the baffling malady had a straightforward explanation. Having seen it once before in an elementary school in Norwood, he diagnosed the episode as a classic instance of mass hysteria.

While social scientists continue to analyze how and why "mass psychogenic illness" takes place, there are other scientists who resist the concept entirely. They are reluctant to endorse a psychological explanation, mostly because of the ambiguity and complexity involved in discerning the true cause of an ailment that has people falling like dominos from no apparent cause.

"But what many people don't understand is that although one may not find a toxic cause for the illness, it's a true illness with true symptoms," said Dr. Bess Miller, a medical epidemiologist for the US Center for Disease Control who studied this year's outbreak of mass hysteria among Arab school children in the Israel-occupied West Bank. "What these people are feeling is real."

Locally, the Templeton and Norwood incidents reflect a growing number of recorded examples of what may be a contagious psychosomatic illness. The phenomenon, say experts, seems to afflict members of a peer group, mostly women and children who are under emotional pressure—such as a public performance that takes place in a crowded atmosphere. Some social scientists would extend the scope to other kinds of epidemic obsessional behavior—such phenomena as race-riot frenzy and witch-hunt mania.

In addition to the general lack of violent behavior, the episodes at Templeton and Norwood are different in at least one other critical respect. As assessed by Duke University sociologists Alan Kerckhoff and Kurt Back in a book on the subject, the

Boston Globe, October 17, 1983, pp. 41, 43.

children do not experience "an active response to some element in the situation. It is a passive experience. The actors do not *do* something so much as something happens to them."

Domino effect

Investigators have observed a pattern, however, in which the first person stricken in the public-forum kind of episode is often genuinely ill; it is the others who become caught up in the contagion of a precipitating event.

The Templeton and Norwood incidents are not the only recent Massachusetts cases. A few days after the Norwood incident, for instance, 32 Hopkinton Senior-Junior High School students were rushed to the hospital with stomach cramps, nausea and dizziness after a student fainted while giving a speech in English class.

In an interview, Small said that while reports of epidemic hysteria are turning up more frequently in medical literature, it's uncertain whether this reflects increasing incidence or just sudden attention from researchers.

By all accounts, it is a phenomenon that is difficult to diagnose. The usual symptoms—anxiety, weakness, dizziness, nausea, fainting spells, and hyperventilation—spread rapidly and then recede quickly, often occurring against a backdrop of highly-charged emotions or afflicting a group that is under psychological stress.

"Whenever people under stress gather together, the potential for mass hysteria exists," said Small, who now works at UCLA's medical school in Los Angeles.

Profile of hysteria

In the past few years, medical investigators have pinpointed certain mass-hysteria characteristics:

•A preponderance of illness among girls or women, perhaps, suggests Small, "because it is more (socially) acceptable for women to complain, and it is not acceptable for men to express discomfort."

•A preponderance of illness in adolescents or preadolescents, presumably, investigators believe, because children in this age group are especially vulnerable to peer pressure.

•A tendency for outbreaks to occur in schools or factories "in which there are no immediate means of escaping the stress," Small said.

•Some scientists have observed, too, that the behavior seems to sweep through members of cohesive groups. In the Templeton case, for example, hospitalized children were more likely than others to have noticed close friends becoming sick. Elsewhere, researchers have also noted that the first person who falls ill is frequently a group leader.

Exactly how unusual behavior like this becomes accepted in a group and spreads is unclear. One pattern, said Small, seems to be that the first person to become sick —at a class performance, for example, or in some other stressful situation— becomes legitimately ill. Another child observes it, becomes anxious about the fact that he too has a headache or a nervous stomach, assumes the symptoms, and sets off a chain reaction.

album Paul is wearing an arm patch that reads OPD for Officially Pronounced Dead.
- Clue 5. On the back cover of the *Sgt. Pepper* album everyone is facing forward except Paul.
- Clue 6. The *Abbey Road* album cover shows Paul leaving a cemetery, walking barefoot in the way that corpses are buried in England.

- Clue 7. The license plate on a car on the *Abbey Road* album cover reads "28 IF" suggesting Paul's age *if* he had survived.
- Clue 8. In a picture in the *Magical Mystery Tour* album all the Beatles are wearing red carnations except Paul who wears a black one.
- Clue 9. The walrus (meaning "corpse") in the song "I am the Walrus" is supposed to refer to Paul.
- Clue 10. In the song, "Glass Onion," John Lennon gives numerous clues including his announcement that the walrus was actually Paul.
- Clue 11. When the picture of Paul, alive and well, on the cover of *Life* Magazine was held up to the light, a car from the ad on the reverse side could be seen superimposed across his chest.

leveling The elimination of extraneous detail from rumor as it is passed from person to person.

sharpening The emphasis on certain aspects of a rumor according to the selective perception of participants.

assimilation The modification of a rumor to fit the expectations, habits, and belief systems of participants.

Allport and Postman (1952) have suggested that the transmission of a rumor involves three interrelated tendencies: leveling, sharpening, and assimilation. **Leveling** occurs as a rumor is passed from person to person. All extraneous information is sorted out, so that the rumor becomes more concise and consequently easier to repeat. **Sharpening** is applied to what is left of the rumor as the leveling process goes forward. Certain elements of the rumor are emphasized to fit the selective perception of the participants, that is, those who pass the rumor tend to focus on what they think are its most interesting or important parts. Finally, **assimilation** takes place. The rumor is modified so that it fits into the habits, expectations, and belief systems of the participants. As a result of this final step, the event contained in the rumor tends to become what the transmitters of the rumor expect or desire it to be. Box 7–3 puts the rumor process into everyday perspective.

It is usually difficult, if not impossible, to track down the original source of a rumor. We shall probably never know, for example, who first suggested that fast-food hamburger contains worms, that a rat was found in commercial fried chicken, that bubble gum contains spider eggs, that Procter and Gamble was owned by the Moonies, that a mouse was discovered in a soda bottle, that a certain punk rock group steps on baby chickens or strangles cats during its concerts, or that a carbonated candy explodes in children's stomachs. (see Box 7–3). All the foregoing rumors are erroneous; yet they have spread far and wide during the last few years. Once a rumor gets going, it is difficult to stop!

Psychologists have attempted to explain why rumors are so attractive to many people in the first place. One approach suggests that rumors allow individuals to pass on communication messages in which their own personal anxieties or hostilities are expressed,

but not identified as being their own. Hence the central characteristic that attracts many people to rumors is that they need not take any personal responsibility for the information they are transmitting; they can claim and actually believe that they are merely repeating what someone else is supposed to have thought or done.

The most common form of this type of rumor is gossip about other people. For example, when we say that "George" is a mean so-and-so because of the way he treats people in the office, we may be expressing our *personal* dislike of George under the guise of "reporting the facts." On the other hand, we may be trying to assuage our own feelings of guilt because we too treat other people in the office badly (but less badly, we think, than George). By pointing to *George's* failings we are "telling" ourselves and others that we aren't so bad after all.

Box 7–3   SPREADING THE NEWS: ANATOMY OF RUMORS

They tend to reinforce people's views of the world

By Jean Caldwell
Globe Correspondent

This year, the story went this way in Springfield, Holyoke, Chicopee and Westfield: There was a little old "lady" at the local mall who told patrons that she was sick and needed a ride home. "She" turned out to be a man in disguise who wielded an axe.

In nearby Norwalk, Conn., a different story made the rounds this fall. A small girl supposedly disappeared while shopping in a department store with her mother and was found in a restroom with her hair cut off and dressed in boy's clothing.

Such stories have spread like wildfire this year in the Northeast, ranging from Pittsfield to Pennsylvania. Frightened mothers have flooded police stations, newspapers and mall officials with inquiries.

But the stories have all turned out to be just rumors—a psychological phenomenon that's just beginning to be studied and understood. While the research is sparse, one thing has been established: It is virtually impossible to trace a persistent, widespread rumor back to its source.

The handful of psychologists and sociologists who have looked into it say rumors are spread mostly for subliminal reasons: The teller is isolated and wants to make conversation and get attention: the stories offer entertainment; and, perhaps most of all, the rumor makes all the participants feel safe—or at least a little better in an uncertain world. For unknown reasons, the mall rumor seems to recur about every 10 years and generally starts in the spring.

Recently, the mall story or one of its variations has jumped all over the country. Fredrick Koenig, a sociology professor at Tulane University in New Orleans, says he has heard from friends and associates that the story was circulating in parts of Texas, the Midwest, the Rocky Mountain states, the Far West.

Koenig says most rumors act as a curious kind of balm. When you hear the mall rumor, he says, it is easy "to nod your head, roll your eyes and think, 'It's a jungle out there. You don't know who you can trust. You can't go any where.'" People who view the world as a dangerous place find this an oddly reassuring rumor, says Koenig.

While the hit-and-run rumor can be just a short-lived nuisance for mall shopkeepers and desk sergeants in Western Massachusetts, it can be a stealthy, relentless enemy for major corporations, which have occasionally had to launch national advertising campaigns to wrestle elusive apparitions to the ground.

Fighting back

For instance, McDonalds suffered a 20 percent dip in sales in the Southwest in 1978 when a totally baseless rumor spread that worms had been added to their hamburgers. It began a media campaign that stressed the use of "100 percent pure beef."

Two years ago, Procter & Gamble Co. finally went to court against individuals who had been passing out leaflets and otherwise disseminating the notion that the company was affiliated with Satan. A recent article in Management Review notes that the company received as many as 15,000 calls a month when the outrageous rumor was at its height in late 1981.

Source: Boston Globe, November 21, 1983, pp. 61, 66.

KMart, Jockey shorts and the Entenmann bakery all have been the victims of false rumors. Entenmann's had to launch an anti-rumor campaign complete with a press conference and hundreds of letters to churches to deny a widely-circulated rumor that it was owned by the Rev. Moon's Unification Church—the "Moonies." It isn't and never was.

Koenig, who has been a consultant to a number of large corporations beset by rumor-mongers in recent months, says he is one of the few sociologists who believes the best way to stop a rumor is to deny it publicly and frequently.

Koenig believes, however, that making a rumor "news" changes its character. "It implies that anyone who reads this and passes it on is a fool and knave and up to no good. Most people will refrain from telling it if they know it is not true, even if it is a good story."

A case in point is the Connecticut rumor about the little girl in the department store. Eventually, it circulated so widely in the Berkshires that irate readers called the Berkshire Eagle in Pittsfield demanding to know why the story was being suppressed. Julie Sell, a reporter for the Eagle, said callers insisted that story had to be true because so many people were talking about it. The rumor stopped when Sell wrote an op-ed article under the heading "Anatomy of a Rumor." She said it made those who had spread the rumor look foolish—although she didn't write it to embarrass people.

Dr. Ralph Rosnow of Temple University, who is coauthor of the book, "Rumor and Gossip, the Social Psychology of Hearsay," says the mall-department store rumor is a less gruesome version of the rumor that circulated in Detroit during a time of racial riots. This rumor involved a boy who was abducted into a department store restroom and castrated. The boy and the abductor were always of opposite races and the race of the boy always matched that of the person telling the rumor, which circulated through both the black and the white communities.

Rosnow said his research leads him to believe uncertainty and anxiety are necessary to fuel the rumor. He says one hypothesis of rumors is that they are an effort to make sense of the world and to reduce anxiety. Even a rumor that scares the person telling it to death "gives them consistency in their view as they believe in evil. It gives them psychological solace."

One of the biggest problems with any form of gossip is that, like any form of human communication, it shapes how others are seen and how others see us. Since much gossip is negatively oriented (e.g., pointing out George's alleged failings), it can introduce strain and ill-feeling into a social setting (see cartoon on p. 270).

CONVERGENCE OF ATTITUDES

The **convergence of attitudes** approach accounts for collective behavior by emphasizing that people who act in like manner often already share the same predispositions to action before they ever come together. The event capturing their common attention serves merely to set off their shared dispositions, leading to recognizable collective behavior. Perhaps the best way to examine convergence of attitudes is to examine the main type of collective behavior associated with it, public opinion.

convergence of attitudes The approach to collective behavior that emphasizes that people who act in like manner often already share the same predispositions to action before they ever come together.

SALLY FORTH   by Greg Howard

Sally Forth by Greg Howard, © 1983 Field Enterprises, Inc. Courtesy of
News America Syndicate.

Public Opinion

public opinion The convergence of the separate opinions held by members of a
group in a spontaneous
attempt to resolve a controversial issue that cannot be
decided by existing norms.

When people are confronted with a controversial issue that cannot
be decided on the basis of an existing norm, **public opinion** frequently arises as a spontaneous attempt to find resolution of the
issue. Public opinion is never unanimous nor is it necessarily the
opinion of a majority. But public opinion is a *collective* experience,
forming out of debate and discussion, in short, out of the disagreements that can be found among the members of society as illustrated in Box 7–4. Thus public opinion represents the convergence of all of the separate opinions found in a group (Blumer,
1965).

When examined properly, public opinion is not the mystery it
once was. The political poll organizations, for example, using the
sampling methods of sociology, have made the predicting of public opinion into a very accurate procedure. Polling, in fact, has
become so exact, even in large-scale situations, that the pollsters
rarely miss on their predictions. For example, in the 1972 presidential elections the majority of polls were less than one tenth of
1 percent wrong in predicting the percentage of people who
would vote for candidates Nixon and McGovern across the whole
country! More recent election polls, even when wrong, have typically been off by only a few percentage points.

Especially since the Watergate affair in the early 1970s, Americans have been extremely aware of attempts to detect and measure public opinion. During the final year of the Nixon administration, for example, numerous public opinion polls from such
pollsters as Gallup and Harris clearly documented a sharp loss of
public confidence in the president and majority support for his
impeachment throughout the country.

For more than 45 years pollsters have measured stability and
change in public opinion. The stability of public opinion is illustrated in the case of attitudes toward gun control. Since 1938 the

Box 7-4 DIVIDED PUBLIC OPINION: THE ERA

Issues that propose what appear to be major changes in the way a society works or in the way in which people think about the world often cause serious differences in public opinion. One such issue was raised by the proposed Equal Rights Amendment (ERA) to the Constitution. If approved by two-thirds of the states, the ERA would have made it illegal to treat anyone differently on the basis of sex, race, creed, and so on. The ERA was championed by the Women's Liberation movement as a major step in eradicating discrimination on the basis of sex. In the following quotes (the *Winston-Salem Sunday Journal and Sentinel,* 1975), two North Carolina ministers, each representative of sizable portions of the public, cite the same background material to argue about the ERA, with one finding biblical evidence in favor of its passage and the other finding biblical evidence against it. The ERA was shortly to come before the North Carolina public in a referendum when these articles appeared.

"Neither male nor female . . ."

By the Rev. James R. Reeves,
United Methodist Pastor

It has recently come to my attention that some of my friends and coworkers in the church are opposing the Equal Rights Amendment on theological grounds.

Some say the ERA will destroy the so-called "divine order of the family." Concerning this divine order, I am prepared for considerable prayer and biblical debate with these brethren, for I find this inconsistent with the teachings of Jesus.

Christ dealt with all persons, not as "male" or "female," but as individuals in need of spiritual and/or physical redemp-tion. I find no sexist teachings in the words of Jesus, and even Paul's more sexist tendencies are moderated by his more defined theology.

What greater statement of equality is there than these eloquent verses from Galatians: "For as many of you as were baptized into Christ have put on Christ. There is neither Jew nor Greek, there is neither slave nor free, there is neither male nor female, for you are all one in Christ Jesus" (Chapter 3:27–28 RSV).

I believe that God's love comes equally to both men and women and therefore any distinction that is based on the superior–inferior assumption is contrary to the will of God.

ERA's greatest contribution is in providing for the fundamental dignity and individuality of each citizen. In North Carolina, women's salaries are often thousands of dollars less than men's for the same work!

The presence of women in the labor force is not new. Luke 8:1–3 tells us that at times Jesus and his disciples were supported by their women followers.

Even for those who believe in the so-called "divine order of the family" there should be no plausible argument against ERA. The amendment will not interfere with private family matters. It will force no woman out into the work force.

It will simply provide equal rights under the law to all our citizens.

I urge supporters of ERA to write their legislators calling for quick and positive action on this essential legislation.

". . . Woman is weaker vessel!"

By the Rev. Mike Neal, Pastor,
Broadbay Hills Baptist Church

I am opposed to ERA and would like to consider the biblical aspect rather than the legal one. Former Sen. Ervin, who also opposes ERA, has well stated the latter.

Some religious leaders may criticize my approach, claiming we cannot mix sacred and secular matters. But God never equipped us with "sacred–secular" switches, and all of our lives are to be controlled by the sacred.

Jesus said, ". . . Man shall not live by bread alone but by every word that proceedeth out of the mouth of God" (Matthew 4:4). Spiritual principles are to undergird man's every thought and action.

God has established a divine order for the home and this must be followed to guarantee peace and happiness. It was in the home that Satan first appeared and disrupted.

Eve actually began the first woman's liberation movement, by acting independently of God's order through her husband. This action brought chaos to the human race. Many of the major cults have been founded by and because of women.

The Bible declares that the woman is "the weaker vessel" and her husband's duty is to protect her, loving her as he would his own body. According to the ideal biblical standard, the woman's position is being ". . . keepers at home, good, obedient to their own husbands . . ." (Titus 2:5).

This verse also teaches that violating this order causes the word of God to be blasphemed! It is clear, the "husband is the head of the wife . . ." (Ephesians 5:23).

The weight of biblical evidence is against the women's liberation movement, nonparents and the ERA issue. While people may remain Christians and support ERA, they are doing so in disobedience to the expressed word of God. Christianity was the greatest liberating force that unshackled both men and women from the power of sin.

Ultimately, the opinion championed by the second minister, Reverend Neal, prevailed. The ERA was defeated in North Carolina. It was also defeated in the country-at-large. By the early 1980s ERA supporters had failed to get the number of states needed to ratify the amendment so that it could become part of the Constitution. Disappointed but not discouraged, ERA supporters vowed to introduce the amendment in Congress once again in 1984 and to fight for its adoption as many times as necessary until it became part of the law of the land.

majority of Americans have been informing public opinion interviewers that they favor control of civilian firearms (see Box 7–5). Furthermore, a majority of gun owners themselves have been reporting that they believe guns should be registered (Erskine, 1972; NBC *News*, 1981).

The tendency for public opinion to change can be seen in regard to attitudes toward capital punishment. On more than one occasion, Pollster George Gallup asked a national sample of Americans, "Are you in favor of the death penalty for persons convicted of murder?" In 1965 only 42 percent of all Americans indicated that they were in favor; but this figure increased steadily until 1981, when 65 percent said that they favored the death penalty.

It is possible for those in power to suggest, manipulate, or even create public opinion. An example of an attempt to create public

As shown in the following figures, public opinion since 1938 has favored some kind of official control of access to guns.

Box 7–5   **PERCENT IN FAVOR OF GUN CONTROL**

YEAR	U.S. PUBLIC	GUN OWNERS
1938	79	
1940	74	
1959	75	65
1968	71	65
1972	71	61
1981	71	56

Source: Adapted from Hazel Erskine, "The Polls: Gun Control," *Public Opinion Quarterly,* Fall 1972, p. 455; NBC News and the Associated Press, Poll Results NBC News, Report No. 66 (New York: NBC News, April 28, 1981), p 12.

opinion is provided by Bernstein and Woodward (1974). Members of President Nixon's administration, fearful that one of Nixon's decisions to continue the bombing of North Vietnam in the early 1970s would create large-scale antiadministration public opinion, literally sent thousands of telegrams themselves to the White House in support of the president's policy. Thus, when all the letters to the White House on the bombing action were tabulated, including those sent by "unrehearsed" citizens, it would surely be possible for White House officials to "truthfully" announce to reporters that mail was running "4 to 1 in favor of the president's decision." The reporters would report the White House announcement, thereby creating the impression with the public that Americans supported the policies under question. Through this manipulation of the media, White House officials hoped not only to silence criticism of the president's policies, but to create, by means of suggestion, actual support.

A more recent example involves the Carter administration. When it became very clear that President Carter's energy conservation proposals were going to have an extremely difficult time getting through Congress, Mr. Carter used the power of communications available to him as president. He called a press conference where he discussed at length the reasons why his energy proposals should be passed. Secondly, he had an evening "Report to the American People" in which he went on prime-time television on all networks to explain the rationale for his policies to the public. By employing both tactics, Carter hoped to stimulate interest in the American public so that enough people would write their congressional representatives and sway the potentially antiadministration votes of these representatives. The fact that these efforts failed in large measure to generate the desired support indicates the intricate nature of public opinion and, in this case, its relation to positions of high prestige and power (see Chapter 5). If public opinion is either against or uninterested in an issue, it is extremely difficult for even the most powerful leaders in the society to change that opinion.

In November 1983, President Ronald Reagan's surprise invasion of the island of Grenada received strong support from American citizens who were very much concerned about the possibility of communist influence in the western hemisphere. Having only a few days earlier suffered the loss of 233 marines in Beruit, Lebanon, Reagan's administration took no chances in placing the Grenada invasion in the best possible light. First, Reagan refused to permit members of the press to cover firsthand the early phases of the invasion, until American control of the island had been all but completed. Second, through an effective use of his press conference, he stressed Cuban communist influence on the island; and third, he emphasized that the primary purpose of the invasion was "a rescue mission" to assure the safety of American students on Grenada. With the Iranian hostage crisis still firmly in their minds, many Americans sent letters to President Reagan in which they expressed their wholehearted support for his foreign policy.

emergent norms/alienation The approach to collective behavior that emphasizes (1) norms do in fact come to control some types of collective behavior and (2) these types of collective behavior are classifiable according to the amount of alienation that their members experience.

Emergent norms/alienation   Thus far in this chapter we have examined approaches to the study of collective behavior that have emphasized in large measure the lack of social structure and predictability of such interactions. In contrast, the **emergent norms/alienation** approach to collective behavior asserts that (1) norms for right and proper behavior do in fact come to control some types of collective behavior and (2) these types of collective behavior are classifiable according to the amount of alienation that their members experience. The emergent norms/alienation approach is usually applied to that form of collective behavior known as the social movement.

Social Movements

social movement a collectivity which acts with some continuity to promote or resist a change in the group.

Turner and Killian (1957, p. 308) define a **social movement** as "a collectivity acting with some continuity to promote or resist a change in the society or group of which it is a part." By focusing on the continuity of the social movement, Turner and Killian direct our attention to the enduring structural elements of the group, the characteristic that distinguishes social movements from other types of collective behavior.

A social movement frequently has a spontaneous beginning. It may, for example, begin as an active crowd. This is, in fact, the way youth movements frequently began. In the early sixties at the University of California in Berkeley, for example, young people in relatively small numbers began meeting in public to voice their support of the Civil Rights movement. Various university and local officials started to protest that such meetings should not be held and tried to keep them from taking place. The young people resisted and suddenly "free speech" became an issue: As time progressed, the entire spectrum of "student rights" became a key focus, then the American involvement in the war in Vietnam. The protests spread across the country. An active crowd had spawned a powerful social movement.

Over time, however, a social movement tends to take on more and more of the stable characteristics that we associate with structured forms of interaction. Most important of these characteristics are the emerging norms of the group. Such norms are necessitated by the direction of the movement. If it is to attain its goal of altering society, it must have some sort of "rules and regulations" for how to proceed toward that goal.

In its early stages, the movement usually develops a shared set of attitudes toward its problem (e.g., a hippie slogan "All people over 30 are members of the establishment and not to be trusted."). Sharing such attitudes gives the members of a social movement a means of identifying themselves, the "enemy," and the goal toward which they are striving.

The next developments likely to take place within a movement are a hierarchy of authority and a specialization of tasks. Leaders and followers tend to become identified and leaders do certain things (like planning), whereas followers do others (like going out to the streets to convert people). At this point in the development of a social movement a set of specific norms begins to appear. For example, it becomes the main task of leaders to specify what procedures to take with converts and with the "enemy" and to indicate what followers of the movement should do and think in their role as members.

As the movement continues to develop, it may generate norms to cover almost all of life's activities. The movement tends to become an encompassing way of life for its adherents. For example, what began in the 1950s as a series of largely unrelated antisegregation demonstrations in the South fast became the Civil Rights movement of the 1960s, complete with formally organized groups such as the Southern Christian Leadership Conference

One of the most effective tactics employed by Dr. Martin Luther King (center) in his struggle to obtain equality for black Americans was the mass march. King and his supporters would meet at an appointed place and march together to another place, en route being highly visible and, usually, highly publicized by the media as well. Over a period of years, these marches and other tactics created such a groundswell of support that laws regarding treatment of blacks were changed throughout the country. Although by no stretch of the imagination has racial prejudice disappeared in the United States, the role Dr. King and his supporters played in the movement for equal rights has been crucial.

headed by Dr. Martin Luther King and the Student Non-Violent Coordinating Committee (SNCC). This movement eventually developed highly specialized tactics of confrontation, plans for large-scale operations such as registering millions of blacks to vote, and whole philosophies of life such as Dr. King's nonviolent beliefs.

The message is clear enough: In order for its members to meet their needs over time, any group must develop a stable social structure (however, much flexibility on "ways to proceed" may be built into that structure). Consequently, all enduring human interactions, as we have already seen, tend to become patterned and, to the degree that they do, predictable (Chapters 2 to 6).

Social movements that have difficult goals to attain, that entail the changing of public opinion and the changing of norms, are no exception to this process of emerging norms.

Of course, not all social movements follow the course of development just described. Many terminate as quickly as they arise, especially if the changes they seek are attained. For example, a movement for prisoners' rights might quickly disband if prison officials were to meet its participants' demands. Similarly, some social movements have a way of "petering out" either because the task they face is too formidible or there is not enough mass support to keep the movement going. Many youth communes established in the late 1960s and early 1970s disbanded for the former reason and the failure of the ecology/environmental protection movement to move beyond a few dedicated groups is more than likely an example of the latter reason.

If, however, the goals of a social movement are not quickly met, but still appear to be ultimately attainable to movement members and generate enough mass support to keep the movement going, there is a strong tendency for the emergent norms process to begin. An example concerns the Civil Rights movement. After Dr. Martin Luther King's assassination in 1968 the public aspects of the Civil Rights movement became much less visible. People who supported the movement took many of their concerns to the local, "grass-roots" level. However, as the 1970s progressed it became evident that the ultimate goals of the movement—full equality for blacks and other minority groups—had not been attained. Hence a need to "go public" and stimulate nationwide interest in civil rights once again arose. One instance of the Civil Rights movement resurfacing occurred in the summer of 1983, on the fifteenth anniversary of Dr. King's death. In August hundreds of thousands of people descended on Washington, D.C., near the Lincoln Memorial, where Dr. King had given his famous "I have a dream" speech, and heard emotional and revitalizing speeches by the present leaders of the Civil Rights movement and Coretta Scott King, Dr. King's widow.

Once a social movement is well established, it may be difficult for members of the group to disband the movement even if its goals are attained. As the norms of the movement become more encompassing, its members become more deeply committed to their role-status positions in the movement; termination of the movement would also mean termination of their new way of life. In order to preserve the normative structure of the group, and the life-styles it supports, the movement may undergo a transformation of goals. One laudable example of such a transformation is the shift by the Mother's March on Polio to an organization dedicated to the eradication of all childhood diseases. In the 1950s the

Mother's March was formed to gain funds for conquering polio, a disease that had killed and maimed many children. In the 1960s, however, partially as a result of the funding provided by the Mother's March, virtually every child in the United States was vaccinated against polio. When polio ceased to be a major problem, the very reason for existence of the movement was threatened. The Mother's March met this challenge by converting itself into an organization designed to conquer *all* childhood diseases.

As Turner and Killian (1957) note, a social movement is focused on changing its relationship to society. In psychological terms this means that the members of the movement are more or less in opposition to the way in which the dominant culture is operating. In a word, they are **alienated.** The amount of alienation provides us with a basis for the classification of such groups as shown in Figure 7–1.

alienation The psychological state of nonattachment.

There are essentially two major types of social movements: those oriented to "progress," that is, to establishing a new way of life in the society, and those oriented to "return," that is, to reestablishing a past way of life.

Within these major types, specific movements differ in degree of alienation from the status quo. Reform and revival movements are characterized by the least amount of alienation on our continuum; they seek to change only a particular aspect of society, not its basic structure. These groups are usually committed to legal or semilegal methods for effecting change. For instance, they might attempt to convince others by argument, by example, or by tactics such as sit-ins or marches. An example of a return-oriented revival movement is the Young Americans for Freedom (YAF), a group of students who advocate a return to the state of laissez-faire capitalism, individualism, and local government that existed some time

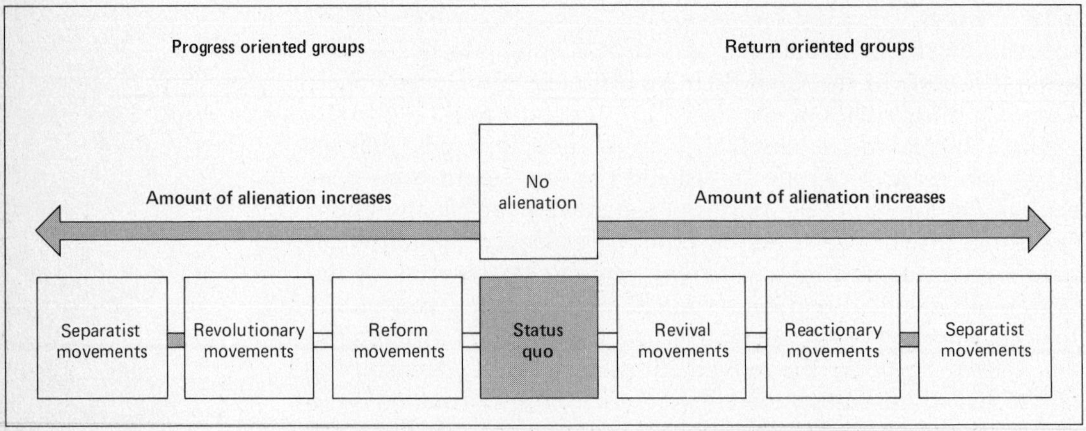

Figure 7–1 A Classification Scheme for Social Movements

ago. Another example of a revival movement is the "Born-Again" Christian sect. These people feel contemporary Americans have strayed too far from the religious (specifically Christian) way of life that used to form the basis of ethical decision making and action in everyday life. They feel that if only people would be "born again," that is, return to the true Christian way of life, the ills of modern society would be quickly resolved. On the reform movements side, there are the already mentioned Civil Rights and ecology movements, and the ever-growing antinuclear weapons movement.

The members of revolutionary and reactionary movements are generally so alienated from society that they seek to remake its basic structure in the image of their ideology. The degree of alienation is such that these groups often do not feel bound by the laws and norms of society and thus feel justified in engaging in either illegal or violent tactics to attain their ends—tactics such as fraud, kidnapping, murder, and the like. Among the return-oriented groups, the Ku Klux Klan represents a reactionary movement seeking to reestablish a pattern of white supremacy in race relations. A more recent progress-oriented group, the Symbionese Liberation Army—responsible for the "kidnapping" of heiress Patty Hearst—advocated the violent overthrow of the U.S. government. (For more on revolutionary movements, see Chapter 8.)

At the extreme ends of the continuum there are separatist movements, generally so alienated from their dominant culture that they seek to dissociate themselves completely from it and establish an alternative way of life. In American history the secession of the South before the Civil War was a classic example of a return-oriented separatist movement. The South opposed not only the breakdown of slavery but the destruction of the old agricultural way of life by encroaching industrialization. In more recent years religious groups, such as the Amish, the Mennonites, and the Children of God, all represent attempts at setting up separatist communities to reestablish a life-style in keeping with what are perceived to be the true dictates of the Bible. In a similar way, the exodus of the various Protestant sects of Europe to the New World in the sixteen and seventeen hundreds, were examples of progress-oriented separatist movements. Lastly, the already discussed hip-radical movement of recent years represents a progress-oriented separatist movement whose members chose to "drop out" rather than participate in the corruption they saw around them.

As you may have gathered from this discussion, if social movements gain enough mass support, they may also be analyzed as valuational subcultures or as countercultures (see Chapter 2). To conclude this chapter, we turn to a more detailed example of a recent and continuing reformist social movement: the Women's Liberation movement.

THE WOMEN'S LIBERATION MOVEMENT: COLLECTIVE BEHAVIOR IN ACTION

According to most researchers (Polk, 1972; Freeman, 1973; Carden, 1974; Friedan, 1983), the new feminist wave began in earnest in American society in the late 1960s. At that time, not unlike the Civil Rights and hip counterculture movements of the same era, women's protest activities began to get massive press coverage.

At first, the appearance of women, relatively well organized and attacking the main tenets of American society, was surprising. As Carden (1974, p. 1) puts it:

> Men and women with traditional views gasped. These must be sick, unbalanced women, or at best, just bored housewives. Everyone knew that American women were better off than women anywhere else in the world or at any time in history; they were spoiled and pampered. What did they have to fuss about? What were they after? What did they mean by "liberation" or "oppression"?

Fundamentally, the goals of the new Women's Liberation movement are the same as those of previous feminist groups, such as those set forth by the first women's convention at Seneca Falls (New York) in 1848, led by Elizabeth Cady Stanton and Lucretia Mott (see Box 7–6). According to Polk (1972, p. 321), the contemporary movement "seeks equality between the sexes—an end to the male chauvinist myth that men are superior to women and an end to the institutions and practices of society which perpetuate this myth."

In other words, the fact that women have long felt to some degree *alienated* from the main social structural elements of American society and have simultaneously felt discriminated against by antifemale norms is the principal reason that they banded together as a vital *reformist* social movement (see Figure 7–1).* Among other things, women in the forefront of the movement in the 1960s and 1970s were specifically requesting an end to the prejudicial assumption that "a woman's place is in the home." They argued that there was no reason that women had to limit themselves to marriage and family care as a "career" (Greene, 1963; Bergquist, 1966). Moreover, there was no reason why women should not have equal access to all occupational ca-

---

*Although there are some elements of the Women's Liberation movement that argue for full separation from male society—thus fitting our classification of a separatist, progress-oriented movement—this group is decidedly in the minority in the contemporary movement.

Box 7–6 THE WOMEN'S MOVEMENT: 1848

The following excerpts from the "Declaration of Sentiments and Resolutions" produced by the Seneca Falls Convention of July 1848, and purposefully echoing the "Declaration of Independence," illustrate key philosophical issues in the Women's Liberation movement. Many of these issues are as vital today as they were in 1848.

When, in the course of human events, it becomes necessary for one portion of the family of man to assume among the people of the earth a position different from that which they have hitherto occupied, but one to which the laws of nature and of nature's God entitle them, a decent respect to the opinions of mankind requires that they should declare the causes that impel them to such a course.

We hold these truths to be self-evident: that all men and women are created equal; that they are endowed by their Creator with certain inalienable rights; that among these are life, liberty, and the pursuit of happiness; that to secure these rights governments are instituted, deriving their just powers from the consent of the governed. Whenever any form of government becomes destructive of these ends, it is the right of those who suffer from it to refuse allegiance to it, and to insist upon the institution of a new government, laying its foundation on such principles, and organizing its powers in such form, as to them shall seem most likely to effect their safety and happiness. . . .

The history of mankind is a history of repeated injuries and usurpations on the part of man toward woman, having in direct object the establishment of an absolute tyranny over her. To prove this, let facts be submitted to a candid world.

He has never permitted her to exercise her inalienable right to the elective franchise.

He has compelled her to submit to laws, in the formation of which she had no voice. . . .

He has made her, if married, in the eye of the law, civilly dead. . . .

He has monopolized nearly all the profitable employments, and from those she is permitted to follow, she receives but a scanty remuneration. He closes against her all the avenues to wealth and distinction which he considers most honorable to himself. As a teacher of theology, medicine, or law, she is not known. . . .

Resolutions

Resolved, That all laws which prevent woman from occupying such a station in society as her conscience shall dictate, or which place her in a position inferior to that of man, are contrary to the great precept of nature, and therefore of no force or authority.

Resolved, That woman is man's equal—was intended to be so by the Creator, and the highest good of the race demands that she should be recognized as such. . . .

Resolved, That the equality of human rights results necessarily from the fact of the identity of the race in capabilities and responsibilities.

reers—from academics and the professions (Epstein, 1973;
Hughes, 1973), to science (Rossi, 1965), to politics (Haavio–Man-
nila, 1970), to the military (Goldman, 1973), to *anything* else.

As Tuchman (1975) puts it, women had not been involved in the
central cultural and occupational roles of American society because their more circumscribed role of being wives and mothers
had *systematically prevented* them from entering into such activities. Moreover, if past women did dare to be different and enter
into such activities against all odds, they were usually classified in
some manner that set them off from society at large: they were
"gifted," "odd," "unfeminine," and the like. Such sanctioning of
course, simultaneously, served the purposes of warning other
women against undertaking such activities and resolidified the
traditional definition of sex roles (see the section on "Sanctions,"
Chapter 2). Consequently, the central issue for the Women's Liberation movement in reducing the alienation they feel is to re-
structure (reform) the cultural barriers that prevent women from
having full choice and control over their lives.

Yet, as the "Declaration of Sentiments and Resolutions" (Box
7–6) showed, sexual inequality and discriminatory interaction patterns against women have existed for a very long time. Why, then,
has the Women's Liberation movement arisen now and not 20 or
30 years ago? To answer this question, we need to examine four
key historical factors: the effects of (1) fertility decline; (2) the pill
("the perfect contraceptive," Ridley, 1972); (3) the popularization
of the findings of social science concerning sex roles; and (4) the
rise of a unique communications network that allowed mass transmission of movement information among women.

1. *The effects of fertility decline.* The major advances in medicine in the past 85 years have led to a unique situation in modern
societies: Newborns no longer die as frequently before reaching
maturity and those who reach maturity live longer and healthier
lives than ever before. As a result, there has been a major decline
in fertility in American families. That is, because more people are
living longer, fewer babies need be produced to do the same
amount of work in society. To illustrate this, consider that white
women born during 1835 to 1839 had an average of 5.3 children
during their fertile years, whereas the same social category had an
average of only 2.3 children during the 1910 to 1914 period (Ridley, 1972, p. 376). The same downward trend in family size has
continued to the present day. The consequence of this fertility
decline has been a "freeing" of women from unnecessary preg-
nancies, unwanted babies, and many of the unending chores of
child care. This has allowed women, particularly white women,
more freedom to become involved in extrafamilial concerns, such
as work and membership in civic organizations. Simultaneously,

The secondary status of women in most societies has been an established fact for centuries (for some of the reasons for this situation, see Box 6-6, "Why Men Dominate Women)". In the painting (top), this role is poignantly portrayed: While the well-dressed man sits inside with all his possessions and his parrot, the women, in various roles (as seductress/whore, as a caretaker of children, and as generally hapless) are relegated to the street. In recent years, however, much of this has changed. Women in modern industrialized nations communicate with one another about their situations. The overall result has been a general "raising of consciousness" concerning women's roles in society and the development of a large women's movement, well-organized and ready to work for equal treatment of women throughout society (bottom).

this situation has made women *potentially available* for mass social movements of any kind as the twentieth century has progressed.

2. *The effects of the pill.* If advances in medicine initiated the downward trend in fertility, introduction of the technological miracle of a completely effective birth control pill in the early 1960s allowed the trend to develop into a fact of life. With the pill, women for the first time in history were able to enjoy sexual relationships without concern over pregnancy and the socially limiting condition of child care. For example, the historical evidence is clear that women involved in higher education who became pregnant were very likely to discontinue their education, thereby being deprived of the major criterion for high-status occupational employment in this country (Ridley, 1972, pp. 380–381). The effects of the pill, therefore, only augmented those initiated by the decline in fertility: it allowed women to remain in the mainstream of cultural activity as long as it was their own choice to do so.

3. *The effect of the popularization of social science research on sex roles.* As more and more young women remained in the cultural mainstream in the 1960s, they faced the antiwoman bias of many occupations and interactions. They also became increasingly aware that these biases were totally arbitrary: that is, unsubstantiated by any conclusive evidence that men were more "suited" for certain types of occupations and life-styles than women. This awareness was furthered by the dissemination of social science research results, such as that of Margaret Mead (see Chapter 3) and in such popularized works as Betty Friedan's *The Feminine Mystique* (Freeman, 1975, p. 798). This information, which soon became part-and-parcel of the generalized radical critique of American society that developed in the 1960s, had the effect of "raising the consciousness" of many women as to the reasons for their situation and made these women much more desirous of immediate and radical solutions to these conditions.

4. *The effect of a unique communications network among women.* In 1961 President Kennedy established a Commission on the Status of Women that produced a report in 1963 entitled *American Women.* This report indicated that women were still denied many of the basic freedoms supposedly available in American life. The concern that this report stirred led to the establishment of 50 similar state commissions whose purpose was to see how widespread such discriminatory practices were and how they were being implemented. One of the important side-effects of these commissions was, as Freeman puts it, that they "brought together many knowledgeable, politically active women who otherwise would not have worked together around matters of direct

concern to women" (1975, p. 798). This communications network led, in June 1966, to the formation of the National Organization of Women (NOW) which ever since has been a primary means of communication among women (Freeman, 1975, pp. 798–799).

In a less traditional way, a communications network was also established among younger women. These women, some of whom were originally associated with the Civil Rights and counterculture movements, began, in the late 1960s, to argue that more attention be paid to the alleviation of *their* oppression. When little came of such demands, they banded together into small consciousness-raising groups across the country—primarily in cities and on college and university campuses. In time, these groups became aware of each other and established regular newsletters and conferences to transmit their concerns (Freeman, 1975, pp. 799–802).

The effect of all this communication has been a massive sensitizing of the whole country to women's issues in recent years and a great growth in the number of women deeply involved in the movement. The two subgroups of the movement that arose in the 1960s—the women's rights groups [such as NOW, the National Women's Political Caucus (NWPC), and the Women's Equity Action League (WEAL)], and the consciousness-raising groups—continue to form the main elements of the Women's Liberation movement (Carden, 1974).

Moreover, these groups and local groups affiliated with them have developed *enormous* political clout. Although the Equal Rights Amendment to the Constitution failed to get ratification by the necessary complement of states, it was reintroduced into Congress in 1983 and the battle for ratification is likely to begin again —with passage more likely. The very fact that the amendment came *close* to ratification in the early 1980s is testimony to the increased political importance of American women. Imagine the fate of such a bill in 1955! Furthermore, polls indicate that women were instrumental in electing Mario Cuomo as governor of New York in 1982 (his opponent was an outspoken antifeminist) and contributed to the defeat or near defeat of antifeminist candidates in Texas, New Jersey, and Missouri in the same year (Friedan, 1983, p. 36). Not insignificantly, the Reagan administration—not known for a favorable stance on women's rights issues—appointed Elizabeth Dole as Secretary of Transportation, Margaret Heckler as Secretary of Health and Human Services, and Sandra Day O' Connor as the first woman Supreme Court Justice. Not to be outdone, the Democratic party took an even more historic step in July, 1984, at their convention in San Francisco. Walter Mondale named Geraldine Ferraro as his vice-presidential running mate. It had taken over two hundred years, but at last a woman was on the ticket for the second highest office in the land.

Has the women's movement succeeded on other levels? There is every indication that it has. All across the country women are participating more in business and are making new decisions about how to structure their careers and families. As seen in Chapter 6, women have made significant strides in their attainment of college and graduate degrees. But there is more. For example, in 1970, women under the age of 25 accounted for 81 percent of the "first births" recorded in that year; by 1980, that figure had shrunk to 68 percent. Or, considered another way: in 1970, for women aged 30 to 34, 10 percent of the babies born were "first births"; in 1980, the figure was 20 percent (Hacker, 1983, p. 58). Clearly, women are choosing to have babies later in life. Then, there is marriage: In 1970, 43 percent of all 20-year-old women were married; in 1980, the figure was 34 percent. In 1970, 86 percent of all 25-year-old women were married; in 1980, the figure was 72 percent. In 1970, 95 percent of all 40-year-old women were married; in 1980, the figure was also 95 percent (Hacker, 1983, p. 105). Conclusion: Women are still choosing to marry but marry at later ages. Finally, take employment patterns: In 1960, women composed 33 percent of the labor force; by 1980, that figure had risen to 42 percent. Women's participation increased in all main areas of the work force—professional and technical workers, managers and administrators, salespeople, and clerical workers. Of most interest was their increase in the areas of "professional and technical" work—in 1970, women's participation was 40 percent; in 1980, 44 percent—and in the area of "managers and administrators"—the 1970 figure was 17 percent, that for 1980, 26 percent —both areas long dominated by men (Hacker, 1983, pp. 130–31). Even more specifically, the proportion of women in some professions rose dramatically between 1970 and 1980, as Table 7–1 indicates.

The changes go deeper than raw statistics can point out. A recent study has shown that contemporary women, often engaged in both career *and* child-rearing, have attained a level of psychological well-being noticeably higher than women of previous decades, those who were almost exclusively engaged in child-rearing. As importantly, women in their thirties and forties who have both careers and family rate higher than males of the same age in scales measuring psychological well-being. Apparently, the males, committed since their twenties almost *exclusively* to careers have a particularly hard time with a life-cycle phenomenon known as the "midlife" crisis—a period of intense questioning that follows one's initial success in a profession. Although some contemporary women have become "overachievers" like many careerist males, most seem to be avoiding the "superwoman" syndrome and balance the different aspects of their life very well indeed (Friedan, 1983, p. 55).

Table 7-1 THE PROPORTION OF WOMEN IN SELECTED PROFESSIONS, 1970-1980

| | *Percentages* | | |
PROFESSION	1970	1980	RISE IN WOMEN'S PROPORTION
Barbers	4.7%	15.7%	234.0%
Lawyers	4.8	12.8	166.7
Compositors and typesetters	15.0	34.5	130.0
Insurance adjusters	26.7	57.5	115.4
Advertising agents	19.5	41.8	114.4
Computer operators	29.2	59.8	104.8
Bank and financial managers	17.6	33.6	90.9
Social scientists	19.2	36.0	87.5
Stock and bond sales agents	9.1	16.4	80.2
Bus drivers	28.0	44.9	60.4
Real estate agents	31.9	50.7	58.9
Shipping clerks	14.5	21.6	49.0
Bakers	29.8	42.9	44.0
Educational administrators	26.4	37.1	40.5
Accountants	26.0	36.2	39.2
Decorators and window dressers	57.6	71.1	23.4

Source: Andrew Hacker, *U/S: A Statistical Portrait of the American People* (New York: Viking, 1983), p. 132.

So, on many levels, it appears the women's movement is a decided success. Although more equality can certainly be attained —and almost certainly will be—it seems unlikely that American society will "slip back into" its previous days of "male dominance/-female submissiveness." The movement has established such momentum and the *idea* that women should be given equal opportunity with men has become so deeply engrained (if not fully supported) in American *culture* that further "liberation" seems a foregone conclusion.

And this is just the problem facing the women's movement at present as *a social movement.* The old goals have been largely attained; many barriers, previously thought insurmountable, have been crossed. There are now major publications addressed to feminist issues (e.g., *Ms.* magazine), an ever-increasing amount of scholarly work devoted to feminist issues, and major women's groups in most areas of the country. In addition, there are yearly women's conferences at the state, national, and international levels. These *emerging norms* of the movement mean, on the one hand, that the movement is more powerful than ever before at applying political pressures. On the other hand, such emerging social structure downplays the original diversity, spontaneity, and flexibility of the movement.

Perhaps more worrisome for movement participants is the fact that the question of "What now?" has not been answered. Like the

Mother's March on Polio after the coming of the Salk vaccine, the women's movement is at a moment of decision. What will the next issue be? Or, will there *be* a next issue? Should the issue be "Equal pay for work of comparable value? Child care? Displaced home-makers? Rape? Lesbian rights? Discrimination in social security, in pensions?" (Friedan, 1983, p. 57) Or, is the movement too faction-alized to refocus on a common goal?

The answer is not clear. Writing a decade ago, Maren Lock-wood Carden (1974, pp. 168–170) foresaw the dilemma: If the movement stayed "radical," that is, committed solely to women's issues, it might survive but, in the process, lose the support of many whose immediate goals—better jobs, greater personal free-dom—had been attained. If, on the other hand, the movement went "conservative," that is, gave up the exclusive interest in *women's* rights but took up the cause of human liberation in all areas of society, then the movement would be likely to be "co-opted" by society-at-large and lose its primary *raison d'être* from another direction.

Betty Friedan, author of the movement galvanizing *Feminine Mystique* in 1963, believes this second option is the only way to go. She feels that, in the last decade and a half, not only have women's "rights" become a focus of society, but women's *sen-sibilities* have as well. Most importantly, such sensibilities—such as a humane concern for the welfare of others—now have been accepted by many *men* in our society. As men have begun to "develop the flexibility and sensitivity to their own feelings and the feelings of others—the attunement to life that has been consid-ered up to now feminine—" the central issues of the 1980s have become common to both sexes—"the basic issues of war and peace, and economic survival, of quality of life for young and old" (Friedan, 1983, p. 57). By focusing on issues of concern to all humanity, Friedan neither intends for a moment to give up the continuing fight for women's rights nor thinks such a position is a "selling out" of feminism. But many in the women's movement disagree. On publication of her book, *The Second Stage* in 1981, in which the preceding argument first appeared, Friedan was attacked by many ardent feminists who thought her "generaliz-ing" of the movement's original women's goals was a death knell.

The debate has yet to be settled. Until it is, the fate and direc-tion of the women's movement in America hangs in the balance.

SUMMARY

In previous chapters we were concerned with highly structured and relatively stable elements of social interaction such as status, role, primary group, and social stratification. In this chapter we turned to forms of collective behavior—gatherings of people whose behavior tends to be more spontaneous and relatively unsupported by conventional norms and values.

The study of collective behavior reflects three different approaches, each of which tends to be applicable to certain types of collective action. The contagion approach emphasizes that individuals may be temporarily transformed under the pressures of the group into something they may not be in everyday life. This phenomenon can be easily seen in the crowd—a temporary cluster of people who react together to a common stimulus while in close physical contact. Some crowds are active in that they form to act out a shared feeling toward persons or events. Other crowds are expressive, existing only to release tension.

Three processes of contagion are often at work in crowd behavior: imitation, suggestibility, and emotional contagion. These processes also operate in the type of collective behavior known as mass hysteria, where the same fear motivates a large number of individuals to react even when they are not all physically together. A classic example of mass hysteria is the audience reaction to Orson Welles' 1938 radio dramatization of *The War of the Worlds*.

The contagion approach can also be applied to study rumor, an interpersonal communication that develops in response to some extraordinary circumstance among individuals who attempt to make sense of their situation. According to Allport and Postman, the serial transmission of a rumor involves the tendencies of leveling, sharpening, and assimilation. The rumor tends to change its content as participants pass on a communication in which their anxieties or hostilities are expressed.

The convergence of attitudes approach to collective behavior emphasizes that people who act collectively often already share the same predispositions to action before they come together. This approach is particularly useful in understanding public opinion, the convergence of all the separate opinions held in a group.

The emergent norm/alienation approach is useful for examining the social movement—a collectivity acting with continuity to promote or resist a change in society. Unlike other forms of collective behavior, social movements tend to take on greater structure with time and often appeal to the alienated members of society. Movements can be classified in terms of the direction of change desired, either a return or progress orientation, and the degree of change desired, reformation (reform or revival), revised structure (revolutionary or reactionary), or new system (separatist).

The Women's Liberation movement is an example of a current reformist social movement. Like all social movements, its members are alienated to a degree from the society in which they live. A consideration of the movement's development suggested that various factors—a decline in per capita fertility, the pill, the spread of social science research findings regarding sex roles, and the development of vital communications networks among women—contributed to the rise and spread of the movement in the 1960s and 1970s. The movement has now entered a second major stage of development—the emergent norms stage—which has not only made it more powerful at applying political pressure to attain its ends but which also threatens to dilute the original intent such that it may lose its potential to effect truly major change in the society. The debate over which way the movement should go in the mid- and late 1980s has not been settled.

QUESTIONS, EXERCISES, PROJECTS

1. What are the characteristics of collective behavior that distinguish it from other forms of social interaction?
2. Define and illustrate the three approaches to the study of collective behavior.
3. Distinguish between active and expressive forms of crowd behavior.
4. What are the conditions under which crowd behavior emerges?
5. Why are people likely to act differently in a crowd than elsewhere? Give two examples of such different behavior from your personal experience.
6. The following rumor project requires four or five persons. Person 1 reads the following paragraph to person 2 so that others cannot overhear it.

    Two boys and two girls were fishing, when the boat in which they were riding overturned. Only the girls knew how to swim; they grabbed hold of the boys and guided them back to shore. Both boys were very grateful.

    Person 2 repeats what he remembers of the story to person 3. Person 3 repeats it to person 4, and so on. After the story has been transmitted to the last person, examine its final form for evidence of the leveling, sharpening, and assimilation to which rumors are subject. In what ways did the story change as it was transmitted from person to person?
7. Give two recent examples of differences in public opinion. Analyze each group sociologically and explain why these differences arose. Predict the future of these differences in later interactions between the groups.
8. Identify three characteristics that are shared by the members of a social movement.

9. Distinguish between three local social movements according to the amount of alienation that characterizes each. Explain why the differences in alienation exist in the first place.

10. Explain the rise of the Women's Liberation movement to prominence as a major American social movement in the 1960s and 1970s. What implications does this movement have for American society if it is fully successful?

11. Think of women's groups in your hometown and on your college campus. Are there any? If not, why not? If there are, what are the stated goals of these groups? Is there disagreement between "radical" and "conservative" factions? Which group seems to have more support? Why?

SOCIAL CHANGE

The study of collective behavior informs us that social interaction can be relatively spontaneous—that is, not fully controlled by everyday norms and values. Moreover, at least two types of collective behavior—the active crowd and the social movement—are centrally concerned with changing the relationship of the group to society. If either of these forms of collective behavior is effective in attaining its goal, even partially, then it may be said that social change has occurred.

As an example, the Civil Rights movement of the 1950s and 1960s eventually resulted in some important legal and normative changes with respect to inequalities between black and white Americans. New laws made various white employers and school administrations adopt new ways of dealing with inequality (such as providing equal opportunity hiring policies and school busing). The growing awareness of racial discrimination against blacks (and its costs for whites) made some blacks and whites change their ways of acting toward one another in the direction of eliminating that discrimination. Although the Civil Rights movement has not been as "public" in the past few years, the changes it helped institute are nonetheless very real. For example, according to the U.S. Census Bureau, in the decade between 1970 and 1980, the percentage of black homeowners rose to 45 percent as compared with a 26 percent rise for whites. Blacks also have made significant gains in education. Thus the proportion of blacks aged 25 to 34 who were high school graduates was only 53 percent in 1970; by

1982 that figure had risen to 79 percent. (During the same period the figures for whites rose from 76 to 87 percent.)

We may define **social change** as any continuing alteration in the interaction patterns that exist between two or more people. The word "continuing" is important in this definition if we are to exclude those spontaneous changes in behavior that may occur once or twice but produce no lasting effect on the overall pattern of interaction. Note, too, that this definition does not limit social change to alterations induced by collective action groups, such as active crowds and social movements. Although such groups are often important in effecting social change, alterations in patterns of interaction may occur as a result of long-term *trends* in the society that may not be associated with collective behavior at all (such as technological advance) or as a result of the relatively subtle alterations in people's behavior that occur in everyday life (such as acting differently toward others because of what they may have said to you).

The study of social change must be undertaken in order to reach a full understanding of the social world. The sociologist who ignores processes of cultural and social alteration can never hope to understand fully the nature of social interaction or to create effective strategies for altering the undesirable elements of society. However, by its very nature, any description of the structure of social interaction can be no more than a "snapshot" of social reality, a static representation of a dynamic and changing experience.

Consequently, in this chapter we turn our attention to the central processes of social change. More specifically, we shall be interested in the following questions: What are the major types of social change? What are the source points of social change? By what process, at what rate, and to what degree does social change spread? What directions may social change take in human history?

social change Any continuing alteration in the interaction patterns that exist between two or more people.

MAJOR TYPES OF SOCIAL CHANGE

Sociologists generally recognize that there are three main types of social change—revolutions, trends, and everyday changes. Of these, the most noticeable, and most spectacular, is a revolution.

Revolutions

As we indicated in our discussion of revolutionary movements in Chapter 7, because of their extreme alienation from the status quo, participants in these movements seek the complete transformation of the existing social order, rather than a mere reformation. Because of this orientation, revolutionary groups are likely to be resisted vehemently by mainstream members of society. Consequently, we may define a true **revolution** as a violent attempt at total restructuring of most of the institutions (e.g., the economic and political spheres) and values of a society. In other words, if a revolution is successful, the whole society is likely to undergo a sudden and drastic overhaul: Capitalism may give way to communism, feudalism may be overturned in favor of democracy, or fascism may replace socialism.

It is important to note that this definition does *not* include many social changes that are frequently referred to in common parlance as "revolutions." Thus, today, many Americans are speaking of the "computer revolution," as people all over the country buy their Ataris and Apples and type away with them on their laps in buses and on airplanes. However widespread and significant such a change may be, it is not a "revolution" in sociological terms—it is part of a trend, though a relatively speedy one.

Many of the preconditions for a true revolution can be specified. Prior to its onset, there tends to be a "crisis of confidence" in which the current leadership, usually the government, is widely perceived as having failed to meet the needs of its citizens. This perception may or may not be accurate, but frequently the existing machinery of prerevolutionary government is actually inefficient and fails to make the changes in its old institutions that would be necessary to alleviate the pressures on the populace (Brinton, 1952).

Obviously, revolutions do not occur in societies where most of the members are content with their social order. Also, a revolution is not an inevitable consequence of extreme oppression or impoverishment. When a society has been impoverished over a prolonged period of time, the members may come to accept their plight fatalistically. Also, the energy of impoverished people may be focused largely, if not exclusively, on the process of survival (Tocqueville, 1946).

Revolution seems to occur most frequently when the members of a group experience serious **relative deprivation** —a feeling of dissatisfaction by comparison with either their own past history or the more favorable situation of another group. The importance of the concept of relative deprivation is that it emphasizes the difference between *actual* and *felt* deprivation. If *actual* deprivation were the determinant of revolution, we would find that revolutionary movements arise exclusively and inevitably among the lowest status, most disadvantaged, or most exploited members of society. Clearly, this is not always the case (consider, for example, why the impoverished masses of Indonesia or India do not continually revolt or why the American Revolution had a middle-class base). Using the concept of relative deprivation, however, we

revolution A violent attempt at total restructuring of most of the institutions and values of a society.

relative deprivation A feeling of dissatisfaction arising from comparison with the past history of a group or with the more favorable situation of another group.

would instead look for the preconditions of revolution among any group in society whose members *feel* disadvantaged or exploited, regardless of their *actual* circumstances.

According to Davies (1962, p. 6), revolution is most likely when a lengthy period of economic and social progress is interrupted by a short period of sharp reversal.

> The all-important effect on the minds of people in a particular society is to produce, during the [long period of progress], an expectation of continued ability to satisfy needs—which continue to rise—and, during the [period of reversal], a mental state of anxiety and frustration when manifest reality breaks away from anticipated reality. The actual state of socio-economic development is less significant than the expectation that past progress, now blocked, can and must continue in the future.

In providing evidence for this hypothesis, Davies examines the conditions that led up to the Russian revolution of 1917. A long period of rising expectations of economic and social development began with the emancipation of the serfs in 1861 and continued until the limited revolution in 1905. Then, a downward trend of expectations began and continued until the massive revolution of 1917 overthrew the tsar and replaced the feudal society with communism.

During the period of sharp reversal, from 1905 to 1917, peaceful proletarian petitioners were murdered by the hundreds by the tsar's army, thousands were given death sentences for their offenses against the government, censorship was reimposed, crop failures occurred on a fairly large scale, and the army and navy were defeated in their war with Japan. As the existing government continued to suppress the needs of Russian citizens, a conscious awareness of relative deprivation (in comparison with the previous period of rising expectations) became both pervasive and intense among the Russian people. There was widespread discontent among many who feared that important ground gained over the long period of time until 1905 would be completely swept away. As a result, revolution became widely regarded as the only alternative and in 1917 became the reality itself.

Karl Marx's influential view of revolution also stresses the importance of relative deprivation in producing social change, although not so much according to losses or gains over a period of time. The Marxian version of revolution instead emphasizes the social tension that occurs when the "enjoyments" of the workers decline in comparison with the increasing "enjoyments" of the capitalist (see the more detailed discussions of Marx in Chapter 5 and later in this chapter). As Marx and his coauthor Frederick Engels suggest, "Our desires and pleasures spring from society; we measure them, therefore, by society and not by the objects which serve for their satisfaction. Because they are of a social nature, they are of a relative nature" (1955, p. 94).

The concept of relative deprivation, then, provides one of the clues to why all social change occurs. Humans being instinctless, are not "locked into" social patterns by any force other than society itself (as Marx and Engels suggest). Consequently, when people become aware of what they perceive to be a better way of life, that is, when they experience relative deprivation, they may decide to seek that better way. As indicated by Davies, the role of relative deprivation in determining revolutionary social change is controlled by its *sudden* rise to awareness because of variance in condition—crop failure, wartime defeat, and the like.

Revolutionary activities are often spectacular in their immediate effect. However, in long-established, complex, and relatively stable societies, such as our own, they do not often occur. The reason that they do not, ultimately, is connected to these factors: (1) There is the tremendous ability of modern societies to socialize the young into a belief in and commitment to the basic values of the society (recall our discussion of socialization in Chapter 3); (2) Just as importantly, there are modern societies that, whatever their social structural inequities, have developed an unparalleled ability to satisfy the basic needs (food, drink, shelter) for the *majority* of their population (see Chapter 6). Consequently, revolutionary changes are unlikely because most people are too "well-padded" to entertain such a possibility seriously. (3) There is a tendency for the media and commercial aspects of modern societies to so misrepresent and water-down revolutionary-type activities that they lose their symbolic power to convert people to their ranks.

For example, if we return to the hip counterculture of the 1960s once again, we shall remember that within it there was at least one group—the political radicals—that might have potentially formed a revolutionary vanguard. Yet, in their presentation of this group, the American media left no stone unturned, illustrating the group's "bizarreness"—articles and TV programs centered on the lengthy hairstyle of this group's members, the fact that they smoked marijuana, listened to loud music, wore paint on their faces, didn't work—rather than on the philosophical and symbolic reasons for doing all these things. As a result, within a year or two, millions of young Americans had adopted the style of the counterculture without any real knowledge of or commitment to its beliefs. Similarly, once rock music began to be big business, the record industry lost no time selling rock records, using hip counterculture jargon. For example, in the late 1960s a Columbia records ad appeared that pictured a group of long-haired young people sitting in a darkened room in a circle, presumably smoking marijuana, and listening to the rock music of a Columbia group. The ad said: "The man (the police) can't bust our music!" The net result of these procedures was to undermine or destroy the original meaning of the hip philosophy and make it into another fad.

Indeed, about the only sudden changes that occur in modern industrial societies *are* fads. As a result of some Madison Avenue brainstorm, Americans in the last two decades have alternated between skate boards, hula hoops, frisbees, quadraphonic hi-fi equipment, European cars, CB radios, T-shirts with vital insignias, and, most recently, video cassette recorders and personal computers (see Box 8–1). Needless to say, other than on the pure entertainment level, and for some people the economic level, most of these sudden changes produce no lasting alteration in the main interaction patterns of the society as a whole. (Computers might.)

Trends

trend A relatively long-term and gradual alteration in interaction patterns.

In other words, in the modern context, sometimes much more important than revolutionary change is the effect of a **trend**—a relatively long-term and gradual alteration in interaction patterns. (See Box 8–2.)

Specialization.   To illustrate how trends can effect widespread social change, let us examine one important general trend that seems to occur in every society as it becomes more complex, **specialization**. Specialization is the division of functions at one time carried out by a single institution or group among one or more new institutions or groups. Over the years, through the process of specialization, Western society has created a wide range of institutions—schools, families, political systems, corporations, legal units, and religions—each of which carries out highly specialized functions for its members.

specialization The assignment of some of the functions previously carried out by one institution to other institutions, so that the original institution carries out fewer functions.

One of the consequences of specialization for our society can be seen in the changing nature of the middle-class American family, an institution that has been stripped of many of its original economic functions in the last century (see Chapter 6). At the present

---

Box 8–1   IT'S A SIGN OF THE TIMES (BUT IT'S ONLY A FAD)

Recently a *New York Times* reporter (Sept. 14, 1983, p. B6) was walking through Chinatown, only to see two fads "interacting." Passing by him were a Chi- nese boy and his father. Both had on T-shirts. The father's read "Hong Kong!" The boy's read "Donkey Kong!"

Box 8–2 TRENDS IN CRIME: AN "AGE YOUNG" QUESTION?

Silberman (1978) argues that violent crime has always been as American as Jesse James. It is true that violence is nothing new to our society. We have long been known as the "Wild, Wild West"—as a nation in which crime flourishes and the law is routinely ignored. In fact, when foreigners think of the United States, they often still conjure up images of Al Capone's Chicago and organized crime. Americans seem to agree: A recent Gallup poll reports that 48 percent of all Americans are afraid to walk the streets in their own neighborhoods.

Although the rate of serious crime has fluctuated over the years, it rose more than 150 percent from 1960 through the middle 1970s. To explain this dramatic increase, many people claimed that our courts and prisons have been incompetent or that judges have been soft on crime. Criminolo-

gist James A. Fox (1978) argues instead that the soaring crime rate may have been mostly a result of important changes in the age of people in our population. He shows that due to an increase in the birthrate following World War II, there was a very large number of teenagers after 1963. It is precisely this group—the baby-boom generation aged 14 through 21—that was most involved in violent crime.

Recent FBI reports show that a new trend in crime has been set in motion. The rate of violent crime has been on the decline since 1982, mainly because there have been fewer teenagers around. According to criminologist Fox, the level of violent crime should continue its decline until 1990, when the children of the baby-boom generation themselves reach a crime-prone age. At that time the crime rate will once again increase.

time most goods and services consumed by family members are produced and distributed outside the familial sphere of influence in highly specialized economic institutions (e.g., General Motors, Westinghouse, IBM, and the like). Less than 100 years ago, however, the family was a functioning economic unit for many Americans, in the form of either a family firm (a business enterprise) or the family farm. In present-day America the family unit is no longer a significant part of our economy. Specialization has produced two separate institutions where originally there was one: a family, specializing in the functions of expressivity and early child training, and a firm, specializing in instrumental tasks. Regarding the family, the single function of child rearing does not require and even makes impractical the larger unit previously necessary to carry out both economic and child-rearing functions. Thus before World War II it was not unusual for many American families to have five, six, even seven or eight children. This was because children often performed an economic function. As they got old enough, they worked on the family's farm or in the family business. Today, with the advent of businesses primarily outside the family, such participation is no longer necessary in most cases. As a result, families with more than four children are becoming a

Numerous fads have caught the public imagination in recent years. Essentially recreational diversions, such fads often pass from the scene in a year or two. Cabbage Patch Kids and Videogames have been particularly long-lived fads, reaching their peak of popularity during the early 1980s.

great rarity in our culture. Interestingly, even the remaining function of the nuclear family has been affected by the trend toward specialization. It now focuses mainly on *early* childhood training, whereas other specialized units such as the school, the peer group, the Sunday school, and the day-care center have increasingly intervened in the training of the developing child.

Emile Durkheim's (1933) analysis of the division of labor in society relates occupational specialization to the nature of the solidarity of a group. In simple, preliterate societies, there is little division of labor and tradition dominates the culture. The individuals are bound together by what Durkheim called **mechanical solidarity,** that is, by the similarity of their life-styles and values. Societies with a developing technology tend to increase their division of labor. When the division of labor becomes complex, the members of society no longer all perform similar functions or live in similar styles. Instead, they play highly specialized roles, each of which is a part of and necessary to the functioning of the society as a whole. Thus they are bound together by what Durkheim calls **organic solidarity,** that is, by their interdependence on one another's specialized roles for survival.

Clearly, organic solidarity is the predominating feature of our society. With few exceptions, each of us is dependent on a complex web of other people, many of whom we do not know, for our day-to-day lives. Our houses are built by individuals with specialized training. Our wiring and plumbing are installed and cared for by still other specialized occupations. Similarly, our furniture, entertainment, food, clothing, transportation, communications systems, and so on are all provided by people whose specialized function is to provide and maintain these goods and services for us.

mechanical solidarity Feeling of identity and unity among the members of a society based on the similarity of their values and life-styles.

organic solidarity Feeling of identity and unity among the members of a society based on their interdependence.

A Detailed Example: Two American Megatrends.   One way to see how trends can extensively transform the way of life of a society is to examine their development in detail. For example, without stretching the imagination, one can claim that, since World War II, much of American society has been transformed by the development of and insinuation into every part of our lives of two widespread changes, or "megatrends," both centered around cities—decentralization and the move to the Sunbelt (Spates and Macionis, 1982, pp. 219–228). Let us consider these phenomena.

Decentralization

It is no secret that Americans have been moving to the suburbs for decades. As Table 8–1 suggests, that movement continued unabated in the decade between 1970 and 1980. The real question is, "Why?" The answer isn't so hard to find.

Table 8–1 POPULATION OF SUBURBAN AREAS FOR SELECTED U.S. CITIES, 1970–1980

NORTHERN INDUSTRIAL CITIES	1980 POPULATION (IN THOUSANDS)	CHANGE SINCE 1970 (IN THOUSANDS)	PERCENT CHANGE SINCE 1970[a]
Baltimore	1,380	+ 215	+ 16
Boston	2,197	− 61	− 3
Chicago	4,071	+ 466	+ 11
Cleveland	1,323	+ 10	+ 1
Detroit	3,146	+ 226	+ 7
Philadelphia	3,019	+ 146	+ 5
New York	2,045	− 33	− 2
SOUTHERN CITIES			
Atlanta	1,588	+ 398	+ 25
Birmingham	552	+ 86	+ 16
Dallas–Fort Worth	1,680	+ 540	+ 32
Houston	1,317	+ 552	+ 42
Miami	1,238	+ 305	+ 25
New Orleans	626	+ 173	+ 28
Orlando	567	+ 213	+ 38
Tampa–St. Petersburg	1,048	+ 453	+ 43
WESTERN CITIES			
Los Angeles–Long Beach	4,136	+ 265	+ 6
Phoenix	739	+ 352	+ 48
Portland	871	+ 244	+ 28
Salt Lake City	707	+ 248	+ 35
San Francisco–Oakland	2,213	+ 182	+ 8
Seattle–Everett	1,055	+ 215	+ 20

[a]Percentages are rounded.
Source: U.S. Department of Commerce.

Economic Considerations. By about 1950 more and more businesses, particularly industry and manufacturing, were leaving the industrial districts of the center cities. The costs of refurbishing older buildings were high, and with high rents in the center city area, expansion was not always economically feasible. In addition, concerns over rising crime rates, taxes, and traffic congestion played a part in the proliferation of new "industrial parks" in the outer urban areas. When such businesses disappeared, they more frequently than not pulled their labor force after them. The result was a growth in suburban population and a decline in center-city population.

Technology. Key technological changes have stimulated the flow outward from center cities. For instance, unlike steam power, which must be used within the immediate area of its production, electric power can be transmitted over long distances. This makes it possible for both industries and residential areas to spread widely across the metropolitan area. Similarly, cars and trucks provide far greater flexibility in mobility and location than the rail transportation system that dominated late nineteenth-century America. This has been expecially true since the 1950s and the development of the interstate highway system and its ubiquitous outer-city "loops" (such as those surrounding Washington, D.C., Baltimore, Md., and Columbus, Ohio). As rail lines pushed out of the cities in earlier decades, the first suburbs clustered around the stations. But motor vehicles have made living in a far wider area possible while still providing access to the urban area as a whole. As late as 1920, the average commute was only about 1.5 miles. By 1960, however, this distance had grown to almost 5 miles, and it is not uncommon today to travel more than 20 miles to work.

These technological changes have combined to produce a common result: a change in the meaning of urban space. Because we move more easily across space—in minutes by car or milliseconds by telephone—physical proximity is not so necessary as it once was for joining together all the activities of the urban area.

Suburban Housing.   Although American suburbs had existed before World War II, their growth following that conflagration was nothing short of stupendous. At that time, millions of Americans returned from overseas to find their old city neighborhoods in increasing disrepair (in the war effort many neighborhood maintenance projects had been shelved and the ability of private homeowners to maintain full upkeep was curtailed). In many instances, returning white soldiers also found minority groups, particularly blacks, living in or close to their previous homes. (Numerous blacks had migrated north during the war to work the industrial machinery vacated by whites.) Finally, like many Americans, these veterans had their version of the classic American dream— their own place outside the congested city, a home with a little more room where they could raise their children in cleaner air and send them to good schools, without fear of crime and other perceived urban ills.

This dream became a reality when, after the war, the Federal Housing Authority (FHA) made low-interest loans for construction available to veterans or to anyone who could provide assurance of their ability to repay the loans. Millions of veterans accepted the FHA offer and, fulfilling their dream, elected to build their new homes in suburban areas.

Inner-City Decay.   The irony of all this movement outward, of course, was that the central cities themselves began to disintegrate (in many cases, literally). As the white middle classes moved out in droves to separately incorporated suburbs, the cities lost more of the tax base that departing industry had already eroded, becoming increasingly strapped financially.

To add to the difficulties, the population left behind in the city core was composed of an ever-growing number of minorities and the poor—people who could not pay much in taxes in the first place. In time, many of them lost jobs (as businesses moved out) and went on welfare. Thus, the city was faced with an ever-*increasing* demand for services and ever-*shrinking* ability to provide them. In the 1970s the financial straits of many American cities—among them New York and Cleveland—led to major cutbacks in city services.

Rural Growth. The decentralization of the American population has done more than spread urban settlement outward from the center cities, however. Small towns and rural areas are experiencing a precipitous boom as well. During the 1960s rural America lost 2.8 million people, but during the 1970s the trend changed sharply: Rural areas gained 8.4 million people, up some 15.4 percent.

But the people moving to these rural areas are in no way traditionally rural. Most are well-educated, have sophisticated tastes, and often work in nearby cities. Problems of adjustment when the "city-slickers" descend on such areas, have been rife, as illustrated in Box 8–3.

The Sunbelt Phenomenon

Decentralization has not affected all American urban regions equally. In general, the old industrialized North is in dire straits. The South, by comparison, is sitting pretty (at least for the moment). First, Sunbelt cities are often the direct beneficiaries of northern cities' problems. Northern cities characteristically have old industrial systems, poor inner-city transportation for products, deteriorating services, and skyrocketing costs. Most Sunbelt cities, in contrast, have new plants, are surrounded by new and efficient superhighways, have good or brand new service systems, and offer lower costs—particularly for energy and labor. Hence many decisions to move out of northern cities have been made *simultaneously* with decisions to move south.

The census makes this indubitably clear. Table 8–2 compares the raw population figures and national rankings for the 10 largest American cities of 1980 and compares those figures for the same cities and their rankings to the 1950 census. Although northern industrial giants such as New York, Chicago, Philadelphia, and Detroit have manged to stay in the top 10, all have lost a significant

Box 8–3 THE INVASION OF THE CITY SLICKERS

[What city people who move to the country] bring along is a series of unconscious assumptions. It might be better for rural America if they brought a few sticks of dynamite, or a can of arsenic.

Take a typical example. Mr. and Mrs. Nice are Bostonians. They live a couple of miles off Route 128 in a four-bedroom house. He's a partner in an ad agency; she has considerable talent as an artist. For some years they've had a second home in northern New Hampshire. The kids love it up there in Grafton County.

For some years, too, both Nices have been feeling they'd like to simplify their lives. They look with increasing envy on their New Hampshire neighbors, who never face a morning traffic jam, or an evening one, either; who don't have a long drive to the country on Friday night and a long drive back on Sunday; who aren't cramped into a suburban lot; who live in harmony with the natural rhythm of the year; who think the rat race is probably some minor event at a county fair.

One Thursday evening Don Nice says to Sue that he's been talking to the other partners, and they've agreed there's no reason he can't do some of his work at home. If he's in the office Wednesday and Thursday every week, why the rest of the time he can stay in touch by telephone. Sue, who has been trapped all year as a Brownie Scout leader and who has recently had the aerial snapped off her car in Boston, is delighted. She reflects happily that in their little mountain village you don't even need to lock your house, and there is no Brownie troop. "You're wonderful," she tells Don.

So the move occurs. In most ways Don and Sue are very happy. They raise practically all their own vegetables the first year;

Sue takes up cross-country skiing. Don personally splits some of the wood they burn in their new woodstove.

But there are some problems. The first one Sue is conscious of is the school. It's just not very good. It's clear to Sue almost immediately that the town desperately needs a new school building—and also modern playground equipment, new school buses, more and better art instruction at the high school, a different principal. Don is as upset as Sue when they discover that only about 40 per cent of the kids who graduate from that high school go on to any form of college. The rest do native things like becoming farmers, and mechanics, and joining the Air Force. An appalling number of the girls marry within twelve months after graduation. How are Jeanie and Don, Jr., going to get into good colleges from this school? . . .

Pretty soon Sue and Don join an informal group of newcomers in town who are working to upgrade education. All they want for starters is the new building ($2.8 million) and a majority of their kind on the school board.

As for Don, though he really enjoys splitting the wood—in fact, next year he's planning to get a chainsaw and start cutting a few trees of his own—he also likes to play golf. There's no course within twenty miles. Some of the nice people he's met in the education lobby feel just as he does. They begin to discuss the possibility of a nine-hole course. The old farmer who owns the land they have in mind seems to be keeping only four or five cows on it, anyway. Besides, taxes are going up, and the old fellow is going to have to sell, sooner or later. (Which is too bad, of course. Don and Sue both admire the local farmers, and they're sincerely sorry whenever one has to quit.)

Over the next several years, Don and Sue get more and more adjusted to rural living—and they also gradually discover

Source: Noel Perrin, "Rural Area: Permit Required," *Country Journal,* April 1980, pp. 34–35.

more things that need changing. For example, the area needs a good French restaurant. And it needs a *much* better airport. At present there are only two flights a day to Boston, and because of the lack of sophisticated equipment, even they are quite often canceled. If Don wants to be sure of getting down for an important meeting, he has to drive. Sue would be happy with more organized activities for the kids. There's even talk of starting a Brownie troop.

In short, if enough upper-middle-class people move to a rural town, they are naturally going to turn it into a suburb of the nearest city. For one generation it will be a nice and truly rustic suburb, with real farms dotted around it, and real natives speaking their minds at town meeting. Then as the local people are gradually taxed out of existence (or at least out of town), one more piece of rural America has died.

percentage of their population since 1950. If present trends continue, it might not be surprising to see only New York and Chicago on the 1990 list. In comparison, Los Angeles has continued to grow and, "out of nowhere," Houston, Dallas, San Diego, and San Antonio have leaped onto the list. The process is reshaping the face of urban America and having deep ramifications for the entire country. The South has risen again; the West has followed suit. The process is feeding itself and all indications are that it will continue throughout the 1980s. Business follows business; family follows family. Joe Delbova has moved to the Sunbelt (see Box 8–4), and others will follow him.

In conclusion, then, as a result of these two continuing trends, American cities generally, despite recent "comeback" indications, face at least two more decades of financial troubles. Cities like New York will continue to try to hold its heads above water in finding ways to adapt to smaller tax revenues and a changing population. Though the Sunbelt will continue to ride high, that

Table 8–2 THE TEN LARGEST AMERICAN CITIES

	1980		1950	
	POPULATION[a]	RANK	POPULATION[a]	RANK
New York	7,035	(1)	7,892	(1)
Chicago	2,970	(2)	3,621	(2)
Los Angeles	2,950	(3)	1,970	(4)
Philadelphia	1,680	(4)	2,072	(3)
Houston	1,555	(5)	596	(14)
Detroit	1,192	(6)	1,850	(5)
Dallas	901	(7)	434	(21)
San Diego	870	(8)	334	(28)
Baltimore	783	(9)	950	(6)
San Antonio	783	(10)	408	(24)

[a]Population in thousands; center city data only.
Source: U.S. Bureau of the Census, 1976, pp. 24–25; 1980.

Source: Newsweek, April 27, 1981, p. 67.

Box 8–4 JOE DELBOVA'S ESCAPE TO THE SUNBELT

Laid-off rubberworker Joe Delbova will soon leave his home town to seek a new job in the booming Southwest. Making the move may involve giving up a special education program for a handicapped daughter, but with local unemployment now at 9.3 percent, he believes he has no choice. "I'm pretty much against the wall," says Delbova, who has been out of work for a year. "I've no buying power, and I feel I've been abused. I'm an optimistic person, but I can't make it in Akron, Ohio."

Folks in Detroit, Cleveland and other once burly centers of production in the industrial Midwest feel much the same way. . . . That's hardly surprising: while more than half a million people are out of work in Michigan, Houston has relied on North-ern emigres to fill many of the 70,000 new jobs that have opened each year for the past five years. "At least here you have a chance," says V. J. Clay, a former Michigander now living in the nation's energy capital.

In large measure, the loss of jobs from the old industrial states stems from the sickness of the auto business and its ripple effects in steel, rubber, and other supplier industries. Making matters worse, however, is the flight of healthier companies unwilling to pay the region's high tax and wage rates. . . . Small firms have even more reason to move. "It's got to the point where a small business cannot survive in Michigan," says Lewis Snook, who moved his tool-and-die company from Livonia, Michigan to Dallas last year. "Here we can pay $2 to $2.50 less per hour and get the same quality work, if not better."

picture is not completely rosy. The growth of the Sunbelt has been so quick that, in many instances, the region has outstripped its ability to keep up with the incoming throngs. Pollution is on the rise; water, particularly in the Southwest and West, is getting scarce; services cannot cope; and racial tensions are on the rise as Hispanics cross the border from Mexico and blacks move back to the South to take advantage of greener pastures.

Everyday Change

Probably the most pervasive, but least noticed, type of social change is contained in the **everyday changes** that continually affect our social lives. We use the word "everyday" here not to imply that such changes are unimportant nor even that they are happening all the time to everybody, but to suggest that in all our lives there exist relatively small, commonplace changes that alter our behavior, sometimes quite markedly (recall our discussion of "The Dynamic Nature of Social Interaction," Chapter 2).

For example, in order to save money, a couple may decide not to go to the movies every Friday night as they have in the past. Such a decision affects their interaction patterns on Friday evenings; they may start playing board games or going for walks or

everyday change The subtle or unremarkable alterations in interaction patterns that occur from time to time in our daily experiences.

watching television or working on their interpersonal problems or visiting more often with friends. If they chose to visit more, their decision obviously affects the interaction patterns of others as well. Or, to take another case, an employee of a company may start bringing yogurt in his or her bagged lunch. Other people in the office try it and start bringing it as well. Or, a member of a small group starts using a particular expression repeatedly, such as "awesome" or "fantastic," and soon a new pattern of speech has become established in the group.

Such everyday changes in how we relate to one another are often so subtle or unremarkable that they may appear and disappear without anyone consciously focusing on them as changes. Yet changes they are. They may endure for days, weeks, months, or years. After a time they may disappear from our lives or shade into other everyday changes just as subtly as they appeared. In fact, we usually become aware of such changes only when we compare our behavior now to what it was in the past ("We used to go to the movies a lot. When did we stop?") or when someone outside of our situation points them out to us ("When did you people turn into a bunch of yogurt nuts?") Box 8–5 shows how subtle and gradual everyday changes can be: Did you know that "night" is the new frontier?

Occasionally, of course, everyday social changes can become

Box 8–5   AN EVERYDAY CHANGE THAT HAS CREATED A NEW FRONTIER

For most people the word frontier conjures up images of the wild and woolly west of a century ago; of settlers and pioneers, of cowboys and Indians. According to sociologist Murray Melbin (1978), however, there is a new frontier of the here and now —located not in space or territory, but in time. He suggests that night is our newest frontier; that the pioneers of the night are those who populate the night-time hours of our cities—not hunters and trappers, of course; but shift workers, nurses, dancers, airline personnel, and the like.

In fact, there are strong similarities between the western frontier of the nineteenth century and the night time hours today. For example, both are populated mostly by young men, both tolerate individualism and eccentric behavior. Both have reputations for danger and lawlessness, not always deserved, and, in both frontiers, people are uncommonly helpful and friendly toward one another.

With many advantages over the daylight hours, it is not surprising that growing numbers of Americans are working and playing during the night-time hours. Around the clock services now include radio and TV broadcasting, convenience stores, cinemas, automobile repair shops, and insect exterminators. Night-time business calls have increased by more than 50 percent during the last few years.

Thousands of young people still go west; they pack their bags and head for California. For some, however, it may be more convenient simply to work by night and sleep by day. They don't even need a covered wagon—only an alarm clock!

the source of or merge with either revolutionary or trend changes. For example, in the section on the women's movement in the last chapter, we indicated that one of the reasons the contemporary movement arose when it did was because women began communicating with each other about their problems. Consider the specific example of the consciousness-raising groups—it began when a few women saw the analogy between the oppression of blacks, the poor, youth, and themselves. They talked about this in small groups. For numerous reasons these groups proved effective in changing how these women thought, felt, and acted. This was clearly what we are calling everyday change. However, as we also saw, the process did not stop there. The women in the consciousness-raising groups communicated with other women about the success of their sessions. Soon other women experimented with the format and their success was passed on to still others. Before very many years had passed, the everyday changes put into motion by all these small groups developed into the nationwide women's movement.

SOURCE POINTS OF SOCIAL CHANGE

Having described the major types of social change, we now try to understand just where in a society social change is likely to appear. Or, to phrase it as a question: What are the source points of change? Earlier in this chapter we said that social change may arise when the feeling of relative deprivation experienced by members of a group is intense enough to move them to changing their patterns of social interaction. Although the degree of such feelings is highly variable, they are likely to become intensive enough to motivate action toward social change in only three types of social systems: (1) in social systems where the pattern of interaction is not yet fully defined (as in the first year of marriage or in the relationship of a new member to a clique); (2) in social systems where members have become ambivalent about the interaction pattern (as in the hesitance of some Catholics to accept the antiabortion laws); (3) in social systems where change is expected and is regarded as normal (as in the area of politics and international affairs).

In addition to these characteristics, other factors may influence where (or whether) social change occurs. One such factor is the physical environment. San Francisco, before the earthquake of 1906, was widely regarded as the most corrupt city on the West Coast. After the earthquake had destroyed virtually the entire city, the returning population of San Francisco tried to make sure that the "undesirable elements" that were responsible for the degradation of the city either did not return or were strictly controlled and negatively sanctioned if they did. Similarly, other non-cultural factors may result in social change, such as rapid population growth and the spread or control of disease (recall the discussion of "The Influence of Other Factors on Culture," Chapter 2).

To say exactly where social change arises is still, nonetheless, a difficult process. Sociologists have come to recognize that no one factor, regardless of how persuasive it may be, is likely to account for the complex forces that actually produce social change in various groups and societies. However, many sociologists have come to agree that, because of their central importance in working out essential elements of human interaction, the economic system and religious values are frequently the source points of important social change.

The Economic System

From the Marxian standpoint, social change results from the dialectical process of economic forces in history, an evolutionary movement having three distinct phases at every stage of development. The first phase, called the *thesis*, is a period of order and stability in society that occurs when one system is established as the dominant economic order, for example, the order imposed by capitalism when it replaced feudalism. In this phase almost everyone accepts the dominant economic system, even though one or several groups within the society may be subject to exploitation by that established system. The second phase, called *antithesis*, arises when the exploitation becomes more intense and the exploited group becomes more aware of its situation. In this phase all the groups in society are no longer in agreement about their relationship to the economic system. Thus Marx predicted that the order and stability of early capitalism would give way to a period of intense class conflict between the bourgeoisie and the exploited proletariat. As described in Chapter 5, when the workers became conscious of themselves as a class and recognized their common economic interests, they would band together in order to overthrow the capitalist system. This action would initiate the third and final phase of the dialectical process, *synthesis*, the establishment of a new system to resolve the conflicts of the previous one. Thus the revolution of the workers would successfully overturn capitalism and establish the communist order in which the workers would own as well as work all the means of production. It was a "synthesis" because the new order would combine parts of the old order and the revolutionary order. Thus the synthetic communist society would be likely to maintain capitalism's focus on industrialism, but it would not let the profits of that productive system be controlled by the few. Rather, a mechanism would be established in which the surpluses of production would be shared among all members of society.

For Marx, then, conflict, change, and revolution were fundamentally economic in nature. In every period of history the requirements of the prevailing economic system determine the character of all the other institutions, including family, government, press, education, and religion. These institutions existed only to serve and maintain the economic status quo. In Marxian theory the evolution of the nuclear family described in Chapter 6 would not be seen as being caused by other trends, such as specialization, or as having independent status at all. It would be seen as a shift in relationships to provide the most efficient and willing labor force for capitalist exploitation.

Religious Values

Many sociologists continue to accept major aspects of Marx's economic theory. Others believe that noneconomic institutions are important source points of social change and that, contrary to the Marxian argument, changes in these institutions allow for developmental changes in economic spheres of society.

The classic study of the manner in which religious ideas may become a source point for social change is Max Weber's (1958) *The Protestant Ethic and the Spirit of Capitalism.* Weber tried to show that the central ideas of both Protestantism and capitalism were compatible and that capitalism could never have become the primary mode of economic activity in the Western world without Protestant ideas to support it. Essentially, his argument went as follows.

Capitalism is a set of economic ideas, the goal of which is making a profit, that is, receiving more for a product than is paid to produce or acquire it. In its ideal type the capitalist philosophy sets no limit on profit: The capitalist is expected to make as much profit as possible and to reinvest it so that still more profit can be made at a later time. Thus the acquisition of money or the things that produce money (labor, land, material resources) becomes an end in itself.

In order to continue increasing profit, a capitalist has to labor at peak efficiency throughout life; setting any limits on the effort expended or trying merely to maintain a particular level of profit would give other capitalists an opportunity to usurp that profit. In addition, the capitalist has to analyze continually his or her activities by rational means to ensure that each investment brings maximum profit.

The capitalist philosophy of never-ending acquisition of wealth differs from the prior systems that had guided the economic activity in the West (e.g., feudalism). Most other economic systems viewed economic activity as a necessary evil undertaken to support life. One worked as much as needed to survive and no more. In such societies those engaged in capitalist activity frequently were regarded as mercenary and perhaps even deranged. For example, the portrait of Shylock in Shakespeare's *The Merchant of Venice*, when shorn of its antisemitic elements, shows a great bias against "money lending" as a profession. Thus capitalistic activities lacked moral support and remained a practice of only a few.

With the spread of Protestantism in the sixteenth century, however, these conditions began to change. According to Weber, the central ideas of this religious movement were essentially identical to those of capitalism and gave general moral support to all Protestants who engaged in capitalistic economic endeavor. Weber shows this connection by focusing on the main precepts of Calvinism, the denomination of Protestantism that took the reformative ideas to their logical extreme.

Calvinist ideology revolved around the doctrine of predestination. God was said to have predestined all human souls to either eternal salvation or damnation by an unknown and unknowable process of divine grace. The human species was put on earth solely to glorify Him. To this end, all human beings were directed to labor incessantly to build the Kingdom of God on earth. Moreover, all things of this world, particularly human nature and the desires of the flesh, were agencies of evil from which only God's grace could give salvation.

Such stringent principles had important social and psychological consequences for those subscribing to them. First, because of the purported sinful nature of the human species, all things of this world—material goods, physical pleasure—were supposed to be utilized as little as possible. Second, work was regarded as a "calling," as the means by which persons could glorify God, not as a means for personal gratification. Furthermore, enjoyment of the fruits of one's labor was seen as being "idolatrous." Consequently, according to the Protestant ethic, hard work and self-denial became the accepted mode of behavior.

According to Calvin's dictates, all souls are predestined to heaven or hell prior to birth, but because God's ways are unknowable, no one can ever know *which* fate is to befall him or her. Belief in such a doctrine would obviously result in great anxiety within the individual, strong feelings of possible unworthiness, and a tremendous drive to know, somehow, what one's fate is. Because the pressures of not knowing were so anxiety-producing for Calvin's congregation, it gradually came to be held that "good works," that is, activities undertaken for the glory of God, could provide at least a clue to the individual's fate. After all, it was reasoned that a person who was damned would hardly be expected to be doing good all the time. Thus a tremendous motivation for undertaking hard work in the service of forces outside the individual was provided. One could not earn salvation through good works, but success came to be viewed as a "sign" of salvation; if one produced enough good works perhaps she or he could rest somewhat more easily about the question of personal salvation. Of course, one could not rest very long. Any reduction of work was seen as sure evidence of predestined damnation, so never-ending hard work became the order of the day.

Thus Protestants in the sixteenth century and after were particularly well suited in terms of their religious ideology to become capitalists. For them, capitalist activity was certainly not mercenary or deranged but, rather, an orientation of the highest moral character—a means of showing constant devotion to God. Protestant capitalists were not operating out of any desire to acquire material goods or to serve any hedonistic desires. The capitalist goal of the never-ending acquisition of wealth became equated with the Protestant ethic of never-ending work for the glory of God (see Box 8–6).

THE SPREAD OF SOCIAL CHANGE

Essentially, there is only one way in which social change can spread. It must be passed on from individual to individual in the group by the transmission of the new ideas or actions. This process is known as **diffusion** and ranges from the simple communication that may occur between members of a family to the rapid spread of a fad or a revolutionary fervor to the slower passage of important attitudes and actions down through the ages.

diffusion The process by which social change is spread, the transmission of new ideas and actions from individual to individual in a group.

In other words, although the diffusion process is the same from group to group, the actual *rate* of social change may differ considerably. Even with a thorough knowledge of a social system, predicting the rate of change is a difficult task. This predictive problem exists also with the *degree* of social change, or the amount of important social reorganization that occurs in a group as a result of being influenced by new ideas and actions.

Factors Affecting Rate and Degree of Change

Sociologists have identified three factors that influence the rate and degree of social change in all social situations where change is likely to occur: the *duration* of the interaction between those advocating change and those not yet committed to it, the *influential strength* of each party in the interaction, and the *ideational nearness* of the people involved in the change. The actual effect

Box 8–6   BEN FRANKLIN'S PECUNIARY PHILOSOPHY

The following comments are from Benjamin Franklin. They indicate the deep commitment to capitalist ideas held by early Protestants. In addition, they give indication of why America, primarily a Protestant nation from its inception, has also been a major capitalist power in the world. Today, most sociologists would argue that the Protestant connection to capitalism is nowhere near as important as it used to be and, because of socialization, all Americans, regardless of religious, ethnic, or racial background, are expected to be successful exponents of an instrumental ethic.

Remember, that *time* is money. He that can earn ten shillings a day by his labour, and goes abroad, or sits idle, one half of that day, though he spends but sixpence during his diversion or idleness, ought not to reckon *that* the only expense; he has really spent, or rather thrown away, five shillings besides.

Source: Max Weber, *The Protestant Ethic and the Spirit of Capitalism* (New York: Scribner's, 1958).

Remember, that *credit* is money. If a man lets his money lie in my hands after it is due, he gives me the interest, or as much as I can make of it during that time. This amounts to a considerable sum where a man has good and large credit, and makes good use of it.

Remember, that money is of the prolific, generating nature. Money can beget money, and its offspring can beget more, and so on. Five shillings turned is six, turned again it is seven and threepence, and so on, till it becomes a hundred pounds. The more there is of it, the more it produces every turning, so that the profits rise quicker and quicker. He that kills a breeding-sow, destroys all her offspring to the thousandth generation. He that murders a crown, destroys all that it might have produced, even scores of pounds.

Remember this saying, *The good paymaster is lord of another man's purse.*

cultural diffusion The process by which cultural elements are borrowed when one culture interacts with another.

of these factors may be more easily seen if we examine some well-known instances of **cultural diffusion**—the process of cultural borrowing that occurs when one society comes into contact with another (see Box 8–7).

Some South Sea island societies on out-of-the-way shipping lines have changed relatively little in the last 100 years because the duration of their contact with other cultures, specifically Western culture, has been short and intermittent. Other islands, more centrally located, have undergone drastic changes as a direct result of their continuing interaction with Western ideas and behavioral patterns. Hawaii, for example, in little more than a 100 years, has been transformed from a relatively easy-going, agrarian, politically independent island with an indigenous population to a fast-paced, commercial-industrial American state with a polyglot population from all over the world.

The rate and degree of change will also be affected by the relative influential strength of the group desiring change and the

Box 8–7 CULTURAL DIFFUSION IN THE LIFE OF THE AVERAGE AMERICAN

Our solid American citizen awakens in a bed built on a pattern which originated in the Near East but which was modified in northern Europe before it was transmitted to America. He throws back covers made from cotton, domesticated in India, or linen, domesticated in the Near East, or wool from sheep, also domesticated in the Near East, or silk, the use of which was discovered in China. All of these materials have been spun and woven by processes invented in the Near East. He slips into his moccasins, invented by the Indians of the Eastern woodlands, and goes to the bathroom, whose fixtures are a mixture of European and American inventions, both of recent date. He takes off his pajamas, a garment invented in India, and washes with soap invented by the ancient Gauls. He then shaves, a masochistic rite which seems to have been derived from either Sumer or ancient Egypt.

Returning to the bedroom, he removes his clothes from a chair of southern European type and proceeds to dress. He puts on garments whose form originally derived from the skin clothing of the nomads of the Asiatic steppes, puts on shoes made from skins tanned by a process invented in ancient Egypt and cut to a pattern derived from the classical civilizations of the Mediterranean, and ties around his neck a strip of bright-colored cloth which is a vestigial survival of the shoulder shawls worn by the seventeenth-century Croatians. Before going out for breakfast he glances through the window, made of glass invented in Egypt, and if it is raining puts on overshoes made of rubber discovered by the Central American Indians and takes an umbrella, invented in southeastern Asia. Upon his head he puts a hat made of felt, a material invented in the Asiatic steppes.

On his way to breakfast he stops to buy a paper, paying for it with coins, an ancient Lydian invention. At the restaurant a whole new series of borrowed elements confronts him. His plate is made of a form of pottery invented in China. His knife is of steel, an alloy first made in southern India, his fork a medieval Italian invention, and his spoon a derivative of a Roman original. He begins breakfast with an orange from the eastern Mediterranean, a cantaloupe from Persia, or perhaps a piece of African watermelon. With this he has coffee, an Abyssinian plant, with cream and sugar. Both the domestication of cows and the idea of milking them originated in the Near East, while sugar was first made in India. After his fruit and first coffee he goes on to waffles, cakes made by a Scandinavian technique from wheat domesticated in Asia Minor. Over these he pours maple syrup, invented by the Indians of the Eastern woodlands. As a side dish he may have the egg of a species of bird domesticated in Indo-China, or thin strips of the flesh of an animal domesticated in Eastern Asia which have been salted and smoked by a process developed in northern Europe.

When our friend has finished eating he settles back to smoke, an American Indian habit, consuming a plant domesticated in Brazil in either a pipe, derived from the Indians of Virginia, or a cigarette, derived from Mexico. If he is hardy enough he may even attempt a cigar, transmitted to us from the Antilles by way of Spain. While smoking he reads the news of the day, imprinted in characters invented by the ancient Semites upon a material invented in China by a process invented in Germany. As he absorbs the accounts of foreign troubles he will, if he is a good conservative citizen, thank a Hebrew deity in an Indo-European language that he is 100 percent American.

Source: Ralph Linton, *The Study of Man* (New York: Appleton, 1936) pp. 326–327.

The effects of cultural diffusion are everywhere, often reciprocal, and often unnoticed. In the left photograph, Chinese women play basketball, a game invented in America. In the right photograph, a New York restaurant offers Chinese *and* American *and* Spanish food.

group it is confronting. For example, defeated and occupied nations throughout history have been the object of enforced cultural diffusion. One objective of Hitler in World War II, for example, was to spread the basic patterns of his *Third Reich* to the entire world. As the German war machine conquered Belgium, France, and other European countries, the process of enforced "Nazification" began: Citizens were forced to swear allegiance to Hitler, businesses were forced to supply German troops and stock German goods, and so on. Another example is the attempt of some societies (our own included) to convert the local populations of occupied territories to the religious beliefs of the dominating society. Thus, in the nineteenth century and continuing until the present, many churches have sent out missionaries whose sole task was to change the religious beliefs of an indigenous society to those of the missionary's society. Even more immediate is the case of Canada which in recent years has been trying to limit the influence of American business and people on its economic and social structure. The fear of many Canadians is that such "creeping

Americanism" was slowly, but inevitably, undermining the identity of Canadians and Canada as a separate people and nation.

Both the rate and degree of social change are likely to be *increased* if the essential value pattern of the changing force is similar to that of the group to be changed. An interesting example of this ideational nearness has occurred between what would appear to be two dissimilar societies: the United States and Japan. According to Bellah (1958), the reason for such a rapid dissemination of change between the two nations is their similar basic philosophies. Despite Japan's oriental background and the United States' occidental one, both are essentially committed to the instrumental pattern described in Chapter 2. Consequently, when friendly relations between the two nations were resumed at the end of World War II, Japan developed into a major industrialized nation almost overnight. Japanese society has been so successful in adopting the American model that it now controls much of the world market in goods it specializes in: cars, electronic gear (steroes, TVs), and cameras.

Acceleration in Change

One pattern in the rate of social change seems to emerge in any careful examination of the sociological facts. Over the broad sweep of human history, change has taken place at an increasingly *faster* rate. This acceleration has been most pronounced and visible in relation to advances in technology, for instance, in inventions and discoveries associated with cutting-tool efficiency, the speed of travel, the power to kill and destroy, and the current high-tech/computer "revolution."

According to William Ogburn (1922), there is a general tendency for parts of culture to change and adapt at different rates when diffusion occurs producing a phenomenon known as **cultural lag**. During periods of accelerating technological change, cultural lag may be widespread. Material culture (e.g., destructive technology) tends to change before ideational culture (e.g., norms governing the use of destructive technology), creating a period of time when society has not yet fully adapted itself to the new material conditions.

cultural lag The tendency for the parts of culture to change and adapt at different rates.

Hornell Hart (1957b p. 417) has dramatized the critical importance of this cultural lag. Imagine a hydrogen bomb suspended in the air over the United Nations building in New York City:

> The bomb represents the towering upsurge of military technology—the vastly multiplied power of destruction which modern science has placed in the hands of the Soviet as well as of the American government. The glass-faced building of the United Nations symbolizes the frail structure of international law

Since the turn of the century, social change has been extremely rapid. Some social observers, like Alvin Toffler, argue that such tremendous change is very difficult to assimilate, both on the individual and social levels. What results is a condition that he calls "future shock." These photographs depict just a few of the major changes that have occurred.

Technology (top left): The first powered flight was barely able to carry a man and lasted 13 seconds. Today, jumbo jets carry hundreds of passengers (not to mention cargo) and can stay airborne for a day or longer.

Fashion and Entertainment (bottom left): These two photographs depict the tremendous changes in acceptable fashion and entertainment pleasure that have occurred in recent years. No longer an "underground" phenomenon, sexual enticement of nearly unrestricted nature is available in most major cities.

Art (top): Representational art is not as important in contemporary sculpture as it once was. Instead, much greater emphasis is placed on form and symbol. This sculpture, by American artist John Raimondi, is entitled "Erma's Desire." It is constructed of cor-ten steel and measures 47 × 33 × 26 feet. It is situated on Interstate 80 in Grand Island, Nebraska. The fact that it was commissioned as part of the Bicentennial Celebration in 1976 indicates how our understanding of art has changed in this nation in the last two centuries.

and order, groping upward, uncertain and as yet feeble—yet embodying the best aspirations and collective achievements of mankind until now in our struggle to bring collective intelligence to mastery over colossal brute force. Quite evidently, the growth of world law and order is lagging disastrously behind the upsurge of destructive technology.

Toffler (1970) used the term *future shock* to refer to the stressful, disorienting effects of rapid and accelerating technological change—a condition in which anchors are lacking, standards of conduct are in a state of conflict, and normlessness abounds. (Toffler's concept is quite similar to Durkheim's concept of anomie discussed in Chapter 1)

> The final, qualitative difference between this and all previous lifetimes is the one most easily overlooked. For we have not merely extended the scope and scale of change, we have radically altered its pace. We have in our time released a totally new social force—a stream of change so accelerated that it influences our sense of time, revolutionizes the tempo of daily life, and affects the very way we "feel" the world around us. We no longer "feel" life as men did in the past. And this is the ultimate difference, the distinction that separates the truly contemporary man from all others. For this acceleration lies behind the impermanence—the transience—that penetrates and tinctures our consciousness, radically affecting the way we relate to other people, to things, to the entire universe of ideas, arts and values. (Toffler, 1970, p. 17)

In our society an accelerating rate of change has generated pervasive future shock and members of the society have had tremendous difficulty in adjusting to the impact of change. However, some changes have enhanced the quality of our lives and other positive changes, such as full equality of the races and sexes, are long overdue. Rather than retard the rate of change overall, we might follow Toffler's advice and find means to aid those who attempt to cope with rapid change.

THE DIRECTION OF SOCIAL CHANGE

Sociologists have long sought to discover some overall direction of social change that operates on the basis of an underlying principle or law. Unfortunately, there is little agreement regarding the nature of this general trend; indeed, there is little agreement about whether such a principle or law even *exists*. Nevertheless, theorists have conceptualized social change as moving in a *linear* di-

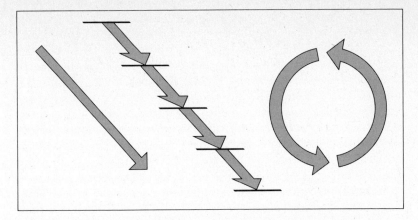

Figure 8–1 Directions of Change: Linear, Successive-Stage, and Cyclical

rection, through *successive stages,* or in a *cyclical* pattern (see Figure 8–1).

Linear Model

As Miller (1957, p. 93) suggests, **linear models of social change** characteristically posit "a total movement which constantly advances toward a definite goal." Drawing a parallel between biological evolution and societal change, many linear models have asserted that the development of society has been toward greater and greater progress.

In the nineteenth century, for example, the English sociologist Herbert Spencer (1820–1903) published many volumes on all the major disciplines of his day—biology, psychology, ethics, and the fledgling sociology—in an attempt to convince the scientific world of the ubiquitousness of the single principle of evolution. Spencer regarded **evolution** as the process whereby matter moved from an incoherent, unstable, homogeneous state to a unified, stable, heterogeneous state. He felt that everything in the universe conformed to this principle, not only in the physical and biological world, but in the social world as well.

From this notion the idea of societal evolution appeared. Spencer attempted to show that human societies, like plant and animal species, developed toward greater complexity and interdependence of their parts. They evolved from relatively simple, unstable groups, where everyone was essentially alike, to complex, stable groups, where everyone did essentially what she or he was best suited for. To Spencer's mind, tribal societies—which he called "primitive tribes"—represented the lesser evolved societies and civilized modern states such as Western industrial nations repre-

linear model of social change A conception of the overall direction of social change in which societies are seen as moving in a straight line from lower to higher levels of development.

evolution In sociology, the progress of human societies from simple, unstable groups to complex, stable, interdependent groups.

sented the highly evolved societies. In his later writings Spencer also argued that the evolutionary law of "the survival of the fittest" (his concept originally, not Darwin's) was applicable to societies and that better adapted social groups would eventually transform or absorb lesser adapted ones. Finally, Spencer felt that within the most evolved societies the best social order was that which did not interfere in any way with the efforts of its members. He predicted that the emergence of an industrialized social order would protect individual rights and decrease oppressive governmental functions. Since Spencer's day, the doctrine of inevitable social evolution, called Social Darwinism, has been severely criticized.

First of all, Spencer's ideas seemed unnervingly self-serving. His theory touted Western societies as being more evolved than others, English society as being among the most evolved of the Western group, and *his* social class and ideas as being more evolved than those of other groups in society. (For more on this problem—of social scientists consciously or unconsciously praising *their* way of life as the best—see Chapter 9.) Second, cumulative evidence suggests that most societies, if anything, *are inherently conservative,* not progressive (Parsons, 1937). There is a tendency for social norms, once in place, to stay in place. Tradition is often valued for its own sake and innovation shunned. Third, as the anthropologists have shown, notably Levi-Straus (1961), tribal societies are *not* less complex than modern societies in anything more than technological terms. Their culture, language, and social structural arrangements are frequently as sophisticated, if not more so, than those of so-called "modern" societies. Finally, as for the idea of the "survival of the fittest," our analysis of social stratification in Chapter 5 should have explained that those "on top" in a social order are not always there for reasons of skill. Often they have attained and maintained their vaunted positions by the unequal use of wealth, prestige, or power. For example, the wealthy, whatever their innate abilities, can "buy" opportunities not afforded poorer members of society—sending their children on world cruises, thereby increasing their understanding of the world; buying their children the best books and, by making contributions, getting them into the best schools; and so on. Likewise, prestige opens many doors irrespective of talent. Rockefellers and Kennedys have more opportunities than others simply because of their name; Harvard graduates have the same advantage over equally (or better) qualified graduates from lesser-known universities. In short, the idea of social evolution seems patently wrong.

Nevertheless, although the idea of continuing progress in social change has fallen into disrepute, many elements of the linear model continue to be applied to the study of social change, as in the linear theory of Ferdinand Tönnies (1855–1936). Tönnies (1957) viewed the large-scale societal changes beginning in the Middle Ages as a result of population growth and industrialization as a linear trend away from simple, traditional, communal societies, **gemeinschaft,** and toward complex, urbanized societies, **gesellschaft.** In fact, Tönnies' model of the characteristics of gemeinschaft and gesellschaft (see Box 8–8) are based fundamentally on the distinction between what Cooley called primary and secondary groups.

gemeinschaft Tönnies's conception of simple, traditional, communal societies.

gesellschaft Tönnies's conception of complex, urbanized societies.

Successive Stage Model

Another approach to depicting large-scale social change is the **successive-stage model,** which holds that societies inevitably move through a sequence of stages, each providing the preconditions for the next.

successive-stage model of social change A conception of the overall direction of social change according to which societies move through a sequence of stages.

Marx.   Marx identified four stages of history—in the economic development of society—that differed in regard to their methods of production: primitive communism, slavery, feudalism, and capitalism.

  Primitive communism, the first stage of human history, was based on collective ownership and utilization of all goods. Since the economy was at the subsistence level of hunting and gather-

primitive communism Marx's first stage of the economic development of society, in which there is collective ownership and utilization of all goods.

Box 8–8   GEMEINSCHAFT AND GESELLSCHAFT

A. Gemeinschaft
  1. Family life: concord. Man participates in this with all his sentiments. Its real controlling agent is the people (Volk).
  2. Rural village life: folkways and mores. Into this, man enters with all his mind and heart. Its real controlling agent is the commonwealth.
  3. Town life: religion. In this, the human being takes part with his entire conscience. Its real controlling agent is the church.

B. Gesellschaft
  1. City life: convention. This is determined by man's intentions. Its real controlling agent is *gesellschaft* per se.
  2. National life: legislation. This is determined by man's calculations. Its real controlling agent is the state.
  3. Cosmopolitan life: public opinion. This is evolved by man's consciousness. Its real controlling agent is the republic of scholars.

Source: Ferdinand Tönnies, *Community and Society,* trans. and ed., Charles P. Loomis (East Lansing, Michigan: Michigan State University Press, 1957), p. 233.

To Herbert Spencer (1820–1903) social evolutionism (see text) was based on a direct analogy with a living body. Societies, Spencer felt, were living organisms, only of a different sort than physical bodies. Consequently, their organization was extremely similar to that of living bodies. Thus, each society had its sustaining system, analogous to the elimination system in physical bodies. Productive industries often played this role in modern society. In addition, all societies had their distributing and regulating systems. An example of the former was the division of labor in the society; of the latter was the government. These were analogous to the circulatory and nervous systems in the physical body. Few, if any, sociologists today would continue to subscribe to Spencer's biological analogy. Despite the lack of support for Spencer's theories today, his importance to sociology is assured for another reason: Because his theories found widespread support in the latter part of the Nineteenth Century—mainly by industrialists who saw in his "survival of the fittest" theory "scientific" justification for their monopolistic activities—and because he called himself a sociologist, he made the discipline well known. At around the turn of the century, sociology began being taught as a regular course in many colleges and universities.

slavery Marx's second stage of development, in which human beings could be privately owned.

feudalism Marx's third stage of development, in which serfs were directly controlled but not owned by feudal landlords.

ing, collective pursuits were necessary for the survival of the group, that is, every individual's existence depended on securing the cooperation of his or her neighbors. Societies organized around primitive communism tended to be small, isolated, and self-sufficient. They engaged in little or no trade, contained no political institutions, and organized most of their activities within a large family unit.

The transformation from primitive communism to **slavery** is best illustrated by ancient Egypt, where both land and human beings could be privately owned. As history progressed, technological advances in agriculture led to an economic surplus. Often this surplus came under the control of a few members of society —the king and/or the ruling class. These individuals realized that even more surplus could be generated if others could be forced to work for those in power. Primitive communism was abandoned and, for the first time in history, true social classes with different interests (a key to the whole Marxist schema) appeared. As a result, wars of conquest were frequently conducted in order to acquire large numbers of slaves.

Under the next stage, **feudalism**, slavery as such was abolished. Land and serfs (workers) were directly controlled but not *owned* by feudal landlords who answered to the king. Serfs were legally obligated to the estate of a feudal lord to whom they gave service or a share of the goods they produced.

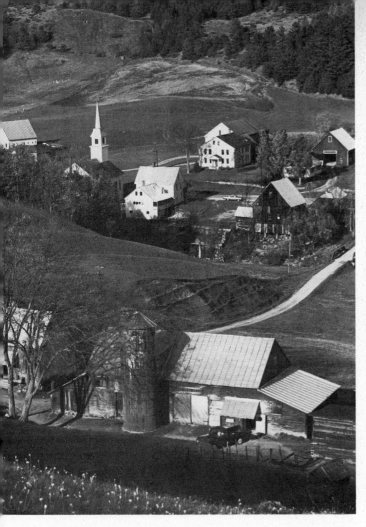

Ferdinand Tönnies (1855–1936) is best remembered today for his clear-cut distinction between two types of community: the gemeinschaft (left), or small town, and the gesellschaft (right), or modern city. Some of the main distinctions between these two polar types are outlined on p. 323.

The feudal economy was based on the strength of local economic units (estates) and the self-sufficient production of goods by serf labor. By contrast, **capitalism** is the stage of development in which one class of individuals owns the means of production to make profit while another class of individuals operates the means of production to receive a wage. Whereas feudalism was a barter economy, capitalism characteristically uses money as a medium of exchange in the market place. Also unlike feudalism, the capitalist economy entails a complex division of labor based on the role competence of individuals rather than their heredity (see Box 8–9).

Marx saw these four stages as the necessary preconditions for

capitalism Marx's fourth stage of development, in which one class owns the means of production while another class operates the means of production.

Box 8-9   MARX AND THE RISE OF CAPITALISM

Marx (1888, pp. 13–14) argued that the rise of modern capitalism was the inevitable product of a long course of development, of a series of stages in the mode of production that would ultimately produce the rise of the proletariat.

> We see . . . that the means of production and of exchange, which served as the foundation for the growth of the bourgeoisie, were generated in feudal society. At a certain stage in the development of these means of production and of exchange, the conditions under which feudal society produced and exchanged, the feudal organization of agriculture and manufacturing industry—in a word, the feudal relations of property—became no longer compatible with the already developed productive forces; they became so many fetters. They had to be burst asunder; they were burst asunder.

> Into their place stepped free competition, accompanied by a social and political constitution adapted to it and by the economic and political sway of the bourgeois class.

> A similar movement is going on before our own eyes. Modern bourgeois society, with its relations of production, of exchange, and of property—a society that has conjured up such gigantic means of production and of exchange—is like the sorcerer who is no longer able to control the powers of the nether world whom he has called up by his spells. For many a decade past, the history of industry and commerce is but the history of the revolt of modern productive forces against modern conditions of production, against the property relations that are the conditions for the existence of the bourgeoisie and of its rule.

socialism Marx's final stage of development in which all members of society own the means of production together and share equally in all products of the social order.

the emergence of a final stage, **socialism** in which economic inequality and hence conflict would disappear. This would occur in two phases: First, after the successful "revolt of the proletariat" (see Chapter 5), the newly empowered "dictatorship of the proletariat" would oversee the destruction of traces of capitalist institutions and the resocialization of society's members. Second, the utopian state of communism would be ushered in.

Parsons.   Among contemporary sociologists who subscribe to the successive-stage theory is Talcott Parsons (1977)—although his version is definitely non-Marxist. Essentially Parsons argues that human beings are continually trying to improve their lot in life. This process, which he calls "adaption," will inevitably lead, on the societal level, to the potential for social change to occur. However, Parsons does not, as did Spencer and Marx, believe that social evolution is inevitable. Rather, he feels that there ensues a process by which members of the society attempt to find better adaptations to the problems they face. If they are successful, society will pass on to the next stage of social evolution as, for example, Western society did when it surmounted the limitations of feudalism by moving into a capitalistic mode of production (see Chapter 6). If the society is not successful, it does not evolve further, becoming "stuck" at its present stage (Parsons would argue that contemporary British society is in this predicament) or the society may dissolve under external and internal pressures (as did, e.g., ancient Greece and Rome). The solutions to adaptive problems, which Parsons calls "evolutionary breakthroughs," are the events that permit societies to pass through Parsons's three successive-stages: primitive societies (e.g., the Arapesh, Mundugumor, and Tchambuli societies discussed in Chapter 3), intermediate societies (e.g., ancient Greece and Rome), and modern societies (e.g., the United States today).

There are also numerous critics of the successive-stage view. Some argue that the Parsonian view, although somewhat more sophisticated than the Spencerian linear perspective, only looks at the facts that are amenable to its assumptions of adaption and evolutionary breakthroughs. Others argue that it is merely a sophisticated way of coming to the same type of conclusion that Spencer came to, namely, American society is the best society in the world. Furthermore, these critics argue that the Parsonian theory conveniently overlooks the fact that our society is very restrictive of the human rights of many of its members—for example, blacks, women, and homosexuals. (For more on this controversy, see Chapter 9.) Still others argue that it is an incorrect interpretation of the nature of social change altogether. This leads us to a consideration of the third theory of social change.

Cyclical Pattern Model

The **cyclical model of social change** rests on the assumption that history, in at least some aspects, tends to repeat itself. The pattern of change is seen as cyclical, usually in a sequence of progress, stagnation, and decline.

In Pitirim Sorokin's (1947) cyclical view of the rise and fall of societies, he identifies three recurring cultural themes, the ideational, sensate, and idealistic. Each of these themes is a shared conception of truth that is capable of maintaining itself for centuries. Each is important for its capacity to give meaning to the lives of society's members.

cyclical model of social change A conception of the overall direction of social change that assumes history tends to repeat itself. The pattern is seen as cyclical.

ideational cultural theme
Sorokin's notion of a cultural system in which spiritual needs are emphasized.

Being grounded in the sacred, the **ideational cultural theme** centers on spiritual needs and is based on a belief in the validity of faith. This theme emphasizes the spiritual perfection of the human being and minimizes the attainment of physical pleasure. An excellent example of ideational culture is medieval Europe, a culture within which religious and spiritual concerns predominated.

sensate cultural theme
Sorokin's notion of a cultural system in which sensual and physical needs are stressed.

The **sensate cultural theme** emphasizes sensual and physical needs and is based on rationality and empiricism. This theme stresses physical pleasure and minimizes moral commitment to spiritual ideals. What is more, the sensate theme ascribes ultimate validity to information gained by the senses. Recent America exemplifies this theme as reflected in the lives of many of its members. Thus numerous Americans tend to adjust themselves to the use of sex to achieve pleasure and to the consumption of goods and services. So predominant had this theme become in the 1970s that Christopher Lasch (1978) spoke of our society as one embodying a "culture of narcissism"—a culture where self-gratification was primary and all other concerns were secondary. The hedonistic, sex-oriented life-style associated with the Roman Empire is another example of the sensate cultural theme.

idealistic cultural theme
Sorokin's notion of a cultural system in which the ideational and sensate themes are balanced.

The **idealistic cultural theme** is seen as a combination of the ideational and sensate and exists in the intervals separating them. It is during the dominance of the idealistic system that the creative efforts of human beings are nurtured and given expression. Art and music flourish. During this transitional phase of culture, reason is generally accepted as a method for achieving truth. According to Sorokin, Greek culture was idealistic during the fifth and fourth centuries B.C., including the Golden Age of Athens. The Renaissance would be a similar period.

Sorokin claims to show cyclical changes in the achievements of Western societies that can be traced to the growth and decline of ideational, idealistic, and sensate cultural systems. He holds that the pendulum of change swings back and forth through the idealistic phase to an extreme stage of sensate or ideational culture. Cyclical change may be in either direction. According to Sorokin, ours has been an era of advanced sensate culture that will gradually move toward the ideational extreme—A prediction perhaps born out by the resurgence in recent years of groups such as the moral majority, groups whose avowed purpose is to counter our amoral, narcissistic society's tendencies by reintroducing the old "God-fearing, God-faring" ways of the past.

The three models of social change—linear, successive-stage, and cyclical—are summarized in Figure 8–1.

SUMMARY

Any sociologist who seeks to understand the nature of interaction cannot afford to ignore processes of social change. Knowledge of such social dynamics yields a running account of the important causal influences in history.

Social change may be defined as any continuing alteration in the interaction patterns existing between two or more people. Three main subtypes are: revolution, trends (such as urbanization), and everyday changes (such as a joint decision to stop going to the movies in order to save money). As an important example of change, revolution is a violent attempt at total restructuring of many of society's institutions, values, and legal codes. Many of the preconditions for revolution can be specified, including a crisis of confidence and relative deprivation.

Social change is likely to arise only in certain types of social systems: those in which interaction patterns are not yet fully defined, in which members are ambivalent about the interaction pattern, or in which change is expected as part of the pattern. It may also be a result of environmental factors, such as natural disasters. Although predicting exactly where social change will arise is difficult, it can be said that economic and religious institutions are more likely than others to be source points of social change.

The spread of change occurs through the process of diffusion, whereby information about new ideas and actions is passed from individual to individual in a group. Three factors are influential in determining the degree and rate of social change: (1) the duration of interaction between those advocating change and those who as yet are not, (2) the influential strength of the participants in the interaction, and (3) the ideational nearness of the participants. Modern societies seem to be altering at an accelerating rate of change, resulting in the closely related phenomena of cultural lag and future shock.

Three models have been used to depict the overall direction of social change. The linear theories often assert that the development of society has been toward greater and greater progress. Spencer attempted to show that society evolved toward greater complexity and interdependence of its parts. Although the idea of progress in social change has fallen into disrepute, many elements of the linear model continue to be applied to the study of change. For example, Tönnies summarized large-scale societal changes as a linear trend away from *gemeinschaft* and toward *gesellschaft*.

The successive-stage model for depicting the direction of change is illustrated by Marxian history. Marx identified a sequence of four stages of history through which societies move on their way to the utopian stage of communism—primitive communism, slavery, feudalism, and capitalism. Talcott Parsons' theory of primitive, intermediate, and modern stages in social evolution is a contemporary example of this model of social change.

The cyclical model assumes that history tends to repeat itself. Sorokin identifies three recurring cultural themes—the ideational, sensate, and idealistic—which he feels are capable of maintaining themselves for centuries. In Sorokin's view, cyclical changes in the achievements of Western societies can be traced to the growth and decline of these three cultural systems.

QUESTIONS, EXERCISES, PROJECTS

1. What are the three main types of social change? Give examples of each and explain how each example differs from the others.
2. Explain the part played by relative deprivation as a factor in the occurrence of revolutionary change.
3. Discuss some of the important changes in American society that have occurred as institutions have become more specialized.
4. Describe the megatrends of decentralization and the Sunbelt phenomenon. Have these trends changed your life or the life of anyone you know? How?
5. The "computer revolution" is supposedly reshaping how America does business, how people amuse themselves, and how families interact. Is this true in your experience? What are the long-term implications of increasing "computerization" for your life, for your family's life, for your city or town? Should the process be stopped? *Can* it be stopped?
6. Summarize Durkheim's analysis of division of labor and group solidarity.
7. Discuss the Marxian notion of social change as a dialectical process of history.
8. Summarize Weber's argument that Protestant religious values influenced the development of capitalism in the modern world.
9. Illustrate the process of cultural diffusion by tracing the origin and subsequent cultural transference of any aspect of American culture. Discuss such factors as the date of original usage

or discovery and the date when it was first introduced into American society.

10. Give examples of at least two cultural lags in American society that have influenced your life.

11. Explain Spencer's concept of evolution as he applied it to social change. Why was Spencer wrong?

12. Discuss the three cultural themes specified by Sorokin in his cyclical view of the rise and fall of societies.

13. Define and briefly illustrate the three general directions in which social change has been conceptualized to move.

CONTROVERSIES IN SOCIOLOGY

Throughout this book we have tried to show not only the main concepts, theories, and methods that sociologists use when analyzing the social world, but the often conflicting and controversial elements in their approaches and findings as well. For example, regarding theoretical approaches, in Chapter 3 we indicated the very different approaches that would be taken to the study of the self by theorists such as Sigmund Freud and George Herbert Mead; in Chapter 5 and again in Chapter 8, we pointed out the different focal points of the Marxian and Weberian approaches to the study of social stratification and social change; also in Chapter 8 we indicated the lack of agreement among sociologists on the appropriate way to study social change. Regarding the findings of social research, many sociologists, to say nothing of lay people, have found themselves involved in heated discussions of issues raised by various investigations, for example, studies on the effects of television on children, the influence of pornography on deviant sexual behavior, the causes of revolution, or the deterrent effects of capital punishment on criminality.

Sociologists not only continue to debate their theories and results but, more importantly, also differ with respect to their basic conceptions of the nature of sociological inquiry. Should sociologists focus on harmony and order or conflict and change? Must sociology commit itself to a value-free position? What is the relation of sociology to social problems and social policy? What is the relation of social life to biological inheritance? Let us deal with each of these questions.

FUNCTIONAL VERSUS CONFLICT SOCIOLOGY

Sociologists are not in agreement regarding the basic nature of social interaction and society. The *functional* school of thought emphasizes the order, consensus, and harmony in social life. Proponents of this view (such as Talcott Parsons, see Chapter 8) frequently argue that society tends to move toward balance or equilibrium. They assert that the parts of a society—its institutional arrangements—tend to adjust and readjust themselves in such a way that society not only survives but, over time, comes to operate smoothly as well.

In sharp contrast *conflict* sociologists, such as Karl Marx and C.

The difference between the functional and conflict perspectives in sociology (see text) is symbolically represented in the two photographs. The functionalist perspective focuses on social structure and is interested in the general relationships that exist between actors—on how they are organized and how they maintain their interactions. Conflict in this perspective is usually seen as a matter of "adjustment" of the interests of the actors to one another. These theorists would argue that the vast majority of social relationships proceed in an orderly manner. Conflict theorists, on the other hand, are not convinced of the essentially "harmonious" nature of interaction. Rather, they tend to see interaction as a series of ongoing negotiations between individuals and groups. Furthermore, many of these negotiations are not sanguine and orderly, but actual out-and-out struggles for power and position. They believe the functionalist perspective is a sophisticated way of saying that the status quo—what already exists in society—is a natural and inevitable consequence and that those in power "deserve" to be where they are. Finally, conflict theorists would claim that the real relationships between many members of society are nowhere near as harmonious as they appear on the surface; that subterfuge and chicancery are at work to protect wealth, prestige, or power.

Wright Mills (see, for Marx, Chapters 5 and 8; for Mills, Chapter 5) lay stress on disorder and change rather than on harmony and balance. From the conflict perspective, social conflict is regarded as basic to the core of society, a constant in all forms of social life. The reason is simple: The valued resources of society—land, money, power, raw materials—are almost always in short supply. Hence people are in competition to get their "share" of those resources. As a result, social change is seen as resulting from conflict among competing factions in society and social integration is tenuous (Eitzen, 1974).

Conflict sociologists criticize the functional approach for an inability to deal adequately with processes of change and for an ideological conservatism that supports the status quo (Martindale, 1960). In contrast, functionalists see those who subscribe to the conflict view as "leftist ideologues" who overemphasize the role of conflict in social life (see Table 9–1).

The distinction between functional and conflict sociology can be illustrated by considering the study of social stratification (Chapter 5). Functional sociologists have frequently asked: How does the presence of inequality with respect to wealth, social honor, or power help to assure the survival of a society? They suggest that stratification arises in a society to assure that the most capable persons (in regard to ability and training) are placed into society's most important positions and are adequately motivated to perform their tasks in such positions. Thus greater wealth, honor, and power accrue to members of society who perform its important occupational roles (Davis and Moore, 1945).

Conflict sociologists tend to view stratification in a different way. Some might argue, for example, that social hierarchies are associated with certain types of economies (e.g., with feudalism and capitalism) and that they would disappear under the impact of communism. Others might assert that social stratification (e.g., inequality between owners and workers) serves the interests not of society in general, but of the power elite in particular, limits the development of talent in a society, and ultimately leads to conflict, revolution, and change in the basic fabric of society (Tumin, 1953). Thus, whereas functionalists view stratification as a mechanism that strengthens and integrates society, conflict sociologists see

Table 9–1 FUNCTIONAL VERSUS CONFLICT SOCIOLOGY

	FUNCTIONAL	CONFLICT
Fundamental relationship among the parts of society	Harmony and cooperation; complementary interests of parts; basic consensus on societal norms and values	Disorder and conflict; competition for things people want; dissensus on societal norms and values
Degree of integration	Highly integrated	Loosely integrated; whatever integration is achieved is the result of force and fraud
Type of social change	Gradual, adjustive, and reforming	Abrupt and revolutionary
Degree of stability	Stable	Unstable

Source: Adapted from D. Stanley Eitzen, *Social Structure and Social Problems in America* (Boston: Allyn & Bacon, 1974), p. 10.

stratification as conflict generating, as serving the few as opposed to the many, and as dysfunctional for society as a whole.

It is important to recognize the distinction between the functional and the conflict approach, but it should also be pointed out that many sociological works contain elements of both perspectives. An interesting example of this convergence is Lewis Coser's (1956) analysis of the functions of social conflict. Taking his hypotheses from the work of the German sociologist George Simmel, Coser argues that "conflict within a group . . . may help to establish unity or to re-establish unity and cohesion where it has been threatened by hostile and antagonistic feelings among the members" (p. 151). He suggests that under certain conditions conflict is capable of clarifying issues, increasing communication, or reducing tension among group members. Thus Coser proposes that social conflict itself may serve to assure group survival, consensus, and solidarity. Clearly, it would be difficult to pigeonhole his analysis as belonging exclusively to either the functional or the conflict school of thought.

VALUE-FREE, VALUE-COMMITTED, OR BIAS-FREE SOCIOLOGY

Beginning with Max Weber, sociologists have repeatedly called for a value-free sociology, in which personal preference, moral judgment, and ideology are eliminated from the conduct of sociological inquiry. The image of a value-free sociology assumes that in order to be scientific, sociologists would also have to be ethically neutral. (See Box 9–1) That is, they would have to direct their efforts toward the pursuit of *objective knowledge* about how society operates, regardless of how they feel about the issues, consequences, or reactions of those involved. As noted by an early figure in the history of sociology, William Graham Sumner (1906, p. 10), those advocating value-free sociology believe that "it is the pursuit of truth which gives us life, and it is to that pursuit that our loyalty is due."

Many sociologists no longer accept the value-free position. Some argue instead for a value-*committed* position, whereby sociologists focus their efforts on changing society, influencing public policy, or improving the quality of social life. They feel that accumulated sociological knowledge should serve to better our social lot and are dissatisfied with the idea of an ivory tower scientist who seeks knowledge "for its own sake." According to the value-committed position, it is not enough for the sociologist to be a scientist, the sociologist must also be a critic and an activist as well. For example, Ernest Becker (1971, p. 120) argues that there is "an

BOX 9–1   ROLES OF THE SOCIAL SCIENTIST

Norman Denzin (1970) identifies several different roles that sociologists may play, depending on how they define their relationship to the discipline. Denzin notes that every sociologist actually performs at least a little of each role and that the problem is to achieve an effective balance among them.

One role [the sociologist] may play is that of critic, both within and outside the discipline. The work of other scientists comes under his attack, as can the products and various social arrangements present in society. The critic should serve two functions: he should show what is wrong and offer as many valid alternatives as possible.

A second role, related to but distinguishable from the critic, is that of activist. Here criticism is carried over into meaningful and alternative social action programs. Again this work can be done within the discipline and in society generally, though activists today are concerned mostly with the latter. Their activities can range from involvement in protest movements, to strikes, political proposals, to petitions and fund raising. The activist supposedly has some knowledge of those situations he protests and has information on the implications of the various actions he proposes.

The third role calls for a vigorous separation (often a denial) of the roles of critic and activist. The aloof observer of social action is a scientist in the purest sense. He pursues those problems he finds intellectually intriguing and does so independent of any outside political or social pressures. This too is an ideal type.

The fourth role is sociologist as salesman. Here social problems, translated through the lenses of a client, takes precedence. These problems may range from the mundane (marketing surveys) to the profound (the effects of different educational programs in the ghetto). The client may be private industry or the federal government. In any event a significant reversal of the sociological act occurs. The sociologist ceases to define how and what he will study. This power is relinquished and placed in the hands of the client. Too often this leads to relatively meaningless social findings. But more importantly it inevitably places the sociologist one step behind society and the client. It makes him a complacent partner in the social problems so many abhor.

Each of these roles seldom is acted out in pure form. Every social scientist is a little of each. The problem is to achieve the proper mix. The solution cannot be made scientifically, although certain rules and canons of scientific procedure are relevant. These hold that the cardinal criterion of every sociological act is its theoretical and empirical grounding. Above all the sociologist should never abdicate these standards for money, prestige or political pressure.

Source: Norman K. Denzin, *The Values of Social Science* (Chicago: Transaction, 1970), pp. 9–11.

authentic tradition for the science of man," that sociology *must* be a science that examines societies in order to develop a model of "a new moral code." What is relevant in establishing this moral code? That is, how do we know how to judge between better and worse social conditions? By no other way, argues Becker, than by asking the question, " 'What are the differences in *human freedom* in societies across the span of history?' It is only when we ask this question that we can see the moral usefulness of the science of man."

Another alternative to the value-free position recognizes the complexity of human values. Furthermore, it acknowledges the inevitable (and frequently positive) influences of values on the conduct of scientific inquiry. Proponents of this viewpoint seek to eliminate *bias,* values that interfere with objectivity in the scientific process. Bias occurs when an investigator maintains a position, belief, or judgment independently of the evidence of the case. The key characteristic of bias is prejudgment—a conclusion reached and maintained without regard for the research findings related to it.

But bias is *not* the only expression of values in the scientific process. Sociologists frequently select their research problems on the basis of personal values without necessarily losing their objectivity. For instance, someone concerned about the adverse impact of poverty on American society might decide to study social stratification; someone who seeks to reduce prejudice and discrimination might specialize in the sociology of minorities. In this connection it is interesting to note that white southerners are *overrepresented* in research that deals with black Americans. As suggested by Gaston and Sherohman (1974, p. 81), "Perhaps childhood socialization in the South makes problems of race relations more salient to a would-be sociologist, which increases the probability that when he goes to graduate school in the North, he will later study blacks, regardless of . . . his institutional location."

The influence of bias must also be distinguished from the impact of professional ethics on the scientific process. As noted by the eminent philosopher of science Abraham Kaplan (1963), values in the ethics of a scientifically oriented discipline frequently operate to minimize bias. With reference to their ethical standards, sociologists are expected to be committed to those values associated with objectivity, honesty, and truth.

To an increasing extent sociologists are learning to recognize that some bias can exist in their work in spite of professional ethics stressing objectivity and truth. For an early example of bias in sociology, we return to the work of Herbert Spencer as introduced in Chapter 8. As you may recall, Spencer's evolutionary view of social change has been essentially discredited. Observations of

It is extremely difficult for social scientists to maintain total objectivity in studying social life. In some respect, whenever we study social life we are studying either ourselves directly or things that reflect upon ourselves. For example, take the photograph reproduced here, which depicts inner-city poverty. If, in our sociological analysis, we conclude that poverty is a product of the oppression of certain groups by others, and if we are a member of the oppressing group, how are we to feel or act? If, on the other hand, we conclude that poverty is a result of a certain group being lazy or self-indulgent, then isn't this a justification for the belief that we have no *responsibility* for the poor? If, to take a third possibility, we merely *describe* the nature of poverty and don't take a position one way or the other concerning it (that is, we attempt to be value-free to the end), isn't this ignoring the human suffering involved and the consequences of our research from yet another direction? There is no easy answer to this predicament, but, one way or another, sociologists must work out how they will deal with these crucial issues.

societies since Spencer's time do not indicate that his linear theory of evolution applies to the social world. Yet Spencer was convinced, with relatively little evidence, that it did. Why?

Spencer's viewpoint is much more comprehensible if we examine the social conditions under which he worked. In the first place, the idea of evolution was virtually omnipresent in the scientific circles of his day. Most serious scientists agreed that evolution was a major breakthrough in understanding the world. Since Spencer was among the first to employ the concept of evolution (Darwin, e.g., noted Spencer's influence on his thinking) and was highly interested in society, it was less than surprising that he would apply the theory to social behavior.

Moreover, Spencer was born and brought up in a middle-class setting in a rapidly industrializing English society. He was educated at home for the most part and was thoroughly socialized to be a "self-made man"—an extreme individualist who did everything for himself and who thoroughly resented any imposition of outside authority from society. As a result of this socialization, Spencer came to believe strongly that it was right and proper for humans to be self-made and improper for them not to be.

Thus Spencer "theorized" that the individual best develops his or her own potentialities when there is no interference from any outside agency of society. He portrayed the "highly evolved" society as one characterized by this very laissez-faire quality. In addition, Spencer wrote that it was perfectly natural and right that the "evolved" society—the "fit"—should control the "unevolved" or "primitive" society—the "unfit." Spencer's England was certainly acting on such a principle during the nineteenth century, its greatest period of nationalistic imperialism in Africa, India, and other areas of the globe.

What we are suggesting is that Spencer as social analyst was a victim of his own biases. These biases were developed during his own early socialization and were reinforced by the groups with which he was later associated. In other words, under the guise of "science" and "objectivity," he was really seeing the world through the eyes of his own culture. Moreover, he utilized any and all evidence he could find to buttress his theory. Any evidence to the contrary he either ignored or misinterpreted (see Box 9–2).

A more recent example of the way that bias can operate in the work of behavioral science is provided by psychologists' reactions to Arthur Jensen's (1969) hypothesis that "genetic factors are strongly implicated in the average Negro–white intelligence difference." From a scientific standpoint, a psychologist's acceptance or rejection of Jensen's hypothesis regarding race differences in intelligence should be based entirely on the cogency of research evidence and not on exposure to the culture in which the psychologist has been socialized. To determine whether this was in fact the case, Robert Friedrichs (1973) sent a mail questionnaire to members of the American Psychological Association, asking whether they agreed with Jensen's position. Freidrichs reports that over two thirds of the psychologists responding disagreed with Jensen's thesis. What is significant is that he found that agreement with Jensen could be related to such factors as age, regional residence, and ethnicity. For example, psychologists from Alabama and Mississippi were more likely than others to accept Jensen's argument whereas Jewish psychologists were especially likely to disagree with him. In addition, psychologists who disagreed were significantly younger than those who agreed with Jensen. How could such results be obtained if the decisions of psychologists were totally free of bias? Friedrichs' results indicate that "behavioral scientists—as much as they may be consciously committed to a 'value-free' perspective in their professional work —demonstrate much the same tendency to allow demographic, ethnic, and peer-group factors to influence their professional judgment as they have so thoroughly catalogued in their studies of laymen" (p. 429).

Box 9–2 SPENCER'S VIEW OF BIAS IN SOCIAL SCIENCE

The following is an excellent statement by an early sociologist about the reasons why social scientists must control personal bias in their work if they are ever going to reach objective conclusions. As we have seen, Spencer was not completely able to exercise such control.

However, the author of the passage is Herbert Spencer. This fact not only makes the passage's statements all the more poignant, but points up very clearly the phenomenal difficulty social scientists have in realizing and overcoming their own biases.

> The difficulties of . . . Social Science . . . drew our attention. We saw that in this case, though in no other case, the facts to be observed and generalized . . . are exhibited by an aggregate of which [the social scientist] forms a part. In his capacity of inquirer he should have no inclination towards one or other conclusion respecting the phenomena to be generalized; but in his capacity of citizen, helped to live by the life of his society, imbedded in its structures, sharing in its activities, breathing its atmosphere of thought and sentiment, he is partially coerced into such views as favour harmonious cooperation with his fellow-citizens. Hence [there are] immense obstacles to the Social Sciences, unparalled by those standing in the way of any other science.
> . . .
> For the interpretation of human conduct as socially displayed, every one is compelled to use, as a key, his own nature—ascribing to others thoughts and feelings like his own; and yet, while this automorphic interpretation is indispensable, it is necessarily more or less misleading. . . . From the emotional, as well as from the intellectual part [of a person's] nature, we saw that there arise obstacles. The ways in which beliefs about social affairs are perverted by intense fears and excited hopes, were pointed out. . . . A contrast was drawn showing, too, what perverse estimates of public events men are led to make by their sympathies and antipathies—how, where their hate has been aroused, they utter unqualified condemnations of ill-deeds for which there was much excuse, while, if their admiration is excited by vast successes, they condone inexcusable ill-deeds immeasurably greater in amount. . . .

Source: Herbert Spencer, *The Study of Sociology* (London: Kegan Paul, Trench, 1873), pp. 385–387.

Clearly, then, contemporary behavioral scientists, including sociologists, can be influenced by the same cultural factors that operate on other members of society. (See Box 9–3.) In some respects we have not progressed very far beyond Spencer's day. Scientific objectivity is an essential *goal*, but it is not a reality that sociologists can *take for granted*. Sociologists must be willing to scrutinize their own work for the presence of biases that they tend to associate with nonsociologists.

One way to do this is for the sociologist to alert the reader, after careful scrutiny of his or her possible biases, of what these biases are. In this way the reader can attempt to judge from the evidence presented whether these biases have effected the results. An example of this approach is provided by sociologist Maren Lockwood Carden in the preface to her book, *The New Feminist Movement* (1974, p. xvii):

> In any study of such a contemporary and controversial topic as feminism, it is important for the reader to know the author's viewpoint and possible biases. I should therefore say at the outset that I am, in general, sympathetic with the goals of the new feminist groups I describe. I shall not attempt to state my own views in detail: some of my ideas are distinctly "radical" while others are distinctly "conservative." In the account which follows I have tried to allow for the possibility that my own views might color my description and analysis; my aim throughout has been to produce an objective sociological study.

SOCIOLOGY AND SOCIAL PROBLEMS

One of the most important areas of modern life in which sociology has had an impact is race relations. Beginning with the Supreme Court decision of 1954, the work of sociologists has been employed to document the harmful and costly effects of segregation and to justify social change in black–white relations. In the 1960s and early 1970s, many sociologists argued for the implementation of court-ordered busing and other efforts to integrate education. However, the overall impact of sociology on social problems has been less than spectacular. Several factors can be offered to explain this lack of substantial impact.

First of all, sociologists do not always have viable solutions to the problems they study. (See Box 9–4.) Allan Mazur (1968) has called sociology "The Littlest Science," meaning that it is a young science, whose knowledge of social behavior is relatively primitive, especially by comparison with the state of knowledge in the physical sciences. Many of the genuine breakthroughs in our understanding of social problems have yet to be made. A perfect exam-

BOX 9-3 SCIENTISTS OPPOSE SURVEY OF CHROMOSOME DISORDER

by Richard A. Knox
Globe Staff

A group of Harvard and MIT scientists is attempting to halt the genetics research project of a Harvard colleague, charging that the work is "worthless" and poses serious psychological and social dangers to the children and parents involved.

The issue, now pending before a Harvard Medical School committee on medical ethics, revolves around the long-standing controversy over the behavioral effects —if any—of a genetic quirk in which a male child is born with an extra "Y," or male, sex chromosome.

Since it was discovered more than a dozen years ago, the "XYY syndrome" has generated fierce debate. In the mid-1960s some studies purported to show a markedly higher incidence of "XYYs" among inmates of institutions for the criminally insane.

This finding, which has been sharply questioned for its scientific validity, invited the inference that the genetic disorder somehow predisposed its victims to violent or antisocial behavior.

The theory was given spurious support by an erroneous report that Richard Speck, the convicted killer of eight Chicago nurses, was an "XYY." The report turned out be false, but it stuck in the public mind and colored subsequent scientific debate on the matter.

While most scientists agree that "XYY" research to date doesn't prove anything, the suspicion remains among some that the disorder, which may afflict some 100,-000 American males, may be associated with some behavioral difficulties.

In an attempt to resolve this and other controversies in the area of sex chromo-some abnormalities, Dr. Stanley Walzer, a child psychiatrist at the Children's Hospital Medical Center, has been following a small number of affected children for up to five years.

Because of the stigma attached to the "XYY syndrome," Walzer's critics have focused on this portion of his research. In a critique submitted Oct. 4 to a closed-door hearing of the 32-member Harvard ethics panel, the five scientists who have spear-headed opposition to the work stated:

"We feel that the study cannot yield significant information, that already published studies cannot be interpreted, and that it is difficult to imagine a study which would be useful." Their specific objections to the study can be boiled down to three major points:

—The way in which parental permission to participate in the massive screening program was gained constituted "deceit" and "subtle coercion." Up until recently, they said, women were presented with a noninformative "informed consent" form upon admission to the hospital prior to delivery. The form, they charge, gave parents "no clues as to what they might be getting themselves into."

—The fact that parents of "XYY" individuals were told that their children were suffering from the disorder, and might evidence behavioral problems, may create a self-fulfilling prophecy. In other words, parents in their anxiety may foster behavioral difficulties in the child which would not otherwise appear. It also "biases" the study, the critics charge, and renders its conclusions invalid.

—The labeling of XYY children by the researchers might compromise their civil rights throughout life.

Source: Boston Globe, November 16, 1974, p. 3.

Walzer, the butt of the criticism, was reluctant to issue a public defense to the charges while the matter is pending before the Harvard faculty committee.

However, in a telephone conversation last night he said the project has been reviewed annually by human experimentation committees of the Boston Hospital for Women and the Children's Hospital, as well as by site visitors from the National Institutes of Mental Health.

Walzer said the informed consent procedure had been changed since the criticism mounted. Women no longer are asked to sign a consent form, permitting the chromosome analysis, until after they give birth.

Walzer also defended the practice of telling parents of affected children about the disorder. "We feel we have an ethical obligation to tell them," he said. "We feel there is no place for secrets in medicine." However, the research group is careful not to reveal the information to any other person or agency, such as school officials, to avoid stigmatizing the child.

Asked if the children exhibited any tendencies toward violent behavior, Walzer said: "Oh, God, no. There has been no tendency toward violent behavior. Let's just say that they have experienced difficulty with certain parameters of behavior. But with help and guidance most of them are doing just beautifully."

ple concerns the busing of children to promote integration. After more than a decade of busing in major cities around the country, James Coleman, one of the sociologists in the forefront of busing implementation, retracted his support of the program. The evidence, Coleman suggested, showed that, on the whole, busing did not have the desired effect. It broke up natural neighborhood relationships, posed hardships on children and parents alike, and did not seem to make people more racially tolerant. Consequently, although still holding that segregation was most deleterious in social life, Coleman suggested that busing was not a particularly good means of alleviating it.

A second factor in sociology's lack of impact on social problems is that policymakers tend to ignore the work of the sociologist unless it can be employed to justify their preconceived notions. An interesting illustration of this phenomenon can be found in *The Report of the President's Commission on Obscenity and Pornography* (1970). Based on its massive research evidence, the commission recommended that "federal, state, and local legislation prohibiting the sale, exhibition, or distribution of sexual materials to consenting adults should be repealed" (p. 51). Here was a case in which sociologists might have made an important contribution. The overwhelming weight of evidence at the time led to a single conclusion: Exposure to or use of "explicit sexual materials" does not contribute to crime, delinquency, sexual, or nonsexual deviance. Yet the recommendations of the commission were either ignored or condemned by government officials. No politician was enthusiastic about letting hard core pornography run rampant in *their* district. (A wise reservation as it turns out, for more recent

One would expect, of course, that social scientists examining the data about genetic factors related to intelligence differences between social groups would reach similar conclusions. As Friedrichs determined (p. 341), this is far from the case. The interpretations reached by the social scientists differed because of *scientists'* social characteristics!

evidence—discussed later in this chapter—has indicated that the commission was only *partially* right in its observations and recommendations.)

A third factor that may reduce the impact of sociology on social problems involves questions of an ethical nature. Laud Humphreys' (1970) study of homosexual encounters in public restrooms is a case in point. Humphreys' investigation provided information about the characteristics of a group of people in our society who had previously been known only through police records, but his method of investigation was highly criticized. Humphreys used

> *Research conducted by behavioral scientists is not always regarded in a favorable light by those who hold power in a society.*

Box 9–4   RESEARCHER DEFENDS HIS DATING STUDY

Associated Press

A Harvard researcher says he is upset at suggestions that his Federally funded research into the private relations of dating couples is a waste of money.

Zick Rubin, a social psychologist, defended his work yesterday in Cambridge after Sen. William Proxmire (D-Wis.) called the $121,600 Harvard study and two similar programs "a futile and wasteful attempt to define the impossible."

The research is funded by the National Science Foundation. Proxmire said the Federal agency should arrange its priorities to address our scientific, not our erotic, curiosity."

Rubin said he is using the Federal money to follow the development of the relationships of several hundred dating couples at four Boston area colleges.

"We are trying to study close relationships as they affect people's lives in many important and vital ways," he said.

"My research is directly related to the issues of marriage and divorce, which are crucial social issues nowadays."

Rubin said, "We are engaged in basic research into the dynamics of close interpersonal relationships. These are national concerns."

Source: Boston Globe, March 19, 1975, p. 5.

the technique of participant observation, assuming the role of a "lookout" to warn of approaching police or strangers, in order to study the encounters. He also conducted personal interviews with those he had observed by changing his appearance to avoid recognition and introducing himself as a researcher studying community health behavior. The publication of his work was regarded by many as an invasion of privacy that unnecessarily exposed a set of respondents to the possibility of police detection and intervention.

Community studies by sociologists have been especially likely to receive criticism on ethical grounds. For instance, Vidich and Bensman (1960) studied "Springdale," a small community in upstate New York. Springdale townspeople expressed their shock and anger with the published version of the study. They felt that Stein and Vidich had presented an inaccurate picture of their town. More importantly, perhaps, they were surprised by the ease with which key townspeople could be identified despite the pseudonyms used. We cannot help but wonder whether Stein and Vidich's study of Springdale may have had some harmful effects on community life (see Box 9–5).

A classic example of ethical problems encountered in the conduct of sponsored research is Project Camelot, a venture carried out by social scientists that proposed to focus on the determinants of revolution with special reference to Latin American nations. Project Camelot was initiated during 1965, a time when the United States had recently sent marines to the Dominican Republic. The project was under the sponsorship of the U.S. Army, a fact that quickly became a point of contention for its critics. As a matter of fact, many persons condemned the United States and American social science for what they believed to be an effort to interfere in the internal affairs of Latin American countries (Horowitz, 1967). Project Camelot was canceled, but the debate continued to rage. For example, sociologist Myron Glazer (1972, p. 39) condemned the project on the following counts: "for simply assuming that the United States military has a legitimate role in dealing with social problems of other countries, for asserting that this country's foreign policy was a major factor in determining the site(s) of research, and for implying that internal war is always the greatest threat to a population's well-being."

Whatever its motivation and consequences, the "bruhaha" surrounding Project Camelot informs us that sociologists who investigate important social issues may unwittingly harm those whom they set out to help. In sponsored research—whether funded by industry, political groups, or an agent of government—the possi-

---

Box 9–5   A GUIDELINE FOR ETHICAL CONCERNS

Research into the social order of a community, organization, group, or entire society may uncover some evidence of *publicly unacknowledged activity:* forms of deviant behavior such as white-collar crime, shady business practices, or political corruption; organizational incompetence; and hidden inequities of power and wealth. What constitutes an invasion of privacy in a psychological study of individual behavior may be regarded in sociological research as no less than subversive activity. Why? Because it may undermine institutions by exposing their weaknesses.

Becker (1964) once suggested that good sociology will always make someone angry, because it reveals that a group or organization is less than it claims to be. The ethical problem, for Becker, is one of deciding which people to harm rather than of avoiding harm altogether.

Taking his direction from the work of Diener and Crandall (1978), McAllister (1980) suggests one guideline for the ethical problems of research. He argues that ethical risks can be justified only if they do not exceed the commonplace or ordinary risks of everyday life. Thus, for example, most of us expect some loss of privacy simply because we have a listed phone number, walk in a public place, or ride a crowded elevator. The ethical issues arise only when research exceeds the ordinary risks. Using McAllister's criterion, however, sociology may be caught on the horns of a dilemma: whether to exceed the everyday standard and risk being unethical or to remain within it and fail to say anything of importance.

bility always exists for the sociologist to become the servant of those who hold the power in a society or to those who seek to hold it.

THE SOCIOLOGY DEBATE

In Chapter 3 we introduced an argument with which we feel most sociologists would agree: namely, that it is primarily social factors that determine human behavioral patterns and not other factors, such as biological traits. As evidence for this position we cited the studies by Kingsley Davis on the isolated children Anna and Isabelle and Margaret Mead's analysis of sex role development in three New Guinea societies.

In recent years, however, this fundamental sociological argument has been challenged by a group of scholars claiming that inherited biological characteristics can account for some central human behavioral patterns, such as aggression, territoriality, and social stratification. This stance, which we shall call the sociobiological position, after Edward O. Wilson's book *Sociobiology* (1975), is now the center of a major debate in sociological circles. Because it is, we shall examine it in some detail.

Probably the person most influential in reopening the debate was the German ethologist, Konrad Lorenz. In his book, *On Aggression* (1966), Lorenz argues that aggression is a deeply rooted biological instinct present in human beings just as it is in other species. By aggression, however, he does not mean the belligerance that is often shown between animals of *different* species when they attack or prey on one another. Rather, he means it to characterize "the fighting instinct in beast and man which is directed *against* members of the same species" (1966, p. ix). Thus the struggle between a cheetah and an antelope would not be aggression in Lorenz's definition, whereas the pecking of a lower-status chicken by a higher-status chicken would be. Moreover, Lorenz asserts, it is incorrect to assume that aggression is always a negative trait, destructive of the species. For example, in an environment where the material resources necessary for survival are in short supply, aggressive behavior can help maintain a balanced distribution of that population over the available land space. Each individual or group will fight for its "turf" against others, thereby forcing some of the population into less competitive areas. Similarly, aggression ensures the selection of the physically strongest members of the species in reproducing offspring and results in the physically strongest members of a species being in a position to protect the young or other weak members when they are threatened (1966, p. 40).

As evidence for his position, Lorenz spends much time examin-

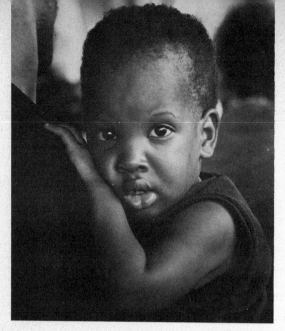

The bio-sociology controversy has rekindled the most fundamental of all sociological debates: the nature of the relationship between biological inheritance and the effects of culture on the human being. Are the human differences we observe in these photographs of a genetic or cultural origin? While, to some degree, the answer is obviously "both," we feel that the evidence still suggests that the cultural influence is by far the greater (see text).

ing the instinctually aggressive behavior of many animal species. He suggests that because human beings have extremely similar behavioral patterns, their behavior must be determined by instinct as well. For example, chickens develop a "pecking order" where, within a group, the most aggressive rooster dominates the rest of the roosters and, consequently, has first access to females and the best food. Similarly, Lorenz points to the fact that human societies (as we spent a good deal of time describing in Chapter 5) are invariably stratified, with some groups dominating other groups in many ways. Moreover, as we saw in the Gans discussion of the positive functions of poverty (Chapter 6), many benefits, such as wealth, power, and prestige, accrue to these dominant groups and there is little doubt that individual and group aggression often have been fundamental behaviors in obtaining and maintaining higher social status positions (see, as one example, our discussion of reactions to the hip counterculture of the 1960s in Chapter 2). As further evidence, Lorenz suggests that our earliest human ancestors—for example, Cro-Magnon man—were highly aggressive and that this genetic trait has been passed down to modern human beings (1966, Chapter 13).

In conclusion, Lorenz feels that the best solution to the problem of human aggression is self-knowledge. That is, since aggression is an instinct demanding occasional release, we should be aware that it will continually surface and take measures to control and redirect it from its most dangerous forms of expression, such as war. More specifically, Lorenz suggests that we should redirect individual and group aggressive tendencies into such relatively "harmless" activities as competitive sports and ideological causes, as art, beauty, truth, and medicine (1966, Chapter 24).

A slightly different position is that taken by sociologist Pierre van den Berghe (1974). He argues that aggression is a "biological predisposition" in human beings (thus making it somewhat less powerful than Lorenz's claim that aggression is an inevitably appearing instinct). This aggressive predisposition develops into actual behavior under conditions of resource competition. Resource competition can be of two main types: for material goods, such as food, or for socially valued "goods," such as gold or prestige. In either case, however, the scarcity of the valued objects brings forth competition between human beings and hence aggressive behavior. In order to control unbridled competition, van den Berghe argues, human beings have invented territoriality, as a means of gaining exclusive access to the resources in a given area, and social hierarchies (stratification), as a means of maintaining access over time to these resources.

Interestingly, van den Berghe indicates that both these means of control over aggression also tend to increase it. Thus by making a certain space "off-limits" for part of the population because of its valuable resources, the *desire* for that space is increased in those without access to it—and these people are more likely to become aggressive to obtain these resources in the future. Similarly, by giving preferred access to resources to those in higher social strata, the desire for those resources is increased in those people in lower social strata (1974, p. 778). Thus aggression "is a mechanism making for both stability and change, the two ubiquitous sides of social organization" (1974, p. 784).

As evidence for his argument, van den Berghe suggests, first, that "homicidal aggression exists in all or practically all cultures," and that there "is hardly a culture which is not riddled with interpersonal or inter-group conflict"; second, that "all human societies are clearly hierarchized *at least* by age and sex (adult males being dominant over adult females, adults of either sex being dominant over younger children)," and that many societies are also clearly stratified along class lines; and, third, that space is arranged in a territorial fashion "in all or nearly all human societies"—for example, in the insistence on the privacy of one's own room or home, or the group's focus on both local territory—the "neighborhood" —or wider territory—the village, the city, the state, the nation (1974, pp. 782–783). Finally, like Lorenz, van den Berghe finds similar behavior in nonhuman species, especially the primates, and suggests that human beings are quite analogous to these species in aggressive, territorial, and hierarchical behavior. Box 9–6 reports the kind of evidence often advanced by sociobiologists.

Because arguments such as these criticize some of the most fundamental axioms of social science, there have been heated debates about the types of reasoning and evidence that have been used to arrive at the sociobiology position. (See, e.g., Alland, 1972; Montagu, 1973; Fischer, 1975; Mazur, 1975; Moberg, 1975; van den Berghe, 1975; Reynolds, 1976.) Three common critiques are the following: first, both Lorenz, van den Berghe, and other sociologists base much of their biological evidence for human aggression on the observation of similar behavioral patterns in nonhuman species. By *analogy,* they imply that because these behaviors are at least partially genetically determined in these nonhuman species, the same is probably true of these behaviors in human beings. The problem with this argument is that there is no *direct* biological evidence indicating that human beings have such instinctual apparatus. Whereas genes for hair color, skin color, and so on have been isolated in human as well as nonhuman species, the same cannot be said for any gene for aggression. Consequently, the critics of sociobiology argue, it is just possible that human beings behave aggressively because they have found by *experiment* and *learning* that these behaviors produce certain

The following study might very well be used to support the position of those who argue that biology determines social class or dominance in human beings. The same research might just as easily be used, however, to support the view that a social characteristic (social class) influences body chemistry (a biological characteristic). More objectively, the research probably supports neither position: animal dominance can hardly be equated with social class in human beings.

Box 9–6

TESTS LINK SUBSTANCE IN BRAIN TO SOCIAL STATUS

The New York Times

NEW YORK—Studies of monkeys and college students suggest that social status is reflected in the chemistry of the brain.

Scientists say studies show that the dominant males in colonies of vervet monkeys had twice as much circulating serotonin in their blood as any other males. Serotonin is a neurotransmitter, a chemical used in sending information from cell to cell in the brain.

And when a dominant monkey was put by himself, his blood serotonin level dropped. In a solitary situation he had no need or opportunity to show dominance. With the dominant male removed, scientists at UCLA found, another male soon assumed the role. His blood serotonin also rose to about twice the normal level.

When the original dominant male returned, however, he became dominant again; the level of serotonin in his blood went up and that of his rival went down.

Just what serotonin has to do with animal dominance is unknown, but the scientists found hints of something similar in humans. Measurement of blood serotonin levels in a college fraternity showed that officers had higher levels than the others.

The scientists said social interactions seem to influence serotonin levels.

"We don't believe for a moment that serotonin is the only factor," said Dr. Michael T. McGuire. Of UCLA's Neuropsychiatric Institute. "But we just can't find out what else is going on."

The team plans to study humans further next summer with the help of a 17-man Swedish yacht crew who will be contestants in an around-the-world sailing race out of London.

Source: The *Evening Bulletin,* September 30, 1983, p. A-5

effects on other people or gain them certain goods they desire. In other words, until a direct biological link between aggression and human behavior is found, the critics feel it is wiser to focus on what the direct evidence does suggest: namely, that aggression is of social, not biological, origin.

Second, because of the lack of direct biological evidence once again, there is a tendency for the sociobiologists to utilize available evidence from early humanlike species (such as "Cro-Magnon" and "Neanderthal") to suggest aggression as a biologically inherited trait in contemporary *homo sapiens*. The problem with such evidence, the critics say, is at least threefold: (1) Our evidence about prehuman species is extremely scanty and specific descriptions of behavioral patterns are very difficult to make with any degree of certainty. (2) Even if prehuman species were highly aggressive, there is no way of deducing, by direct evidence, that they were so for biological, and not social learning, reasons. (3) Even if it could somehow be established that these prehuman species exhibited aggressive behavior for reasons of biological determinism, there is no cause to assume, without specific biological evidence, that contemporary human beings, a biologically different species, exhibit the same behaviors for the same reasons.

The last argument developed by the critics of the sociobiological position concerns the "overgeneralization" of evidence by scholars such as Lorenz and van den Berghe. To say that some, even most, human beings act in a certain manner—for example, aggressively—is not to say that *all* do and, to admit exceptions, especially to a trait that is claimed to be biological in nature, means that those exceptions need to be explained. (By reexamining the section describing van den Berghe's theory, you will see clearly, in van den Berghe's own words, this tendency to overgeneralize: using statements about "most" human beings to imply a biological predisposition in the species *as a whole*.) Either the exceptions are biological aberrations or variations (a very difficult case to prove), or the exceptions have had their biological instincts or predispositions "overridden" by other, presumably social, considerations. Van den Berghe, for example, takes this latter tack when he argues that the peacefulness of an African pygmy tribe is a result of its being intimidated by more aggressive neighbors (1974, p. 782). However, if a biological determinist takes such a position, it significantly weakens the deterministic element in the thesis. In addition, the sociobiology critic would add, if you can *explain* the behavior by utilizing social factors alone, what is the necessity to hypothesize biological instincts or predispositions that cannot be demonstrated? Thus, if the African pygmy tribe is intimidated by its aggressive neighbors, this could easily be the result of each group's possession of differing amounts of *power*—a *social* relationship—not the result of the biologically predisposed aggressivity of one tribe holding in check the biologically predisposed aggressivity of another.

Moreover, there is no reason that the widespread fact of aggression in many societies cannot be explained as a product of social learning. Aggression is one possible response to conditions of scarce resources or need-frustration; cooperation, as the Arapesh show (see Chapter 3) is another. If, by trial and error, aggressive behavior is found to be rewarding to the group or individual using it—that is, if it decreases resource scarcity or need-frustration—this response will tend to be repeated in similar circumstances. In time, it is likely to take on the character of a normative obligation for a given group in certain situations. As other individuals or groups see the "positive" effects of aggression in solving the problems of scarce resources or need-frustration, they, not being unintelligent, may experiment with it as well and also develop normative aggressive behavior patterns. (This is the process of diffusion described in Chapter 8.) Finally, some societies may develop aggressive patterns for purely defensive reasons as well. If the sociobiologists would only pay more attention to the crucial roles played by environment, social learning, and tradition (culture) in forming aggressive behavioral patterns, it is argued, they would find little reason to resort to as yet undiscovered biological factors in explaining those patterns.

Despite the strength of these arguments, perhaps the strongest critique of the sociobiological position comes from cross-cultural studies that very clearly link aggressive behavioral patterns to social definitions of the situation. Russell (1972) examined data from over 400 societies to see which, if any, social factors, such as child-rearing practices, might be related to warlike behavior. (The sociobiological hypothesis would suggest that specific social factors would have little to do with aggression, the trait being innate and in need of expression under any circumstances.) Russell found, first, that societies varied a great deal on the amount of warfare they engaged in and, second, that the more warfare any society had, the more likely it was also to have certain highly aggressive social practices in its day-to-day routines. More specifically, he found that warlike societies tended to have punitive child-rearing practices, an emphasis on interpersonal competition for prestige, a belief in the rights of the individual and his or her desires as being more important than those of the group, high levels of anxiety and fear between individuals and groups within the society, and punishment of pre- and extramarital sexual behavior. From this evidence, he argued that it appears that societies *create* and *enhance* their level of aggression by the invention of social practices that contain within them behaviors that produce aggressive personalities and the normative expectation that aggressive behavior is "natural."

Similarly, Spies (1973), in a direct attempt to indicate the inadequacies of the instinctual theory of aggression, examined 20 societies, 10 of which were classified as warlike and 10 of which were classified as nonwarlike. He examined the incidence of combative sports (sports where the individuals or groups involved had actual physical or symbolic physical contact) in these societies. He reasoned, following Lorenz's lead, that if a society was warlike, there would be no need for combative sports to exist because the instinctual aggressive tension would be "discharged" in the war activities. Conversely, if a society was not warlike, the instinctual aggressive tension would build up inside the individuals of that society and "alternative" discharge mechanisms—in this case, combative sports—would have to be invented to "drain off" the instinctual energy. Consequently, Sipes hypothesized that, if Lorenz was right about the instinctual nature of aggression, warlike societies would not have a high incidence of combative sports and nonwarlike societies would.

He found almost exactly the opposite. Specifically, in his 10 warlike societies, he found that 9 of them had combative sports and, in his nonwarlike societies, he found that only 2 had such sports. From this he concludes that:

> [This] refutes the hypothesis that combative sports are alternatives to war as discharge channels of accumulated aggressive tension . . . It casts strong doubt on the idea that there is such a thing as accumulable aggressive tension, certainly on the social level and perhaps, even on the individual level. It clearly supports the validity of the [social learning] Model and as clearly tends to discredit the Drive Discharge Model. (1973, p. 71)

These findings are quite similar to Russell's. They suggest that societies that have, for whatever environmental or social reason, developed a highly aggressive set of behaviors will maintain these behaviors by inventing mechanisms of socialization that teach its members when and how to be aggressive.

The sociobiology controversy is not likely to disappear for some time—as it should not, until all parties are convinced of the evidence one way or the other. It is our feeling, however, that the burden of proof still rests on those who would argue against the position that human beings are primarily social beings.

CONCLUSION

We have briefly examined several of the major controversies in the field of sociology. The presence of widespread controversy and debate partially reflects sociology's relatively immature status among the behavioral sciences. At the same time, it should be emphasized that controversy can be a dynamic force in the scientific process. It provides the occasion for social scientists representing diverse perspectives and backgrounds to come together for the purpose of dissecting a significant problem. In the process, issues are often clarified and hidden complexities and biases revealed. (See Box 9–7.)

Box 9–7 THE SCIENTIFIC MANIPULATION OF JURIES: HELPFUL OR HARMFUL?

Man has taken a new bite from the apple of knowledge, and it is doubtful whether we all will be better for it. We may not choke on the mouthful, but it will take quite a bit of collective chewing until our system comes to terms with this latest ingestion of scientific bounty. This time it is not religion, the family or the village community that is being challenged by a new application of science; instead; that venerable traditional institution of being judged by a jury of one's peers. The impartiality of the jury is threatened because defense attorneys have recently discovered that they can manipulate the composition of the jury by the use of social science techniques, so as to significantly increase the likelihood that the defendants will be acquitted.

An example of how such social science teams work is the jury selection accomplished by Jay Schulman and Richard Christie at the trial of Indian militants at Wounded Knee. First, a detailed profile of the community's sociological composition was assembled through interviews with 576 persons chosen at random from voter lists. The interviews allowed the research team to cross-tabulate social background characteristics (such as occupation, level of education, etc.) with attitudes favorable to the defense (especially toward the Indians) and select out the best "predictor variables." Such analysis is vital because people of the same social background hold different attitudes in different parts of the country and, hence, a generalized sociological model does not suffice (e.g., women in Harrisburg, where the Berrigan trial was held, proved to be more friendly toward the defense than men, but the reverse was true in Gainesville).

Next, observers were placed in the courtroom to "psych out" the prospective jurors, using anything from the extent to which they talked with other prospective jurors to their mode of dress to evaluate each individual juror, rather than relying only on the sociological category of which he was a member. (In the Angela Davis case, handwriting experts were used to analyze the signatures of prospective jurors.)

Information gained in this way was compared to what the computer predicted about the same "type" of person, on the basis of the interview data fed into it. This double reading was further checked, especially when the two sources of information did not concur, by field investigators who interviewed people acquainted with the prospective jurors. The results were used by the defense attorneys to question jurors and to challenge them, as well as to provide the judge with questions he or she may have wished to ask of prospective jurors.

Now, social scientists did not invent the idea of using challenges to help obtain a favorable jury. Lawyers have used it as far back as records go. But, until recently, lawyers commonly could not use much more than rule of thumb, hunches and some experiences.

Source: Amitai Etzioni, "Out-Psyching Justice, Seen in Perspective," *Human Behavior,* September 1974, p. 10.

Ideally, scientists assume a skeptical or questioning attitude toward the world. They are expected to accept conclusions provisionally (i.e., with less than absolute certainty) and then only after lengthy testing has been carried out. Such an attitude is particularly important in the social sciences, among them sociology.

Throughout this book we have seen that (1) the social scientist often has biases about his or her social world that, unintentionally, often creep into supposedly "objective" studies; (2) the social scientist generally "interacts" with those whom he or she is observing, in the process creating a different phenomenon—the reactions of people who know they are being "watched" as opposed to the reactions of those in an unobserved setting; (3) the social world is incredibly complex, and sociologists frequently do not have definitive answers to many of the questions they ask and may not have them for some time to come. For all these reasons, caution is recommended (see Box 9–8).

Still, the world goes on, and the sociologist, however imperfect the findings, does know *something.* It seems to us (Levin and Spates) that action *based on what we do know,* should not be avoided just because further experience *may* prove us wrong. Let us take a couple of examples.

In recent years there has been considerable research into the

---

Can we objectively evaluate the results obtained in scientific research? How do you think an advocate of male supremacy would handle the following article?

Box 9–8   FEMALE VS. MALE BRAIN DEBATED

United Press International

The scientist who discovered that a key portion of the brain is larger in women than in men said yesterday it does not necessarily mean women are intellectually superior to men.

M. Christine De Lacoste, a neurobiologist at the University of Texas Health Science Center, found within the past year that the corpus callosum—a part of the brain that scientists think ferries information from one side of the brain to the other—is 40 percent larger in women than men.

"We don't know enough to say what the implications of this discovery are," she said. "We can only say there is a difference . . ."

Source: The *Boston Globe* November 12, 1983, p. 4.

However, a radical faction of women scientists attending a Boston forum Thursday on the differences between male and female brains tried through a series of questions to convince her to speculate that the difference signifies superiority.

Some women, such as Candace Pert, chief of the brain biochemical section at the National Institute of Mental Health, said the larger organ suggests that females are better able to communicate between the two sides of the brain.

Neuroscientists theorize that one side of the brain governs creativity while the other side governs logic. Therefore better integration would mean that women are better able to use their logic and creativity together.

effects of explicit sexual and violent material in the media. A book that summarizes the findings of these investigations has been published by Eysenck and Nias (1978). In essence, the authors conclude that the situation is more complicated than either side of the previous controversy had known or admitted. As it turns out, *most* violent material and *some* sexual material in media—television, films, books—seem to have a negative effect on viewers or readers and some has more positive effects. On the negative side, Eysenck and Nias note that gratuitous violence—that perpetrated for its own sake, for pleasure in hurting, or out of a desire for revenge (whether perpetrated by the "baddies" *or* the "goodies")—made viewers or readers tense, angry, and prone to violence themselves. On the other hand, defensive violence—that undertaken by a character for her or his own defense, for the protection of a family or group—did not have the same effect: Viewers or readers of such scenes were not so tense, saw some ultimate justice in the action taken by the character, and became only somewhat more violent themselves.

It was the same for sexual material. When sexual encounters were depicted as exploitive, as domineering, when they showed people using each other as mere objects of pleasure, Eysenck and Nias noted that the viewers or readers became uneasy and took on such attitudes themselves. In contrast, when sexuality was portrayed as a loving and caring encounter between two human beings, with no hint of domination or objectification of the other, most viewers and readers reacted much more positively. Their experience became a kind of catharsis and they reported feeling positive emotions, such as an increase in love and care for *their* sexual partners.

Such findings suggest that both sides of the violence/pornography debate have been too extreme in their positions. Not all sex and violence is negative, as those who would censor all instances of both would have us believe. On the other hand, not all of it is positive or harmless, as those who take the "freedom of speech" position hold. Thus it would seem that the responsible sociological position, assuming agreement with Eysenck and Nias' findings, would be to make these findings as public as possible and speak out against the negative instances of sexual/violent material in the media—hard core, exploitive pornography, the excessive and gratuitous violence of many films and children's programming (e.g., many Saturday morning cartoons).

Similarly, as reported in Chapters 5 and 6, the social stratification and economic systems of the United States literally lock in many people at the lower levels and make it nearly impossible for them to improve their lot *no matter what they do.* Furthermore, all available research suggests that people at the bottom of our prestige and economic hierarchies have the same aspirations and, except for an extremely small minority, work as hard or harder than most other Americans simply to survive (compare Reissman, 1969; Goodwin, 1971; Aldrich, 1973; Davidson and Gaits, 1974; Stack, 1974). Therefore to make things more difficult for such people would seem unconscionable.

Yet recent cutbacks in federal aid programs have done just this. Such cutbacks have made the requirements for receiving welfare benefits more stringent, reduced accessibility to food stamp programs, cut subsidies for school lunch programs (which have hit the poor neighborhoods the worst), and reduced the number of households receiving Medicaid. In other words, the cutbacks have reduced household support, food, and health services for those who are *least* able to provide these services for themselves—generally, the poor of all races, minorities, and the aged. Moreover, such cutbacks first came in 1982 when unemployment nationwide was at a post-Depression high (more than 12 million Americans out of work) and the national poverty rate was 15 percent, the highest since 1965. Finally, the cutbacks came as the percentage of those receiving aid who were below the poverty level rose. For example, in 1979, 41 percent of those receiving some kind of aid were below the poverty level ($9,862 for a family of 4); by 1982 that figure had risen to 50 percent (*New York Times*, September 23, 1983, p. A3).

Once again, the sociological evidence seems clear: A great deal of human suffering in our society is caused by the inequities in our stratification system and unequal access to wealth and power channels. To increase the financial, nutritional, and health-related problems of people who suffer from such *system-created* problems is categorically inhumane. The concerned sociological position, then, would be to make such findings more public and to find ways actively to resist such cutbacks.

What we are suggesting is that the sociologist is an actor on the local, national, and world stage like any other actor. True, sociologists do not have all the answers and may suffer James Coleman's fate. Certainly, there will be those who disagree with our position and/or interpretation of the evidence. Nevertheless, *not to act on the basis of our considered interpretation of the available evidence is to let the situation as it exists perpetuate itself with all its problems and potential for real injustices.*

Sociology, as discussed in Chapter 1, is the study of human interaction and the consequences of that interaction. As such, it is more than a "fact-finding mission"; it is the study of *our own* life situation and, ultimately, of the *quality* of that life situation. As we gather the facts, we are learning that some types of interaction and social structure facilitate an enjoyable life for most or all of a group's members, whereas other types of interaction and social structure frustrate such enjoyment. In both the long and the short run, however controversial such judgments may be, we believe that the sociologist is also responsible for finding ways to help effect the first of these conditions—an equitable and enjoyable social life for all of society's members.

QUESTIONS, EXERCISES, PROJECTS

1. Distinguish between the functional and conflict approaches to sociology.

2. What is the key difference between bias-free and value-free conceptions of sociology.

3. Argue *both* in favor of and against the value-free position as applied to sociology.

4. Examine the role that sociologists have played in regard to any social issue or social policy, for instance, in court-ordered busing to achieve school desegregation, the 1954 desegregation decision of the Supreme Court, the President's Commission on Obscenity and Pornography, the National Commission on the Causes and Prevention of Violence, Project Camelot, the surgeon general's commission on television and violence.

5. What are the basic contentions of the sociobiologists? Why do these contentions reach the heart of the sociological enterprise? What have been the critical reactions to the sociobiological position?

6. Can—or should—sociologists take a position on controversial issues even when they are not sure all the evidence is available?

BIBLIOGRAPHY

Adams, Bert N. (1971). *The American Family.* Chicago: Markham.

Aldrich, H. E. 1974. "Employment Opportunities for Blacks in the Black Ghetto." *American Journal of Sociology* 78:1403–1425.

Alland, Alexander (1972). *The Human Imperative.* New York: Columbia University Press.

Allport, Gordon W., and Postman, Leo F. (1952). "The Basic Psychology of Rumor." In G. E. Swanson, T. M. Newcomb, and E. L. Hartley (eds.), *Readings in Social Psychology.* New York: Holt, Rinehart and Winston.

Anastos, Ernie with Levin, Jack (1983). *Twixt: Teens Yesterday and Today.* New York: Franklin Watts.

Aronson, Sidney H. (1974). "The Sociology of the Telephone." In Marcello Truzzi (ed.), *Sociology for Pleasure.* Englewood Cliffs, N.J.: Prentice-Hall.

Asch, Solomon E. (1952). "Effects of Group Pressures upon the Modification and Distortion of Judgment." In G. E. Swanson, T. M. Newcomb, and E. L. Hartley (eds.), *Readings in Social Psychology;* 2nd ed. New York: Holt, Rinehart and Winston.

Axelrod, Morris (1956). "Urban Structure and Social Participation," *American Sociological Review* 19:267–272.

Babbie, Earl R. (1973). *Survey Research Methods.* Belmont, Calif.: Wadsworth.

Bach, George Leland (1971). *Economics: An Introduction to Analysis and Policy,* 7th ed. Englewood Cliffs, N.J.: Prentice-Hall.

Bahr, Howard M. (1980). "Changes in Family Life in Middletown." *"Public Opinion Quarterly* 44(1): 35–52.

Bakan, David (1971). "Adolescence in America: From Idea to Social Fact," *Daedalus* 100, 4:-979–966.

Barber, Bernard (1957). *Social Stratification.* New York: Harcourt Brace Jovanovich.

Becker, Ernest (1971). *The Lost Science of Man.* New York: George Braziller.

Becker, Howard S. (1964). "Problems in the Publication of Field Studies." In A. J. Vidich, J. Bensman, and M. R. Stein (eds.), *Reflections on Community Studies.* New York: Wiley.

Becker, Howard S., and Geer, Blanche (1970). "Participant Observation and Interviewing: A Comparison." In William J. Filstead (ed.), *Qualitative Methodology.* Chicago: Markham.

Bell, Daniel (1956). "The Theory of Mass Society." *Commentary* 75:83.

Bellah, Robert N. (1958). *Tokugawa Religion.* New York: Free Press.

Bellah, Robert N. (1967). "Civil Religion in America," *Daedalus,* (Winter): 1–21.

Bensman, Joseph, and Rosenberg, Bernard (1960). "The Meaning of Work in Bureaucratic Society." In Maurice Stein, Arthur J. Vidich, and David M. White (eds.), *Identity and Anxiety.* New York: Free Press.

Berelson, Bernard, and Salter, Patricia J. (1946). "Majority and Minority Americans: An Analysis of Magazine Fiction." *Public Opinion Quarterly* (Summer): 168–190.

Berger, Peter L. (1963). *Invitation to Sociology.* Garden City, N.Y.: Doubleday.

Berger, Peter L. (1967). *The Sacred Canopy.* New York: Anchor.

Berger, Peter L. (1971). "Sociology and Freedom." *The American Sociologist* (February): 1–5.

Bernstein, Carl, and Woodward, Bob (1974). *All the President's Men.* New York: Warner.

Berquist, Laura (1966). "How Come a Nice Girl Like You Isn't Married?" *Look* (January 11): 48–50.

"Big Jump in Fraternity Rolls Forecast by 2 Researchers" (1983). *The Chronicle of Higher Education* (November 16): 3.

Blumer, Herbert (1965). "Collective Behavior." In A. M. Lee (ed.), *New Outline of Principles of Sociology.* New York: Barnes & Noble.

Boston Globe (1973). "TV—A Distorted View of Us," June 20, p. 2.

Boston Globe (1975). "Researcher Defends His Mating Study," March 19, p. 5.

Bowden, Elbert V. (1974). *Economics Through the Looking Glass.* San Francisco, Calif.: Canfield.

Bower, Donald W., and Christopherson, Victor A. (1977). *Journal of Marriage and the Family* 39:3.

Brinton, Crane (1952). *The Anatomy of Revolution.* New York: Norton.

Brockton Daily Enterprise (1973). February 27, p. 2.

Brown, Roger (1965). *Social Psychology.* New York: Free Press.

Carden, Maren Lockwood (1974). *The New Feminist Movement.* New York: Russell Sage Foundation.

Centers, Richard (1949). *The Psychology of Social Classes.* Princeton, N.J.: Princeton University Press.

Chinoy, Ely, and Hewitt, John P. (1975). *Sociological Perspective.* New York: Random House.

Clayton, Richard R., and Voss, Harwin L. (1977). *Journal of Marriage and the Family* 39:2.

Coleman, Richard, and Rainwater, Lee (1978). *Social Standing in America.* New York: Basic Books.

Collins, Glenn (1983). "Stranger's Stare." *New York Times,* April 11, 1983, p. D1.

Cooley, Charles H. (1909). *Social Organization.* New York: Free Press.

Coser, Lewis (1956). *The Functions of Social Conflict.* New York: Free Press.

Coverman, Shelley (1983). "Gender, Domestic Labor Time, and Wage Inequality." *American Sociological Review* 48(5): 623–636.

Cowgill, Donald O., and Holmes, Lowell D. (1972). *Aging and Modernization.* New York: Appleton-Century-Crofts.

Darley, John M., and Latane, Bibb (1968). "Bystander Intervention in Emergencies: Diffusion of Responsibility." *Journal of Personality and Social Psychology* 8:377–383.

Davidson, C. and Gaitz, C. M. (1974). "Are the Poor Different?" *Social Problems* 22 (December): 229–245.

Davies, James C. (1962). "Toward a Theory of Revolution." *American Sociological Review* (February 27) 1:5–18.

Davis, Kingsley (1947). "Final Note on a Case of Extreme Isolation." *American Journal of Sociology.* 52:432–437.

Davis, Kingsley (1949). *Human Society.* New York: Macmillan.

Davis, Kingsley, and Moore, Wilbert E. (1945). "Some Principles of Stratification. *American Sociological Review* (April): 242–249.

Denzin, Norman K. (1970). *The Values of Social Change.* Chicago: Transaction.

Diener, E., and Crandall, R. (1978). *Ethics in Social and Behavioral Research.* Chicago: University of Chicago Press.

Dollard, John (1937). *Caste and Class in a Southern Town.* New Haven, Conn.: Yale University Press.

Drabek, Thomas E., and Haas, J. Eugene (1974), *Understanding Complex Organizations.* New York: Brown.

Durkheim, Emile (1933). *The Division of Labor*

in Society. New York: Free Press. *American Journal of Sociology* 78:912–935.

Durkheim, Emile (1951). *Suicide: A Study in Sociology.* Translated by John Spaulding and George Simpson. New York: Free Press.

Durkheim, Emile (1964). *The Rules of Sociological Method.* Translated by Sarah Solovay and John Mueller. New York: Free Press.

Durkheim, Emile (1965). *The Elementary Forms of Religious Life.* New York: Free Press.

Edwards, Alba M. (1943). *Comparative Occupational Statistics for the United States, 1870–1940.* Washington, D.C.: U.S. Government Printing Office.

Eitzen, D. Stanley (1974). *Social Structure and Social Problems in America.* Boston: Allyn & Bacon.

Epstein, Cynthia Fuchs (1973). "Positive Effects of the Multiple Negative: Explaining the Success of Black Professional Women."

Erskine, Hazel (1972). "The Polls: Gun Control." *Public Opinion Quarterly* (Fall): 455.

Etzione, Amitai (1974). "Out-psyching Justice, Seen in Perspective." *Human Behavior* (September): 10.

Eve, Raymond S. (1975). " 'Adolescent Culture,' Convenient Myth or Reality?" *Sociology of Education* 48:152–167.

Eysenck, H. J. and Nias, D. K. B. (1978). *Sex, Violence, and the Media.* New York: St. Martin's.

Farber, Jerry (1969). *The Student as Nigger.* North Hollywood, Calif.: Contact.

Faris, Robert (1953). "Small-Group Research Movement." In Muzafer Sherif and M. O. Wilson (eds.), *Group Relations at the Crossroads.* New York: Harper & Row.

Festinger, Leon (1957). *A Theory of Cognitive Dissonance.* Stanford Calif.: Stanford University Press.

Festinger, Leon, Riecken, Henry W., and Schachter, Stanley (1956). *When Prophecy Fails.* New York: Harper Torchbooks.

Feuer, Lewis S., ed. (1959). *Marx and Engels: Basic Writings on Politics and Philosophy.* New York: Anchor.

Fischer, Claude S. (1975). "The Myth of 'Territoriality' in van den Berge's 'Bringing Beasts Back In.' " *American Sociological Review* 40:674–676.

Fischer, David H. (1977). *Growing Old in America.* New York: Oxford University.

Flacks, Richard (1971). *Youth and Social Change.* New York: Markham.

Fox, James A. (1978). *Forecasting Crime Data.* Lexington, Mass.: Lexington Books.

Freeman, Howard E., Dynes, Russell R., Rossi, Peter H., and Whyte, William Foote (1983). *Applied Sociology.* San Francisco: Jossey-Bass.

Freeman, Jo (1975). "The Origins of the Women's Liberation Movement." *American Journal of Sociology* 78:792–811.

Freud, Sigmund (1920). *A General Introduction to Psychoanalysis.* Translated by C. S. Hall. New York: Boni & Liveright.

Freud, Sigmund (1922). *Beyond the Pleasure Principle.* London: International Psychoanalytical Press.

Freud, Sigmund (1930). *Civilization and Its Discontents.* Translated by Joan Riviere. London: Hogarth.

Freud, Sigmund (1961). *The Future of an Illusion.* New York: Anchor.

Friedan, Betty (1963). *The Feminine Mystique.* New York: Dell.

Friedan, Betty (1983). "Twenty Years After the Feminine Mystique." *New York Times Magazine.* (February 27)35–58.

Friedrichs, Robert W. (1973). "The Impact of Social Factors upon Scientific Judgement: The 'Jensen Thesis' as Appraised by Members of the American Psychological Association." *Journal of Negro Education* (Fall): 429–438.

Fromm, Erich (1941). *Escape from Freedom.* New York: Avon.

Gallup, George H. (1981). *The Gallup Report No. 636.* Princeton, N.J.: The Gallup Poll, p. 17.

Gans, Herbert (1962). "Urbanism and Suburbanism as Ways of Life: A Re-evaluation of Definitions." In Arnold M. Rose (ed.), *Human Behavior and Social Processes.* Boston: Houghton Mifflin, pp. 625–648.

Gans, Herbert J. (1972). "The Positive Functions of Poverty." *American Journal of Sociology* 78:275–289.

Gans, Herbert J. (1973). *More Equality.* New York: Pantheon.

Gaston, Jerry and Sherohman, James (1974).

"Origins of Researchers on Black Americans" *American Sociologist* 9:75–82.

Gerbner, George, Gross, Larry, Jackson-Beeck, Marilyn, Jeffries-Fox, Suzanne, and Signorielli, Nancy (1978). "Cultural Indicators: Violence Profile No. 9." *Journal of Communication.* 28 (3):176–207.

Gerth, H. H., and Mills, C. Wright, eds. and trans. (1946). *From Max Weber: Essays in Sociology.* New York: Oxford University Press.

Glazer, Myron (1972). *The Research Adventure.* New York: Random House.

Goffman, Erving (1959). *The Presentation of Self in Everyday Life.* Garden City, N.Y.: Doubleday.

Goldberg, Stephen (1974). *The Inevitability of Patriarchy.* New York: Morrow.

Goldman, Nancy (1973). "The Changing Role of Women in the Armed Forces." *American Journal of Sociology* 78:892–911.

Goode, William J. (1963). *World Revolution and Family Patterns.* New York: Free Press.

Goodman, Ellen (1972). "Babies in Pink Are So Girlish." *Boston Globe* February 23, p. 16.

Goodwin, L. (1971). "Research Reported in 'Viewing the Poor.'" *Transaction* 5(May): 16.

Gough, E. Kathleen (1974). "Nayar: Central Kerala." In David Schneider and E. Kathleen Gough (eds.), *Matrilineal Kinship.* Berkeley, Calif.: University of California.

Gouldner, Alvin W. (1963). "Anti-Minotaur: The Myth of a Value-Free Society." In Maurice Stein and Arthur Vidich (eds.), *Sociology on Trial.* Englewood Cliffs, N.J.: Prentice-Hall.

Greeley, Andrew M. (1972). *The Unsecular Society.* New York: Schocken.

Greeley, Andrew M., and McCready, William (1975). "Are We a Nation of Mystics?" *New York Times Magazine* (January 26):12, 15 f.

Greene, Gael (1963). "A Vote Against Motherhood: A Wife Challenges the Importance of Child Bearing." *Saturday Evening Post* 36–37.

Gross, Edward (1953). "Some Functional Consequences of Primary Controls in Formal Work Organizations" *American Sociological Review* 18:60–69.

Gross, McEachern, Alexander W., and Mason, Ward S. (1957). *Explorations in Role Analysis: Studies of the School Superintendency Role.* New York: Wiley.

Haavio-Mannila, Elina (1970). "Sex Roles in Politics." *Scandinavian Political Studies* 5:209–238.

Hacker, Andrew (1983). *U/S: A Statistical Portrait of the American People.* New York: Viking.

Haney, Craig, Banks, W. Curtis, and Zimbardo, Philip G. (1973). "Interpersonal Dynamics in a Simulated Prison." *International Journal of Criminology and Penology* 1:69–97.

Happold, F. C. (1955). *Adventure in Search of a Creed.* London: Faber and Faber.

Harris, Louis (1972). "Levels of Alienation Still High." *Boston Globe,* November 30, p. 64.

Harris, Marvin (1977). "Why Men Dominate Women," *New York Times Magazine* (November 13):46, 115 f.

Hart, Hornell (1957a). "Acceleration in Social Change." In Francis R. Allen, Hornell Hart, Delbert C. Miller, William F. Ogburn, and Meyer F. Nimkoff (eds.). *Technology and Social Change.* New York: Appleton.

Hart, Hornell (1957b). "The Hypothesis of Cultural Lag: A Present Day View." In Francis R. Allen, Hornell Hart, Delbert C. Miller, William F. Ogburn, and Meyer F. Nimkoff (eds.), *Technology and Social Change.* New York: Appleton.

Havighurst, Robert J., and Neugarten, Bernice L. (1957). *Society and Education.* Boston: Allyn & Bacon.

Heilbroner, Robert L. (1968). *The Making of Economic Society,* 2nd ed. Englewood Cliffs, N.J.: Prentice-Hall.

Hodge, Robert W., Siegel, Paul M., and Rossi, Peter H. (1964). "Occupational Prestige in the United States: 1925–1963" *American Journal of Sociology* (November): 286–302.

Hoffman, Abbie (1968). *Revolution for the Hell of It.* New York: Dial.

Hoge, Dean R. (1971). "College Students' Value Patterns in the 1950s and 1960s," *Sociology of Education* 44:170–197.

Homans, George C. (1950). *The Human Group.* New York: Harcourt Brace Tovanovich.

Horowitz, Irving Louis (1967). *The Rise and Fall of Project Camelot.* Cambridge, Mass.: M.I.T. Press.

Howe, Florence, and Lauter, Paul (1972). "How the School System Is Rigged for Failure." In Richard C. Edwards, Michael Reich, and Thomas E. Weisskopf (eds.), *The Capitalist System.* Englewood Cliffs, N.J.: Prentice-Hall.

Howell, Joseph T. (1973). *Hard Living on Clay Street.* New York: Anchor.

Hughes, Helen MacGill, (1973). "Maid of all Work or Departmental Sister-in-Law?" *American Journal of Sociology* 78:767–772.

Humphreys, Laud (1970). *Tearoom Trade.* Chicago: Aldine.

Hunt, Raymond, Gurrslin, Orville, and Roach, Jack L. (1958). "Social Status and Psychiatric Service in a Child Guidance Clinic," *American Sociological Review* 23:81–83.

Hunter, Floyd (1953). *Community Power Structure: A Study of Decision Makers.* Chapel Hill, N.C.: University of North Carolina Press.

Hyman, Herbert H. (1974). "Mass Communication and Socialization." In W. Phillips Davison and Frederick T. C. Yu (eds.), *Mass Communication Research.* New York: Praeger.

James, William (1958). *The Varieties of Religious Experience.* New York: Mentor. (Original published 1902).

Jensen, Arthur R. (1969). "How Much Can We Boost I.Q. and Scholastic Achievement?" *Harvard Educational Review* (Winter): 12–123.

Kahl, Joseph A., and Davis, James A. (1955). "A Comparison of Indexes of Socio-Economic Status." *American Sociological Review* (June):20.

Kandel, Denise B., and Lesser, Gerald S. (1972). *Youth in Two Worlds.* San Francisco: Jossey-Bass.

Kaplan, Abraham (1963). *The Conduct of Inquiry.* New York: Chandler.

Kaplan, H. Roy (1978). *Lottery Winners: How They Won and How Winning Changed Their Lives.* New York: Barnes & Noble.

Katz, Elihu, and Lazarsfeld, Paul F. (1955). *Personal Influence.* New York: Free Press.

Kelley, Jonathan (1974). "The Politics of School Busing." *Public Opinion Quarterly* (Spring):23–39.

Killian, Lewis (1964). "Social Movements." In E. L. Faris (ed.), *Handbook of Modern Sociology.* New York: Rand-McNally.

Kluckhohn, Clyde (1951). "Values and Value-Orientations in the Theory of Action." In Talcott Parsons and Edward Shils (eds.), *Toward a General Theory of Action.* New York: Harper & Row.

Kluckhohn, Florence R., and Strodtbeck, Fred L. (1961). *Variations in Value Orientations.* New York: Harper & Row.

Knox, Richard A. (1974). "Scientists Oppose Survey of Chromosome Disorder." *Boston Globe,* November 16, p. 3.

Koch, Howard (1970). *The Panic Broadcast.* Boston: Little, Brown.

Krause, Elliott (1980). *Why Study Sociology?* New York: Random House.

Kunen, James (1969). *The Strawberry Statement.* New York: Pantheon.

Lasch, Christopher (1978). *The Culture of Narcissism.* New York: Norton.

Lamy, Philip (1983). "Punk Values and the Middle Class: A Content Analysis," An unpublished masters paper, Department of Sociology and Anthropology, Northeastern University.

Largey, Gale Peter, and Watson, David Rodney (1972). "The Sociology of Odors." *American Journal of Sociology* 77(6):1021–1034.

Lebon, Gustave (1895). *The Crowd: A Study of the Popular Mind.* New York: Viking.

Lenski, Gerhard (1963). *The Religious Factor.* New York: Doubleday.

Leonard, George B. (1968). *Education and Ecstasy.* New York: Delacorte.

Levin, Jack, and Levin, William C. (1980). *Ageism: Prejudice and Discrimination Against the Elderly.* Belmont, Calif.: Wadsworth.

Levin, Jack, and Taube, Gerald (1970). "Bureaucracy and the Socially Handicapped: A Study of Lower Status Tenants in Public Housing." *Sociology and Social Research* 54:-209–219.

Levi-Strauss, Claude (1961). *A World on the Wane.* New York: Criterion.

Libarle, Mark, and Seligson, Tom (1970). *The High School Revolutionaries.* New York: Random House.

Liebow, Elliot (1967). *Tally's Corner.* Boston: Little, Brown.

Linton, Ralph (1936). *The Study of Man.* New York: Appleton.

Lipset, Seymour M., and Bendix, Reinhard (1959). *Social Mobility in Industrial Society*. Berkeley: University of California Press.

Lorenz, Konrad (1966). *On Aggression*. New York: Bantam.

Lynd, Robert S., and Lynd, Helen Merrell (1929). Middletown. New York: Harcourt Brace Jovanovich.

McAllister, Ronald J. (1980). "Research Ethics," unpublished manuscript, Department of Sociology, Northeastern University.

MacDonald, Bob (1981). "A PhD's Lament," *Boston Globe*; p 1, 16.

Martindale, Don (1960). *The Nature and Types of Sociological Theory*. Boston: Houghton Mifflin.

Marx, Karl (1888). *Manifesto of the Communist Party*. Chicago: Kerr.

Marx, Karl and Engels, Friedrich (1930). *The German Ideology*. New York: International.

Marx, Karl, and Engels, Frederick (1955). *Selected Works in Two Volumes*. Moscow: Foreign Languages Publishing House.

Marx, Karl, and Engels, Frederick (1964). *On Religion*. New York: Schocken.

Mauss, Armand L. (1969). "Anticipatory Socialization Toward College as a Factor in Adolescent Marijuana Use." *Social Problems* (Winter):357–364.

Mazur, Allan (1968). "The Littlest Science." *American Sociologist* 3:195–199.

Mazur, Allan (1975). "Cross-Species Comparisons of Aggression." *American Sociological Review* 40:677–678.

Mead, George Herbert (1934). *Mind, Self and Society*. Chicago: University of Chicago Press.

Mead, Margaret (1939). *Sex and Temperament in Three Primitive Societies*. New York: Morrow.

Melbin, Murray (1978). "Night as Frontier." *American Sociological Review*. 43(1):3–22.

Milgram, Stanley (1965). "Some Conditions of Obedience and Disobedience to Authority." *Human Relations* 18:57–76.

Miller, Delbert C. (1957). "Theories of Social Change." In Francis R. Allen, Hornell Hart, Delbert C. Miller, William F. Ogburn, and Meyer F. Nimkoff (eds.), *Technology and Social Change*. New York:Appleton.

Mills, C. Wright (1956). *The Power Elite*. New York: Oxford University Press.

Moberg, Dennis J. (1975). "A Comment on van den Berghe's Biosocial Model of Aggression."*American Sociological Review* 40:676–677.

Montagu, Ashley (1973). *Man and Aggression*, 2nd ed. New York: Oxford University Press.

Morris, Charles, and Small, Linwood (1971). "Changes in the conception of the Good Life by American College Students from 1950 to 1960," *Journal of Personality and Social Psychology* 22:254–260.

Murdock, George (1949). *Social Structure*. New York: Free Press.

Neumann, Franz (1960). "Anxiety and Politics." In Maurice Stein, Arthur J. Vidich, and David M. White (eds.), *Identity and Anxiety*. New York: Free Press.

Oakley, Ann (1974). *The Sociology of Housework*. New York: Pantheon.

Ogburn, William F. (1922). *Social Change*. New York: Viking.

Palmore, Erdman (1975). *Honorable Elders*. Durham, N.C.: University of North Carolina.

Parsons, Talcott (1937). *The Structure of Social Action*. New York: McGraw-Hill.

Parsons, Talcott (1955). "The American Family." In Talcott Parsons and Robert F. Bales (eds.), *Family: Socialization and Interaction Process*. New York: Free Press.

Parsons, Talcott (1963). "Introduction." In Max Weber, *The Sociology of Religion*. New York: Free Press.

Parsons, Talcott (1964). "Youth in the Context of American Society." In Talcott Parsons (ed.), *Social Structure and Personality*. New York:-Free Press.

Parsons, Talcott, with White, Winston (1964). "The Link Between Character and Society." In Talcott Parsons (ed.), *Social Structure and Personality*. New York: Free Press.

Parsons, Talcott (1977). *The Evolution of Societies*, Englewood Cliffs, N.J.: Prentice-Hall.

Parsons, Talcott, with White, Winston (1964). "The Link Between Character and Society." In Talcott Parsons (ed.), *Social Structure and Personality*. New York: Free Press.

Petty, R. E., Williams, K. D., Harkins, S. G., and Latane, B. (1977). "Social Inhibition of Helping Yourself: Bystander Response to a Cheeseburger." *Personality and Social Psychology Bulletin* 3:575–578.

Phillips, David P. (1983). "The Impact of Mass Media Violence on U.S. Homicides." *American Sociological Review* 48(4):560–568.

Polk, Barbara Bovee (1972). "Women's Liberation: Movement for Equality." In Constantina Satilios-Rothschild (ed.), *Toward a Sociology of Women.* Lexington, Mass.: Xerox, pp. 321–330.

Radcliffe-Brown, A. R. (1957). *A Natural Science of Society.* New York: Free Press.

Ransford, H. Edward (1968). "Isolation, Powerlessness, and Violence: A Study of Attitudes and Participation in the Watts Riot." *American Journal of Sociology* 73:581–591.

Reich, Charles (1969). *The Greening of America.* New York: Random House.

The Report of the Commission on Obscenity and Pornography (1970). Washington, D.C.: U.S. Government Printing Office.

Reynolds, Vernon (1976). *The Biology of Human Action.* San Francisco: Freeman.

Ridley, Jean Clare (1972). "The Effects of Population Change on the Roles and Status of Women: Perspective and Speculation." In Constantina Safilios-Rothschild (ed.), *Toward a Sociology of Women,* Lexington, Mass.: Xerox, pp. 372–386.

Riesman, David (1950). *The Lonely Crowd.* New Haven, Conn.: Yale University Press.

Riesman, David, and Glazer, Nathan (1971). "Apathy and Involvement in the Political Process." In Bernard Rosenberg, Israel Gerver, and F. William Howton (eds.), *Mass Society in Crisis.* New York: Macmillan.

Riesman, L. (1969). "Readiness to Succeed: Mobility Aspirations and Modernism Among the Poor." *Urban Affairs Quarterly* 4 (March): 379–395.

Roethlisberger, F. J., and Dickson, W. J. (1939). *Management and the Worker.* Cambridge, Mass.: Harvard University Press.

Rose, Arnold (1962). "Reactions Against the Mass Society." *The Sociological Quarterly* 3:-310–319.

Rosnow, Ralph L. (1974). "On Rumor." *Journal of Communication* 24:26–38.

Rosnow, Ralph L., and Fine, Gary Alan (1974).

"Inside Rumors." *Human Behavior* (August:64–68.

Rossi, Alice (1965). "Women in Science: Why so Few?" *Science* 148:1196–1202.

Roszak, Theodore (1968). *The Making of a Counterculture.* Garden City, N.Y.: Doubleday.

Russell, Elbert W. (1972). "Factors of Human Aggression." *Behavior Science Notes* 7:275–312.

San Francisco Sunday Examiner and Chronicle (1975). April 27. This World section, p. 2.

Schoenstein, Ralph (1974). "It Was Just a Joke, Folks." *TV Guide* (May 18):6–7.

Schwartz, Barry and Barsky, Stephen F. (1977). "The Home Advantage." *Social Forces* 55:-641–661.

Scott, Robert A. (1967). "The Selection of Clients by Social Welfare Agencies: The Case of the Blind." *Social Problems* 14:248–257.

See, Carolyn (1975). "California Children," *New Times* (January 10):35–39.

Shearer, Lloyd (1974). "Intelligence Report." *Parade Magazine,* (December 1):8.

Sherif, Muzafer (1936). *The Psychology of Social Norms.* New York: Harper & Row.

Shibutani, Tamotsu (1966). *Improvised News: A Sociological Study of Rumor.* Indianapolis, Ind.: Bobbs-Merrill.

Silberman, Charles E. (1978). *Criminal Violence, Criminal Justice.* New York:Random House.

Sipes, Richard G. (1973). "War, Sports, and Aggression." *American Anthropologist* 75:64–86.

Sjoberg, Gideon, Byrne, Richard A., and Farris, BuFord (1966). "Bureaucracy and the Lower Class." *Sociology and Social Research* 50:-325–337.

Slater, Philip (1970). *The Pursuit of Loneliness.* New York: Beacon.

Sorokin, Pitirim A. (1947). *Society, Culture and Personality.* New York: Harper & Row.

Spates, James L. and Macionis, John J. (1982). *The Sociology of Cities.* New York: St. Martin's.

Spiro, Melvin E. (1956). *Kibbutz: Venture in Utopia.* Cambridge, Mass.: Harvard University.

Stack, Carol B. (1974). *All Our Kin.* New York: Harper & Row.

Stein, Maurice R. (1960). *The Eclipse of Community.* New York: Harper & Row.

Stouffer, Samuel A. (1949). *The American Soldier: Studies in Social Psychology in World War II.* Princeton, N.J.: Princeton University Press.

Sumner, William Graham (1906). *Folkways.* Boston: Ginn.

The Sunday Journal and Sentinel, Winston-Salem, N.C., 1975, March 2, p. 6.

Suttles, Gerald (1968). *The Social Order of the Slum.* Chicago: University of Chicago Press.

Swados, Harvey (1957). *On the Line.* Boston: Little, Brown.

Szilard, Leo (1952). "Report on Grand Central Terminal." *University of Chicago Magazine* (June):7–8.

Takooshian, Harold, Haber, Sandra, and Lucidio, David J. (1977). "Who Wouldn't Help a Lost Child? You, Maybe." *Psychology Today,* 10:67–68, 88.

Tavris, Carol (1974). "A Conversation with Stanley Milgram." *Psychology Today* (June):71–80.

Tocqueville, Alexis de (1946) *Democracy in America,* New York: Knopf.

Toffler, Alvin (1970). *Future Shock.* New York: Bantam.

Tönnies, Ferdinand (1957). *Community and Society.* Translated and edited by Charles P. Loomis. East Lansing, Mich.: Michigan State University Press.

Tuchman, Gaye (1975). "Women and the Creation of Culture." In Marcia Millman and Rosabeth Moss Kanter (eds.), *Another Voice: Feminist Perspectives on Social Life and Social Science.* Garden City, N.Y.: Anchor.

Tumin, Melvin M. (1953). "Some Principles of Stratification: A Critical Analysis" *American Sociological Review* 18:387–394.

Turnbull, Colin M. (1972). *The Mountain People.* New York: Simon & Schuster.

Turner, Ralph H., and Killian, Lewis M. (1957). *Collective Behavior.* Englewood Cliffs, N.J.: Prentice-Hall.

van den Berghe, Pierre L. (1974). "Bringing Beasts Back In: Toward a Biosocial Theory of Aggression." *American Sociological Review,* 39:777–788.

van den Berghe, Pierre L. (1975). "Reply to Fischer, Moberg, and Mazur." *American Sociological Review* 40:678–682.

Vidich, Arthur J., and Bensman, Joseph (1960). *Small Town in Mass Society.* Garden City, N.Y.: Doubleday.

Ward, Lester Frank (1906). *Applied Sociology.* Boston: Ginn.

Warner, W. Lloyd, and Lunt, Paul S. (1941). *The Social Life of a Modern Community.* New Haven, Conn.: Yale University Press.

Webb, Eugene, Campbell, Donald T., Schwartz, Richard D., and Sechrest, Lee (1966). *Unobtrusive Measures.* Chicago: Rand McNally.

Weber, Max (1946). *Essays in Sociology.* Translated by H. H. Gerth and C. W. Mills, New York: Oxford University.

Weber, Max (1958). *The Protestant Ethic and the Spirit of Capitalism.* Translated by Talcott Parsons. New York: Scribner.

Weber, Max (1963). *The Sociology of Religion.* New York: Free Press.

Wilensky, Harold L. (1961). "Orderly Careers and Social Participation: The Impact of Work History on Social Integration in the Middle Mass." *American Sociological Review* 26:-521–539.

Williams, Robin (1971). *American Society: A Sociological Interpretation.* New York: Knopf.

Wilson, Edward O. (1975). *Sociobiology: The New Synthesis.* Cambridge, Mass.: Harvard University Press.

Wolfe, Tom (1968). *The Electric Kool-Aid Acid Test.* New York: Farrar, Straus, & Giroux.

Yablonsky, Lewis (1968). *The Hippie Trip.* New York: Pegasus.

Yinger, J. Milton (1960). "Contraculture and Subculture." *American Sociological Review* 25:625–635.

Zurcher, Louis A., Sonenschein, David W., and Metzner, Eric L. (1966). "The Hasher: A Study of Role Conflict." *Social Forces* 44:505–514.

GLOSSARY

ability grouping The sorting of students into homogeneous groups on the basis of their ability to perform classroom tasks such as reading or arithmetic.

achieved status Position based on role competence rather than ascribed characteristics.

active crowd A crowd that forms in order to act out a shared feeling toward persons or events and to effect a change in relationship or situation.

actual norms Concepts that specify the degree of latitude a participant may take in conforming to ideal norms without becoming subject to the hostility of other group members.

alienation The psychological state of nonattachment.

altruistic suicide The variety of suicide that occurs when the individual's social integration is excessively high.

anomic suicide The variety of suicide that occurs when an individual's social integration is suddenly disrupted causing extreme confusion about how to act.

anomie A state of society where, because of sudden or continuing social change, knowledge of the correct ways to behave is disrupted.

anticipatory socialization The influence on an individual of the norms and values of a group that an individual aspires to jion.

ascribed status A position based on hereditary or developmental characteristics.

assimilation The process by which participants in the transmission of rumor change the information relayed to fit their expectations and norms.

bilateral A descent system where descent is recognized through both the mother's and the father's family lines.

bourgeoisie The capitalist class, those individuals who own property and the machinery of production.

bureaucracy A formal structure that contains well-defined roles, is ruled by a few, has written rules and goals, and evaluates its members on the basis of their specialized role performance.

capitalism Marx's fourth stage of societal development in which one class owns the means of production while another class operates the means of production.

career mobility Changes in an individual's occupational status.

caste A closed system of stratification in which vertical mobility is not permitted.

charisma A special, magnetic quality that a

person has by virtue of natural endowment or because of some extraordinary means.

church The most highly structured and conventional form of religious organization whose membership is drawn from the mainstream of society.

class According to Weber, that form of stratification having to do with the possession of material wealth.

class consciousness An awareness among the members of a social class of their place in the social stratification system.

collective behavior The behavior of groups of people who come together in a relatively spontaneous manner. Their actions are not fully controlled by conventional norms, values, and sanctions.

colonization The process of exploration, settlement, and annexation of foreign lands to a parent nation.

communism A classless society in which everyone owns and works the means of production.

comparative analysis A method that examines the characteristics of groups or countries and compares them with other groups or countries.

concept A basic idea of a discipline. Sociological concepts include role, status, norm, primary group, and culture.

conscience The negative side of the superego resulting from parental proscriptions about behavior, the source of feelings of guilt.

consciousness The individual's awareness of self.

contagion A process whereby emotions, attitudes, and actions from one participant to another transform the separate individuals into a uniform mass that thinks and acts in concert.

content analysis A method that studies forms of communication, such as books, films, radio or TV broadcasts, diaries, and the like.

control group The subjects in an experiment who are not exposed to changing conditions devised by the experimenter.

convergence of attitudes The approach to collective behavior that emphasizes that people who act in like manner often already share the same predispositions to action before they ever come together.

core human problems Those problems that demand social answers for the continued existence of any society.

counterculture A group whose members totally reject the values of the dominant culture and seek to develop an alternative set of values by which to guide their lives.

crowd A temporary cluster of people who react together to a common stimulus while in close physical contact.

cult A small number of people banded together to express a revolutionary religious cause.

cultural diffusion The process by which cultural elements are borrowed by interacting cultures.

cultural lag The tendency for the parts of culture to change and adapt at different rates.

cultural relativism The doctrine that other cultures can only be understood on their own terms.

culture A way of life that is learned and shared by human beings and that endures from one generation to the next.

cyclical model of social change A conception of the overall direction of social change that assumes history tends to repeat itself. The pattern is seen as cyclical.

democratic-humanitarian complex A value pattern that stresses democracy, equality, justice, freedom, and humanitarianism.

dependent variable A variable to be explained or accounted for.

deviant behavior Any behavior that violates the norms or values of a group.

diffusion The process by which social change is spread, the transmission of new ideas and actions from individual to individual in a group.

division of labor The assignment of different specialized activities to different groups of people in society.

dominant culture Ideas and actions are shared by the majority of people in a group, the most powerful people in the group, or both.

economy, the The social institution that provides the answer to the basic needs problem by developing ways of procuring the material necessities of life.

education The social institution in modern societies that provides the answers to the problems of formal socialization—specialized occupational knowledge and generalized citizen knowledge.

ego The element of personality that enables the individual to devise and evaluate possible plans of action.

ego ideal The positive side of the superego resulting from parental prescriptions about behavior; the source of feelings of pride.

egoistic suicide The variety of suicide that occurs when the individual's social integration is excessively low, so that life loses meaning.

emergent norms/alienation The approach to collective behavior that emphasizes (1) norms do in fact come to control some types of collective behavior and (2) these types of collective behavior are classifiable according to the amount of alienation that their members experience.

emotional contagion A radical solution to the ambivalence felt by active crowd members. Emotional expression quickly spreads throughout a crowd.

ethnocentrism The tendency for a person to regard his or her own culture as a standard for judging any other culture.

everyday change The subtle or unremarkable alterations in people's interaction patterns that occur from time to time in our daily experience.

evolution In sociology, the progress of human societies from simple, unstable groups to complex, stable, interdependent groups.

experiment A method of research in which the investigator manipulates an independent variable.

experimental group The subjects in an experiment who are exposed to changing conditions devised by the experimenter.

expressive crowd A crowd that exists to provide a release of tension for its members through their reaction to an observed event.

extended family A family unit consisting of numerous blood relatives and their nuclear families.

face restoration An effort to reestablish the appearance of capability or strength after an individual has experienced social embarrassment.

face-saving behavior Tactics and strategies de-

signed to avoid or prevent social embarrassment.

family, the The social institution that provides the answers to the love, marriage, and children problems; usually characterized by a group sharing a common residence and working in economic cooperation.

family of orientation The child's original family unit in which early socialization occurs.

family of procreation The new family unit established by the individual at marriage.

feudalism Marx's third stage of development, in which serfs were directly controlled but not owned by feudal landlords.

folkways Norms that state the traditionally accepted way of conducting the routine affairs of everyday life.

formal organization A secondary group established to serve a specialized set of goals, such as schools, corporations, prisons, and hospitals.

formal structure The set of norms and objectives that define the roles and procedures to which members of a formal organization are officially expected to comply.

game Mead's second stage of self-development in which the child learns to take a number of roles simultaneously and achieves a unified self-conception.

gemeinschaft Tönnies's conception of simple, traditional, communal societies.

general system values Concepts that identify the desirable goals of the group and specify the appropriate behavior of group members as they work toward those goals.

generalized other The viewpoint of a group or community as a whole.

general knowledge That component of ideational culture that provides the basic data about reality that enables individuals to conduct their everyday affairs; the most commonplace elements of general knowledge are facts and usages.

generational mobility Changes in social rank between parents and their children.

gesellschaft Tönnies's conception of complex, urbanized societies.

government A legitimately recognized set of statuses and procedures for implementing and obtaining the goals of the group.

group Two or more persons who are mutually aware of one another's presence and orient their actions toward one another.

growth economy An economy where people work harder in procuring the material resources of life than is necessary for mere subsistence; other pursuits, such as religion, assume a distinctly secondary role in daily activity and interest.

guidelines for behavior That part of ideational culture that suggests how the members of a group should or should not act in social situations.

health The social institution that provides the answer to the problem of how to care for the ill of society.

horizontal mobility Any change in position that does not involve a change in social rank.

hypothesis A statement of relationship between two or more phenomena that can be submitted to test.

I Mead's concept of the spontaneous, impulsive, and innovative aspects of the self.

id A reservoir of psychic energy whose primary aim is to reduce pain and heighten pleasure.

ideal norms Concepts that specify the precise behavior that individuals are expected to exhibit if they are to fulfill the group ideals.

ideal type An abstract model of a social phenomenon.

idealistic cultural theme Sorokin's notion of a cultural system in which the ideational and sensate cultural themes are balanced.

ideational cultural theme Sorokin's notion of a cultural system in which spiritual needs are emphasized.

ideational culture A learned and shared set of ideas that provide general knowledge about the world and guidelines for social behavior.

identification A child's attempt to become like the parent of the same sex in order to gain the affection of the parent of the opposite sex.

imitation A radical solution to the ambivalence felt by active crowd members. They unthinkingly copy the actions of one another.

independent variable A variable presumed to be a cause or an influential factor.

industrialism The process of manufacturing goods such as clothing, dishes, etc., in large quantities for mass consumption.

informal structure The unofficial norms that arise in a formal organization from informal, primary ties.

in-group solidarity The positive feeling among members of a group that their way of doing things is right.

inner-directed Riesman's term to characterize an individual who has an internal source of normative guidance.

instinct An inborn, automatic, and unvarying response to stimuli.

institutions A cluster of interrelated norms that center around some human activity.

instrumental complex A value pattern emphasizing the most efficient use of means in attaining the ends of society.

interpretation The process whereby human beings think, organize, and evaluate their thoughts and choose a course of action appropriate to the stimuli.

legal system A subinstitution charged with interpreting the rules of society and with the right to punish deviants.

leveling The process by which participants in the transmission of rumor eliminate extraneous elements in the information relayed.

linear model of social change A conception of the overall direction of social change in which societies are seen as moving in a straight line from lower to higher levels of development.

market system An economic arrangement characterized by individual initiative, the profit motive, competition, and a focus on the general wants of consumers.

mass hysteria Form of collective behavior in which the same fear motivates a large number of people to react, whether or not they are physically together.

mass society A society characterized by large-scale urbanization, bureaucratization, and industrialization.

material culture Products of human activity.

matrilineal A descent system where descent is recognized through the mother's family line.

matrilocal A family residence pattern where the married couple resides with the wife's parents.

me Mead's concept of the aspect of the self that is the internal agent of conformity and social control.

mechanical solidarity Feeling of identity and unity among the members of a society based on the similarity of their values and lifestyles.

media, the The social institution in a modern society that provides the answers to the problem of how to communicate with the population-at-large.

military, the The social institution that provides the answers to the problems of national security and procurement of scarce resources from other societies that do not wish to part with such resources.

monogamy A form of marriage where the man and the woman are permitted only one marriage partner at a time.

mores Norms that specify essential behavior and to which the members of the group demand conformity.

nationalization The process that transforms previously scattered political units into centralized political units.

neolocal A family residence pattern where the married couple does not live with either set of parents but resides alone in an independent household.

normative subculture A group within the dominant culture that focuses at least part of its existence around a set of norms different from those of the members of the dominant culture.

norms Those guidelines for behavior that inform the participants in social situations specifically what is right and proper to do.

nuclear family A family unit consisting of a husband and wife and their children.

Oedipus complex A sexual desire for the parent of the opposite sex coupled with a feeling of hostility for the parent of the same sex.

opinion leaders Key persons in primary groups.

organic solidarity Feeling of identity and unity among the members of a society based on their interdependence.

other-directed Riesman's term to characterize an individual whose source of guidance is the peer group.

out-group hostility The negative feeling members of a group have about other groups.

participant observation A method of research in which the sociologist participates in the activities of the group under study.

patrilineal A descent system where descent is recognized through the father's family line.

patrilocal A family residence pattern where the married couple resides with the husband's parents.

peer group People who are similar to an individual in age, sex, economic, political, and religious background.

personality The configuration of habits, expectations, and attitudes that is both enduring and characteristic of an individual.

play Mead's first stage of self-development in which the child begins role-taking.

political process The procedures that exist for filling vacancies in government when they occur.

political system The social institution that provides the answers to the problems of goal attainment and rule enforcement in a society.

polyandry A form of marriage where the woman is permitted more than one husband.

polygamy A form of marriage where one or both of the partners are permitted other marriage partners.

polygyny A form of marriage where the man is permitted more than one wife.

power That form of stratification having to do with the ability of an individual to make decisions affecting the lives of other members of society.

power elite A group of high status members of the military, industry, and politics who make policy decisions.

primary group A group characterized by relatively small size, cohesion, and intimate, informal, and influential interaction.

primitive communism Marx's first stage of economic development of society, in which there is collective ownership and utilization of all goods.

profane In contrast to the sacred, the designation of beliefs, practices, or objects as being everyday, mundane, and of this world.

proletariat The worker class, those individuals who sell their labor.

public opinion The convergence of the separate opinions held by members of a group in a spontaneous attempt to resolve a controversial issue that cannot be decided by existing norms.

randomization An experimental procedure

whereby subjects are assigned on a chance basis to the experimental and control groups.

rationalization An emphasis on rules and procedures for maximizing efficiency.

reference group A group that influences an individual but in which he or she does not necessarily hold membership.

relative deprivation A feeling of dissatisfaction arising from a comparison with the past history of a group or with the more favorable situation of another group.

religion The social institution that provides the answers to the ultimate questions of human life; a unified system of beliefs and practices relative to sacred things.

retrospective socialization The influence on an individual of the norms and values of a group in which an individual no longer holds membership.

revolution A violent attempt at total restructuring of most of the institutions and values of a society.

role A specific set of norms and expected behaviors associated with a status.

role conflict Situation in which an individual becomes the recipient of incompatible or contradictory role requirements, that is, the individual is expected to behave in ways that are inconsistent with one another.

role set All the role relationships in which an individual is involved by virtue of occupying a single status.

role-taking The mental process whereby an individual determines the standpoint of others based on their gestures.

rumor Face-to-face communication of unauthenticated information as a form of collective problem solving in order to provide a definition of an ambiguous situation.

sacred A set of beliefs, practices, or objects set apart or forbidden because of their special, divine, or other-worldly nature.

sample A small number of individuals who are somehow representative of a larger population used in research in order to make generalizations about the larger population without studying all its members.

sanctions Rewards and punishments that are employed to keep deviant behavior at a minimum.

scientific method A method of inquiry based on systematic and objective observation.

secondary group A group characterized by formal relationships, little influence on personality, and specialized interaction.

sect A small religious association that generally appeals to poor, propertyless, or otherwise marginal members of society.

self The individual's capacity for self-awareness and self-evaluation.

sensate cultural theme Sorokin's notion of a cultural system in which sensual and physical needs are stressed.

sharpening The process by which participants in the transmission of rumor emphasize certain aspects of the information relayed.

significant others The people with whom an individual interacts frequently and emotionally.

significant symbols A set of symbols that is shared by the members of a language community.

simulation A method that creates artificial social conditions.

slavery Marx's second stage of development in which human beings could be privately owned.

social The primary quality of human interaction. A social situation is one in which individuals orient their behavior toward one another.

social category Any classification of individuals who share characteristics but who are not interacting.

social change Any continuing alteration in the interaction patterns that exist between two or more people.

social class An aggregate of persons who perform essentially the same activities in daily life.

social honor (prestige) That form of stratification having to do with the amount of social recognition accorded an individual by other members of society.

social institutions The representative ways that society's members have developed to solve certain core human problems.

social mobility The dynamic aspects of stratification.

social movement A collectivity that acts with

some continuity to promote or resist a change in the group.

social stereotype   A socially agreed-upon definition of a group in terms of general characteristics that may or may not be accurate in reality.

social stratification   A ranked set of strata or social classes that reflect inequality in the things that society's members consider valuable.

social structure   Interaction that acquires a patterned and stable character, so that many of its elements are repeated over time and are shared by many members of the society.

social system   A group whose parts are interdependent.

socialism   Marx's final stage of development in which all members of society together own the means of production and share equally in all products of the social order.

socialization   The process whereby culture is transferred to and internalized by individual personalities.

society   A group that seeks to provide the means for satisfying all the needs of its members.

sociology   The scientific study of the behavior of people when they interact with one another, of the characteristics that people develop as a result of such interaction.

specialization   The assignment of some of the functions previously performed by one social institution to other institutions, so that the original system carries out fewer functions.

status   Any social position that involves prescriptions and expectations for behavior.

status inconsistency   A lack of coincidence or overlap among the three characteristics of stratification, wealth, prestige, and power.

status set   The totality of an individual's concurrent statuses.

stereotyping   Characterizing members of a group according to some traits all members are presumed to possess.

subculture   People who accept only some of the aspects of the dominant culture while also sharing values or norms peculiar to itself.

subsistence economy   An economy where people work as hard as is necessary to produce the material resources of life and then devote the rest of their time to other pursuits.

successive-stage model of social change   A conception of the overall direction of social change according to which societies move through a sequence of stages.

suggestibility   A radical solution to the ambivalence felt by active crowd members. Suggestions are uncritically accepted.

superego   The internal representative of cultural norms, values, and sanctions.

survey   A method of research in which a record of behavior is obtained by the investigator after it has occurred.

theory   A general statement of relationships among variables that explains a number of observations or hypotheses.

trend   Relatively long-term, gradual alterations in interaction patterns.

unconscious processes   Emotions and urges of which an individual is unaware.

unobtrusive measures   A method of observation that does not require the cooperation of the respondent.

urbanization   The process of increasing population and trade that transforms villages and towns into cities.

valuational subculture   A group within the dominant culture that disagrees with the priority given to certain values within the dominant culture.

value orientations   Concepts that give members of a group the basic answers to the core problems of human existence.

values   Concepts of the desirable that indicate what activities are good to do and what kind of person it is good to become.

variable   A concept capable of having two or more aspects.

vertical mobility   Any upward or downward change in social rank.

voluntary association   People who come together on a part-time basis to focus on some common interest, need, or problem.

wealth   The possession of material goods.

INDEX